Constructing Identity in and around Organizations

Perspectives on Process Organization Studies
Series Editors: Ann Langley and Haridimos Tsoukas

Perspectives on Process Organization Studies is an annual series, linked to the International Symposium on Process Organization Studies, and is dedicated to the development of an understanding of organizations and organizing at large as processes in the making (see http://www.process-symposium.com/). This series brings together contributions from leading scholars, which focus on seeing dynamically evolving activities, interactions, and events as important aspects of organized action, rather than static structures and fixed templates.

Volume 1: Process, Sensemaking, and Organizing
Editors: Tor Hernes and Sally Maitlis

Volume 2: Constructing Identity in and around Organizations
Editors: Majken Schultz, Steve Maguire, Ann Langley, and Haridimos Tsoukas

Constructing Identity in and around Organizations

Edited by
Majken Schultz, Steve Maguire, Ann Langley,
Haridimos Tsoukas

OXFORD
UNIVERSITY PRESS

OXFORD
UNIVERSITY PRESS

Great Clarendon Street, Oxford OX2 6DP

Oxford University Press is a department of the University of Oxford.
It furthers the University's objective of excellence in research, scholarship,
and education by publishing worldwide in

Oxford New York

Auckland Cape Town Dar es Salaam Hong Kong Karachi
Kuala Lumpur Madrid Melbourne Mexico City Nairobi
New Delhi Shanghai Taipei Toronto

With offices in

Argentina Austria Brazil Chile Czech Republic France Greece
Guatemala Hungary Italy Japan Poland Portugal Singapore
South Korea Switzerland Thailand Turkey Ukraine Vietnam

Oxford is a registered trade mark of Oxford University Press
in the UK and in certain other countries

Published in the United States
by Oxford University Press Inc., New York

© Oxford University Press, 2012

The moral rights of the authors have been asserted
Database right Oxford University Press (maker)

First published 2012

All rights reserved. No part of this publication may be reproduced,
stored in a retrieval system, or transmitted, in any form or by any means,
without the prior permission in writing of Oxford University Press,
or as expressly permitted by law, or under terms agreed with the appropriate
reprographics rights organization. Enquiries concerning reproduction
outside the scope of the above should be sent to the Rights Department,
Oxford University Press, at the address above

You must not circulate this book in any other binding or cover
and you must impose the same condition on any acquirer

British Library Cataloguing in Publication Data
Data available

Library of Congress Cataloging in Publication Data
Data available

Typeset by SPI Publisher Services, Pondicherry, India
Printed in Great Britain
on acid-free paper by
MPG Books Group, Bodmin and King's Lynn

ISBN 978–0–19–964099–7

1 3 5 7 9 10 8 6 4 2

Contents

Acknowledgments	vii
List of Figures	ix
List of Tables	x
List of Contributors	xi
Series Editorial Structure	xvii
Endorsements	xviii

1. Constructing Identity in and around Organizations: Introducing the Second Volume of "Perspectives on Process Organization Studies" — 1
   Majken Schultz, Steve Maguire, Ann Langley, and Haridimos Tsoukas

Part I: Identity and Organizations

2. Rethinking Identity Construction Processes in Organizations: Three Questions to Consider — 21
   Michael G. Pratt

3. Identity as Process and Flow — 50
   Dennis A. Gioia and Shubha Patvardhan

4. Exploring Cultural Mechanisms of Organizational Identity Construction — 63
   Mary Ann Glynn and Lee Watkiss

5. Organizational Identity Formation: Processes of Identity Imprinting and Enactment in the Dutch Microbrewing Landscape — 89
   Jochem J. Kroezen and Pursey P. M. A. R. Heugens

6. Narrative Tools and the Construction of Identity — 128
   James V. Wertsch

Contents

7. Villains, Victims, and the Financial Crisis: Positioning Identities through Descriptions — 147
   Frank Mueller and Andrea Whittle

8. Identity and Time in Gilles Deleuze's Process Philosophy — 180
   James Williams

Part II: General Process Perspectives

9. The Bakhtinian Theory of Chronotope (Time–Space Frame) Applied to the Organizing Process — 201
   Philippe Lorino and Benoît Tricard

10. The Momentum of Organizational Change — 235
    Elden Wiebe, Roy Suddaby and William M. Foster

11. Management Knowledge: A Process View — 261
    Simon Grand and Adrian Ackeret

12. Aligning Process Questions, Perspectives, and Explanations — 306
    Andrew H. Van de Ven and Harry Sminia

Index — 321

Acknowledgments

We would like to express our great appreciation to the following colleagues who have generously offered their time to act as reviewers for the chapters published in this and the previous volume:

Majken Schultz, Steve Maguire, Ann Langley, and Haridimos Tsoukas.

Reviewers Listed Alphabetically:

Francesca Alby, Sapienza University of Rome; Tore Bakken, Norwegian School of Management; Jean Bartunek, Boston College; Olga Belova, Essex Business School; Laure Cabantous, Nottingham University Business School; Andrea Casey, The George Washington University; Robert Chia, Strathclyde Business School; Todd Chiles, Trulaske College of Business, University of Missouri; Marlys Christianson, University of Michigan; Roger Dunbar, Stern School of Business; Martha Feldman, University of California, Irvine; Raghu Garud, Smeal College of Business; Robert Gephart, Uinversity of Alberta; Hélène Giroux, HEC Montréal; Daniel Gruber, Medill at Northwestern University; Cynthia Hardy, University of Melbourne; Tor Hernes, Copenhagen Business School; Petter Holm, University of Tromsø; Robin Holt, University of Liverpool Management School Liverpool; Christina Hoon, Leibniz Universität Hannover; Michael Humphreys, Nottingham University Business School; Muayyad Jabri, University of New England; Claus Jacobs, University of St. Gallen; Esben Karmark, Copenhagen Business School; Dan Kärreman, Copenhagen Business School; Alfred Kieser, Mannheim University; Ioanna Kinti, University of Oxford; Farah Kodeih, ESSEC Business School; Christophe Lejeune, EM-Strasbourg Business School; Philippe Lorino, ESSEC Business School; Steve Maguire, McGill School of Environment; Ajit Nayak, University of Bath, School of Management; Anne Nicotera, George Mason University; David Oliver, HEC Montréal; Brian Petland, Michigan State University; Nelson Phillips, Imperial College London; Marshall Scott Poole, University of Illinois at Urbana-Champaign; Davide Ravasi, Università Bocconi; Robyn Remke, Copenhagen Business School; Claus Rerup, Richard Ivey School of Business; Daniel

Acknowledgments

Robichaud, University of Montréal; Linda Rouleau, HEC Montréal; Jorgen Sandberg, University of Queensland; Georg Schreyögg, Freie Universität Berlin; Majken Schultz, Copenhagen Business School; David Seidl, University of Zurich; John Shotter, University of New Hampshire; John Sillince, Strathclyde Business School; Riitta Smeds, Aalto University School of Science and Technology; Scott Sonenshein, Jesse H. Jones Graduate School of Business; Chris Steyaert, University of St. Gallen; Robyn Thomas, Cardiff Business School; Dennis Tourish, Aberdeen Business School; Mary Tripsas, Harvard Business School; Haridimos Tsoukas, University of Cyprus & University of Warwick; Harald Tuckermann, University of St. Gallen; Timothy Vogus, Owen Graduate School of Management; Sierk Ybema, VU University, Amsterdam; and Cristina Zucchermaglio, Sapienza University of Rome.

List of Figures

2.1	Organizational self and identity processes	33
2.2	Hypothetical self and identity processes	39
4.1	Mapping cultural mechanisms onto organizational identities	79
5.1	Theoretical model of organizational identity formation	99
5.2	Empirical model of organizational identity formation: imprinting and enactment processes	106
6.1	The Bronze Soldier in the Tallinn Military Cemetery	134
8.1	Manifold of the syntheses of time	185
8.2	Deleuze's manifold of time dimensions	188
9.1	The chronotopes of manufacturing	221
9.2	The new chronotopes	222
9.3	The time schedule of the research project	225
9.4	The traditional chronotope of the building industry	225
10.1	Momentum in the flow of time	248
11.1	Management knowledge: a process view	275
11.2	Managerial engagements over time and relevant dimensions of engagement regimes	277
11.3	Enactment of engagement regimes over time	294
11.4	Flow of managerial activities, engagement regimes, emerging controversial issues, and shifting concepts of management	297
12.1	Illustration of events observed over time	307

List of Tables

4.1	Cultural mechanisms in organizational identity construction	70
5.1	Common themes between old institutionalism literature and organizational identity literature, and implications for the identity formation process	94
5.2	Number of interviewees and participating breweries per interviewee role	102
5.3	Description of employed identity claims and number of breweries per claim	105
5.4	Identity formation processes per identity source and corresponding percentage scores for the empirical evidence found	107
7.1	Core tenets of the DP perspective on identity	152
7.2	Participants in Treasury Select Committee meeting February 10, 2009	159
7.3	Comparison of identity positions attributed to bankers in Treasury Select Committee meeting, February 10, 2009	165
9.1	The chronotope of manufacturing	222
9.2	The new chronotopes	223
9.3	The traditional chronotopes of the building industry	226
10.1	Depiction of momentum in the organization studies literature	240
10.2	The temporal interactions of agentic momentum	250
11.1	Multiple managerial engagements	272
11.2a	Patterns of justification: dimensions—success	278
11.2b	Patterns of justification: dimensions—innovation	279
11.2c	Patterns of justification: dimensions—organization	279
11.3a	Patterns of routinization: dimensions—governance	283
11.3b	Patterns of routinization: dimensions—decision-making	284
11.3c	Patterns of routinization: dimensions—resource allocation	285
11.4	Engagement regimes: emerging patterns of change	288
11.5	Emerging controversial issues	291
12.1	Alignment of process questions, perspectives, and explanations	307

List of Contributors

Adrian Ackeret is a Ph.D. student in Management at the University of St. Gallen (HSG), Switzerland, and a research fellow at RISE Management Research in the University's Institute for Systemic Management and Public Governance. He holds a master's degree in business administration and management from the same university. His research is on entrepreneurial management and strategy from a process perspective, with an empirical focus on the software industry.

William M. Foster is Assistant Professor of Management at the Augustana Campus of the University of Alberta. He received his Ph.D. from the University of Alberta. His research interests include rhetorical history, social memory studies, and business ethics. His work has published in *Advances in Strategic Management, Journal of Management Inquiry,* and *Team Performance Management.* He is co-author (with Elden Wiebe) of "Praxis makes perfect: Recovering the ethical promise of Critical Management Studies" in *Journal of Business Ethics.* His current research projects include a study of the activities of corporate historians and a study of how sustainability officers identify and engage with different stakeholders.

Dennis A. (Denny) Gioia is the Robert and Judith Klein Professor of Management in the Smeal College of Business at the Pennsylvania State University. Prior to his academic career he worked as an engineer for Boeing Aerospace at Cape Kennedy during the Apollo lunar program and for Ford Motor Company as corporate recall coordinator. Current research and writing interests focus primarily on the ways in which organizational identity and image are involved in sensemaking, sensegiving, and organizational change. He received his doctorate in Management from Florida State University.

Mary Ann Glynn is the Joseph F. Cotter Professor of Organizational Studies and Leadership, Professor of Sociology (by courtesy), and Research Director of the Winston Center for Leadership and Ethics at Boston College, Carroll School of Management. Her research focuses on the phenomena of organizational identity, institutional dynamics, and leadership, examining how these are shaped by micro-level cognitive processes and macro-level cultural influences.

Simon Grand (Ph.D., University of Zurich) is knowledge entrepreneur, academic director of RISE Management Research at the University of St. Gallen (HSG), founding

List of Contributors

partner of TATIN Scoping Complexity (Zurich), and senior researcher at the Institute for Research in Art and Design (Basel). He researches strategy, entrepreneurship, and management from a process and practice perspective, studying innovative companies "at the edge" in software engineering, information technology, artificial intelligence, life sciences, design, fashion, and art. He is currently finalizing his Habilitation qualification in strategy as process, and two books—one on executive management in practice, and the other on a process theory of organization and management.

Pursey P. M. A. R. Heugens is Professor of Organization Theory, Development, and Change, and Chair of the Department of Strategic Management and Business Environment at the Rotterdam School of Management, Erasmus University. He obtained his Ph.D. from the same university in 2001. His research interests include comparative corporate governance, business ethics, and bureaucracy, institutional, and demographic theories of organization. Pursey serves on the editorial boards of six scholarly journals. His research is published in journals such as *Academy of Management Journal*, *Academy of Management Review*, *Organization Studies*, and *Journal of Management Studies*.

Jochem J. Kroezen is a Ph.D. candidate in the Department of Strategic Management and Business Environment at the Rotterdam School of Management, Erasmus University. Prior to his current appointment, he completed the ERIM Research Master's Program in Business Research (M.Phil.) with distinction. His Ph.D. research deals with the process of organizational identity formation in nascent organizations, with a specific focus on institutional influences on this process. Jochem's research interests include institutional theory, population ecology, and sociology of science.

Ann Langley is Professor of Management at HEC Montréal and Canada Research Chair in Strategic Management in Pluralistic Settings. Her research focuses on strategic change, leadership, innovation, and the use of management tools in complex organizations with an emphasis on processual research approaches. She has published over fifty articles and two books, most recently *Strategy as Practice: Research Directions and Resources* with Gerry Johnson, Leif Melin, and Richard Whittington (Cambridge University Press, 2007).

Philippe Lorino has been Professor of Management Control at ESSEC Business School since 1993. He is a graduate (Sciences) of Paris Ecole Polytechnique and Ecole des Mines and Ph.D. in Management (Paris University). Until 1987, he was a senior civil servant in the French Government, in charge of public industrial policies. From 1987 to 1993, he was in charge of designing new management control systems in an international computer company. His research, inspired by the pragmatist philosophy, currently explores collective activity, processes of organizing as dialogical inquiries, and management systems as semiotic mediations of activity.

List of Contributors

Steve Maguire is Associate Professor of Strategy and Organization in the Desautels Faculty of Management at McGill University in Montreal, Canada. He received his Ph.D. from HEC-Montreal in 2000. His research focuses on institutional, technological, and organizational change resulting when commercial, scientific, and political struggles intersect around social or environmental issues. He has studied the pharmaceutical sector, analyzing the identity work and empowerment of people living with HIV/AIDS as well as their impacts on the commercialization, availability and accessibility of treatments. He has also studied the chemical industry, and is a recognized expert on the application of the precautionary principle in chemical risk management. His research has appeared in the *Academy of Management Journal, Emergence, Global Governance, Greener Management International, Health Care Management Review, Journal of Management Studies, Organization Studies*, and *Strategic Organization*. Most recently, he co-edited the *SAGE Handbook of Complexity and Management* (2011).

Frank Mueller holds a chair in management at the University of St Andrews. His research interests include discourse analysis of workplace change; change in professional organizations, especially health and engineering; theory and practice of teamworking. He has published widely in journals including *Organization Studies, Human Relations, Journal of Management Studies, Accounting, Organizations and Society, Organization,* and *Work,* and *Employment and Society.*

Shubha Patvardhan is a doctoral candidate in the Department of Management and Organization at the Smeal College of Business, the Pennsylvania State University. Her research focuses on organizational and field identity and the processes associated with the development of both. Her broad area of research interests span cognition and strategy-making. She holds an M.B.A. from XLRI Jamshedpur, India.

Michael G. Pratt is the O'Connor Family Professor in Management and Organization, and, by courtesy, Professor of Psychology, at Boston College. He earned his Ph.D. in organizational psychology from the University of Michigan. His research centers on how individuals relate to and connect with their work, occupations, professions, and organizations. He currently explores these connections primarily through the lenses of multiple identities, identification, multiple emotions (ambivalence), sensemaking, and intuition. His work has appeared in various outlets, including the *Academy of Management Annual Review, Academy of Management Journal, Academy of Management Review, Organizational Research Methods,* and the *Administrative Science Quarterly.* He also co-edited a book (with Anat Rafaeli) entitled, *Artifacts and Organizations: Beyond Mere Symbolism.* He recently completed his tenure as the inaugural associate editor for qualitative research at the *Academy of Management Journal.*

List of Contributors

Majken Schultz is Professor of Organization Studies at the Department of Organization, Copenhagen Business School; International Research Fellow at the Centre for Corporate Reputation at Oxford University, Saïd Business School; and partner in the Reputation Institute. Her research focuses on the construction and expression of identity in theory and practice with a special interest in the interplay between culture, identity, and images and the implications for corporate branding processes. She has published several books and more than forty international articles. Among her books (together with Mary Jo Hatch) are *The Expressive Organization* and *Organizational Identity: A Reader* with Oxford University Press. Her most recent book also with Hatch is *Taking Brand Initiative: How Companies Can Align Their Strategy, Culture and Identity Through Corporate Branding* with Jossey Bass. This book has been translated into Danish, Spanish, and Korean. She serves on several company boards and is very active in the public debate on issues related to identity and branding and is a regular columnist in the leading Danish business newspaper *Boersen*.

Harry Sminia is Lecturer in Strategic Management at the Management School of the University of Sheffield, UK. He received an M.Sc. in Sociology from the University of Leiden and a Ph.D. in Business Administration from the University of Groningen, both in the Netherlands. Over the years, he has conducted research in strategy formation, organizational change, competitive positioning, strategy-as-practice, and institutionalization, employing process methods and methodology.

Roy Suddaby is the Eric Geddes Professor of Business at the Alberta School of Business and a visiting professor at Uppsala University. His research is aimed at understanding institutional and organizational change. Current projects include the adoption and diffusion of corporate art collections and the strategic use of history for competitive advantage.

Benoît Tricard is Professor at ESCEM Management School (France). He used to work as a consultant specialized in the analysis of processes and change management. His research currently explores the insights given by the pragmatist philosophy to the study of organizations.

Haridimos Tsoukas holds the Columbia Ship Management Chair in Strategic Management at the University of Cyprus and is a Professor of Organization Studies at Warwick Business School, University of Warwick, UK. He obtained his Ph.D. at the Manchester Business School (MBS), University of Manchester, and has worked at MBS, the University of Essex, the University of Strathclyde, and the ALBA Graduate Business School, Greece. He has published widely in several leading academic journals, including the *Academy of Management Review, Strategic Management Journal, Organization Studies, Organization Science, Journal of Management Studies,* and *Human Relations*. He was the Editor-in-Chief of *Organization Studies* (2003–8). His research interests include: knowledge-based perspectives on organizations, organizational becoming, the management of

List of Contributors

organizational change and social reforms, the epistemology of practice, and epistemological issues in organization theory. He is the editor (with Christian Knudsen) of *The Oxford Handbook of Organization Theory: Meta-Theoretical Perspectives* (Oxford University Press, 2003). He has also edited *Organizations as Knowledge Systems* (Palgrave Macmillan, 2004) (with N. Mylonopoulos) and *Managing the Future: Foresight in the Knowledge Economy* (Blackwell, 2004) (with J. Shepherd). His book *Complex Knowledge: Studies in Organizational Epistemology* was published by Oxford University Press in 2005. He is also the author of the book *If Aristotle were a CEO* (in Greek, Kastaniotis, 2004). He writes regularly on political and social issues for the leading Greek newspaper *Kathimerini*.

Andrew H. Van de Ven is Vernon H. Heath Professor of Organizational Innovation and Change in the Carlson School of Management of the University of Minnesota. He received his Ph.D. from the University of Wisconsin, Madison, in 1972, and taught at the Wharton School of the University of Pennsylvania before his present appointment. He is co-author (with M. S. Poole, K. Dooley, and M. Holmes) of a process research methods book, *Organizational Change and Innovation: Theory and Methods for Research* (2000), and author of *Engaged Scholarship: A Guide for Organizational and Social Research* (2007), both published by Oxford University Press. He was 2000–1 President of the Academy of Management.

Lee Watkiss is a doctoral student at Boston College, Carroll School of Management. His research interests lie at the intersection of cognitive and cultural processes, especially in how actors use cultural resources to cultivate meaning. He focuses on cognitive processes and their cultural dynamics that center around sensemaking, organizational identity, and symbolization within the phenomenon of organizing.

James V. Wertsch is the Marshall S. Snow Professor in Arts and Sciences, Associate Vice Chancellor for International Affairs, Director of the McDonnell International Scholars Academy, and Professor of Anthropology at Washington University in St. Louis. His research is concerned with language, thought, and culture, with a special focus on national narratives and identities. He is the author of over 200 publications appearing in over a dozen languages. These include the volumes *Voices of the Mind* (Harvard University Press, 1991), *Mind as Action* (Oxford University Press, 1998), and *Voices of Collective Remembering* (Cambridge University Press, 2002). After finishing his Ph.D. at the University of Chicago in 1975, Wertsch joined as a postdoctoral fellow in Moscow at the USSR Academy of Sciences and Moscow State University. Wertsch has held faculty positions at Northwestern University, the University of California at San Diego, Clark University, and now Washington University in St. Louis. In addition, he has been a visiting professor at the University of Utrecht, Moscow State University, the University of Seville, the Swedish Collegium for Advanced Study in Social Sciences, Bristol University, and the University of Oslo. Wertsch is a fellow of the American

List of Contributors

Academy of Arts and Sciences, holds honorary degrees from Linköping University and the University of Oslo, and is an honorary member of the Russian Academy of Education. He currently serves as a guest professor at the University of Oslo in Norway, Tsinghua University in Beijing, and at Fudan University in Shanghai.

Andrea Whittle is a Professor at Cardiff Business School, Cardiff University, and a member of the Cardiff Organization Research Group (CORGies). Earlier she was at the Saïd Business School, Oxford University, working as an Economic and Social Research Council (ESRC) post-doctoral fellow. Her research interests focus on discourse, identity, discursive psychology, and management consultancy.

Elden Wiebe (Ph.D., University of Alberta) is Associate Professor of Management at The King's University College, Edmonton, Alberta, Canada. His primary research interests include time in relation to organizations, organizational change, and strategic management; and secondly, spirituality in the workplace. He has published in *Perspective in Process Organization Studies*, *Journal of Business Ethics* (with William M. Foster), *Journal of Management Inquiry*, and *Healthcare Quarterly*. He is also the co-editor (with Albert J. Mills and Gabrielle Durepos) of the recently completed *Sage Encyclopedia of Case Study Research*.

James Williams is Professor of European Philosophy at the University of Dundee. He has written widely on recent French philosophy and its connections to other traditions, in particular process studies. His work includes books and articles on post-structuralism, analytic and continental philosophy, Deleuze, Whitehead, and Lyotard. His most recent books are *Gilles Deleuze's Logic of Sense: A Critical Introduction and Guide* (Edinburgh University Press, 2008) and *Gilles Deleuze's Philosophy of Time: A Critical Introduction and Guide* (Edinburgh University Press, 2011). His current work is on process and time in architecture and planning.

Series Editorial Structure

Series Editors

Ann Langley, HEC Montréal, Canada, ann.langley@hec.ca
Haridimos Tsoukas, University of Cyprus, Cyprus and University of Warwick, UK, process.symposium@gmail.com

Advisory Board

Hamid Bouchikhi, ESSEC Business School, France
Michel Callon, CSI-Ecole des Mines de Paris, France
Robert Chia, University of Strathclyde, UK
Todd Chiles, University of Missouri, USA
Barbara Czarniawska, University of Gothenburg, Sweden
François Cooren, Université de Montréal, Canada
Martha Feldman, University of California, Irvine, USA
Raghu Garud, Pennsylvania State University, USA
Silvia Gherardi, University of Trento, Italy
Cynthia Hardy, University of Melbourne, Australia
Robin Holt, University of Liverpool, UK
Paula Jarzabkowski, Aston Business School, UK
Sally Maitlis, University of British Columbia, Canada
Wanda Orlikowski, MIT, USA
Brian T. Pentland, Michigan State University, USA
Marshall Scott Poole, University of Illinois, USA
Georg Schreyögg, Freie Universität Berlin, Germany
Kathleen Sutcliffe, University of Michigan, USA
Andew Van de Ven, University of Minnesota, USA
Karl E. Weick, University of Michigan, USA

Editorial Officer & Process Organization Studies Symposium Administrator

Sophia Tzagaraki, process.symposium@gmail.com

Endorsements

"As we become more willing to convert reified entities into differentiated streams, the resulting images of process have become more viable and more elusive. Organization becomes organizing, being becomes becoming, construction becomes constructing. But as we see ourselves saying more words that end in 'ing,' what must we be thinking? That is not always clear. But now, under the experienced guidance of editors Langley and Tsoukas, there is an annual forum that moves us toward continuity and consolidation in process studies. This book series promises to be a vigorous, thoughtful forum dedicated to improvements in the substance and craft of process articulation."

Karl E. Weick, Rensis Likert Distinguished University Professor of Organizational Behavior and Psychology, University of Michigan, USA

"In recent years process and practice approaches to organizational topics have increased significantly. These approaches have made significant contributions to already existing fields of study, such as strategy, routines, knowledge management, and technology adoption, and these contributions have brought increasing attention to the approaches. Yet because the contributions are embedded in a variety of different fields of study, discussions about the similarities and differences in the application of the approaches, the research challenges they present, and the potential they pose for examining taken for granted ontological assumptions are limited. This series will provide an opportunity for bringing together contributions across different areas so that comparisons can be made and can also provide a space for discussions across fields. Professors Langley and Tsoukas are leaders in the development and use of process approaches. Under their editorship, the series will attract the work and attention of a wide array of distinguished organizational scholars."

Martha S. Feldman, Johnson Chair for Civic Governance and Public Management, Professor of Social Ecology, Political Science, Business and Sociology, University of California, Irvine, USA

Endorsements

"*Perspectives on Process Organization Studies* will be the definitive annual volume of theories and research that advance our understanding of process questions dealing with how things emerge, grow, develop, and terminate over time. I applaud Professors Ann Langley and Haridimos Tsoukas for launching this important book series, and encourage colleagues to submit their process research and subscribe to *PROS*."

Andrew H. Van de Ven, Vernon H. Heath Professor of Organizational Innovation and Change, University of Minnesota, USA

"The new series—*Perspectives on Process Organization Studies*—is a timely and valuable addition to the organization studies literature. The ascendancy of process perspectives in recent years has signified an important departure from traditional perspectives on organizations that have tended to privilege either self-standing events or discrete entities. In contrast, by emphasizing emergent activities and recursive relations, process perspectives take seriously the ongoing production of organizational realities. Such a performative view of organizations is particularly salient today, given the increasingly complex, dispersed, dynamic, entangled, and mobile nature of current organizational phenomena. Such phenomena are not easily accounted for in traditional approaches that are premised on stability, separation, and substances. Process perspectives on organizations thus promise to offer powerful and critical analytical insights into the unprecedented and novel experiences of contemporary organizing."

Wanda J. Orlikowski, Alfred P. Sloan Professor of Information Technologies and Organization Studies, Massachusetts Institute of Technology, USA

"The recent decades witnessed conspicuous changes in organization theory: a slow but inexorable shift from the focus on structures to the focus on processes. The whirlwinds of the global economy made it clear that everything flows, even if change itself can become stable. While the interest in processes of organizing is not new, it is now acquiring a distinct presence, as more and more voices join in. A forum is therefore needed where such voices can speak to one another, and to the interested readers. The series *Perspectives on Process Organization Studies* will provide an excellent forum of that kind, both for those for whom a processual perspective is a matter of ontology, and those who see it as an epistemological choice."

Barbara Czarniawska, Professor of Management Studies, School of Business, Economics and Law at the University of Gothenburg, Sweden

Endorsements

"We are living in an era of unprecedented change; one that is characterized by instability, volatility, and dramatic transformations. It is a world in which the seemingly improbable, the unanticipated, and the downright catastrophic appear to occur with alarming regularity. Such a world calls for a new kind of thinking: thinking that issues from the chaotic, fluxing immediacy of lived experiences; thinking that resists or overflows our familiar categories of thought; and thinking that accepts and embraces messiness, contradictions, and change as the *sine qua non* of the human condition. Thinking in these genuinely processual terms means that the starting point of our inquiry is not so much about the *being* of entities such as 'organization,' but their constant and perpetual *becoming*. I very much welcome this long overdue scholarly effort at exploring and examining the fundamental issue of *process* and its implications for organization studies. Hari Tsoukas and Ann Langley are to be congratulated on taking this very important initiative in bringing the process agenda into the systematic study of the phenomenon of organization. It promises to be a path-breaking contribution to our analysis of organization."

Robert Chia, Professor of Management, University of Strathclyde, UK

"This new series fits the need for a good annual text devoted to process studies. Organization theory has long required a volume specifically devoted to process research that can address process ontology, methodology, research design, and analysis. While many authors collect longitudinal data, there are still insufficient methodological tools and techniques to deal with the nature of that data. Essentially, there is still a lack of frameworks and methods to deal with good processual data or to develop process-based insights. This series will provide an important resource for all branches of organization, management, and strategy theory. The editors of the series, Professors Ann Langley and Hari Tsoukas are excellent and very credible scholars within the process field. They will attract top authors to the series and ensure that each paper presents a high quality and insightful resource for process scholars. I expect that this series will become a staple in libraries, Ph.D. studies, and journal editors' and process scholars' bookshelves."

Paula Jarzabkowski, Professor of Strategic Management, Aston Business School, UK

1
Constructing Identity in and around Organizations

Introducing the Second Volume of "Perspectives on Process Organization Studies"

Majken Schultz, Steve Maguire, Ann Langley, and Haridimos Tsoukas

It is a great pleasure to present the second volume of "Perspectives on Process Organization Studies," an initiative that celebrates a more complex kind of thinking about organizations by nurturing scholarship that reflects an understanding of the world as in flux, in perpetual motion, and continually "becoming." Process Organization Studies (PROS) is an approach to studying *organizing* that unfolds from process metaphysics—the worldview that sees processes, rather than substances, as the basic forms of the universe. A process orientation prioritizes activity over outcome, change over persistence, novelty over continuity, expression over determination, and becoming over being. Accordingly, flux and transformation as well as creativity, disruption, and indeterminism are key themes within a process worldview.

To engage with the world by seeing process as fundamental does not imply to deny the existence of states, events, entities, or other "things"; it does, however, draw attention to the ways in which any object can be unpacked to reveal the complex processes involved in—the sequences of activities and transactions that take place and contribute to—the object's constitution (Rescher, 1996; Nayak and Chia, 2011). As process philosopher Nicholas Rescher (1996: 29) notes, "the idea of discrete 'events' dissolves into a manifold of processes which themselves dissolve into further processes." A process perspective thus invites us to acknowledge, rather than to reduce, the complexity inherent in the world as well as in our experiencing of the world. It is animated by what philosopher Stephen Toulmin (1990) calls an "ecological style" of thinking (Tsoukas and Dooley, in press). The latter, as Toulmin notes, embraces complexity by reinstating the importance of the particular, the local, and the timely. More broadly, the ecological style acknowledges connectivity, recursive patterns of communication, feedback, nonlinearity, emergence, ineffability, and becoming (Hayles, 1991, 1999; Turner, 1995; Tsoukas, 2005).

In providing an alternative to traditional "entitative" conceptions of reality (Chia, 1999; Tsoukas and Chia, 2002), a process perspective rests on an antidualist and relational ontology. It recognizes that "what is" has no existence apart from its *relating* to other things. Consequently, long established dualisms—for example, mind and body, reason and emotion, humanity and nature, individual and collective, organism and environment, agency and structure, ethics and science, etc.—are recast as barriers to understanding that need to be overcome; materiality and time are also reconceptualized because "structures and objects become secondary to the movement of process" (Cooper, 2007: 1547). Objects are constituted by and in relation to other objects, and in an ongoing manner—temporality is a constitutive feature of the world and human experience. Processes unfold in time, which means that human phenomena cannot be adequately understood if time is abstracted away, but much of our work in organization studies has not directly considered temporality or questioned how time is constructed and lived in organizations.

Each volume in the present Series aims not only to contribute to the development of process organization studies generally but also to explore in more depth the implications of a process perspective for a particular central theme of broad relevance to organization studies. This volume focuses specifically on the concept of "identity" in and around organizations. Part I presents seven chapters dealing explicitly with this theme, while Part II offers four complementary contributions that address broader issues in process organization studies. In this introduction, we elaborate on the relevance of a process perspective to studies of identity, and present the eleven individual chapters.

1.1 Identity as *process*?

Why is our subheading a question? In addition to the fact that it is unusual to view identity *as* process, it is also because this volume is animated by questions. Its chapters not only pose important questions about identity and then explore them to offer tentative answers but, in so doing, also raise new questions. The questions motivating this volume include the following: (*a*) Which theoretical underpinnings are shared across theorizing about identity and processes? In other words, can the identities constructed in and around organizations be theorized from a process perspective? (*b*) Which processes are relevant, or even specific, to constructing identities in and around organizations? Put another way, if identity is conceived as process, what are the implications for theory as well as for designing and conducting empirical studies? (*c*) What are the implications of identity as process for thinking about different levels of analysis? (*d*) How do considerations of identity contribute to process theorizing more generally?

In assembling chapters that address these questions, this volume represents an attempt to amplify—and, possibly, refract—contemporary debates among identity scholars that, in various ways, question established notions of identity as "essence," "entity," or "thing" while calling for alternative ways to approach identity, to understand it, and to grasp its significance in contexts in and around organizations. Rather, conceptualizing identity as process calls for other metaphorical images, such as identity as "flow" or "narrative" or "work" or "play"—that is, identity as continually under construction. The constructing of identities—those processes of social construction through which actors in and around organizations claim, accept, negotiate, affirm, stabilize, maintain, reproduce, challenge, disrupt, destabilize, repair, or otherwise relate to their sense of selves and others—has become a critically important topic in the study of organizations (e.g., Czarniawska-Joerges, 1997, Corley et al., 2006; Lerpold et al., 2007; Gioia et al., 2010). Departing from early conceptualizations that posited organizational identity as those aspects of their organization that members perceive as central, enduring, and distinctive (Albert and Whetten, 1985), recent research has studied identity as relational and dynamic, formed though interactions, associations, and conversations. "[O]rganizational identity is not an aggregation of perceptions of an organization resting in peoples' heads, it is a dynamic set of processes by which an organization's self is continuously socially constructed from the interchange between internal and external definitions of the organization offered by all organizational stakeholders" (Hatch and Schultz, 2002: 1004). With a process perspective, identity is thus an ongoing accomplishment; processes of constructing identity are open to contestation and as productive of fragmented, fluid selves characterized by multiple, contradictory narratives as of convergent, stable ones. Drawing on the dialectic between

Constructing Identity in and around Organizations

organizational being and becoming (Chia, 1996), a process perspective considers organizational identity to be ever emerging from ongoing processes of enacting "how we are becoming" rather than from defining "who we are" as an organization. Further, a process perspective underscores for researchers how identity construction is historically situated in time and space; that is, "the various categorizations that constitute identity and their meanings are not fixed but change over time, in different contexts, and as a result of ongoing language use" (Maguire and Hardy, 2005: 15) such that "informed analysis of identity construction in an organizational setting has to acknowledge the socially and discursively constructed nature of the self" (Kärreman and Alvesson, 2001: 63).

This volume takes the theorizing of identity in and around organizations one step further, as all contributing authors, together representing a notable variety of theoretical perspectives, have pushed their thinking and moved their empirical work forward by using a process perspective. Their insights not only shed light on identity construction processes but also demonstrate how process thinking itself becomes richer when developed in relation to the identity construct. With questioning so prominent in the volume—both the opening and closing chapters explicitly mention questions in their titles—we considered it appropriate to organize our introduction around four questions that motivate our endeavor.

1.2 Which theoretical underpinnings are shared across theorizing about identity and processes?

Our first question asks whether it is possible not only to apply a process perspective to identity but also to illuminate shared underpinnings of the ways in which process and identity are being theorized. One of the fundamental assumptions in process thinking is that organizations consist of mutually interlocking behaviors that develop and transform in relation to each other (Weick, 1979; Langley and Tsoukas, 2010). This implies that a process perspective focuses on overcoming established distinctions, asking instead how these distinctions are being constructed and reconstructed over time. The concept of identity also emerges from a relational understanding of the interrelatedness between self-perceptions and the perceptions of others, as suggested by Mead (1932). In his chapter, Pratt calls for a deeper concern with the construct of "self" as it is more clearly constituted in relationship with "others"; and invites a closer scrutiny of self-processes as underlying identity dynamics.

This relational underpinning of identity can, similar to process thinking, be further analyzed in relation to time and space. The spatial dimension of identity concerns how "others" are constituted in interrelated ways to serve as sources of origin, development, and transformation of identity. This raises questions of how stakeholders, peers, and competitors are constructed when members of organizations define themselves as similar to and/or different from others, as demonstrated in the study of the formation of microbrewers by Kroezen and Heugens, and also addressed by Glynn and Watkiss in their chapter on sources of identity. The role of time and conceptions of temporality are foundational in a process perspective, as illustrated in the chapters by Williams and by Van de Ven and Sminia and elaborated further in chapters by Tricard and Lorino as well as Wiebe, Suddaby, and Foster. But so far the discussion of time in identity studies has mostly concerned whether identity is enduring or not, that is, debating the definition by Albert and Whetten (1985). Building on recent conceptualizations of "identity dynamics" (Hatch and Schultz, 2002), identity as "adaptive instability" (Gioia et al., 2000) and the dynamics between time and space (e.g., Clegg et al., 2007), there is a need to develop our understanding of the flow of time in identity and ask how past, present, and future are connected. The chapters by Pratt and by Mueller and Whittle both discuss the shared underpinnings of process thinking and identity studies, suggesting that temporality might be studied either as shifting interrelations between self and others over time or as sequences of individual identity definitions, which are changing as the positions of individuals change from situation to situation. Similar to process thinking, the flow of events contextualize theorizing about identity. Finally, the importance of origin is stressed, as organizations and their identities are situated in a specific historical context, such as national cultural history (i.e., the chapter by Wertsch) or industrial history (i.e., the chapter by Kroezen and Heugens).

1.3 Which processes are relevant, or even specific, to constructing identities in and around organizations?

The next set of questions asks: if identity is seen as process, how can we further specify the processes that constitute identity in organizations and to what extent are they unique to the phenomenon of identity? As this Series will demonstrate over time, a process perspective can be applied to a rich variety of constructs, such as sensemaking, identity, and materiality. This perhaps poses a conceptual risk of creating an "isomorphic process," where the uniqueness—in our case of the identity construct—is absorbed by generic process thinking. Several of the chapters in this volume address this issue as a motivation to elaborate those processes that are unique to identity, asking: which are the processes that constitute identity?

To identify such processes, contributing authors begin from a range of different positions on the conceptual landscape relevant to "identity." One set of chapters is mostly concerned with the processes connecting organizational identity to a focal organization's external environment, suggesting different directions of influence. Analyzing identity from the level of society, Glynn and Watkins elaborate the multiple processes through which societal cultures influence identity, whereas Pratt, in his chapter, focuses on the unfolding mutual relations between a focal organization's self and specific organizational stakeholders, drawing on a framework that highlights the processes involved in "self-formation." In their chapter, Kroezen and Heugens are also concerned with processes of identity formation, but they take a more specific temporal perspective by elaborating processes that constitute the origin and early stages of identity formation, which they define as imprinting and enactment. The chapter by Mueller and Whittle also elaborates on the micro-moves that constitute self-definitions, but focuses on individual rather than organizational identities as well as the different roles embedded in shifting identity positions. The chapter by Wertsch comes full circle as he shows how individuals use narrative tools embedded in a broader sociocultural setting to "make sense of themselves and the world around them" (Wertsch, Chapter 6).

Together, these chapters pave the way for a much richer understanding of processes unique to identity in and around organizations. The conceptualization of identity as process invites a closer scrutiny of how identities form and develop, whether it is over long periods of time or during shifting situations within a day. By elaborating influences on identity in and around organizations, the authors encourage the exchange of ideas between institutional theory and perspectives emerging from pragmatism and a social constructivism, as they are all enriching the processes that contextualize identity (see also Atken et al., forthcoming). Finally, some of the chapters discuss the processes involved in expressing identity, showing how individuals use narrative tools, and discursive positioning in the construction of self.

1.4 What are the implications of identity as process for thinking about different levels of analysis?

Conceptualizing identity as process has implications for how different levels of analysis are considered and invoked in theorizing. First, the insight that viewing identity as process can shed light on various types of identity at different levels of analysis is confirmed by chapters in this volume. Most chapters in Part I explicitly address organizational identity, but national and individual identities are also addressed. Other levels of analysis such as, for example, professional identities may not be explicitly addressed but theorizing indicates they could be. For example, Wertsch's approach to collective identities, which harnesses the concept of "mnemonic communities," is applicable to collectivities covering a wide range of levels of analysis, from families to professions to nations.

Second, it would appear that a process perspective is generally facilitative of—or even demands—multilevel approaches, and the chapters in this volume indicate that this is the case for the phenomenon of identity. Logically, if organizational or individual or any other type of identity is an emergent property of some underlying processes, then at least two levels of analysis are involved in theory-building. Further, because a process perspective posits that any apparently stable or fixed object of knowledge can be de-reified and opened up to reveal how it is reproduced through processes occurring on faster time scales, a potentially infinite number of levels of analysis and processes operating on different time scales are brought into play. The chapters in this volume explore this complexity. Several explicitly stress the integration of micro- and macro-level perspectives. Glynn and Watkiss, for instance, do so by theorizing how aspects of societal cultural can shape organizational identities and, in turn, how organizations can appropriate cultural mechanisms to construct organizational identities; while Kroezen and Heugens illustrate empirically how organizational identities are shaped by processes involving individuals at a lower level of analysis as well as institutions at a higher level. The chapters by Wertsch and by Mueller and Whittle illustrate the important role of narratives—especially those which construct "villains" and "victims"—in connecting phenomena typically considered as occurring at different levels of analysis and time scales. In fact, Wertsch explicitly parses national narratives into "two levels of narrative analysis, one concerned with specific narratives and the other with narrative templates," to illustrate their cognitive and emotional impacts on individuals.

We believe that a process perspective can facilitate not only the work of researchers interested in exploring how multiple levels of analysis intersect with each other and with time to become constitutive of identities but also the efforts of scholars wrestling with issues of levels of analysis and of temporality as they seek to theorize other phenomena. This brings us to our final question.

1.5 How do considerations of identity contribute to process theorizing more generally?

Process theorizing in general exposes the fragility of assumptions about permanence and stability that seem at the same time to be necessary for activity in the world, and yet that are sustained or undermined continually in every moment, in part through that very activity. The concept of identity appears to imply both in its labeling and in much of its application to research practice, the presence of an essence, some form of continuity or permanence that endures over time (Albert and Whetten, 1985). When that durability is systematically problematized, as in the chapters in this volume, while retaining and even enhancing the value of the concept as a way of understanding individual and organizational selves that has some temporal stickiness, we see how other phenomena with similar connotations of stability (structures, institutions, materiality, organizations) might also be illuminated by a process perspective.

Indeed, several of the general process chapters in this volume reveal this paradox of stability constituted in movement but apply this to different underlying concepts: for example, Grand and Ackeret focus on management knowledge, showing how it is reconstituted and progressively deepened by situated engagement in managerial practices. Lorino and Tricard illustrate how robust time–space narrative frames (or "chronotopes") become sedimented through repeated iterations of organizing activities to the point where their questioning may become as painful and disruptive as the confrontations between national identity narratives described by Wertsch in this volume. In our view, research that interrogates the dynamic processes underlying seemingly entitative constructs such as identity offers one of the most exciting and promising ways of enriching process organization studies. Their particular contribution lies in recognizing the ongoing reconstitution of stability combined with the immanent potential for change, a pattern that we are pleased to find reflected in one way or another in the seven identity-related chapters in this volume as well as in the set of four general process chapters that complete it.

1.6 Introducing the volume

We now present the contents of these chapters in more detail. The volume begins and ends with questions—an appropriate bookending, we think, for a volume in a series emphasizing process, with the unfinished open-endedness it implies! The first two chapters challenge established notions of organizational identity, advocate a process perspective, and offer clear guidance for future scholarship.

Opening the volume with Chapter 2, "Rethinking identity construction processes in organizations: Three questions to consider," Michael G. Pratt invites readers to a reflexive journey through issues central to understanding organizational identity, organizing his trek around three key questions: (*a*) Can we meaningfully talk about identity and process? (*b*) If we can meaningfully talk about identity and process, how should we talk about them? (*c*) If we know how to talk about identity and process, what might be missing from the conversations we are currently having? Arguing that scholarship on both identity and process draws upon similar relational, behavioral, and symbolic "theoretical wellsprings," Pratt shows how much of what underpins the identity construct resonates with a process perspective. The chapter then examines some verbs important to the study of identity, to illustrate how identity becomes process in different ways by untangling these verbs' tacit metaphorical implications (e.g., constructing/ practicing/playing identity). Drawing upon the works of G. H. Mead, Pratt suggests distinguishing identities from the "self"—"a gestalt that is both related to and stands apart from the identities that comprise it"—and discusses "what a 'self-process' would look like" at the organizational level. In developing a framework for exploring organizational identity in terms of self-processes, the chapter introduces an explicit temporal dimension, showing how the self forms in relations with others (i.e., organizational constituencies) that change over time in an ongoing dialogue between character-defining commitments and others' expectations. The chapter thus points toward future research to expand the concept of organizational identity to include collective self-processes and temporality. Pratt's three questions lead him to another one that is critical for scholars adopting a process perspective on organizational identity—"whether identity is simply the 'content' of some processes (i.e., processes about identity), or whether there are processes that are unique to identity?"

Chapter 3 by Dennis A. Gioia and Shubha Patvardhan, "Identity as process and flow," continues in articulating questions fundamental to future scholarship by challenging established notions of organizational identity that assume that "Who we are as an organization" is a "thing" or "entity"—"some*thing*" existing in a "normal state of equilibrium." Drawing on critical self-scrutiny, the authors point out how numerous scholars of identity have been caught up in an "as if" game, in which we pretend to ourselves to be able to see identity as if it was a "static construction made manifest" through our research. They also suggest an alternative approach in which organizational identity is conceived as "flow": "identity is *always* in process, always in a state of 'becoming.'" Actually, the authors advocate a *both-and* framing wherein identity as thing and identity as process are reconciled as duality rather than opposed as dualism. They point to the debate pitting identity as claims (in the social actor view) against identity as construction (in the social constructionist view) as terrain where theory has advanced through arguments initially for the complementarity, and later for the mutual constitution, of the two views. Like Pratt, their intellectual journey leads them to more questions: (*a*) How should we approach our subject of study? (*b*) What research strategies are well suited to studying identity as process? (*c*) How might a compelling identity-as-process study look? In response, they counsel a shift in focus from "organization" to "organizing" as a first step enabling scholars to "capture both elements of identity: the *being* and the *becoming* of identity," call for more "mixed-method" approaches to shed light on identity processes, and advocate process narratives as a means to highlight the temporality and sequencing inherent to identity as organization–constituency relationships shift over time.

The two chapters that follow adopt a macro-level process perspective, emphasizing different aspects of organization–environment relations to identify or explore empirically environmental influences on organizational identity processes.

In the next chapter, Chapter 4, "Identity Exploring cultural mechanisms of organizational construction," Mary Ann Glynn and Lee Watkiss explore the cultural embeddedness of organizational identity, highlighting the role played by "cultural mechanisms" in the construction of a given organization's identity claims. The authors draw on Lamont and Small's (2008) observation that there are six major models of culture—that is, as frames, repertoires, narratives, capital, symbolic boundaries, and institutions—and argue that each suggests a mechanism through which culture can penetrate organizational identities. According to the authors, an organization makes identity claims of "who we are" and "what we do" by appropriating and interpreting cultural resources; and each of the six mechanisms highlights a different facet of culture that can be drawn upon to make an organization's identity sensible, meaningful, and credible. Notably, however, Glynn and Watkiss point out that all six mechanisms are not necessary to identity construction; rather, an organization selectively chooses those mechanisms that best suit its identity. In referencing the societal culture that embeds it in this way, an organization demonstrates social fitness that, in turn, enables legitimation and wealth creation. Interestingly, the various mechanisms described in this chapter each imply a different temporal nature or anchor for organizational identity: the taken-for-grantedness of institutional templates, for instance, implies a generalized timelessness but can usually be traced to prior acts of institutional entrepreneurship while narratives tend to situate and constitute organizations within sequences of actions, cause and effect, as well as concrete settings. This chapter thus provides an array of approaches to understanding the temporality of organizational identity as a process.

The following chapter by Jochem J. Kroezen and Pursey P. M. A. R. Heugens, Chapter 5, "Organizational identity formation: Processes of identity imprinting and enactment in the Dutch microbrewery landscape," examines organizational identities within a particular institutional field—microbreweries in the Netherlands. The chapter presents an empirical study of organizational identity formation, elaborating the institutional influences on microbrewery identities. The authors link organizational institutionalism with organizational identity by theorizing the "normative core" of the organization and its distinctive character, and by conceiving of organizations as "flexible 'organisms' that are continuously 'in flux' but in a given context." On the basis of a qualitative study of fifty-nine recently founded Dutch microbreweries, the authors develop a conceptual model of organizational identity formation that stresses two central processes: (*a*) initial *imprinting* of potential identity attributes upon organizations, and (*b*) subsequent enactment of a *selection* of these attributes by organizational insiders. Their approach incorporates human agency in that founders not only make decisions based on a "reservoir" of possible identity attributes but also play a crucial role in the enactment of specific attributes as the organization engages in particular relations with other actors in the breweries' environment. The study also highlights the crucial roles of peers and external audiences in identity formation. In addition, the authors' approach sheds light on the temporally contingent nature of such reservoirs of identity attributes: "Over time these attributes accumulate due to the mutually constitutive and interactive imprinting roles of the different identity sources." Further, the chapter also highlights how the balance of imprinting and enactment processes changes over time as a given organization matures.

The next two chapters continue to focus on identity as a process, but theorize individual identities with reference to collectivities that extend beyond a given organization—nation-states and professions—while highlighting the central role of narratives.

In Chapter 6, "Narrative tools and the construction of identity," James V. Wertsch builds on MacIntyre's (1984: 216) observation that humans are fundamentally "story-telling animals" to explore ways in which narrative tools are used by collectivities to construct identities as they engage in imagining and reproducing themselves. By using a shared narrative tool when talking about a past constructed as common, humans form and participate in "mnemonic communities" (Zerubavel, 2003), which can be organizations, professions, families, nations, or other groups. Resisting "the temptations of the copyright age to think of narratives as products of individual imagination," Wertsch sees narratives as "instruments provided by the broader sociocultural setting that are taken over by individuals to make sense of themselves and the world around them"—"a kind of off the shelf technology" tying individuals to their institutional, historical, and cultural context. This emphasis sheds light not only on differences in collectives' interpretations of the world, but also on the role of narratives in constituting collectives in the first place. Working at the level of nation, Wertsch uses his framework to examine the underlying cognitive and emotional forces involved a specific clash between the Estonian and Russian mnemonic communities, which have been caught in a long-term "mnemonic standoff" over "what really happened" in the past (Wertsch, 2008b). What William James calls the "integral pulse of consciousness" not only assumes but helps to create and reinforce an imagined group—and not only at the level of nation-state. Rather, "[m]any of the same principles and processes are involved in other groups; it seems that everyone from corporations, universities, and professional organizations to families is concerned with the narrative tools at its disposal for creating collective identity." This chapter thus clarifies and makes important additions to research agenda of organizational scholars interested in narrative approaches to identity as process.

In the next chapter, Chapter 7, "Villains, victims and the financial crisis: Positioning identities through descriptions," Frank Mueller and Andrea Whittle also study identity as a process and at the individual level of analysis but, in contrast to the previous chapter, the reference point for the individuals involved in their case study is their profession, as bankers, and not their nation-state. The authors' theoretical perspective is informed by discursive psychology, which they put to good use in examining the identity positioning employed in the narratives surrounding the recent financial crisis. Because discursive psychology "is sensitive to the *unfolding* and *ongoing* process through which identities are negotiated within interaction," the authors are able to adopt a process perspective on individual identities to show how they evolve in shifting and mutual relationships between participants in specific events. Representations of the processes purported to underlie empirical events themselves are analyzed using a narrative framework, which allows the authors to show how individuals position themselves—both historically and causally—in relation to each other, while acting out their identity in different roles—some as victims which implies, necessarily, others as villains. Although the event described unfolds during a limited period of time, the authors are able nonetheless to illustrate how a variety of what they label "discursive devices" is used by actors in their mutual, micro-level activities of identity construction. The authors' analysis therefore relates micro-level moves with an aim of identity reconstruction to a particular post-crisis moralistic landscape, illustrating how even seemingly small maneuvers in the flow and ebb of identity are embedded in a broader narrative and institutional context.

The next chapter, Chapter 8, "Identity and time in Gilles Deleuze's process philosophy," by James Williams, represents a disjunction of sorts. Here, it must be said, the volume begins to change its tone. Whereas most prior chapters have tended to see identity *as* process and flow, the philosopher Gilles Deleuze sees identity as always *coming after* process and as always *subject to* process. In other words, "there is no identity as such independent of the processes making and unmaking it." Like other chapters, the issue of how scholars of identity are to incorporate considerations of time is therefore raised, but what is time? Williams addresses this question by introducing Deleuze's process philosophy of time and by showing how it can be used to examine, critically, management practices associated with the organizing of time, using an annual performance appraisal and objective setting meeting as an example. Although management technologies for organizing time often appear quite simple, they are in fact designed to tame great complexity because times not only are multiple but also take

Constructing Identity in and around Organizations

other times as constitutive dimensions. Anchored around three "syntheses" of time as well as the more traditional distinctions between past, present and future, Deleuze's philosophy has a ninefold grid of times. This means that an organization is always a multiplicity of becoming. Further, Williams argues that the order of priority of becoming and identity, with becoming primary, bequeaths a value system to Deleuze's philosophy. Practical application of this philosophical framework to organizational activities, therefore, can shed light on the costs and omissions associated with particular management practices.

In line with the mission of this book series, the remaining chapters in the volume broaden the perspective beyond an explicit focus on identity-related phenomena to contribute to process organization studies more generally. The first two chapters in this segment of the book pursue the exploration of time initiated by Williams.

In their chapter entitled "The Bakhtinian theory of chronotope (time–space frame) applied to the organizing process," (Chapter 9) Philippe Lorino and Benoît Tricard begin by offering a view of organizing processes as inherently narrative in form as people enact narratives through their activities and through the sense that they make of them as they unfold. The focus here is not on narratives as discursive productions (as in the previous chapters by Wertsch and by Mueller and Whittle), but rather on narratives as embedded in and constructed through activity. These narratives are underpinned by what Lorino and Tricard call "architextures," that is, generic frames that bound the range of conceivable narrative patterns within a given cultural context. Drawing on Bhaktin and Deleuze, the authors introduce the central notion of the "chronotope," a form of architexture based on distinctive time–space configurations. They argue that breaches in chronotopes create situations that seem senseless to people embedded in them, provoking what they have labeled rather picturesquely, following Deleuze, as "screams"—expressions of disarray that reassert the time–space boundaries expressed in the chronotope. This phenomenon is illustrated with two empirical case studies in which the researchers were attempting to intervene to propose changes to organizing narratives: one involving a transformation of the computer industry's value chain, and the other located within the construction industry where the chronotopes of building designers and site managers prevented them from collaborating in improving safety. The notion of chronotope as presented by Lorino and Tricard is shown to be a powerful way of understanding time–space relations and their embeddedness in established organizing narratives. It has clear value as a conceptual tool for process researchers as well as practical implications for the management of organizational change.

The temporal theme is also central to the next chapter, Chapter 10, on "The momentum of organizational change," authored by Elden Wiebe, Roy Suddaby, and William M. Foster. The authors investigate the various ways in which the notion of "momentum" has been defined in the organizational literature and relate it to the flow of time (past, present, and future). Contrasting their view with narrower conceptions of momentum that imply inertia, they identify three different understandings of momentum—inherent, exploratory, and emergent—grounded respectively in the past, the future, and the present. While inherent momentum suggests the idea of continuity in direction based on the past, exploratory momentum implies persistence in the pursuit of future goals, and emergent momentum suggests the effortful accomplishment of managerial action in the here and now. These conceptions reconnect the idea of momentum with the potential for various types of organizational change. Agency is clearly associated with the last two. However, the authors argue that agency is also contributive to inherent momentum through the way in which views of the past are actively and continuously reconstructed in the present. The authors complete and enrich their conceptual development by examining how past, present, and future all flow together within each of the forms of momentum, drawing on a variety of examples from the organizational literature. Lorino and Tricard, Wiebe, Suddaby, and Foster contribute to process organization studies by introducing and deepening the analysis of an important facet of organizing and changing that explicitly addresses time and temporality.

Although not directly referring to the notion of momentum, the next chapter by Simon Grand and Adrian Ackeret—"Management knowledge: A process view" (Chapter 11)—indirectly reveals many of its elements in an in-depth empirical process study of changes in management practices following the sudden departure of the chief executive of a Swiss software engineering firm. The study shows how management knowledge emerges and is dynamically sedimented over time following this event through successive "engagements," that is, interactions among managers and board members surrounding specific issues. Studying a series of twenty-five such engagements over a period of three years, and drawing on conventionalist theory and on recent process-based theories of routines, the authors reveal a dual process of managerial knowing and sensemaking embedded within these engagements: the use of different types of "justifications" or explanations of behavior combined with the enactment and reenactment of emerging "routines" or management practices. Through the recursive adaptation of justifications and routines over time in successive engagements, a set of "engagement regimes" constituting managerial knowledge emerge, represented by Grand and Ackeret in this case as regimes of formalization, collectivization, normalization, and separation. These regimes in turn generate their own set of controversial issues. Grand and Ackeret contribute to process organization studies by offering a perspective that simultaneously conceptualizes within the same framework notions of managerial knowledge and managerial knowing. Their work also offers a very interesting methodological exemplar of empirical process research involving the real time tracing of managerial interactions resulting in a wonderfully rich data set. The identification of "engagements" as a unit of analysis constitutes a very useful approach to systematic analysis of process data that could be of value to others.

In the final chapter, Chapter 12, "Aligning process questions, perspectives and explanations" by Andrew H. Van de Ven and Harry Sminia, the methodological issues underlying process analysis are made more explicit and linked to different forms of conceptual explanation. Like the opening chapter by Pratt, this chapter orients its analysis around questions. It also echoes the emphasis on time inherent to earlier chapters by focusing on four temporally oriented process questions: (*a*) about the past (how did we get here?), (*b*) about the present (what is going on?), (*c*) about the future (where are we going?), and (*d*) about action (what should we do?). The past-oriented question suggests a need for historical analysis and the development of conceptual explanations in terms of event sequences. Present-oriented questions suggest a conception of process as becoming and a need for ethnographic studies. Future-oriented questions suggest conceptualizations that examine path-dependency and creation and that focus on endogenous forces generative of different futures. Finally, action or intervention-oriented questions appear to be the most complex—yet, for these authors, they are the most interesting ones. Van de Ven and Sminia argue that this perspective demands an understanding of mechanisms underlying event sequences and recall the potential of teleological, life cycle, dialectic, and evolutionary theories as useful conceptual resources for moving in this direction. Overall, the authors illustrate not only both the importance of fitting study approaches and conceptualizations to questions but also the interaction among different kinds of questions, where answers to one may contribute to enriching the answers to others. Their reflections usefully lay out the range of process questions, concepts, and methods available to process scholars in their quest to better capture and understand the temporally fluid nature of organization and organizing.

Whether readers are interested in identity or in process studies more generally, this volume has much to offer. Fittingly, it begins and ends with questions. This is, after all, a volume in a book series dedicated to *process*, so it would be counterproductive in our view, not to mention contradictory, to offer up "answers" in a reified, definitive form. It is precisely the tentative, contingent, hesitant, humble unfolding of theorizing and shedding of light (and hence shadowing) in new ways, as well as the foregrounding (and hence backgrounding) of some phenomena rather than others, by both actors in the world *as well as* scholars seeking to understand them, to which we wish to draw attention.

References

Albert, S. and Whetten, D. A. (1985). "Organizational Identity." *Research in Organizational Behavior*, 7: 263–95.

Atken, K., Howard-Grenville, J., and Ventresca, M. (eds.) (forthcoming). *Organizational Culture and Institutional Theory: A Conversation at the Border*. A dialogue of essays accepted for publication in *Journal of Management Inquiry*.

Chia, R. (1996). *Organizational Analysis as Desconstructive Practice*. Berlin: Walter de Gruyter.

—— (1999). "A 'Rhizomic' Model of Organizational Change and Transformation: Perspective from a Metaphysics of Change." *British Journal of Management*, 10: 209–27.

Clegg, S. R., Rhodes, C., and Kornberger, M. (2007). "Desperately Seeking Legitimacy: Organizational Identity and Emerging Industries." *Organization Studies*, 28/4: 495–513.

Cooper, R. (2007). "Organs of Process: Rethinking Human Organization." *Organization Studies*, 28/10: 1547–73.

Corley, K. G., Harquail, C. V., Pratt, M. G., Glynn, M. A., Fiol, C. M., and Hatch, M. J. (2006). "Guiding Organizational Identity through Aged Adolescence." *Journal of Management Inquiry*, 15/2: 85–99.

Czarniawska-Joerges, B. (1997). *Narrating the Organization—Dramas of Institutional Identity*. Chicago: University of Chicago Press.

Gioia, D A., Price, K. N., Hamilton, A. L., and Thomas, J. B. (2010). "Forging an Identity: An Insider-Outsider Study of Processes Involved in the Formation of Organizational Identity." *Administrative Science Quarterly*, 55/1: 1–46.

—— Schultz, M., and Corley, K. G. (2000). "Organizational Identity, Image, and Adaptive Instability." *Academy of Management Review*, 25/1: 63–81.

Hatch, M. J. and Schultz, M. (2002). "The Dynamics of Organizational Identity." *Human Relations*, 55/8: 989–1018.

Hayles, K. N. (ed.) (1991). *Chaos and Order.* Chicago: Chicago University Press.

—— (1999). *How we became Posthuman.* Chicago: University of Chicago Press.

Kärreman, D. and Alvesson, M. (2001). "Making Newsmakers: Conversational Identity at Work." *Organization Studies*, 22/1: 59–89.

Lamont, M. and Small, M. (2008). *How Culture Matters: Enriching our Understanding of Poverty.* New York: Russell Sage Foundation Publications.

Langley, A. and Tsoukas, H. (2010). Introducing "Perspectives on Process Organization Studies," in T. Hernes and S. Maitlis (eds), *Process, Sensemaking & Organizing.* Oxford: Oxford University Press, pp. 1–26.

Lerpold, L., Ravasi, D., van Rekom, J., and Seonen, G. (2007). *Organizational Identity in Practice.* London: Routledge.

MacIntyre, A. (1984). *After Virtue: A Study in Moral Philosophy.* Notre Dame, IN: University of Notre Dame Press. (Second edition.)

Maguire, S. and Hardy, C. (2005). "Identity and Collaborative Strategy in the Canadian HIV/AIDS Treatment Domain." *Strategic Organization*, 3/1: 11–45.

Mead, G. H. (1932). *The Philosophy of the Present.* Chicago, IL: Open Court.

Nayak, A. and Chia, R. (2011). "Thinking Becoming and Emergence: Process Philosophy and Organization Studies," in H. Tsoukas and R. Chia (eds), *Philosophy and Organization Theory, Research in the Sociology of Organizations*, vol. 32. London: Emerald Group Publishing Ltd., pp. 281–310.

Rescher, N. (1996). *Process Metaphysics.* Albany, NY: State University of New York Press.

Toulmin, S. (1990). *Cosmopolis.* Chicago, IL: The University of Chicago Press.

Tsoukas, H. (2005). *Complex Knowledge.* Oxford: Oxford University Press.

—— Chia, R. (2002). "On Organizational Becoming: Rethinking Organizational Change." *Organization Science*, 13: 567–82.

—— Dooley, K. (in press). Introduction to the Special Issue "Towards the Ecological Style: Embracing Complexity in Organizational Research." *Organization Studies*.

Turner, F. (1995). *The Culture of Hope.* New York: Free Press.

Weick, K. E. (1979). *The Social Psychology of Organizing.* New York: McGraw-Hill.

Wertsch, J. V. (2008b). "A Clash of Deep Memories." *Profession 2008*. New York: Modern Language Association, pp. 46–53.

Zerubavel, E. (2003). *Time Maps: Collective Memory and the Social Shape of the Past.* Chicago: University of Chicago Press.

Part I

Identity and Organizations

2

Rethinking Identity Construction Processes in Organizations: Three Questions to Consider[1]

Michael G. Pratt

Abstract: While an exciting stream of research on identity construction processes in and around organizations has emerged in organizational studies, it may be time to reflect on our current progress to ensure that we are not closing off some avenues for inquiry prematurely. In reflecting upon the field, I address three questions: (*a*) Can we meaningfully talk about identity and process? (*b*) If we can meaningfully talk about identity and process, how should we talk about them? (*c*) If we know how to talk about identity and process, what might be missing from the conversations we are currently having? In addressing these questions, I examine the degree to which identity is amenable to process theorizing, I explore the language we use when talking about process and identity, and I inquire about the role of identity in "identity processes" and processes related to identity. With regard to the latter, I suggest that current process theorizing about organizational identity is impoverished because it rarely considers the role of the self, and I offer some ideas for theorizing about organizational self-processes.

"Identity is such a crucial affair that one shouldn't rush into it."

—David Quammen

I suppose talking about such a fundamental question as "who am I?" in Greece—where "γνῶθι σεαυτόν" ("know thyself") was supposed to have been carved in stone at the Temple of Delphi thousands of years ago—is altogether appropriate. Identity as either something you build (implied

Constructing Identity in and around Organizations

in the epigraph), or something you discover (implied in knowing one's self), may be broadly defined as "identity processes." Given the increased academic interest in identity, as well as the growing number of scholars interested in process, several of us from across the world gathered for the Second International Symposium on Process Organization Studies: Constructing Identity in and around Organizations. Conferences such as these are wonderful vehicles for cross-pollinating ideas and legitimizing topics and conversations. But a side-effect may also be the privileging of some conversations over others. Before scholars head off to continue work on identity construction processes, I wonder if perhaps we have closed off some conversations too soon. In what ways, if any, should we be talking about identity construction processes in and around organizations?

Before following up on that last statement, I want to provide a bit of background to this chapter and its author. My writing comes out of a keynote address given at the aforementioned conference. The Process Organization Studies Conference had three keynote speakers, and all of us were technically "outsiders" to the process theory community. Two of these speakers were also outside of business schools. I was not. I was the "insider–outsider" of the group. While I am not sure that my research conforms to each of the major tenets of process theory (Langley and Tsoukas, 2010), I have been interested in process for a long time—even if I have not labeled it as such, and perhaps not theorized or depicted it as well as I could have. To illustrate, early in my career (pre-tenure), I argued for looking at the process of identifying with organizations (Pratt, 1998), and have since proposed a model of identifying (Pratt, 2000) that remains one of few process-oriented models of identifying (Ashforth et al., 2008). But my interest in process preceded a deep look into Mohr's classic work (1982) on process versus variance models, and it was well before I read more recent treatments of process (e.g., Langley, 1999; Langley and Tsoukas, 2010).

I mention all of this as a way of introducing a few provisos. First, because this is based on a keynote, this chapter reflects my thoughts and musings about identity construction processes in and around organizations. It is meant to be informal, hopefully provocative, and failing all that, to provide some level of intellectual stimulation. Second, my typical approach to thinking and musing about topics is to ask questions. A mentor of mine once told me that the purpose of our profession is to keep important questions alive. I have taken that message to heart. Third, as an insider to the management community, I draw considerably on organizational research on identity and process—acknowledging that there is terrific work being done on identity, process, and identity and processes outside of our field (e.g., Cerulo, 1997, for review). Moreover, while I draw broadly from the management literature, and I have written about both individual- and collective-level identities, most of my process work has been focused on individuals within collectives. Thus, I tend to start "bottom–up" rather than "top–down" in my approach to identity in and around organizations. Finally, as an insider–outsider to the process theory community, I should note that I know more about identity theorizing than process theorizing. I mention this as more than a CYA (cover your assertions) standpoint—though there certainly might be some of that. Rather, I want to mention that I am still on the steep side of the process theorizing learning curve. I do hope, however, that this combination of being both close and distant to the phenomena at hand may provide a unique vantage point on the field.

Returning to my statement about whether and how we should be talking about identity construction processes in and around organizations, I thought I would take a step back from the emerging and exciting work being done in this area—both presented at the conference and in recent publications—to raise three questions. First, *can we meaningfully talk about identity and process?* Clearly, answering "no" to this query would make this a very (and possibly mercifully) short essay. However, this question seems like a good place to start if we are going to build a research stream on identity and process in organizations. What I mean by "meaningfully" talk about identity as a process is this: beyond the fact that identity has been applied to almost everything (see Pratt, 2003, for a critique), and almost anything can be depicted in variance and process terms, what—if anything—about identity that makes it perhaps uniquely suited to process theorizing? Second, *if we can meaningfully talk about identity and process, <u>how</u> should we talk about them?* This question shifts the discussion from "should we" to "how should we" and my focus here will be on the language we use in talking about identity processes or processes related to identity. Third and finally, I ask, *if we know how to talk about identity and process, what might be missing from the conversations we are currently having?* Here, I focus on whether identity is really where the "action" is regarding process or whether we might be better off also talking about "self" processes—or perhaps some other process or set of processes altogether. I also address the role of identity in process about or involving identity.

2.1 Question #1: Can we meaningfully talk about identity and process?

On the face of it, process theories may not jibe well with theories of identity. Drawing from Albert and Whetten's (1985) classic definition of organizational identity as the distinctive, core, and enduring features of an organization (see also Whetten, 2006), such a concept seems to emphasize continuity and cohesion. In addition, identities are often conceptualized in terms of structures. Micro-sociologists, for example, tie identity to social structures, namely roles (Stryker, 1987; Stryker and Burke, 2000); psychologists make links to cognitive structures such as schemas (Markus, 1977). Thus, from a view at 10,000 feet, identity appears to be among those theoretical constructs that attempt to explain how order comes out of chaos: at some level, it appears to serve as an island of stability in an ever-changing sea of reality, opinion, and circumstance. From a social actor perspective on organizational identity, while customers change, and stakeholders may behave erratically, an organization's identity endures. Alternatively, from a more micro-sociological perspective, role identities may endure despite the fact that the tasks that comprise them change. Whether it is about diaper changing, soccer coaching, or providing driving lessons, all of these various and changing behaviors across time are explained in single structural role identity: parent. Therefore, while there may be change all around identity, the identity concept seems to point our attention into what is cohesive and enduring.

Contrast this with terms consonant with a process worldview: "becoming, change, flux... disruption, and indeterminism" (Langley and Tsoukas, 2010: 2). Process perspectives view those things that appear stable and persistent as actually comprised of multitude of activities, expressions, and small (or not so small) changes. It is not denied that we see things as stable, but it points our attention to what is dynamic and ephemeral. Thus, at some level, identity and process seem mismatched (see also Langley's 2009 observation about the surprising juxtaposition of "stable" identity and process).

Mismatched does not necessarily mean incompatible, though. To illustrate, it may be that process and identity researchers have been studying two sides of the same coin: what some have been studying as "identity" is simply a residue of larger structuration processes whereby society produces identity, which, in turn, reproduces society (e.g., Mead, 1934; see also Alvesson and Wilmott, 2002). If true, then process should be evident even in those perspectives on identity that emphasize stability. This appears to be the case. To illustrate, in organizational research, a social actor perspective suggests that if some aspect of an organization's identity is not enduring, it is not identity (Whetten, 2006). However, endurance does not mean a lack of process. Research by Ravasi and Schultz (2006) and Gioia et al. (2010) both suggest that social actor views have their own processes and that these processes are often bound up in social construction processes. Moreover, if we take a process view that things are constantly changing (Tsoukas and Chia, 2002)—including identity—then attempts to "keep the same" would also involve effort and process. Thus, Anteby and Molnar (2010) suggest that organizations have to "remember to forget" some events and ideas in order to maintain an identity over time. Hence, there are processes to be studied even if we do believe that identities are enduring.

The fit between process and identity becomes clearer as we delve more deeply into the theoretical wellsprings from which both draw. To illustrate, Teresa Cardador and I argue that there are three fundamental bases of identification—and by consequence, identifying and identity (Cardador and Pratt, 2006).[2] These bases are relational (e.g., social identity approaches, which include ingroup–outgroup categories), behavioral (e.g., role-based approaches), and symbolic (e.g., narrative approaches). While derived largely from micro research, collective treatments of identity seem to suggest similar bases including relational/categorical (e.g., Porac and Thomas, 1989; Whetten, 2006; Kjaergaard et al., forthcoming), role/behavioral (Pratt and Foreman, 2000; Lerpold et al., 2007), and narrative/symbolic approaches (Czarniawska-Joerges, 1994; Brown, 2006; Cappetta and Gioia, 2006; Schultz et al., 2006), or some combination thereof (Pratt and Rafaeli, 1997; Lerpold et al., 2007; Rindova et al., forthcoming). These bases echo some of the main tenets of a process worldview, such as an emphasis on interactions, experiences, and narratives.

The behavioral component of identity, for example, suggests that identity forms in the act of doing or in "practice" (Lerpold et al., 2007). Thus, psychologists discuss the importance of self-schemas in identity, and note how schemas form in areas where there are repeated behaviors in a given domain (Markus, 1977). Schemas, in turn, are viewed as both process and structure (Markus and Wurf, 1987). Similarly, structural symbolic interactionists discuss the importance of roles, which are organized around behaviors, to identity formation. While some treatments of role are relatively static, research (Turner, 1990) has also emphasized human agency and action by focusing not only role-taking (adopting roles), but also role-making (modifying roles). Thus, even when couched in terms of cognitive or social structures, identity researchers have long viewed these structures as dynamic; and this dynamism is linked to "doing."

More recently, process oriented identity researchers looking at identity work and construction note the importance of doing, acting, and interacting. To illustrate, at the micro level, residents develop professional identity by working, assessing work-identity integrity violations, customizing identities, and having those identities validated or not (Pratt et al., 2006). Thus, constructing identity comes as individuals both act (e.g., working) and react (e.g., customizing) with others in their social environments. Similarly, at the macro level, organizational identities are believed to be forged through articulating visions, experiencing meaning voids, engaging in experiential contrasts, converging on a consensual identity, negotiating identity claims, attaining optimal distinctiveness, performing luminal actions, and assimilating legitimizing feedback (Gioia et al., 2010). As with identity dynamics at the micro level, "doing" is at the heart of identity formation.

"Doing" gets closer to "being"/identity as people come to reflect upon and make sense of their actions. Thus, we see a common triad in dynamic treatments of identity that includes sensemaking, identity, and action (e.g., Fiol, 1991; Gioia and Chittipeddi, 1991; Pratt, 2000; Ravasi and Schultz, 2006; see also Weick, 1995). Entities (individual or collective) act, such actions are selectively validated and invalidated, which leads to a meaning void or "seekership," sensemaking ensues, individuals act on new meanings, which are again validated or not, and so on (see Pratt, 2000; Gioia et al., 2010). As this cycle continues, the entity changes by taking on new meanings about self and others. Building from this action–identity–sensemaking cycle, it is not a big stretch to see linkages here with the importance of experience in understanding process (Langley and Tsoukas, 2010).

In addition, as noted above, action and experience do not take place in a vacuum—they take place in the presence of others. Thus, a second base for identity formation is relational. With regard to relationships, a social identity approach emphasizes categories as a key component of identity; such categories, in turn, are inherently relational—depicting differences between those similar to us (i.e., an ingroup) and those different from us (i.e., an outgroup). Sociologists, in turn, often draw upon Cooley's "looking glass self" in their conceptualization of identity. In particular, structural symbolic interactionists note the importance of the verification of identity by others (Burke, 1991; Stryker and Burke, 2000). Thus, identity is, at its heart, a relational construct (Pratt, 2003). In organizational research, there has been considerable research looking at how organizational identity

Rethinking Identity Construction Processes in Organizations

(who we are) relates to organizational image (how outsiders see the organization—e.g., Hatch and Schultz, 1997, 2002) and to an organization's construed external image (what organizational members believe regarding how outsiders see them—Dutton and Dukerich, 1991). Simply put, how others such as important stakeholders view an organization, strongly impacts the identity of that organization. Building on the notion of acting and inter-relating are key to identity, one again does not have to venture far to see that identity may be especially amenable to a process metaphysics where "focusing on *inter*-actions is preferred to analyzing self-standing actions" (Langley and Tsoukas, 2010: 3).

A third base for identity formation is symbolic. In addition to an emerging interest in artifacts and process (the theme of next year's process conference), the notion of narratives has played a critical role in explaining identity formation both outside of and inside organizations. To illustrate, Singer (1995) and McAdams (2001) have both emphasized how constructing identities involve constructing stories and other narratives about ourselves. In the organizational realm, researches such as Czarniawska-Joerges (1994), Brown (2006), and, more recently, Ibarra and Barbulescu (2010) have championed a narrative approach to examining collective-level identities. In narratives, identity finds another linkage with process theorizing as narrative approaches have been identified as a key strategy for theorizing from process data (Langley, 1999). In sum, the relational, behavioral, and symbolic bases of identity appear to make identity particularly open to process approaches and theorizing.

Perhaps, the one area where the resonance between identity and process is somewhat out of sync is when regarding the critical importance of time to process theorizing. While time is certainly not absent from identity research, it is often used in a somewhat static manner. For example, research has shown that "ideal" or future-oriented identities—especially when compared with current identities—can be very motivating for members of organizations, such as during change attempts (Reger et al., 1994; Pratt and Dutton, 2000; Foreman and Whetten, 2002). Others suggest that past identities, as they relate to nostalgia, can also be motivating, though often to maintain continuity and resist dominant powers (Brown and Humphreys, 2002). However, beyond research on identity work or identity construction, explicitly theorizing about time in identity research is relatively rare (see Heugens and Krozen this volume as a notable exception). Moreover, empirically tracking identity in and around organizations is rarer still (cf. Pratt et al., 2006; Ravasi and Schultz, 2006; Gioia et al., 2010). Past, current, and future identities serve largely as guideposts for attention rather

Constructing Identity in and around Organizations

than showing how present identities becomes past, and how past and future identities become enfolded into the present.

Building from the above, the answer about whether we can meaningfully talk about identity and process appears to be "yes." While identity appears to point out attention to constancy and process to change, the theory that underlies the "bases" of identity seems largely resonant with process theorizing. So far, so good.

2.2 Question #2: If we can meaningfully talk about identity and process, *how* should we talk about them?

Identity is not a verb—there is no "identity-ing." Moreover, while identification can sometimes lead to identity changes, it does not have to (Pratt, 1998), and thus "identifying" may not be the right verb either to describe identity processes writ large.[3] Consequently, researchers who study identity and process need a verb to attach to identity to discuss identity-related/identity processes. Drawing from the conference entries, two popular words to describe these processes are "construction" and "work." While sometimes used synonymously, identity construction (which often borrows from "social construction") is often used generally to refer to how identities come to be formed. Identity work may be more specific. It has been linked to the relationship between identity control attempts (i.e., identity regulation) and the formation of a self-identity, and is defined as "interpretive activity involved in reproducing and transforming self-identity" (Alvesson and Wilmott, 2002: 627). Given the power of language over how we see and understand the world, I wonder what some implications of using words like "construction" and "work" might be on our nascent theorizing. For example, construction is a noun, although it points to the act of constructing; work, by contrast, can be both a verb and a noun. But the fact that neither term is exclusively a verb is interesting.

What is gained and lost by using terms like "construction" or even "work"? On the positive side, construction and work depict potentially ongoing activities, are relational, and involve action as well as learning/experience. Thus, these terms could fit with elements of process and process theorizing reviewed previously. This linkage may even be clearer if we referred to construct*ing* and work*ing* identity (or identity working and constructing). However, to the degree that identity reflects both process and structure, perhaps words like "work" are especially fitting.

Rethinking Identity Construction Processes in Organizations

There may be some drawbacks to using these terms, however. For example, construction, in particular, evokes some permanence either in the materials used (e.g., building from cultural or social structures) or outcomes achieved, such as the building of an "identity" or "identities." Now constructions need not be very permanent; and certainly many social constructionists would find it ironic to think of construction in terms of such permanence. However, on the face of it, construction seems to imply a greater degree of permanence than one may wish, especially for those who see identities as "temporary achievements" or "dynamic structures." But before we discard "constructions" as being too permanent, it may be important to think about the linkage between identity and terms such as "enduring" and "constant." While identities may not be permanent constructions, they do appear to be "sticky" to some degree. For example, the labels may change even if the meanings do not, and vice versa (Gioia et al., 2000). Stories, even if retold, can contain some lingering narrative elements. Thus, perhaps the permanence implied by words like "construction" may be okay—especially if their "outcomes" are appropriately qualified (and if they are tied to social construction).

Another potentially troubling element of work and construction is that both have functional overtones (though not necessarily reflecting the functionalist paradigm—see Burell and Morgan, 1979): both constructing and working are purposeful (e.g., engaging in identity work as a response to identity regulation). As with the permanence described by construction, perhaps the functional overtones are not all bad. I have personally talked about identity as "air bags" that are largely hidden but deployed when individuals are threatened. That is certainly a highly functional take on identity! However, just because identities can serve a function, the language we use raises questions about whether *all* processes of or about identity are ends-oriented in some way. Or in the spirit of providing a less leading question, what verbs can we use that relax this functional assumption? One obvious choice would be identity "playing."

Talking about identity playing/playing identity would highlight some of the same elements as constructing and working, emphasize new ones, and de-emphasize others. For example, playing would definitely reflect the "Other"—as playing involves real or imagined others. Moreover, it would certainly highlight the impermanence of process, or perhaps better said, a process that is more about ongoing and momentary accomplishment—more akin to a performance than something built. Identity playing might also signal that identity (-related) processes can be fun and spontaneous. One downside of playing is that, like work, these processes may not always

29

be fun and spontaneous, and play may not have the "stickiness" often ascribed to identity. Moreover, to the degree that organizations are purposeful, are we likely to see a lot of identity play in them?

Another potential verb to consider when describing identity and process is "practicing" (see Ibarra, 1999). Practicing elicits some of the same purposeful, learning-oriented, and often social, nature of some identity/identity-related processes in organizations. And perhaps more so than working and constructing, practicing highlights the imperfect and iterative nature of these processes. Talking about identity practicing/practicing identity may even highlight elements of identity and process that are currently not highlighted in any research of which I am familiar. For example, practicing suggests that individuals may get better at "doing identity" as they gain experience. Thus, we may have identity novices and identity maestros. This distinction may have some credence at the collective level as some organizations specialize in—and are quite expert in—being "identity transforming organizations" (Greil and Rudy, 1984). The potential downside of talking about "practicing" is that it may be even more goal-oriented than words like "working" or "constructing." Along the lines of "practice makes perfect," it may suggest that there is some idealized "outcome" or end-state that all processes of or about identity are building toward.

Other verbs connecting identity and process have been used as well. For example, identity dynamics that have been associated with "claiming" and "granting" (Albert and Whetten, 1985; Glynn, 2000; Bartel and Dutton, 2001; DeRue and Ashford, 2010) have been used to emphasize the relational aspects of identity—as something that must be asked for and validated by others (see also "mirroring," "expressing," "impressing," and "reflecting"—Hatch and Schultz, 2002). Similarly, I often think of "engaging" whereby individuals actively participate in making/maintaining/changing identity with an "other"—largely as a counter to more top-down approaches where individuals are "identity dopes" that simply assimilate identity information from others around them (Greil and Rudy, 1984). Of course, it is doubtful that any verb will accurately capture the range of identification processes in and around organizations. The point is to think more carefully about the verbs we use to describe these processes, and what those verbs both denote and connote. It may be that we want to employ a richer vocabulary, and to choose verbs that best reflect how entities engaged in identity/identity-related processes view these processes (i.e., do minimal "violence to experience").

2.3 Question #3: If we know how to talk about identity process, *what* might be missing from the conversations we are currently having?

Framing research in terms of identity [insert your verb of choice] processes suggests that identity is "figure" in these processes, and the rest is ground. Of course, scholars always make choices about what to focus on, and what to ignore. However, there is reason to believe that what identity process scholars are potentially ignoring may fundamentally change how we look at how identity is formed, maintained, and changed in and around organizations. To begin, identity is often conceptualized as being intimately connected with a broader self. This begs a first set of questions. In what way, if any, is our research on identity constructing/working/playing/practicing processes impoverished because we view identity as either equivalent to or in isolation of self? What, if anything do we know about "self-processes"? In addition, when reading about identity processes in and around organizations, it appears that these processes are always occurring in relation to or with other processes, such as sensemaking, learning, or control. This begs a second set of questions. What role does identity play in these processes? Is identity simply a descriptor of the outcome of other processes? Or are there some processes inherent or unique to identity dynamics?

2.3.1 Self-processes

While some use "identity" and "self" interchangeably, I draw upon Mead's foundational work (1934) that clearly distinguishes the two. Returning to an earlier point about the relational nature of identity, Mead sees "who we are" as stemming from the relationship between an entity and those in the society/community surrounding the entity. For an organization, this "community" may comprise institutional actors, broadly defined, and more specifically, share holders, buyers, suppliers, and the like. How an entity responds to those in the community becomes the "raw materials" for identities. These identities, in turn, become raw materials for the self.

Identity—or more appropriate, identities—are therefore numerous, and are acted upon or are objects, and refer to the "me" (vs. "I"). "Me" at a collective level has been linked to the interplay of organizational identity and organizational image (see Hatch and Schultz, 2002),[4] or for our purposes here, simply "organizational identity." The self, by contrast, is unifying and holistic, is the actor/subject, and refers to the "I." The role of "I" at the collective level has been linked to the interplay of organizational identity and organizational culture (Hatch and Schultz, 2002) or as used here, metaphorically, to the "organizational self" (Pratt and Kraatz, 2009). Drawing from the latter, the *self* is what allows an entity to perceive itself "as" and to act "as if" it were a coherent whole; thus, the self is a gestalt that is both related to and stands apart from the identities that comprise it. Thus, as Cooley (1902/2006: 182) notes, the self is akin to a "nucleus of a living cell, not altogether separate from the surrounding matter, out of which indeed it is formed, but more active and definitely organized."

Whereas identity *can* be discussed in terms of process, it is difficult to find notions of self that do not directly involve process. To illustrate, Markus and Wurf (1987: 301, emphasis mine), in their review of research on the self-concept, note:

> Whether researchers define the self-concept in terms of hierarchies, prototypes, networks, spaces, or schemas, they generally agree that the self-structure is an active one. What began as an apparently singular, static, lump-like entity *has become a multidimensional, multifaceted dynamic structure* that is systematically implicated in all aspects of social information processing.

Similarly, it is worth noting that Cooley referred to a "looking-glass self" rather than a looking glass identity. By failing to recognize self-processes, or by equating self with identity, research on identity construction in and around organizations would appear to be missing a vital piece of the process puzzle. This missing part centers on the processes by which an entity's various "me's" become a cohesive, but not static, "I."

But what would a "self-process" look like? Drawing from Mead's not-always-clear description (1934) of self-formation in humans in *Mind, Self, and Society*, Matt Kraatz and I (2009) extrapolated a metaphorical self-formation process as best we could to the organizational level. Building on this, in Figure 2.1, I attempt to illustrate how Mead's foundational work (1934) might manifest itself for an organization attempting to manage multiple organizational identities via an organizational self. I then integrate research by Hatch and Schultz (2002) and others to look at three approaches to studying self and identity processes in and around organizations.

In Figure 2.1, there are both an organization and a number of constituents. These constituents may be external (e.g., suppliers, clients, shareholders) or internal (e.g., employees) to the company. This parallels Mead's analysis (1934) of an individual in a community. In particular, it

Rethinking Identity Construction Processes in Organizations

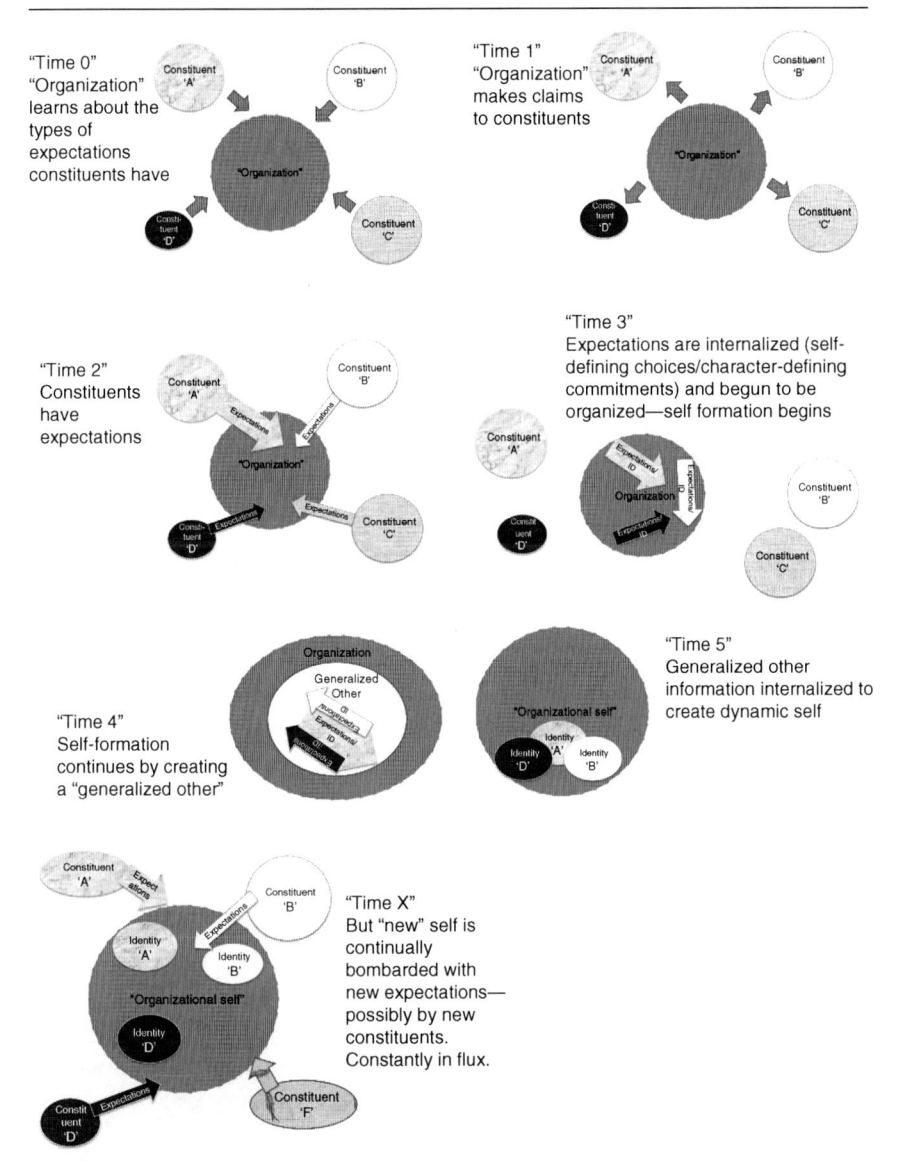

Figure 2.1 Organizational self and identity processes

follows from Mead's assertion that forming a self is only necessary if one has multiple "others" in one's environment who have expectations about who one should be. It is difficult, however, to present a complex process graphically. To facilitate my explanations, I divide self-formation into time periods. These time periods, such as "Time 1," are listed in quotation marks as this is Time 1 for explanatory purposes only. For an organization, the process could start from expectations from others (Time 2) rather than from where I have chosen to start my explanation. [*Note*: For an individual, the self-formation process starts when it is recognized by another living being. Organizations, however, do not emerge as physical bodies all at once, and are composed of a collection of individuals with greater language ability and awareness than an infant. Hence, the starting point for identity formation may be a bit fuzzier.]

Starting with "Time 1," at some point in an organization's lifecycle—perhaps even before it is a "real" organization—it has to claim that it does something or is something. It is important to note that these claims do not come out of thin air when creating an organization, but are likely based on existing categories, or combinations of existing categories that already exist ("Time 0"). This declaring action of "who we are" would be akin to identity "claiming" by some theorists (Glynn, 2000). An example of such a claim can be found in CloudSwitch, a start-up company that does "cloud computing": a process whereby computing is done via external, shared servers—thus computing is done somewhere "in the clouds." During its formative days in January of 2009, one of the company founders, Ellen Rubin, made the following remarks about CloudSwitch:

> Rubin isn't saying much about what they're up to, other than that they're developing software to help enterprises manage cloud computing services. "I don't want to say much for competitive reasons, but we're working with partners and customers now, and building out our offering," she told me today. She said they'll be ready to divulge more in the spring. The company has about ten employees, and office space in Bedford (www.innoeco.com).

These remarks are tentative and ambiguous, but are built from existing categories (e.g., cloud computing, customers, competition). From these remarks, we know that CloudSwitch will develop software for companies to use and manage cloud computing service—but not much else. However, before making a stronger claim, the company is checking with "partners and customers." Thus, claims become refined as constituents start to put expectations on that organization (see "Time 2"). Thus, on the same day the above appears, the following appears:

> Stealth cloud computing company CloudSwitch has taken in $7.4 million in Series A funding co-led by Atlas Venture and Matrix Partners. The news was first reported by Scott Kirsner on his blog, and confirmed by Atlas partner Axel Bichara. Little information is available about Waltham, MA-based CloudSwitch,

whose placeholder website merely says it is in stealth mode. But Bichara called it "a wildly exciting company" that is generally looking at making cloud computing available to companies that already have their own data centers and presumably want to make them more efficient while holding down costs.... CloudSwitch was co-founded by CEO Ellen Rubin and John Considine. Rubin was previously VP of marketing for Marlborough, MA-based Netezza, while Bichara calls Considine a technical "superstar" who was formerly at Pirus Networks, which was sold to Sun Microsystems in 2002. (www.xconomy.com)

Thus, someone from the investor constituency, Bichara, is beginning to set high expectations for the company as both "wildly exciting" and noting that one of the co-founders is a "technical superstar." Some of these expectations may be given to verify claims made by the organization (i.e., identity "granting"—Bartel and Dutton, 2001). Thus, with the talent CloudSwitch has, they can likely follow up on their promise to develop software to better manage cloud computing. However, organizations may also be asked to respond to external demands that may not correspond to existing claims, thus asking an organization like McDonald's to be more conscientious about its use of recyclable materials. For CloudSwitch, the partner is making expectations about efficiency and cost control—issues not in the original claiming of the founder. Thus, there is both verification and new expectation setting.

Over time, there may be more expectations set upon an organization than it can hope to meet. Thus, organizations need to choose to meet some expectations and ignore others. At the micro level, this process is akin to internalizing some roles, thus transforming role expectations into role identities. However, for organizations, this may mean taking on character-defining commitments (Selznick, 1984 [1957]; Whetten, 2006). Such commitments may involve reacting to expectations in Time 2, or reinforcing identity claim-making that began in Time 1. Thus, as early as three months after being in "stealth mode," Rubin begins to provide more detailed claims, and adds chief information officers to the mix of potential constituents, noting that the company is:

> ...focused on the connection between the enterprise data center and all these new cloud providers... By moving things into the cloud, we want to help chief information officers free up space in their data centers, and free up resources, and let companies use that for higher-value purposes. (www.boston.com)

By 2011, the claims on their website have continued to differentiate. Their message picks up the "expertise" thread noted in Bichara's initial expectation setting done two years prior, but does not pick up on the founder's talk about appealing to chief information officers. The website also adds a new claim about "protecting" companies from potential disadvantages of cloud computing:

> CloudSwitch protects enterprises from the complexity, risks and potential lock-in of cloud computing, freeing them to leverage the cloud's advantages in cost and business agility. Backed by Matrix Partners, Atlas Ventures and Commonwealth Capital Ventures, CloudSwitch is based in Burlington, MA and is led by seasoned entrepreneurs from BMC, EMC, Netezza, RSA, SolidWorks and Sun Microsystems. (www.cloudswitch.com)

As organizations continue to take on more internalized expectations and claim more "identities," there begins a need to form some cohesion out of this myriad of identities; in Mead's terms, there is a need to form a self. If an entity had only one constituent in his/her audience who had only a single expectation, then there would not be any need for a self. There would be no complexity to manage, no priorities to set, and no need to make a more integrative "structure."

The first step in this self-building would be to create some sort of minimal structuring, such as a hierarchical prioritization, of existing constituent expectations. This is begun in Time 3 with the internalization of some identities but not others. However, this organization is continued in Time 4 as one attempts to get a unified picture of the expectations of the entire social field. Pratt and Kraatz (2009) suggest that this is akin to an organization getting a gestalt view of all reputational demands placed upon it. Thus, an organization moves from understanding distinct expectations to organizing them into a coherent whole. Mead refers to this process as creating a "generalized other."

Mead suggests that in the process of reacting to this generalized other, an agentic "I" or self is formed (see "Time 5"). Mead is not exactly clear how this happens, but it may be that as one reassesses and integrates one's expectations, one has a better sense of "who one is" in relation to all others, and thus is in a better position to decide how to meet the demands of one's community. This self-based-on-others' expectations resonate with statements made by Honda's CEO who said that his company is striving to be "a company that society wants to exist" (Honda Environmental Annual Report, 2007). Whatever this process of becoming is, it is clear that the self is dynamic and is a momentary and ongoing accomplishment. Because the self is linked to the generalized other, and because this generalized other must change as new constituents enter and leave the picture and as new expectations are asked of the organization, the self must also continue to develop over time ("Time X").

While a relatively rough sketch of how self-processes and identity-processes may work together, this overview highlights several processes that are currently underexamined in the organizational literature and perhaps suggests a few others. I suggest three types of such processes: expecting and accepting, expressing and reflecting, and integrative processes.

2.3.1.1 EXPECTING AND ACCEPTING PROCESSES

To begin, research has emphasized the identity claiming and identity granting (e.g., Glynn, 2000; Bartel and Dutton, 2001; DeRue and Ashford, 2010); and certainly actors such as organizations or individuals may make identity claims, and such claims may or may not be granted by others. However, there might be other actions and reactions as well, such as expecting and accepting. To illustrate, Mead argues that constituents may suggest or demand that certain expectations be met. These expectations may align with identity claims (i.e., what the organization wants to be) but they may not. These unsolicited expectations, in turn, can be granted or not by the organization in the form of accepting. Thus, both organizations and constituents make claims (e.g., actor-requesting and constituent-expecting) and both may grant these claims (e.g., constituent-validating and actor-accepting).

2.3.1.2 EXPRESSING AND REFLECTING PROCESSES

Another way we can look at identity and self-processes is to look at how actors "express" and "reflect"—a distinction at the heart of Hatch and Schultz's theorizing (2002). These processes go on simultaneously and possibly "stand behind" the granting and claiming processes. To illustrate, organizations need to express requests, reflect on expectations, and ultimately express whether or not they accept expectations. More broadly, in the process of requesting and accepting organizations will attempt to shape how constituents see them—thus invoking the "me" element of identity. However, at the same time, in order to choose which expectations to internalize and how to prioritize and organize them, organizations also need to be reflective—which relates to the "I" element of the self.

2.3.1.3 INTEGRATIVE PROCESSES

Past personal experience,[5] that has since been validated by Mead's work and others, suggests that it is not enough to create multiple versions of "who

I am/who we are" that come from multiple "claiming and granting" processes (e.g., "requesting, expecting, validating, and accepting") and "expressing and reflecting," processes. At some point, the entity—be it individual or organizational—has to come to a more integrated understanding of their self. In other words, these integrative processes are critical as any given entity—whether an individual or organization—is expected to be responsive to different constituent demands (i.e., have multiple identities), while at the same time it is being judged as a coherent whole (Love and Kraatz, 2009). Research suggests that there are at least two integrative processes that occur as a part of self-dynamics: those involved in creating a generalized other, and those involved in creating an organizational self.

Unfortunately, extant theory is not clear on how these integrative processes work. Structural symbolic interactionists, for example, are strong on talking about how identities can be organized, but weaker on how these identities can become transformed into a coherent self (Pratt and Kraatz, 2009). And to my knowledge, little if any empirical work has been done on how organizations (or even individuals) come to form a generalized other. While Mead (1934) suggests that the capacity in individuals to form a generalized other comes from early experiences with role playing as a child, it is not clear what the organizational analog might be (perhaps early attempts at mimetic isomorphism?). Thus, for these processes, I leave more questions than answers.

2.3.1.4 THE COMPLEXITY OF IDENTITY AND SELF-PROCESSES

But viewing these integrative and other processes together quickly makes it apparent how undertheorized our notions of identity construction may be. For illustrative purposes, I denote the three sets of processes in a hypothetical interaction between an organization and an "Other" in Figure 2.2. The various verbs in CAPITAL letters reflect different types of CLAIMING/REQUESTING while those that do not are validation/granting processes. *Italicized* versus underlined text distinguish *reflective* versus expressive processes, respectively. Finally, those that are boxed are those that may spark integrative processes.

These processes are, of course, reciprocal. Rather than putting in all of the reciprocal arrows, pretend we are unbundling this process and rolling it out over time. Thus, Time 1 becomes stretched out to include what the organization does, and then how the Other responds, which leads to a response by the organization at Time 2 and a response by the Other at Time 2.

Rethinking Identity Construction Processes in Organizations

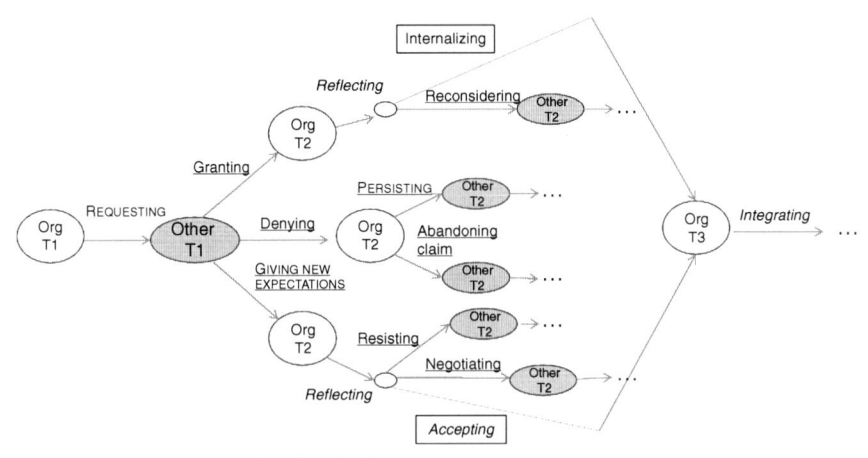

Figure 2.2 Hypothetical self and identity processes

Walking through Figure 2.2, we could begin with an organization making an identity request of some constituent (expressive, claiming). This can lead to at least three responses by the Other in T1: this claim can be granted or denied (expressive, validating responses) and/or new expectations, not related to the claims, may be made (expressive, claiming). This inter-relating process in T1 is akin to mirroring (Hatch and Shultz, 2002) whereby the other comes to recognize the organization in some way.

Moving to Time 2, we can see at least seven organizational responses that may arise, depending on how the Other responded in Time 1. Looking at the top most branch, claims that are granted will likely lead to a reflective response whereby the initial claims will be *internalized* (a reflective process), thus creating an identity; or the initial claims will be further *reconsidered* (i.e., I have changed my mind about my claim)—which will lead to a more expressive response, which, in turn, may lead to further responses from the Other or Others.

The middle branch may occur if the initial claim is denied by the Other, leading to *persistence in claiming* by the organization (expressive, claiming) or to acquiescence or *abandoning*, thus "granting" the denial (expressive, granting). Both will likely lead to additional responses from the Other. The lowest path may occur if the Other gives new expectations. Here, the organization may either *resist*, which fails to grant the expectations. Organizations may also respond by *negotiating*, or to *accepting*. Each of these relate to the granting, or not, of the requests (expressive, granting). If both accepting and internalizing occur during Time 2, then the organization

39

now begins to have multiple identities, which must be prioritized and made to cohere in some fashion as a self begins to form (integrating) in Time 3. The ongoing nature of the process is depicted with "..." in Figure 2.2. Such processes quickly get more complex with the addition of further recursive loops and more than one "Other." Adding multiple "Others," for example, opens the door for the possibility of coalition forming among the organization and some constituents, or among some or all constituents. Moreover, organizations are also constrained by their material resources in terms of how they respond to one or more Others. Organizations cannot be everything that is desired of them.

If adding the self to identity makes process theorizing more complex, the next question that should be asked is whether adding such complexity is worth it. Building from Einstein's maxim, our theorizing "should be as simple as possible, but not simpler." I would argue that removing self from identity theorizing causes us to miss the importance for an entity to feel and to be perceived as whole—be they individual or organizational. And as noted, my own work is not immune from this critique as I have forgotten the self in favor of focusing on identity. Further, I would argue that perhaps the "ultimate goal" of organizing is to get a myriad of individuals with their own needs, skills, and abilities to somehow create something that transcends the simple aggregation of these needs, skills, and abilities. If so, then theorizing about self may facilitate how this might happen.

2.3.2 Identity and _____ processes

At first blush, it appears that identity process are, at minimum, often associated with other processes including sensemaking and sensegiving (Gioia and Chittappeddi, 1991; Pratt, 2000; Ravasi and Schultz, 2006; Gioia et al., 2010), learning and unlearning (Pratt et al., 2006); changing (Fiol, 2002), negotiating (Clegg et al., 2007), communicating (Cheney, 1983), controlling and struggling (Alvesson and Wilmott, 2002; Sveningsson and Alvesson, 2003), comparing/mimicking/legitimizing (Czarniawska and Wolf, 1998; Clegg et al., 2007; Glynn, 2008), and modifying, editing, and deleting (Weber and Glynn, 2006). The presence of so many other processes in identity construction begs the question of what role they play in underlying, intertwining, walking beside, or prefacing and following this construction.

One potential take-away we might draw from the presence of other processes in identity construction is that there are no "identity processes" at all. Rather, identity may simply be the "content" of other processes.

Cheney (1983), for example, argues that identification processes are rhetorical processes; thus identification is the purpose or perhaps the effect of rhetoric, but there are no uniquely "identification" processes per se. Similarly, it may be that what we see as identity construction processes are simply forms of learning, sensemaking, negotiating, and the like. If this is the case, should we actually focus first on what fundamental processes there are, rather than how they manifest in identity construction? I do not think so—but I admit, I am biased. I have spent a fair amount of time on answering social problems related to identity, and believe that adding identity to the mix changes how processes unfold. However, rather than abandoning identity processes/identity and process, we may wish to approach our studies differently, or at least be more conscientious about how we approach identity processes in and around organizations.

2.3.2.1 APPROACH #1: PROCESSES ABOUT IDENTITY

The first approach we might take is to focus on processes *about* identity rather than identity *as* process. For example, identity may be viewed as an outcome, antecedent, or the "content" of a process. If we take this approach, then the first question we need to answer is whether processes about identity alter those processes in significant ways. For example, my colleagues and I have argued that infusing "identity" into conflict processes changes the fundamental nature of how those processes are expressed—so much so that traditional forms of conflict management no longer work (Fiol et al., 2009; Pratt et al., forthcoming). Alternatively, we would need to answer if the processes we use to understand identity fundamentally change how we view identity. But if you add "identity" to an otherwise known process (e.g., learning), and we do not learn anything new about this known process—or about identity—then, it is not clear what value is added in this approach.

2.3.2.2 APPROACH #2: PROCESS UNIQUE TO IDENTITY

A second approach would be to examine whether there were any processes *unique* to identity. I think this is a significantly higher bar, and I am not sure any extant research in organizational studies currently clears it. To be plain, I am ultimately not sure whether there are processes unique to identity or whether it ultimately matters if there are. Perhaps we have enough "basic" processes already without adding identity as process to the mix. That said, I would also argue against the opposite tendency; that is, to see identity and everything else as all one type or processes. I know there are some who argue

Constructing Identity in and around Organizations

that every process is a communication or sensemaking or learning or narrative or... (add a process du jour) process, but I do not find this any more helpful than those who want to argue that identity is about everything (e.g., if economics are all about self-interest, then essentially it is all about identity in some way). In short, I think it is worth looking for and thinking about whether some processes are unique to identity. While I am not entirely sure what these processes might be, my best guess today would be that such a process may be related to the "alchemy," that is, self-formation, specifically, a process that explains how identities can become a self that is both related to and distinct from its component parts. However, even here, the processes might not be unique to identity. Ultimately, though, it is a parts–wholes problem that confounds our human understanding in many fields. Thus, such a process may mirror how neural firings become consciousness, how individual cognitions become a group mind, and the like.

2.3.2.3 APPROACH #3: HOW MULTIPLE PROCESSES INTERPLAY IN IDENTITY DYNAMICS

A third approach, similar to the first, would be to examine how various processes come together during various identity dynamics, such as creating, changing, maintaining, etc. Thus, rather than looking at a single process and view it in terms of identity (e.g., identity construction as a learning process), we might instead look at how multiple processes come together when constructing/practicing/playing identity. Extant research seems to suggest that "doing" identity involves many interweaving processes. To illustrate, maintaining control inherent in identity regulation (Alvesson and Wilmott, 2002) may actually involve mortification, divestiture, selection, and group formation processes that either reinforce or work at odds to create different types of identity work or different forms of identifying (Pratt, 2000). Similarly, changing identity understandings may be a combination of sensemaking, sensegiving, impression management, and managing culture (Ravasi and Schultz, 2006). Alternatively, process may work in tandem when doing identity. For example, learning about work may parallel learning about who one is (Pratt et al., 2006). And sometimes identity creating/maintaining/changing processes may influence (or be influenced by) other process, such as how identification and interpretation processes may influence resource claiming processes (Glynn, 2000). Taken together, we might move ahead by looking at how various processes intersect, trigger, interplay, and so on as identities are formed. Perhaps the key challenge to identity formation/maintenance/change is how to make something unique (either as an individual or collective) out of the same processes that every other entity uses.

2.4 Conclusion

I started this chapter by asking a question about whether we should be talking about identity construction in and around organizations. As is sometimes the case with writing, where you end up is not exactly where you intend. That is certainly the case here. I began feeling like the answer was an unequivocal yes. I ended up with an answer more like, "Yes, but..."

On the one hand, the answer to my first question—Can we meaningfully talk about identity and process?—suggests that there are elements of identity that seem to resonate with a process perspective: both have roots in interactions, inter-relating, experience, and narratives. Moreover, identity theorizing has some temporal elements to it (e.g., ideal identities), though often a more static temporality than what is depicted in process theorizing. In addition, there was nothing in answering the second question that would likely cause us to radically rethink our approach to identity and process. While the field may be prematurely closing in on certain process terms such as "construction" or "work" when discussing identity dynamics, this does not mean that theorizing around identity construction processes is unwarranted—just that it could be opened up a bit.

Things get a bit muddied when addressing my third question about what might be missing from our conversations about identity. It may be that "identity" plays a more minor or perhaps a different role in what we have been considering as "identity processes." With few exceptions, research has largely ignored notions of "self" in treatments of identity—especially at the level of the collective. Thus, focusing on constructing *identity* in and around organizations may be too limiting. We need to ask ourselves as scholars, can we meaningfully talk about identity while ignoring the self?

In addition, once we look at extant research on identity work, identity construction, and even on identifying, it becomes clear that a lot more than just identity is taking place here. It begs the question about whether identity is simply the "content" of some processes (i.e., processes about identity), or whether there are processes that are unique to identity. If all we have are processes about identity, we might ask, "What makes the 'identity' qualifier different or interesting?" If there are unique identity or self-processes, however, they are currently undertheorized in organizational studies.

Constructing Identity in and around Organizations

In closing, whereas conferences are great places to share ideas and insights, chapters are great places to think back on what we have done, and what we intend to do. As we move forward as a field and as a community, this might be a good time to reflect on what it means to look at identity construction processes in and around organization. Returning to the supposed inscription on the Temple of Delphi, does it matter simply that one "knows thyself" (identity as an "outcome" of process) or is it as important as or more important than (*a*) how one knows (identity as process or processes about identity), and/or (*b*) whether how one knows reveals new and interesting insights into other areas of social life? How we answer these questions says a lot about who we are as people and as a profession—does it not?

Notes

1. I wish to thank Mary Ann Glynn, Doug Lepisto, Davide Ravasi, Majken Schultz, and the participants of the Second International Symposium on Process Organization Studies for their comments on and assistance with earlier versions of this chapter.
2. While linking identification dynamics and organizational identity dynamics, my point is simply to argue that various perspectives on identity tend to build from similar arguments. Specifically, that is how one comes to see an organization as self-defining (identifying), how an individual builds identity, and how a collective builds identity tending to use one or a combination of the following arguments: relational, behavioral, or symbolic. That said, there is much too little empirical work on collective identity "construction" dynamics to say with complete confidence that the "bases" for identifying as well as individual and collective identity formation are exactly the same.
3. It is possible that some identify formation processes involve identifying or the process of seeing some target as being self-referential. However, at present, identification seems to be used mostly, if not exclusively, at the individual level to explain how individuals attach themselves to their collectives. It is not clear whether or not collectives such as groups or organizations can "identify," and exploring such a process quickly gets to issues of where identities reside, what they are, where they come from, and the like. I've tried to tackle some of these questions elsewhere (Pratt, 2003). However, these questions are beyond the scope of this chapter.
4. It is important to distinguish between how I am using "I" and "me" from how it has been used by Hatch and Schultz (2002). Hatch and Shultz are looking at the relationship between image, culture, and identity and note that when looking at organizational identity, organizational culture plays the reflective part of "I" and

image plays the reacting part of "me" in relation to identity. As they are not interested in delineating self from identity, they do not associate "I" and "me" with "self" and "identity" respectively. Beyond the differences in terms, we arrive at a similar conclusion about the importance of looking at both self-reflective and image-related (audience-related) processes when looking at identity dynamics in organizations.

5. This need for integration has been made plain in my own work on managing multiple identities. For example, Peter Foreman and I (Pratt and Foreman, 2000) suggested that in managing these multiple organizational identities, organizational decision-makers have to take the following questions into account: (*a*) How many identities that the organization can "afford" to keep or to lose? (*b*) How synergistic are the identities? The answers to these two questions (how many? and how synergistic?) reveal four idealized responses regarding how to manage multiple organizational identities: Compartmentalization (high resources, low synergy) where identities are retained but kept apart either physically, temporally, or symbolically; deletion (low resources, low synergy) where one or more identities are removed from the organization via re-socialization or firing of personnel; integration (low resources, high synergy) where identities are merged into something new; and aggregation (high resources, high synergy) where identities are kept, but are linked in some fashion, such as AOL, Time, and Warner, all being part of a larger "media" identity. One of our main "lessons" for managers was that organizations often try to integrate even if the conditions for integration are not right—usually because identities are not synergistic. While MBAs and executives who were taught our typology of responses understood, they still expressed a strong desire for "bringing the identities together" in some way. I would argue that this need was a recognition that one needs to manage both the parts (identities) and the whole (self), and we had forgotten about the whole.

References

Albert, S. and Whetten, D. (1985). "Organizational Identity," in L. L. Cummings and H. M. Staw (eds.), *Research in Organizational Behavior*. Greenwich, CT: JAI Press, vol. 7, pp. 263–95.

Alvesson, M. and Willmott, H. (2002). "Identity Regulation as Organizational Control: Producing the Appropriate Individual." *Journal of Management Studies*, 39/5: 619–44.

Anteby, M. and Molnar, V. (2010). "Remembering to Forget: Collective Memory Work and Organizational Identity Endurance." Working paper, Harvard Business School, Cambridge, MA.

Ashforth, B., Harrison, S., and Corley, K. (2008). "Identification in Organizations: An Examination of Four Fundamental Questions." *Journal of Management*, 34/3: 325–74.

Bartel, C. and Dutton, J. (2001). "Ambiguous Organizational Memberships: Constructing Organizational Identities," in M. A. Hogg and D. J. Terry (eds.), *Social Identity Processes in Organizational Contexts*. Philadelphia, PA: Psychology Press, pp. 115–30.

Brown, A. (2006). "A Narrative Approach to Collective Identities." *Journal of Management Studies*, 43/4: 731–53.

—— Humphreys, M. (2002). "Nostalgia and the Narrativization of Identity: A Turkish Case Study." *British Journal of Management*, 13: 141–59.

Burke, P. (1991). "Identity Processes and Social Stress." *American Sociological Review*, 56/6: 836–49.

Burrell, G. and Morgan, G. (1979). *Sociological Paradigms and Organisational Analysis*. London: Heinemann.

Cappetta, R. and Gioia, D. (2006). "Fine Fashion: Using Symbolic Artifacts, Sensemaking, and Sensegiving to Construct Identity and Image," in A. Rafaeli and M. G. Pratt (eds), *Artifacts and Organizations*. London: Lawrence Erlbaum Associates, pp. 199–219.

Cardador, M. T. and Pratt, M. G. (2006). "Identification Management and Its Bases: Bridging Management and Marketing Perspectives through a Focus on Affiliation Dimensions." *Journal of the Academy of Marketing Science*, 34/2: 174–84.

Cerulo, K. (1997). "Identity Construction: New Issues, New Directions." *Annual Review of Sociology*, 23: 385–409.

Cheney, G. (1983). "The Rhetoric of Identification and the Study of Organizational Communication." *Quarterly Journal of Speech*, 69/2: 143–58.

Clegg, S., Rhodes, C., and Kornberger, M. (2007). "Desperately Seeking Legitimacy: Organizational Identity and Emerging Industries." *Organization Studies*, 28/4: 495.

Cooley, C. H. (1902). *Human Nature and the Social Order*. New York: Scribner.

Czarniawska-Joerges, B. (1994). "Narratives of Indvidual and Organizational Identities," in S. A. Deetz (ed.), *Communication Yearbook*. Thousand Oaks, CA: Sage, vol. 17, pp. 193–221.

Czarniawksa, B. and Wolf, R. (1998). "Constructing New Identities in Established Organization Fields." *International Studies of Management and Organizations*, 28: 32–56.

DeRue, D. and Ashford, S. (2010). "Who Will Lead and Who Will Follow? A Social Process of Leadership Identity Construction in Organizations." *Academy of Management Review*, 35/4: 627–47.

Dutton, J. and Dukerich, J. (1991) "Keeping an Eye on the Mirror: The Role of Image and Identity in Organizational Adaptation." *Academy of Management Journal*, 34/3: 517–54.

Fiol, C. (1991). "Managing Culture as a Competitive Resource: An Identity-Based View of Sustainable Competitive Advantage." *Journal of Management*, 17/1: 191.

—— (2002). "Capitalizing on Paradox: The Role of Language in Transforming Organizational Identities." *Organization Science*, 13/6: 653–66.

—— Pratt, M., and O'Connor, E. (2009). "Managing Intractable Identity Conflicts." *Academy of Management Review*, 34/1: 32–55.
Foreman, P. and Whetten, D. (2002). "Members' Identification with Multiple-Identity Organizations." *Organization Science*, 13/6: 618–35.
Gioia, D. and Chittipeddi, K. (1991). "Sensemaking and Sensegiving in Strategic Change Initiation." *Strategic Management Journal*, 12/6: 433–48.
—— Price, K., Hamilton, A., and Thomas, J. (2010). "Forging an Identity: An Insider-Outsider Study of Processes Involved in the Formation of Organizational Identity." *Administrative Science Quarterly*, 55/1: 1–46.
—— Schultz, M., and Corley, K. (2000). "Organizational Identity, Image, and Adaptive Instability." *Academy of Management Review*, 25/1: 63–81.
Glynn, M. A. (2000). "When Cymbals Become Symbols: Conflict Over Organizational Identity Within a Symphony Orchestra." *Organization Science*, 11/3: 285–98.
—— (2008). "Beyond Constraint: How Institutions Enable Identities," in R. Greenwood, C. Oliver, and K. Sahlin (eds.), *Handbook of Organizational Institutionalism*. Los Angeles, CA: Sage, pp. 413–30.
Greil, A. and Rudy, D. (1984). "Social Cocoons: Encapsulation and Identity Transformation Organizations." *Sociological Inquiry*, 54/3: 260–78.
Hatch, M. J. and Schultz, M. (1997). "Relations between Organizational Culture, Identity and Image." *European Journal of Marketing*, 31/6: 356–65.
—— —— (2002). "The Dynamics of Organizational Identity." *Human Relations*, 55/8: 989.
Ibarra, H. (1999). "Provisional Selves: Experimenting with Image and Identity in Professional Adaptation." *Administrative Science Quarterly*, 44/4: 764–91.
—— Barbulescu, R. (2010). "Identity as Narrative: Prevalence, Effectiveness, and Consequences of Narrative Identity Work in Macro Work Role Transitions." *Academy of Management Review*, 35/1: 135–54.
Kjaergaard, A., Morsing, M., and Ravasi, D. (forthcoming). "Mediating Identity: A Study of Media Influence on Organizational Identity Construction in a Celebrity Firm." *Journal of Management Studies*, in Press.
Langley, A. (1999). Strategies for theorizing from process data. *Academy of Management Review*, 24/4: 691–710.
—— (2009). "Studying Processes in and around Organizations," in D. Buchanan and A. Bryman (eds), *Sage Handbook of Organizational Research Methods*. London: Sage Publications, pp. 409–29.
Langley, A. and Tsoukas, H. (2010). "Introducing Perspectives on Process Organization Studies," in T. Hernes and S. Maitlis (eds), *Process, Sensemaking and Organizing*. London: Oxford University Press, pp. 1–26.
Lerpold, L., Ravasi, D., van Rekom, J., and Soenen, G. (eds) (2007). *Organizational Identity in Practice*. New York: Routledge, Taylor & Francis Group.

Love, E. and Kraatz, M. (2009). "Character, Conformity, or the Bottom Line: How and Why Downsizing Affected Corporate Reputation." *Academy of Management Journal*, 52: 314–35.

Markus, H. (1977). "Self-Schemata and Processing Information about the Self." *Journal of Personality and Social Psychology*, 35/2: 63–78.

—— Wurf, E. (1987). "The Dynamic Self-Concept: A Social Psychological Perspective." *Annual Review of Psychology*, 38/1: 299–337.

McAdams, D. (2001). "The Psychology of Life Stories." *Review of General Psychology*, 5/2: 100–22.

Mead, G. (1934). *Mind, Self, & Society*. Chicago: University of Chicago Press.

Mohr, L. B. (1982). *Explaining Organizational Behavior*. San Francisco, CA: Jossey-Bass.

Porac, J. and Thomas, H. (1989). "Competitive Groups as Cognitive Communities: The Case of Scottish Knitwear Manufacturers." *Journal of Management Studies*, 26/4: 397–416.

Pratt, M. G. (1998). "To Be or Not to Be? Central Questions in Organizational Identification," in D. A. Whetten and P. C. Godfrey (eds), *Identity in Organizations: Building Theory Through Conversations*. Thousand Oaks, CA: Sage, pp. 171–207.

—— (2000). "The Good, the Bad, and the Ambivalent: Managing Identification Among Amway Distributors." *Administrative Science Quarterly*, 45/3: 456–93.

—— (2003). "Disentangling Collective Identities," in J. Polzer, E. Mannix, and M. Neale (eds), *Identity Issues in Groups: Research in Managing Groups and Teams*. Stamford, CT: Elsevier Science Ltd., pp. 161–88.

—— Dutton, J. E. (2000). "Owning up or Opting out: The Role of Identities and Emotions in Issue Ownership," in N. Ashkanasy, C. Hartel, and W. Zerbe (eds), *Emotions in the Workplace: Research, Theory, and Practice*. London: Quorum Book, pp. 103–29.

—— Foreman, P. (2000). "Classifying Managerial Responses to Multiple Organizational Identities." *Academy of Management Review*, 25/1: 18–42.

—— Kraatz, M. (2009). "E Pluribus Unum: Multiple Identities and the Organizational Self," in L. M. Roberts and J. E. Dutton (eds), *Exploring Positive Identities and Organizations: Building a Theoretical and Research Foundation*. New York: Psychology Press, pp. 385–410.

—— Rafaeli, A. (1997). "Organizational Dress as a Symbol of Multilayered Social Identities." *Academy of Management Journal*, 40/4: 862–98.

—— Rockmann, K., and Kaufmann, J. (2006). "Constructing Professional Identity: The Role of Work and Identity Learning Cycles in the Customization of Identity among Medical Residents." *Academy of Management Journal*, 49/2: 235–62.

—— Fiol, C. M., O'Connor, E., and Panico, P. (forthcoming). "Promoting Positive Change in Physician-Administrator Relationships: Lessons for Managing Intractable Identity Conflicts," in K. Golden-Biddle and J. Dutton (eds), *Exploring Positive Social Change and Organizations*. New York: Routledge, Taylor & Francis Group, in Press.

Ravasi, D. and Schultz, M. (2006). "Responding to Organizational Identity Threats: Exploring the Role of Organizational Culture." *Academy of Management Journal*, 49/3: 433–58.

Reger, R., Gustafson, L., Demarie, S., and Mullane, J. (1994). "Reframing the Organization: Why Implementing Total Quality is Easier Said than Done." *Academy of Management Review*, 19/3: 565–84.

Rindova, V., Dalpaiz, E., and Ravasi, D. (forthcoming). "A Cultural Quest: A Study of Organizational Use of New Cultural Resources in Strategy Formation." *Organization Science*, 1–19.

Schultz, M., Hatch, M. J., and Ciccolella, F. (2006). "Brand Life in Symbols and Artifacts: The LEGO Company," in A. Rafaeli and M. G. Pratt (eds), *Artifacts and Organizations*. London: Lawrence Erlbaum Associates, pp. 141–60.

Selznick, P. (1984 [1957]). *Leadership in Administration: A Sociological Interpretation*. Berkeley, CA: University of California Press. (First published by Harper and Row, New York.)

Singer, J. (1995). "Seeing One's Self: Locating Narrative Memory in a Framework of Personality." *Journal of Personality*, 63/3: 429–57.

Stryker, S. (1987). "Identity Theory: Developments and Extensions," in K. Yardley and T. Honess (eds), *Self and Identity: Psychological Perspectives*. New York: John Wiley & Sons Ltd., pp. 89–103.

—— Burke, P. (2000). "The Past, Present, and Future of an Identity Theory." *Social Psychology Quarterly*, 63: 284–97.

Sveningsson, S. and Alvesson, M. (2003). "Managing Managerial Identities: Organizational Fragmentation, Discourse and Identity Struggle." *Human Relations*, 56/10: 1163–93.

Tsoukas, H. and Chia, R. (2002). "On Organizational Becoming: Rethinking Organizational Change." *Organization Science*, 13/5: 567–82.

Turner, R. (1990). "Role Taking: Process versus Conformity," in D. Brissett and C. Edgely (eds), *Life as Theater: A Dramaturgical Source Book*. New York: Aldine de Gruyter, 2nd edn, pp. 85–100.

Weber, K. and Glynn, M. (2006). "Making Sense with Institutions: Context, Thought and Action in Karl Weick's Theory." *Organization Studies*, 27/11: 1639–60.

Whetten, D. (2006). "Albert and Whetten Revisited: Strengthening the Concept of Organizational Identity." *Journal of Management Inquiry*, 15/3: 219–34.

Weick, K. (1995). *Sensemaking in Organizations*. Thousand Oaks, CA: Sage.

3

Identity as Process and Flow

Dennis A. Gioia and Shubha Patvardhan

Abstract: Rather than viewing organizational identity in the usual fashion as some sort of entity, thing, or "being," we suggest that identity might be better viewed in terms of ongoing process or flow. We argue that such a counterintuitive stance generates a different way of understanding identity, which when viewed in concert with its more usual portrayal, actually produces a more insightful understanding of this key concept. We touch on several of the debates surrounding organizational identity and suggest approaches to studying its dynamics from a process research perspective.

Albert and Whetten (1985) put forth the idea that organizations have identities. In that foundational work they defined organizational identity as that which is central, enduring, and distinctive about an organization. Let us ask you to focus for a moment on that apparently simple and by now widely used definition. If you consider its articulation carefully, you will notice that there is a bit of linguistic legerdemain going on in that definition. The intriguing question prompted by the definition is: What is the referent for the curious phrase "that which is...."? The usual linguistic convention presumes that "that which" refers to some noun, and more specifically to some *thing*. So the usual unquestioned presumption in our tendency to glide over this common definition is that when we are talking about identity, we are referencing some sort of entity, but an entity that does not have physical shape or form.

An alternative definition is also interesting linguistically. Organizational identity has also been defined, perhaps somewhat less precisely, but much more resonantly as "Who we are as an organization." Now, the intriguing aspect of this definition is that although it also is a bit mysterious, it

Identity as Process and Flow

similarly specifies some sort of (apparently embodied) living entity—a "being" at some higher level of understanding and an obvious extension of the individual notion of identity to some higher plane of analysis. What makes this definition resonate more than the sterile, if more precise, central/enduring/distinctive constellation is that it so clearly anthropomorphizes organizational identity. The implication—and assumption—is that organizations have identities in some parallel fashion to the way that individuals have identities. That assumption makes sense, we suppose, because organizations are created by, inhabited by, and function to accomplish the goals of individuals, even if they might soon take on a life of their own. Conceiving of organizations in this way is also comforting because this definition sees organizations as conceptual extensions of ourselves, thus preserving the sense that organizations are by-products of humanity (or at least human agency).

Yet, this definition similarly presumes that there is some entity there. Whatever "who we are" is, it is still intangible. It exists. The entity now is cast as a biological entity with a human face (even if that face is apparitional), but it is nonetheless framed tacitly and compellingly as another form of a thing—a living thing, but a thing nonetheless. Why? Why should we consider identity in either micro or macro forms to be some sort of animate or inanimate thing? If you give any serious consideration to the phenomenological nature of identity, you would soon discover, as Gertrude Stein so famously put it in a different context, that "there is no there there." So, what is going on here in this magnificent collective construction of identity (whether personal or organizational) as a thing?

Our answer to this curious convention is to instead argue that the usual portrayal of identity actually disguises a different way of understanding identity—not as an entity, per se, but rather as a *process*. Not as a static noun, but instead as a dynamic verb. What if we considered identity as an ongoing process of construction, reconstruction, performance, legitimation, etc., rather than a tangible, if ineffable something? All these less comfortable descriptors cast identity as constantly in flux. Or, perhaps more appropriately, they cast it as flow. If we presume the obvious—that identities can change—and go one tentative step further, that the "thing" that is changing is actually fleeting snapshots of a process in constant motion, then we acquire an informative and insightful alternative view of identity itself.

Consider the many conceptual works and studies aimed at explicating identity—and perhaps especially identity change—and it becomes apparent that they presume to be considering an entity as their subject. It is quite a litany in the wake of Albert and Whetten (1985), including Dutton and Dukerich (1991), Gioia and Chittipeddi (1991), Elsbach and Kramer (1996), Gioia and Thomas (1996), Gioia et al. (2000), Fiol (2002), Hatch and Schultz (2002), Corley and Gioia (2004), Brickson (2005), Ravasi and Schultz (2006), Corley et al. (2006), Whetten (2006), Clegg et al. (2007), and Clark et al. (2010) among many others. You will notice that the first author of this chapter is one of the obvious sinners in this listing of well-intentioned guilty parties. And what's more, he will probably sin again, because identity is much more easily understood not just as an entity, but as a possession.

Ironically, although most of his works in this litany are grounded theory models of the processes by which organizational identity can change, they nonetheless might be best characterized as models of how some*thing* (identity) changes over time. Linda Smircich's observation (1983) about organizational culture—that culture is not something an organization *has*, but something an organization *is*—probably is a better casting of organizational identity (but note that she is caught up in the *thing* thing, too—that is, culture as some*thing* an organization is). Our linguistic conventions are both a convenience and a seductive trap, as we all know, for as Lakoff and Johnson (1980) pointed out many years ago, the metaphors we live by tend to create the world with which we must deal. The way we talk about identity is an artifact of the way we think about it. Because we are so inclined to talk about identity as a thing, we both color and constrain the scope of how we consider identity.

We are very much predisposed to freezing identity, to holding it up for examination in a sensemaking fashion and concluding that because we seem to be able to freeze it to a moment in time, it must be a freezable thing. We bracket the experience of identity in the same way that we bracket the flow of ongoing social experience (Schutz, 1967; Weick, 1979), but we should be cognizant of the fact that our epistemological processes invoked to understand that the flow of experience also rouse the discomfiting intrusion of the Heisenberg Principle. That is, our attempts to assess a phenomenon affect our sense of the phenomenon itself. In the case of identity, our processes used for understanding would seem to alter the very ontology of the phenomenon we so very much want to understand—to the point of changing it from apparition to full-blown frozen entity.

As scholars, let us confess a forgivable trait that we share in common with lay people: A default presumption underlying our conception of the social world is that stability is an essential and preferred hallmark. People and institutions conceive of the social world as existing in some "normal" state

Identity as Process and Flow

of equilibrium that is occasionally disturbed by some discontinuity, after which we work very hard to reestablish some new state of equilibrium that generates another static state (that restores our cognitive and emotional equilibrium). Hey, few people like to be off balance and, let's face it, things in motion always retain the nasty possibility of throwing us off balance. Consider, however, that both Weick and Quinn (1999) and Tsoukas and Chia (2002) asked us to consider the possibility that change or disequilibrium was the "normal" state and stability and equilibrium was the "abnormal" state, a simple (if somewhat disconcerting) thought experiment that had the effect of altering how we might conceive of organizational change.

In a parallel fashion, we would ask you to consider the possibility that identity might be usefully construed not as something that exists as a possession, but rather an ongoing state of flux that we enact on an ongoing basis via our constructions and actions. Every once in a while, we stop the motion picture, look at the result of the stop-motion *as if* it were a still photograph and therefore convince ourselves that it is some sort of static thing. We are actually masters of this intriguing "as if" game (Gioia, 2004), and when we look around us, we see everyone else playing the same game, so we presume that the fiction we have created is real. We therefore treat it as real and it becomes real in its consequences (Thomas and Thomas, 1929; Berger and Luckmann, 1966). Yet the essence of identity might better be viewed not as a static construction made manifest, but instead as *flow*. Seeing identity as flow might conjure a river metaphor, but we should be careful even with that metaphor because rivers are simply composed of moving entities (water molecules). Even the old saying that, "you never step in the same river twice" is misleading because it still influences us to see identity as entity-in-motion. Our view is simply that identity is *always* in process, always in a state of "becoming," if you will, as Tsoukas and Chia (2002) so evocatively put it.

Perhaps at this point we should make a small concession. Maybe identity is not best portrayed as *either* a thing *or* a process. Perhaps we are better off— as almost always seems to be the case—by using a *both-and* framing (and, to be fair, in the litany of scholars noted earlier, Hatch and Schultz (2002), Clegg et al. (2007), and Clark et al. (2010) do acknowledge some of the process aspects of identity, as well as the content aspects). Identity can be construed both as some sort of entity and as some sort of process. Surely, at least conceptually, it has hallmarks of both—in the fashion that wave and particle theories of light are necessary to gain a comprehensive understanding of that physical phenomenon. Yet, as we should also acknowledge, the nature of the physical and social worlds are not actually all that similar, despite our sometimes desperate attempts to make them seem as if they are (which is yet another form of our penchant for playing the "as if" game). Our intent in this essay is to try to alter our apparently unwitting emphasis on one way of understanding identity, because it is so clear that we have been blinded by emphasizing the entity character of identity. So, yes, we acknowledge that there are some insights available by viewing identity as an entity, but there are other insights available by considering it as ongoing process and flow. So, we recognize that the *both-and* framing can confer a more comprehensive understanding of our subject.

A debate somewhat analogous to the aforementioned wave/particle views of light has attended the consideration of organizational identity during the first decade of the new millennium. The key question at the heart of that debate has been: Is organizational identity better viewed as a set of *claims* made by the organization acting as an agent in society (what came to be known as the "social actor view") or as a set of *constructions* by the members of an organization (known as the "social construction view")? The claims versus constructions debate has been a marvelous means for working out an understanding of the character of identity. The protagonists in the debate (Gioia et al., 2000; Whetten and Mackey, 2002; Corley et al., 2006; Ravasi and Schultz, 2006; Whetten, 2006) have engaged in some spirited, arms-length trading of countering views. Ravasi and Schultz tried to referee the intellectual battle by arguing that the two views were not mutually exclusive, as had seemed to be the stances by the two warring camps, but rather complementary (a position that was conceptually parallel to the wave/particle views of light).

Yet, identity is such an involved concept that even the complementary view probably does not capture its complexity or its dynamism. Gioia et al. (2010) argued instead that social construction and social actor processes are not merely complementary, but rather that they are mutually constitutive—that is, that each set of processes recursively influences and helps construct the other (even if it is perhaps apparent that social construction processes initially produce the claims made by and for the organization). This mutually constitutive entity/process view of identity holds not only that you get a more complete view of organizational identity, but also that you must understand that each is recursive (and also reflexive) with the other and therefore constitutive of the other before you can grasp the essential character of identity. Even this useful debate, however, tends to elide the flowing nature of identity, unless one recognizes that both claims and constructions constitute an ongoing process of accomplishment.

Consideration of the lively social-construction/social-actor debate leads us to comment on another debate, as well, one which considers the population ecologist's view of identity. Pop ecologists seem essentially to be arguing that "identity is category," or perhaps more appropriately, "category is identity." This argument distills to the following: If an observer can categorize an organization as a member of a given industry, then all the hard work of figuring out the identity of that organization is effectively done, because category so dominates identity that any other features or details of the organization are not worth worrying about. A simple example would be that if an observer can categorize an organization as a bank, then "we know who you are as an organization"—that is, we have established your identity to an adequate degree and that any other features do not supply enough additional information to make any difference in how that bank acts and performs within its industry category. Now, we are oversimplifying here, perhaps to the point of absurdity, but the point to be made is a good one.

Although it is accurate to say that industry constitutes a major component of organizational identity, presuming that the category so dominates that the values and features that are perceived by the members as central and distinctive about them as an organization can be ignored is tantamount to saying that if an observer can establish that a person is female, then her identity is obvious (Gioia et al., 2010). That is, if we know you are a woman, we know your identity and do not need to know anything more about you. We all know that this sort of conclusion-by-stereotypical categorization is so coarse-grained as to be woefully misleading, if not just plain silly for the purposes of understanding identity. We not only need to understand how the person understands herself, but also how her social identity interacts intersubjectively with those around her. Furthermore, we need to understand how her identity is constructed and reconstructed today—perhaps in an equivalent fashion as yesterday. That is, to achieve a truly comprehensive understanding of identity, we need to capture not only the features, but also the flow of her identity in motion.

3.1 Studying identity as process and flow

Now let us take our basic premise a step further. How might we study a phenomenon that is not conceived as a thing? What are the implications of conceptualizing identity-as-process or identity-as-flow for the way we study its dynamics? It seems to us that thinking of identity as process sets up a series of interesting challenges. If identity is not an entity possessed, then where or how should we look or go looking? If no one "owns" identity, then who defines identity and how do they do it? If it is indeed an in-flight process of construction, reconstruction, performance, legitimation, etc., then where or how should the boundaries of such a dynamic construction be drawn? More importantly, how can we hope to capture the essence of an attribute whose very nature is one of change? And what useable lessons might come from the effort? If indeed, as we suggest, our processes used for understanding identity would seem to alter the very ontology of the phenomenon we so very much want to understand, then perhaps this recognition calls for some mindfulness—and perhaps even some judicious alteration in the way we approach the study of identity.

Fortunately for us, in conceiving of identity as process, it seems that we have some pretty good guideposts in the body of work that is now identified as "process research" (see Barley, 1990; Langley, 1999; Pentland, 1999; Smith, 2002; Van de Ven and Poole, 2002; Hernes and Maitlis, 2010; Langley and Abdallah, 2011). Process research is something of an umbrella term for any approach that seeks to uncover the means—the processes—by which change (even in processes) occurs over time. Unlike "variance theories" that purport to answer questions of "what" the character of the relationships between two or more variables are, process theories are directed at unraveling issues of "how" such relationships and patterns emerge (Mohr, 1982). The researcher thus moves from surface to deep structures (or, in our case, from surface to deep *processes*), thereby moving beyond mere description to arrive at explanation. In identity research, this approach would translate to engagement with our phenomenon—not so much in terms of identifying what the core, distinctive, and "enduring" attributes of an individual or organization are, but in pursuing how such an identity is negotiated, constructed, reconstructed, "sustained" and projected backward and forward. In other words, when we speak of identity as process, the ebbs and flows of identity—rather than the features of identity—are our concern. (Or, if the features *are* our concern, then we would ask how those features came to be manifested, maintained, modified, or morphed over time.)

How should we approach our subject of study? Interestingly, process studies accommodate two ontologically diverse grounds: organization-as-entity and organization-as-process. The former perspective is one that sees organizations as *experiencing* change in some elements of their character; the latter is one that sees organizations as *imbued* with change as an existential precondition. From our perspective, organizations do not change, per se, as

Identity as Process and Flow

unfreeze-change-refreeze models would have it (Lewin, 1951). Rather, they are constantly changing (e.g., Weick and Quinn, 1999; Tsoukas and Chia, 2002). A "strong process" view (Chia and Langley, 2004) would even go so far as to posit that there is actually no such thing as an organization because the constant state of flux is not conducive to a portrayal of processes that stop long enough to declare a static state. For that reason, *organizing* rather than organization becomes the phenomenon of interest.

Among process studies, the organization-as-entity stance most obviously focuses on the narration of the sequence of observable change *events* in organizations. On the other hand, the organization-as-process stance focuses on narrating the social construction of such an activity. Although the variance approach is perhaps relatively more familiar to identity scholars, it is the process approach that is most necessary to entertain, although it would take some de-conditioning from our traditional ways of thinking about organizations. In Tsoukas and Chia's provocative words (2002): we would need an "ontological reversal" that would encourage us to rethink our notions about organizations and change: "Change must not be thought of as a property of organization. Rather, organization must be understood as an emergent property of change. Change is ontologically prior to organization—it is the condition of possibility for organization" (2002: 570).

Given our inclination to consider identity as both an entity and a process, we are motivated to suggest an approach that enables us to capture both elements of identity: the *being* and the *becoming* of identity. In fact, given the discovery that the social actor and the social construction views of identity are mutually constitutive (Gioia et al., 2010), we are inclined to suggest that a comprehensive study of identity-as-process would be well served by capturing both the snapshot quality of identity, and the motion-picture quality that details the processes of patterning and construction that lead up to (and also constitute) those snapshots. In other words, snapshots in themselves do not give a complete picture of identity—but without them we would not know where to look for identity. Such snapshots serve to circumscribe the process and act as reference points against which we examine the flow of identity over time. It is essential to remind ourselves, however, that such bracketing is mainly a tool of convenience (albeit an inevitable and important one!). It is the *"as if"* that we rely on—both as theorists and practitioners—to get by in the precarious world of ongoing identity construction.

What research strategies are well suited to studying identity as process? Process research has been conducted using many different specific methods:

grounded theory (e.g., Corley and Gioia, 2004; Clark et al., 2010), analytic induction (e.g., Langley, 1999), ethnography (e.g., Barley, 1990), and so on. Langley (1999) suggests three groups of strategies for process theorizing: grounding strategies (including grounded theory, alternate template strategies), organizing strategies (narrative and visual mapping strategies), and replicating strategies (such as temporal bracketing, quantification, and synthesis strategies). Some strategies are suited for explorations of meaning (grounded theory and narrative); some are better for tracing patterns (visual mapping, quantification, and grounded theory); some reveal mechanisms (alternate templates, temporal bracketing, quantification); and some are better for prediction (synthetic studies).

We are persuaded by Langley's observation that multiple strategies might be combined to achieve better explanatory theories. Although a significant number of studies that we have cited employ a grounded approach, one of the early works on identity (and the process of strategy formation) is in fact a "mixed-method" study that involves a study of micro-processes using an initial grounded theory development approach that is subsequently supplemented with a test of some of these relationships using a more quantitative, nomothetic approach (Gioia and Thomas, 1996). Our take is this: as long as the strategy helps us unearth the deep structure (Chomsky, 1964) or especially the deep processes (Gioia et al., 2010) of a phenomenon, it is likely to be adequate for the purposes of studying identity as process.

How might a compelling identity-as-process study look? We reckon that an exemplary study of identity-as-process would bear all the hallmarks of a well-done process study (Van de Ven and Poole, 2002). First, it will tell a "story." According to Pentland (1999), stories are critical constructs in process research and help "explain the relationships between events in a process or a narrative" (1999: 711). Stories are process theories in waiting. And process theories are stories told systematically. Reflecting on many of the works noted in this essay and borrowing from Van De Ven and Poole's list of ingredients (2002) for process narratives, we add that a compelling identity story is likely to elaborate on (*a*) temporal sequences: *when and in what order processes emerge*, (*b*) focal actors: *who constructed or performed identity work*, (*c*) an identifiable narrative voice: *a reflexive note by the observer or interpreter*, and (*d*) other indicators of content or context: *a reasonable focus on the historical backdrop in which the phenomenon emerges or is played out*.

Needless to say accomplishing the above could be a Herculean task. We are with Langley (1999) when she points out that process data are "notoriously challenging" (1999: 706) because they have features that make them difficult to analyze: that is, they deal with "events" and they often involve multiple levels of analysis. There is also the difficulty of obtaining access to organizations and organizational members for long periods of time (see also Langley and Abdallah, 2011). And then, of course, identity-as-process studies would invite the predictable common criticism that it might harbor no predictive power. All these factors might be seen as grounds for avoiding the study of identity-as-process, but there is a more optimistic way of viewing these challenges: they also might just create the opportunity to conduct some rather original organizational identity research that could generate a unique view of a unique phenomenon.

3.2 Conclusion

Given that organizational identity is a metaphor extended from the idea of individual identity, let us end where we began. Consider your own identity, that is, yourself. Are you static? Or, are you a "work in progress"? Framed in terms of these straightforward questions, it is apparent that we all are more appropriately cast as dynamic. Yet that simple recognition at the individual level gives us some insight into the nature of identity as a process rather than an entity. Can you find in yourself that kid of 10 now that you are your present age? Yes, of course you can. Does that mean that you are the same person you were when you were 10? Of course not. Things change! You change! Yet we are given to maintaining the appearance of stability, even as we are changing. We present ourselves as the same person over time. Our self-descriptions have a lot of sameness about them, leading us to view ourselves as not merely consistent over time but also to present ourselves and our descriptions of ourselves as stable over time. As Gioia et al. (2000) put it a while back: Our labels are stable, but their meanings change. So despite our attempts to maintain the fiction that we are who we were yesterday, the reality is that identity shifts. When juxtaposed with the related recognition that identity is an ongoing accomplishment of construction and reconstruction (even if the reconstructions frequently generate similar interpretations over time), we see that the essence of identity has a stealth dynamism about it.

Are we all then just shape-shifters? The same person in different forms? Or does the fact that we take different forms imply that something has changed about who we are? Our argument is yes to both. Yet the revelational part of that stance is the admission that different guises can constitute changing identities. When we elevate these kinds of observations to the organizational level and ask, "What then is the character of organizational identity?" we discover that because organizations comprise so many different constituent actors and because they have such a diversity of stakeholders and outside referents, they have an even greater capacity for dynamism than individuals do. Such dynamism further enhances the dynamism of identity. And that recognition suggests that identity (whether individual or organizational) is more appropriately viewed not as entity, but as process and flow.

References

Albert, S. and Whetten, D. A. (1985). "Organizational Identity," in L. L. Cummings and B. M. Staw (eds), *Research in Organizational Behavior*. Greenwich, CT: JAI Press, vol. 7, pp. 263–95.

Barley, S. R. (1990). "Images of Imaging: Notes on Doing Longitudinal Field Work." *Organization Science*, 1: 220–47.

Brickson, S. L. (2005). "Organizational Identity Orientation: Forging a Link between Organizational Identity and Organizations' Relations with Stakeholders." *Administrative Science Quarterly*, 50: 576–609.

Berger, P. L. and Luckmann, T. (1966). *The Social Construction of Reality: A Treatise in the Sociology of Knowledge*. Garden City, NY: Doubleday.

Chia, R. and Langley, A. (2004). "The First Organization Studies Summer Workshop: Theorizing Process in Organizational Research (Call for Papers)." *Organization Studies*, 25/8: 1486.

Chomsky, N. (1964). *Syntactic Structures*. The Hague: Mouton.

—— (1964). "The Nature of Structural Descriptions," *Current Issues in Linguistic Theory*. The Hague: Mouton, pp. 65–110.

Clark, S. M., Gioia, D. A., Ketchen, D. J., Jr., and Thomas, J. B. (2010). "Transitional Identity as a Facilitator of Organizational Identity Change during a Merger." *Administrative Science Quarterly*, 55: 397–438.

Clegg, S. R., Rhodes, C., and Kornberger, M. (2007) "Desperately Seeking Legitimacy: Organizational Identity and Emerging Industries." *Organization Studies*, 28: 495–513.

Corley, K. G. and Gioia, D. A. (2004). "Identity Ambiguity and Change in the Wake of a Corporate Spin-off." *Administrative Science Quarterly*, 49/2: 173–208.

—— Harquail, C. V., Pratt, M. G., Glynn, M. A., Fiol, C. M., and Hatch, M. J. (2006). "Guiding Organizational Identity through Aged Adolescence." *Journal of Management Inquiry*, 15: 85–99.

Dutton, J. E. and Dukerich, J. M. (1991). "Keeping an Eye on the Mirror: Image and Identity in Organizational Adaptation." *Academy of Management Journal*, 34: 517–54.

Elsbach, K. D. and Kramer, R. M. (1996). "Members' Responses to Organizational Identity Threats: Encountering and Countering the BusinessWeek Rankings." *Administrative Science Quarterly*, 41: 442–76.

Fiol, C. M. (2002). "Capitalizing on Paradox: The Role of Language in Transforming Organizational Identities." *Organization Science*, 13: 653–66.

Gioia, D. A. (2004). "A Renaissance Self: Prompting Personal and Professional Revitalization," in R. E. Stablein and P. J. Frost (eds), *Renewing Research Practice*. Stanford, CA: Stanford University Press, pp. 97–114.

—— Chittipeddi, K. (1991). "Sensemaking and Sensegiving in Strategic Change Initiation." *Strategic Management Journal*, 12: 433–48.

—— Thomas, J. B. (1996). "Identity, Image, and Issue Interpretation: Sensemaking during Strategic Change in Academia." *Administrative Science Quarterly*, 41: 370–403.

—— Schultz, M. and Corley, K. G. (2000). "Organizational Identity, Image, and Adaptive Instability." *Academy of Management Review*, 25: 63–81.

—— Price, K. N., Hamilton, A. L., and Thomas, J. B. (2010). "Forging an Identity: An Insider-Outsider Study of Processes Involved in the Formation of Organizational Identity." *Administrative Science Quarterly*, 55: 1–46.

Hatch, M. J. and Schultz, M. (2002). "The Dynamics of Organizational Identity." *Human Relations*, 55: 989–1017.

Hernes, T. and Maitlis, S. (2010). *Process, Sensemaking and Organizing: An Introduction*. Oxford: Oxford University Press.

Lakoff, G. and Johnson, M. (1980). *Metaphors We Live by*. Chicago, IL: University of Chicago Press.

Langley, A. (1999). "Strategies for Theorizing from Process Data." *Academy of Management Review*, 24/4: 691–710.

—— Abdallah, C. (2011). "Templates and Turns in Qualitative Studies of Strategy and Management." In D. Bergh and D. Ketchen (eds), *Research Methodology in Strategy and Management*, vol. 6. Bingley: Emerald Group Publishing.

Lewin, K. (1951). *Field Theory in Social Science*. New York: Harper & Row.

Lincoln, Y. S. and Guba, E. G. (1985). *Naturalistic Inquiry*. Newbury Park, CA: Sage.

Mohr, L. B. (1982). *Explaining Organizational Behavior*. San Francisco, CA: Jossey-Bass.

Nag, R., Corley, K. G., and Gioia, D. A. (2007). "The Intersection of Organizational Identity, Knowledge, and Practice: Attempting Strategic Change via Knowledge Grafting." *Academy of Management Journal*, 50: 821–47.

Pentland, B. T. (1999). "Building Process Theory with Narrative: From Description to Explanation." *Academy of Management Review*, 2: 711–24.

Ravasi, D. and Schultz, M. (2006). "Responding to Organizational Identity Threats: Exploring the Role of Organizational Culture." *Academy of Management Journal*, 49/3: 433–58.

Schutz, A. (1967). *The Phenomenology of the Social World*. Evanston, IL: Northwestern University Press.

Smircich, L. (1983). "Concepts of Culture and Organizational Analysis." *Administrative Science Quarterly*, 28: 339–58.

Smith, A. (2002). "From Process Data to Publication: A Personal Sensemaking." *Journal of Management Inquiry*, 11/4: 383–406.

Thomas, W. I. and Thomas, D. S. (1929). *The Child in America*, 2nd edn. New York: Alfred Knopf.

Tsoukas, H. and Chia, R. (2002). "On Organizational Becoming: Rethinking Organizational Change." *Organization Science*, 13: 567–82.

Van de Ven, A. and Poole, M. S. (2002). "Field Research Methods for Studying Processes of Organizational Change," in J. Baum (ed.), *Blackwell Companion to Organizations*. London: Basil Blackwell, pp. 867–88.

Weick, K. E. (1979). *The Social Psychology of Organizing*. New York: Addison-Wesley.

—— (1995). *Sensemaking in Organizations*. Thousand Oaks, CA: Sage Publications.

—— Quinn, R. E. (1999). "Organizational Change and Development." *Annual Review of Psychology*, 50: 361–86.

Whetten, D. A. (2006). "Albert and Whetten Revisited: Strengthening the Concept of Organizational Identity." *Journal of Management Inquiry*, 15: 219–34.

—— Mackey, A. (2002). "A Social Actor Conception of Organizational Identity and its Implications for the Study of Organizational Reputation." *Business and Society*, 41: 393–414.

4

Exploring Cultural Mechanisms of Organizational Identity Construction

Mary Ann Glynn and Lee Watkiss

Abstract: We explore the cultural embeddedness of organizational identity and highlight the role of cultural mechanisms in the construction of the organization's identity claims. We conceive of an organization as a social actor who functions as a skilled cultural operative, sufficiently agentic so as to select those cultural elements that align with its internal character, but not so insensitive as to adopt those elements that are culturally inappropriate or illegitimate. By appropriating and interpreting cultural resources, the organization makes identity claims of "who we are" and "what we do." Drawing from the organizational and social science literatures, we identify six cultural mechanisms—framing, repertoires, narrating, symbolization and symbolic boundaries, capital and status, and institutional templates—whereby organizations incorporate cultural elements into their identities and show their correspondence to identity elements.

4.1 Introduction

The smell of natural gas was unmistakable. It was a smell you could see. The vapours rose clearly in the sunlight, and stank of rotten eggs. But to the explorer George Reynolds it was the best thing he had smelled in seven years. He instructed the men to keep drilling... Back in England, William D'Arcy (a principal investor in Anglo-Persian Oil Company, which would one day become BP) was close to despair. He had gambled his considerable fortune on oil, and now he was on the verge of losing it all... It seemed that the geologists and experts who had wagged their heads encouragingly at him since 1901 had all been wrong about the oil beneath the sands of Persia[1] (BP 1901–8).

As a century drew to a close and a whole new millennium approached, people around the world turned their thoughts to the future...Scientists did the same, naturally, and many of them didn't like what they saw. Climate change, they said, posed a genuine and growing threat to the earth...These developments were not brushed over lightly in a speech Lord Browne, then BP's group chief executive, gave in California in 1997. He called for "a balance between the needs of development and the need for environmental protection." But a different statement took the headlines. Lord Browne had become the first CEO of a major energy company to acknowledge the near consensus among scientists about the global threat posed by climate change. And BP, he said, had a share in the responsibility for addressing the problem[2] (BP 2000s).

The identity claims (above) made 100 years apart by the same oil and gas organization, BP plc. (BP), highlight the role that societal culture plays in crafting organizational identity claims and the social fitness of these claims when aligned with the cultural sentiments of the times. The early twentieth century was a period of geographic exploration and appropriation; this was expressed in the expansionist desires of European colonialists and associated with cultural values of courageousness and bravery, as seen in Reynolds' command to "keep drilling" and to risk a fortune. A century later, expansionism gave way to restraint and a concern with "the need for environmental protection." Accordingly, BP's identity reflected this shift, recharacterizing its identity claims as responsible, progressive, innovative, and performance-driven.[3] Despite being sorely tested by the catastrophic oil leak in the Gulf of Mexico in the spring and summer of 2010, BP's identity claims have continued to include commitments to community, business, and environmental restoration, and emphatically asserting a concern with "making it right" again.[4]

The evolution of BP's identity claims, over time and in accord with prevailing cultural sentiments, suggests that organizational identity is embedded in, and responsive to, broader sensibilities and meanings of the societies in which they operate. While the BP example suggests the possibility that organizational identity is shaped by cultural sentiments, there has been little scholarly exploration of this idea. Instead, researchers have tended to focus on organizational identity as a reflection of the *internal character* of the organization, consisting of those "central, distinct, and enduring" attributes (Albert and Whetten, 1985) claimed by its members (Dutton and Dukerich, 1991), or as an *external perception or judgment* by outside audiences or interested stakeholders (Zuckerman, 2004; Glynn, 2008a). We seek to find a middle ground between these two perspectives and, especially, how organizations construct identities using cultural elements that can both reflect their internal character and align with external perceptions.

We explore the cultural embeddedness of organizational identity and highlight the role of cultural mechanisms in the construction of the organization's identity. We conceive of an organization as a social actor who functions as a skilled cultural operative, sufficiently agentic so as to select those cultural elements that align with its internal character, but not so insensitive as to adopt those elements that are culturally inappropriate or illegitimate. Thus, we view the organization neither as a "cultural dope," passive and constrained by culture, nor the "hyper muscular hero," that functions independently from culture (Powell and Colyvas, 2008; Scott, 2010).

We build on research that demonstrates the effects of societal culture on a diverse set of organizational actions and meanings. For instance, researchers show that cultural-cognitive institutions exert pressures for organizational conformity (e.g., Scott, 2001), that cultural changes in tastes and preferences shape professional identities (e.g., Rao et al., 2003), and that new venture formation and success is predicated upon cultural entrepreneurship (Lounsbury and Glynn, 2001; Martens et al., 2007; Zott and Huy, 2007). This body of work demonstrates that societal culture affects the organization but stops short of articulating the particular mechanisms by which culture exerts its influence. Our objective in this chapter is to offer an initial foray into understanding these processes and mechanisms; our focus is on how an organization's identity is culturally constituted by elements from the broader society.

Broadly speaking, culture consists of "the meanings and practices produced, sustained and altered through interaction" (Van Maanen, forthcoming). Culture is important because it "provides orientation, wards off chaos, and directs behavior toward certain lines of action" (Griswold, 2008: 24). Culture provides meaning and order in a number of different ways. From their review of the relevant social science literatures, Small et al. (2010) identify six different cultural forms and the mechanisms by which they influence. These consider culture as frames, repertoires, narratives, capital, symbolic boundaries, and institutions. This typology not only serves as an analytical tool (Small et al., 2010) but also can be viewed processually as a set of six cultural mechanisms that can shape organizational identity elements. For instance, the cultural form of the narrative functions as a mechanism because it enables storytelling or sensemaking that articulates the organization's identity (e.g., Lounsbury and Glynn, 2001). Although each of the six mechanisms highlights a different facet of culture, all enable organizations to make their identities sensible, meaningful, and credible.

We envision the organization as a social actor embedded in a cultural field, claiming elements that align the identity of the organization with cultural values, beliefs, and understandings but choosing them selectively to differentiate the organization from other firms within the field. In essence, the various manifestations of culture, for example symbols, traditions, stories, and other collective representations, function as a set of resources (Swidler, 1986) for identity. By incorporating these resources, an organization references the societal culture that embeds it (Swidler, 1986; Lamont and Lareau, 1988) and thus demonstrates the social fitness that can enable legitimation and wealth creation (e.g., Lounsbury and Glynn, 2001; Glynn and Abzug, 2002; Navis and Glynn, 2010). As we refer to "culture" in this chapter, we refer to the broader societal, national, institutional, or industry culture rather than the organizational culture per se (e.g., Fiol, 1991; Ravasi and Schultz, 2006).

Our approach complements more sociological approaches to organizations and identity. By focusing on the cultural embeddedness of the organization's identity, our chapter complements existing work focusing on the structural (e.g., Uzzi, 1997) or cognitive embeddedness (Kennedy, 2008) of organizations. For instance, institutional theory focuses on large-scale cultural forces, rules, or templates that shape the organizational field as a whole and homogenize the identities of organizations within (e.g., Glynn and Abzug, 2002; Glynn, 2008*b*), thereby overlooking the tailoring of culture by particular organizations in constructing and defining their identities. We explore intermediate ground, between identity homogeneity precipitated by institutional isomorphism and identity heterogeneity of strategic differentiation (Glynn, 2008*a*), recognizing that an organization selectively appropriates different features of culture (e.g., Rao et al., 2003) and incorporates these features dynamically as they use "culture in interaction" in everyday functioning (e.g., Eliasoph and Lichterman, 2003). Such an approach necessitates a processual perspective on culture and its influence on organizational identity in order to explain "how things evolve over time and why they evolve this way" (Langley, 1999: 692).

A processual perspective on organizational identity investigates how identities "come to be constituted, reproduced, adapted and defined through ongoing processes" (Langley, 2007: 271), a dynamic that Tsoukas and Chia (2002) refer to as "organizational becoming," a seeming parallel to the "theory of being" (Livengood and Reger, 2010: 51) describing organizational identity. We focus on the dynamic and interactive interplay between societal culture and organizational identity, asking: *How* does an organization incorporate cultural forms into its identity as it engages in ongoing organizing (Weick, 1995)? *How* do different cultural mechanisms shape the organization's identity?

We address these questions by first examining the social constructionist nature of organizational identity and its dynamic relationship to societal culture. Next, we review relevant literatures from management and the social sciences to develop a conceptual framework of how different cultural mechanisms can shape organizational identities. Finally, we conclude with preliminary theorization on the processual mechanisms that link organizational identity to societal culture.

4.2 A processual perspective on organizational identity

Research on organizational identity in the management literature was launched by Albert and Whetten (1985), who defined the construct in terms of three criteria: "claimed central character," "claimed distinctiveness," and "claimed temporal continuity." Evident is the centrality of "claim-making" as an identity process (Glynn, 2000: 286), an assertion that can illuminate how an organization appropriates cultural scripts (Cerulo, 1997) within its environments (Czarniawska and Wolff, 1998; Glynn, 2008a). The distinctly processual flavor of Albert and Whetten's classic formulation is made clear in the following quote:

> "An identity distinctive framework underscores the need to examine *how* new roles come into existence, *how* organizations choose (or back into) one role rather than another, and *how* that action affects the organization's internal and external identity." (1985: 273; emphasis added)

However, this has been overlooked in subsequent scholarship (for an exception, see Gioia et al., 2000). This is the focus of our inquiry.

4.2.1 Organizational identity as a socially constructed process

In his foundational work on institutionalization, Selznick (1957) offers a processual perspective, detailing *how* organizations become infused with value beyond that of their technical function to form a distinctive organizational character or identity. An integral part of Selznick's theorization is that an organization endures because it incorporates values, ideals, and purpose that align with societal norms and needs (Albert and Whetten, 1985). In the sociological literature, Cerulo (1997: 387) similarly views identity in terms of processes of social construction such that: "every collective becomes a social artifact—an entity molded, refabricated, and mobilized in accord with reigning cultural scripts and centers of power."

Within the management literature, organizational identity has only infrequently been conceptualized in terms of processes that link it to the broader cultural environment. Although institutionalists have formulated this identity–culture relationship in broad strokes of isomorphic conformity (e.g., Czarniawska and Wolff, 1998; Glynn, 2000), less attention has been paid to the more enabling aspects of culture (e.g., Lounsbury and Glynn, 2001; Navis and Glynn, 2010). Hence, we look beyond the management literature to the social sciences to explicate culture and its relevance to organizational identities.

4.2.2 Societal culture and organizational identity

The construct of culture has a long and rich history in the social sciences. One of the earliest definitions appeared in anthropology, where culture was defined as "that complex whole which includes knowledge, belief, art, law, morals, custom, and any other capabilities and habits acquired by man as a member of society" (Tylor, 1871: 1). This conceptualization frames culture symbolically, emphasizing its collective nature and its function as a kind of "glue" that binds societal members together. Nearly a century later, Geertz (1966: 89) draws attention to the fluidity of culture, observing that cultural patterns both shape themselves to reality and are shaped by it; he defines culture as "an historically transmitted pattern of meanings embodied in symbols, a system of inherited conceptions expressed in symbolic forms by means of which men communicate, perpetuate, and develop their knowledge about and attitudes toward life." Geertz's focus on cultural "models" or "templates" was elaborated by cognitive anthropologist Bradd Shore (1996: 44) who argues that such cultural models "exist both as public artifacts 'in the world' and as cognitive constructs 'in the mind' of members of a community," giving them a "twice born character" (Shore, 1996: 68). Thus, societal culture can exist apart from an organization, but also can be appropriated and adapted by the organization.

Sociologists have generated a plethora of ways of studying culture that include its cognitive, symbolic, structural, and pragmatic aspects. Early approaches defined culture as a set of collective beliefs and values, that is, "a system of shared cognitions" (Goodenough, 1971: 20). Subsequent theorists made the leap from an exterior, somewhat objectified, perspective on culture to an internalized representation of that culture (Parsons and Shils, 1951). Durkheim's conception (1984) of culture as "collective representations" expanded cognition to a macro-level, but continued to represent culture as a strong, homogenizing force on social actors. Recently, this assumption of isomorphic reproduction has been relaxed, permitting a view of culture to be more fluid and dynamic, noting how culture is shaped as it is used in interactions among social actors, that is, as "a set of publicly shared codes or repertoires, building blocks that structure people's ability to think and to share ideas" (Eliasoph and Lichterman, 2003: 735). More generally, cultural sociologists have pointed out how cultural models or forms can take on different meanings, in different contexts, and be deployed by social actors as resources shaped to their needs (e.g., Swidler, 1986).

While cognitive approaches emphasize individuals' internalization of culture, pragmatic approaches emphasize socially organized practices, objective rituals, and symbols. Bourdieu (1977) shows how deeply internalized cultural styles, skills, or "habitus" motivates individuals' actions, thereby recreating and innovating culture in meaningful ways. Similarly, cultural psychologists have observed how culture exists publicly—as "cultural frames"—and privately, as individuals appropriate and act on what culture means to them. In other words, culture can be considered both the "product of action" and the "conditioning elements of further action" (Kroeber and Kluckhohn, 1952: 357). Overall, then, this brief overview suggests that conceptions of culture have evolved to acknowledge the dynamism and fluidity of culture, over time and across various social actors. Moreover, theorizations of culture have widened to acknowledge its dual nature, as both a publicly accessible resource, available to actors (e.g., Swidler, 1986), and as an individuated, actor-specific appropriation that is used to frame and interpret the world (Shore, 1996). The interplay between cultural models of a society and the organization drives the cultural constitution of organizational identities. We next examine the cultural underpinnings and underlying mechanisms.

4.2.3 Cultural mechanisms and organizational identity

Small et al. (2010), from their review of the literature, observe that culture is resident in frames, repertoires, narratives, (cultural) capital, symbolic boundaries, and institutions. We view these variants of culture as mechanisms that can generate and explain how societal culture and organizational

Constructing Identity in and around Organizations

Table 4.1 Cultural mechanisms in organizational identity construction

Cultural mechanism	Definitions, assumptions, and functions of cultural mechanism
Framing	Culture is a cognitive filter, drawing attention to some aspects and not to others in the cultural environment, enabling actors to see and understand their world (e.g., Goffman, 1963; Berger and Luckmann, 1967; Snow and Benford, 1992). A frame is "an interpretive [schema] that simplifies and condenses the 'world out there' by selectively punctuating and encoding objects, situations, events, experiences, and sequences of actions within one's present or past environment" (Snow and Benford, 1992: 137). Prominent in social movement research, frames are shown to mobilize collective action by suggesting that a cause is possible and also necessary and legitimate (Small et al., 2010). Framing tends to suggest appropriate action but not necessarily cause it, thus making a multiplicity of alternative frames possible (Small et al., 2010); thus, culture frames may be varied, contested, complementary, or changing even for a single organization or actor. Cultural frames can articulate an ideology, that is, "A set of interconnected beliefs and their associated attitudes, shared and used by members of a group or population, that relate to problematic aspects of social and political topics" (Fine and Sandstrom, 1993: 24); this often occurs in narratives or myths.
Repertoires	Culture as a resource offers a "toolkit" of practices, beliefs, skills, and attitudes that can offer possibilities for "strategies of action," that is, "persistent ways of ordering action through time" (Swidler, 1986: 273). Like frames, cultural resources direct attention but, unlike frames, narrow actions to those for which one is culturally equipped with appropriate tools (Small et al., 2010). Because cultural repertoires offer a variety of strategies for action, they allow for diversity across actors or in different contexts, such as settled or unsettled times (Swidler, 1986).
Narrating	Culture as a sensemaking device that narrates, interprets, and explains an actor's particular course of action, both to themselves (as self-narration) and to others (as shared narratives). Action is made possible through narrative: those actions more consistent with one's self-narrative are more likely to be enacted (Small et al., 2010). Identity stories are a particular form that ties together the past, present, and future (Zilber, 2002), linking the self-concept to behavior.
Symbolization and symbolic boundaries	Culture symbolically bounds the conceptual distinctions made to categorize objects, people, events, or practices. Cultural boundaries function as a "system of rule that guide interaction by affecting who comes together to engage" (Lamont and Fournier, 1992: 12). Boundaries partition those who are more (or less) worthy of economic success, cultural sophistication, social class, and morality, to create "cultural categories of worth" that are hierarchically differentiated and meaningful as collective identities (Small et al., 2010). Symbolic classification reproduces class privileges (Bourdieu, 1984) and thus can endow different groups with different levels of social or cultural capital.
Capital and status	Cultural capital consists of the "institutionalized, i.e., widely shared, high status cultural signals" used to exclude others in various contexts (Lamont and Lareau, 1988: 156). Cultural

	preferences often serve as class markers in a cultural universe (Small et al., 2010); DiMaggio (1982) has shown how the elite legitimated and sanctioned their preferences as high class and differentiated it from popular or low class. Those with cultural capital have the capacity to define and legitimize cultural, moral, and artistic values, standards, and styles (Anheier et al., 1995) and often function as cultural authorities. Cultural capital can be objectified as transmittable goods, such as art or books (Bourdieu, 1984) or signaled with high status cultural markers, such as tastes, preferences, cultural expertise, or social or familial relationships.
Institutional templates	Culture as constructs drawn from institutions, whether defined robustly as taken-for-granted rules, routines or practices, interpretively as legitimated social constructions in cognitive and normative templates, or narrowly as organizations, enables and constrains shared definitions of experience and the possibility and appropriateness of actions (Small et al., 2010). Institutions are both material and symbolic; symbolic systems categorize activities and infuse them with meaning and, importantly, "are available to organizations and individuals to elaborate" (Friedland and Alford, 1991: 248); the authors identify five major institutions in Western society—family, capitalism, religion/science, democracy, and the bureaucratic state. Because actors negotiate the same institutional hurdles, they tend to act in culturally uniform ways even if their experiences are not shared (Swidler, 1995).

identity are associated or inextricably linked; mechanisms are inherently processual, offering explanations of how societal culture can affect an organization's identity. As Davis and Marquis (2005: 336) put it:

> Mechanisms describe "a set of interacting parts—an assembly of elements producing an effect not inherent in any one of them. A mechanism is not so much about 'nuts and bolts' as about 'cogs and wheels'...—the wheelwork or agency by which an effect is produced" (Hernes, 1998: 74).

As a set, these cultural mechanisms function to encode shared frames of reference, to direct attention, to make the organizational identity meaningful and normative, and to promote organizational capabilities. Individually, the six cultural mechanisms accomplish these in a somewhat different ways. Before describing them in detail, we present the definitions, assumptions, and functions associated with each of the cultural mechanisms in Table 4.1. The table presents each cultural mechanism as though it were distinct and independent, consistent with the approach adopted by Small et al. (2010). Realistically, however, these mechanisms are unlikely to be independent, but rather, overlap and can reinforce (or conflict with) each

Constructing Identity in and around Organizations

other, interactively and interdependently. Moreover, all six cultural mechanisms are not necessary to identity construction; rather, an organization selectively chooses those mechanisms that best suit its identity, an argument we take up subsequently.

4.2.3.1 CULTURAL MECHANISM OF FRAMING

This mechanism emphasizes how a particular schema (or frame) selectively draws attention to, and interprets, some elements in the cultural environment while overlooking or ignoring others (e.g., Goffman, 1963; Berger and Luckmann, 1967; Snow and Benford, 1992). Cultural frames articulate an ideology, that is, a "set of interconnected beliefs and their associated attitudes, shared and used by members of a group or population, that relate to problematic aspects of social and political topics" (Fine and Sandstrom, 1993: 24). Gamson (1992) suggests "harmony with nature" as a popular theme threaded throughout American culture. More generally, Swart (1995: 466) highlights master frames, that is, "general symbolic frames that are culturally resonant to their historical milieux." Cultural frames aid in the creation of a common definition of reality, and, within the frame, guide logical action.

Cultural frames are appropriated and used to define organizational identities in a number of different ways. Dutton and Dukerich's study (1991) of the Port Authority of New York and New Jersey reveals how an organization reframed the issue of homelessness with regard to its identity. Glynn's study (2000) of an orchestra beset with a musician's strike shows how the conflict centered on the framing of the identity of the organization, either as a "World Class Symphony," by the musicians, or the "Best Orchestra We can Afford," by the board and administrators. Rao et al. examine how changes in French cuisine shifted the identities of restaurants and chefs, fueled by an identity movement framing classical cuisine as "the enemy" (2005: 985).

Identities can also be framed by "who we are" as well as "who we are not." Elsbach and Bhattacharya (2001) investigate how individuals can disidentify with an organization as an identity-defining frame. The social movement literature offers robust evidence of how cultural frames can define the identity of a collective in terms of salient social issues (e.g., feminists, civil rights activists) and mobilize collective action in accord with that identity (e.g., Snow and Benford, 1992).

The potency of cultural framing for organizational identity not only is definitional but also associates meanings that are culturally sanctioned. For instance, in American culture, organizations displaying the US flag suggest an identity of patriotism or nationalism, and those telling success stories of "rags to riches" align with the American Dream as personified by Horatio Alger. Moreover, by framing their identities with prevailing cultural sentiments like corporate social responsibility, organizations can enhance their appeal. By appropriating and deploying cultural frames in their identities, organizations signify their cultural fitness and facilitate audience's evaluations of them as credible. Clearly, though, framing an identity that is inconsistent with organizational actions or image may lack authenticity and thus potency or credibility.

4.2.3.2 CULTURAL MECHANISM OF REPERTOIRES

In contrast to the cognitive thrust of frames, theorizing culture as repertoires is pragmatic in orientation, focusing on how actors use cultural "toolkits" of practices, beliefs, skills, and attitudes to craft "strategies of action" (Swidler, 1986: 273). Like cultural frames, cultural repertoires direct attention toward possible actions, but only those for which the actor is culturally equipped and appropriately tooled (Small et al., 2010). This perspective offers an "identity model of culture" predicated upon how people use cultural repertoires to structure their "self," their behavioral practices, and their "cultural capacities" (Swidler, 1986).

The organizational literature shows the relevance of cultural repertoires to identity. Fine (1996) demonstrates how organizational and professional rhetorics are resources that identify workers as artists, laborers, professionals (chefs), or business people. Harris and Sutton (1986) show how practices and rituals characterize dying organizations and that parting ceremonies enable workers to edit their schemas about the organization.

A number of scholars conceptualize culture as a strategic resource that can enable the organizational identity to serve as an "inimitable strategic resource" (e.g., Fiol, 1991) that is instrumental in market positioning and filtering strategic issues (e.g., Dutton and Dukerich, 1991; Gustafson and Reger, 1995; Elsbach and Kramer, 1996; Gioia and Thomas, 1996; Fox-Wolfgramm et al., 1998). Generally speaking, cultural repertoires can craft an organizational identity as a "theory of being" (or perhaps "becoming"; Tsoukas and Chia, 2002) that articulates "'who' they are as a firm, 'what' they stand for, and 'why' they are successful" (Livengood and Reger, 2010: 51). Thus, culture can be resourced in identity to rationalize an organization's identity and purpose and demonstrate its alignment with the social context in which it operates.

4.2.3.3 CULTURAL MECHANISM OF NARRATING

This mechanism focuses on the act of narrating during sensemaking or interpretive processes which can make the organizational identity story understandable (Small et al., 2010). Identity stories are interpretive packages composed in a "fictive history" that is neither fully history nor fully fiction (Ricoeur, 1991). In American culture, a dominant narrative is the American dream (Small et al., 2010), of which a distinguishing motif is that of redemption. McAdams explains the potency of the storytelling and its association with deep-rooted cultural sensibilities:

> Adults who tell a redemptive story tap into a stream of unique inspiration and sustenance in the rich store of redemptive tales that American culture offers. The stories of upward mobility, recovery, fulfillment and release that come from Hollywood, 12-step programs, self-help experts, political speeches, business gurus and Oprah can trace their roots directly to the autobiographies of Massachusetts Puritans, Benjamin Franklin and escaped African-American slaves.[5]

One form of narrative, myth, is a paradoxical combination of truth and fiction, relating "something that is arguably true along with something that is arguably not true...a particular mix of fact and fiction" (Shore, 1996). Myths can be sacred histories and often regarded as transcendent, but they can also have a dark side, promoting "myth-conceptions"—crucially erroneous or misleading images packaged in rhetorical forms that suggest truth. However, these myths can act as a crucial resource for the organization. Through the act of narrating a myth, an organization can use this symbol of the past (Glynn and Watkiss, 2011) to overcome formidable challenges and reach its goals.

Myths tap into an organizational identity by articulating the meanings and values that underlie it. Conceptualizing organizations as "secular religions" (e.g., Ashforth and Vaidyanath, 2002) highlights how organizational myths can function as identity mechanisms that are a touchstone for individuals' identification with the firm. Organizational identity narratives are often populated with saviors, heroes, and occasionally, villains. Constructing heroic narratives of corporate leaders such as Apple's Chief Executive Officer, Steve Jobs, serves to provide a personal face to an organization's identity. Culturally valorized heroes signify not only the individual hero but also the values and identity that are mythologized:

> These heroic figures represented our best images of our selves. Thus George Washington, despite all of his faults, is used to symbolize the American republic

to citizens. Even though few knew Washington personally, he could be taught and presented in a variety of ways that convinced members of the polity that they did know and, of greater significance, admired him with a passion that could brook no dispute. It is relatively easy to understand how those who are defined as great come to define a people through collective representations. (Fine, 2002: 228)

Narrative cultural mechanisms can be key in the identity work of organizational storytelling (e.g., Weick, 1995; Van Maanen, 1998; Ashforth, 2001; Ibarra and Barbulescu, 2010) in which a "culturally appropriate self" is created (e.g., Sutton, 1991; Kunda, 1992). Identity narratives can be particularly potent under uncertainty (Lounsbury and Glynn, 2001; Martens et al., 2007) because they not only explain the organization but also lend it authenticity and credibility by appropriating legitimating cultural scripts (Ibarra and Barbulescu, 2010).

4.2.3.4 CULTURAL MECHANISM OF SYMBOLIZATION AND SYMBOLIC BOUNDARIES

This mechanism emphasizes the classificatory function of culture that partitions and sorts actors into social or demographic classes, or tastes and preferences (e.g., DiMaggio, 1982). Bourdieu (1984) shows how "taste classifies" as a cultural boundary by making distinctions "between the beautiful and the ugly, the distinguished and the vulgar, in which their position in the objective classifications is expressed or betrayed." Theorizing culture in symbolic terms, specifically its symbolic boundaries, suggests that maximizing distinctions into categories of worth can function to define identities.

Symbols and symbolic boundaries constitute the identity of actors (Tajfel and Turner, 1979; DiMaggio, 1997) and are used by organizational members and interested stakeholders to decipher the organizational identity (e.g., Glynn and Abzug, 2002). Boundaries refer to "the physical, temporal, and cognitive limits that define domains as separate from one another" (Kreiner et al., 2006: 1318). Rao et al. show how the partitions that divided French cuisine into two distinct categories—classic and nouvelle—differentiated chefs and their organizations, observing that "A canonical axiom in the social sciences is that categories establish social and symbolic boundaries, and thereby constitute the identity of actors" (2003: 970). Moreover, boundaries make categories clear (e.g., Zuckerman, 1999) and, by implication, pure and uncontaminated (Rao et al., 2003).

Constructing Identity in and around Organizations

For organizational identity, symbolic boundaries can raise interesting issues for hybrid identities that contain elements that typically do not fit together (Albert and Whetten, 1985). In such a case, an organization can avoid or compartmentalize potential conflict by utilizing the boundaries that separate the symbolic from the instrumental and the aesthetic from the commercial. Rao and colleagues (2003) demonstrate how cultural changes in French cuisine threatened the sanctity of ideologically pure classic cuisine, particularly when the boundary with nouvelle cuisine became blurred. Glynn (2000) shows how an organizational crisis reinforced the boundaries between potentially conflicting identity elements within an organization, increasing contestation. Generally speaking, boundaries partition identities of both an organization and the market category in which it operates (e.g., Navis and Glynn, 2010). Understanding how an organization perceives a cultural boundary in the construction of its identity claim, that is, a choice of "who I am" (Santos and Eisenhardt, 2005) and a demarcation of the limits of identity (Ashforth, 2001), is important in positioning its identity within the field and relative to its audience.

4.2.3.5 CULTURAL MECHANISM OF CAPITAL AND STATUS

This mechanism affords an explanation of high status or elite positioning and associated connotations of superiority (Small et al., 2010). Cultural capital can lend authority to the social actor who defines and legitimizes her/his preferred cultural styles and standards (for a thorough review, see DiMaggio's (1982) fascinating study of the Boston Brahmins). Bourdieu (1984) illuminates how cultural capital can extend to taste and lifestyles that are defined as superior and, by implication, the actor's identity as superior. Coleman (1988) shows how family, and particularly, relationships among family members (e.g., parent-and-child), supplies cultural capital.

Theorizing culture as capital suggests that status signals or authoritative statements of elite taste can function as touchstones for organizational identities and render them elitist. Reputational status has been shown to be an important aspect of organizational identity (Fombrun and Shanley, 1990). Elsbach and Kramer's study (1996) of organizational members' responses to status changes, assessed by Business Week rankings, suggests that elite standing is important to perceptions of an organization's identity. The mechanism of cultural capital can shape organizational identity in two different ways: as selection criteria for appropriating particular cultural elements into the organizational identity, and as a characteristic of the organizational identity as a whole. Organizations select those cultural elements that not only align with "who we are" but also lend high value or distinctiveness to their identity. For instance, each of the two organizations that competed in the market category of satellite radio claimed superiority over the other, using descriptive terms like "best" or "leader" in identity comparisons (Navis and Glynn, 2010). Through the accumulation or bricolage of identity elements connoting high cultural capital, organizations can enhance their own cultural authority or legitimacy. This is evident in the following identity claimed by a new restaurant:

> Gabri's Lounge & Restaurant is a 60 seat fine-dining restaurant with a 20 seat lounge.... We will be located in the booming, and rapidly expanding, borough of Long Branch, New Jersey 'on the shore'... The menu will be inspired from different countries' specialties and appeal to a diverse clientele. You can get Swedish specialties like herring, gravlax and meatballs, or you can go a little bit more International and choose a red curry chicken with basmati rice, or an Asian grilled shrimp with spinach, tofu and black bean sauce. We will also have a special pasta dish entree every day plus the 'all American meal' such as barbecue beef ribs and baked beans... Warm colors, fresh flowers, soft music, candles and amazing artwork from some of the areas most notable new artists. ...will contribute to a sense of community and give new artists a chance to show their work for a diverse clientele.[6]

4.2.3.6 CULTURAL MECHANISM OF INSTITUTIONAL TEMPLATES

This mechanism offers insights into the complex interplay among actors, actions, and meanings (Zilber, 2002). Institutions are cultural constructions themselves, undergirded by a core logic that is "symbolically grounded, organizationally structured, politically defended, and technically and materially constrained" (Friedland and Alford, 1991: 248–9). Friedland and Alford (1991: 232) note the contextual and historical embeddedness of institutions and identify five that are core in Western society: Markets, the "accumulation and the commodification of human activity"; Family, "community and the motivation of human activity by unconditional loyalty to its members and their reproductive needs"; Religion or Science, "truth, whether mundane or transcendental, and the symbolic construction of reality within which all human activity takes place"; Bureaucratic State, "rationalization and the regulation of human activity by legal and bureaucratic hierarchies"; and Democracy, "participation and the exercise of popular control over human activity." Thus, institutional logics, both material and symbolic, are "available to organizations and individuals to elaborate" (Friedland and Alford, 1991: 248).

The institutional environment that embeds organizations can be a constraint or an enabler of identity (Garud et al., 2007; Glynn, 2008a). Glynn and Abzug (2002) show how a key marker of the organization's identity—it's name—conforms to the prevailing institutional standards; an effect they show transcends the drive to be strategically distinctive (Glynn and Abzug, 1998). Navis and Glynn (2011) theorize how nascent entrepreneurial identities are attuned to the maturity of the market in which they locate their venture, striving to be "legitimately distinctive," and neither too isomorphic nor deviant. However, institutional mechanisms need not engender blind conformity (Glynn, 2008a). Organizational identities are typically pluralistic (Pratt and Foreman, 2000) and can incorporate elements from diverse institutional environments, such as art and commerce (e.g., Glynn, 2000). In turn, such acts of "institutional entrepreneurship...[can] create new institutions or 1.1.1.1 transform existing ones" (Maguire et al., 2004: 657).

Of the six mechanisms we identify, institutional mechanisms may be most potent in enabling identity resonance for organizations. By appropriating sanctioned and institutionalized templates, norms, values, or standards, organizational identities signal their social fitness, increasing their comprehensibility and acceptance. For instance, an identity claimed as "First National Bank" signals greater organizational credibility than "Fred's Bank" (Glynn and Marquis, 2005). Beyond pressures for conformity, however, institutions also supply logics that can be creatively assembled to create a distinctive organizational identity or to change that identity as environments change (e.g., Maguire and Hardy, 2009). Thus, institutional mechanisms can serve as sources of stability and flux and of legitimation and doubt, in organizational identities, implicating that it is the processes of bricolage, assembly, and alignment that regulate the formation of organizational identities.

4.3 Embedding organizational identity: Cultural mechanisms in identity construction

Taken together, the six cultural mechanisms (identified in Table 4.1) help to explain the cultural construction of organizational identities. Here, we describe more explicitly how each of the mechanisms shapes particular organizational identity elements; this is shown in Figure 4.1.

Figure 4.1 depicts how different forms of culture function as mechanisms to shape particular elements of the organization's identity as well as how

Exploring Cultural Mechanisms of Organizational Identity Construction

Cultural Mechanism	Organizational Identity Elements	Theorization of Organizational Identity (OID)
Framing	Names or Labels	OID as a shared definition of (and for) the collective and identifiable as a unique entity or social actor.
Repertoires	Capabilities, Strengths, Qualities, or Potential Strategies for Action	OID as guide for action or a filter for making decisions; demonstrates mastery of culture and its potential stakeholders or audiences. OID selectively highlights tools that can be competitively advantageous.
Narrating	Identity Narrative, Myths, or Accounts	OID as historical and potentially coherent or authentic, particularly important under ambiguity or uncertainty.
Symbolization & Symbolic Boundaries	Prototyping or Membership	OID as a categorical claim with similarities to other organizations in the same category.
Capital & Status	Superlative Standing; Leadership over other Categorical Members	OID differentiates the organization within the membership category.
Institutional Templates	OID Legitimation	OID as a touchstone for legitimate and audience perceptions of credibility and appropriateness.

Figure 4.1 Mapping cultural mechanisms onto organizational identities

this relates to the theorization of organizational identity. For the sake of clarity and parsimony, we have depicted the mechanisms in the figure as if they were independent; however, in reality, there is probably overlap among them, such that narratives can function as frames, while cultural capital is itself a cultural resource. Moreover, the mechanisms can be combined to enhance the alignment between "symbols on a specific issue and more enduring cultural themes" (Gamson, 1988: 243), making the organizational identity more recognizable and appealing because it seems "natural and familiar" (Gamson, 1992: 135). Organizational identities that align with cultural sensibilities do so by appropriating cultural themes, claiming distinctive categories that are valued, appropriating cultural repertoires or competencies, offering a coherent or authentic narrative, and signaling status, social capital, or cultural authority, and are more likely to gain audience acceptance and legitimacy. In line with this argument, we advance two general propositions that suggest the effects of cultural mechanisms:

Proposition 1: By aligning its identity with prevailing cultural sentiments, through the use of the cultural mechanisms of frames, resources, narratives, symbols, capital, or institutional templates, organizations are more likely to gain audience acceptance and legitimacy.

Proposition 2: Organizations appropriate cultural mechanisms of frames, resources, narratives, symbols, capital, or institutional temples in order to be recognized and valued by a specific cultural group or audience.

The organizational appropriation of potent cultural forms acknowledges both the agency of the organization as a cultural operative and the complexity and richness of culture as a source of the organization's identity. Thus, although isomorphic alignment enables cultural credibility, it is not deterministic; actor's agency and appropriation of cultural forms affect the construction of organizational identities and their capacity for cultural expression.

4.4 Discussion

We have argued that an organizational identity is shaped by broader cultural sentiments and that the organization actively cultivates an identity using a number of cultural mechanisms available to demonstrate its social fitness. Our articulation of six cultural mechanisms—frames, resources, narratives, symbolic boundaries, capital, and institutions—provides a general framework for understanding these dynamics. More research is clearly warranted to understanding the nuances of such processes, and the interrelationships among the various cultural mechanisms. Here, we offer some ideas for future work.

1.4.1 Cultural mechanisms and contextual contingencies

Our core idea centering on how cultural mechanisms align an organization's identity with prevailing cultural sensibilities can be extended in a variety of ways. For instance, different types of cultural mechanisms may be more or less influential or effective depending upon the type of organization or the context in which it operates. Young, entrepreneurial firms, for instance, may rely more on cultural narratives and labels (e.g., Lounsbury and Glynn, 2001; Martens et al., 2007) than more mature or established firms. Navis and Glynn (2010) find that new ventures in emergent markets tend to focus more on their similarities than differences in the early stages of development and that they tend to use cultural and linguistic framing during this period more often than in later periods of market growth and establishment. Walsh and Bartunek (forthcoming: 21) find that the demise of an organization is "reinforced by symbolic cues, such as locked factory doors, final paychecks and new corporate names, which signaled an end of organizational life." Walsh and Glynn (2008) theorize how legacy organizational identities—"who we were as an organization"—can serve as a resource for members' present and future work. Moreover, Glynn and Watkiss (2011) describe how it is the symbol of the organization's past—and not simply past organizational history—that can enable resilience in the face of formidable challenges.

What this stream of research suggests is the feasibility of a contingency approach such that different cultural mechanisms may be associated with different stages of the organizational life cycle, different periods of organizational crisis, change, or conflict, or different moments of organizational transition. We can speculate, for instance, that cultural frames or narratives may be particularly effective mechanisms for crafting an aspired identity for new ventures that do not yet have a performance history; they may be tools for taking the organizational identity into existence (Taylor and Van Every, 2000; Weick et al., 2005). For more mature (or even "dead" organizations), it may be the symbols of the past, memorialized in cultural objects and artifacts, that can be particularly potent as identity legacies.

Beyond organizational contingencies, we can look for explanations to broader contextual contingencies that embed the organization. The national, industry, or societal contexts in which organizations operate might influence the degree and type of cultural mechanisms formative in the organization's identity. Organizations in cultural industries, for example, may have identities that display a greater degree of, or more varied forms of, cultural capital and cultural competence than organizations in manufacturing or high technology. As well, broader contextual influences, from economic, political, or world systems, may affect the cultural composition of organizational identities. In more stable contexts, or what Swidler (1986) terms "settled times," identity construction may draw on rich and complex cultural forms, when environments are more munificent and supportive of greater organizational variety. Conversely, in less favorable or unstable contexts, or "unsettled times" (Swidler, 1986), identities may become simpler, communicating only "who we are" as an organization or more pointedly, "what we do." More generally, we believe that such a contingency perspective may prove fertile ground for explicating the role of cultural mechanisms in organizational identities.

4.4.2 Organizations as cultural operatives

An organization, like other social actors, selectively draws upon cultural resources from available toolkits (Swidler, 1986), favoring some cultural resources and ignoring others. Moreover, *how* they appropriate, interpret, and assemble these cultural resources into a coherent identity suggests that there will be variations in identity construction even among organizations operating in the same cultural environment.

Constructing Identity in and around Organizations

Our theorization of organizational identity brings the audience (or public) explicitly into processes of sanctioning and legitimating identities; generally speaking, audiences favor identities that are associated with meaningful symbols and enduring cultural themes (Gamson, 1988: 243). Research addressing the interrelationship of the organization as a social actor and the sanctioning by relevant audiences can inform theories of identity stability and endurance. Identity persistence over time may arise not only because of organizational inertia or the endurance of identity attributes (Albert and Whetten, 1985) but also because societal pressures sanction certain types of identity symbols as potent and organizations claim these in a demonstration of cultural adaptation and a claim of legitimacy. As Rogers (1999: 6) explains:

> A cultural icon means, then, that a piece of culture—a cultural object that exemplifies some set of values, beliefs and norms in a society—gets a strong grip on a sizeable part of the population... an icon is no mere idea in people's lives... it is an experienced presence, a memorable something.

Given that cultural resources are social constructions subject to reinterpretations and changes in accord with prevailing times and values, they may be reconfigured to suit the needs at hand. Thus, cultural influences themselves may be a source of organizational identity change or stability.

4.4.3 Cultural forms

Finally, we acknowledge that, although we have treated the six cultural mechanisms as distinct, there are likely overlaps or interrelationships that can bring identity elements into synergy or conflict. For instance, cultural narratives can conflict with cultural resources when an organization's aspiration for the future may be inconsistent with present operations or outcomes. More likely, cultural mechanisms may be more effective when they function in concert, reinforcing each other, and being in synch with the cognitive understandings and cultural norms of the times.

4.5 Conclusion

In this chapter, we explored the role of societal culture in shaping organizational identity, treating the organization as a social actor who not only reflects broader cultural themes but also appropriates and interprets cultural resources to construct "who we are" and "what we do." Drawing from the organizational and social science literatures, we identified six mechanisms by which public forms of culture supply the building blocks for organizational identity construction. In turn, we showed how the iterative process of crafting these culturally composed organizational identities could function as touchstones for organizational legitimacy and social fitness. Moreover, understanding the complexities of these processes, the interrelationships among different cultural mechanisms, and the contextual contingencies that affect organizational identity construction are key areas that await future research. Our hope is that our ideas provoke future research in these areas.

Notes

1. BP 1901–8, http://www.bp.com/printsectiongenericarticle.do?categoryId=9014440&contentId=7027520#top retrieved January 14, 2011.
2. BP New Millennium, http://www.bp.com/sectiongenericarticle.do?categoryId=9014445&contentId=7027526 retrieved January 14, 2011.
3. http://www.bp.com/sectionbodycopy.do?categoryId=2&contentId=7065607 retrieved January 14, 2011.
4. http://www.bp.com/liveassets/bp_internet/globalbp/globalbp_uk_english/incident_response/STAGING/local_assets/downloads_pdfs/BP_Communities_DCNational.pdf retrieved January 14, 2011.
5. http://www.sesp.northwestern.edu/newsCenter/?NewsID=146 accessed August 31, 2008.
6. http://www.bplans.com/fine_dining_restaurant_business_plan/executive_summary_fc.cfm retrieved January 15, 2011.

References

Albert, S. and Whetten, D. A. (1985). "Organizational Identity." *Research in Organizational Behaviour*, 7: 263–95.

Anheier, H., Gerhards, J., and Romo, F. (1995). "Forms of Capital and Social Structure in Cultural Fields: Examining Bourdieu's Social Topography." *American Journal of Sociology*, 100/4: 859–903.

Ashforth, B. E. (2001). *Role Transitions in Organizational Life: An Identity-Based Perspective*. Mahwah, NJ: Lawrence Erlbaum.

—— Vaidyanath, D. (2002). "Work Organizations as Secular Religions." *Journal of Management Inquiry*, 11/4: 359–70.

Berger, P. L. and Luckmann, T. (1967). *The Social Construction of Reality: A Treatise in the Sociology of Knowledge*. New York: Anchor.

Bourdieu, P. (1977). *Outline of a Theory of Practice*. New York: Cambridge University Press.

—— (1984). *Distinction: A Social Critique of the Judgement of Taste*. Cambridge, MA: Harvard University Press.

Cerulo, K. A. (1997). "Identity Construction: New Issues, New Directions." *Annual Review of Sociology*, 23/1: 385–409.

Coleman, J. (1988). "Social Capital in the Creation of Human Capital." *American Journal of Sociology*, 94/1: 95–120.

Czarniawska, B. and Wolff, R. (1998). "Constructing New Identities in Established Organization Fields: Young Universities in Old Europe." *International Studies of Management & Organization*, 28/3: 32–4.

Davis, G. and Marquis, C. (2005). "Prospects for Organization Theory in the Early Twenty-First Century: Institutional Fields and Mechanisms." *Organization Science*, 16/4: 332–43.

DiMaggio, P. (1982). "Cultural Entrepreneurship in Nineteenth-Century Boston: The Creation of an Organizational Base for High Culture in America." *Media, Culture & Society*, 4/1: 33–50.

—— (1997). "Culture and Cognition." *Annual Review of Sociology*, 23: 263–87.

Durkheim, E. (1984). *The Division of Labor in Society*. New York: Free Press.

Dutton, J. and Dukerich, J. (1991). "Keeping an Eye on the Mirror: Image and Identity in Organizational Adaptation." *Academy of Management Journal*, 34/3: 517–54.

Eliasoph, N. and Lichterman, P. (2003). "Culture in Interaction." *American Journal of Sociology*, 108/4: 735 94.

Elsbach, K. and Bhattacharya, C. (2001). "Defining Who You Are by What You're Not: Organizational Disidentification and the National Rifle Association." *Organization Science*, 12/4: 393–413.

—— Kramer, R. M. (1996). "Members' Responses to Organizational Identity Threats: Encountering and Countering the Business Week Rankings." *Administrative Science Quarterly*, 41/3: 442–76.

Fine, G. (1996). "Justifying Work: Occupational Rhetorics as Resources in Restaurant Kitchens." *Administrative Science Quarterly*, 41/1: 90–115.

—— (2002). "Thinking About Evil: Adolf Hitler and the Dilemma of the Social Construction of Reputation," in K. A. Cerulo (ed.), *Culture in mind: Toward a Sociology of Culture and Cognition*. New York: Routledge.

—— Sandstrom, K. (1993). "Ideology in Action: A Pragmatic Approach to a Contested Concept." *Sociological Theory*, 11/1: 21–38.

Fiol, C. (1991). "Managing Culture as a Competitive Resource: An Identity-based View of Sustainable Competitive Advantage." *Journal of Management*, 17/1: 191–211.

Fombrun, C. and Shanley, M. (1990). "What's in a Name? Reputation Building and Corporate Strategy." *Academy of Management Journal*, 33/2: 233–58.

Fox-Wolfgramm, S. J., Boal, K. B., and Hunt, J. G. (1998). "Organizational Adaptation to Institutional Change: A Comparative Study of First-Order Change in Prospector and Defender Banks." *Administrative Science Quarterly*, 43/1: 87–126.

Friedland, R. and Alford, R. R. (1991). "Bringing Society Back in: Symbols, Practices, and Institutional Contradictions," in W. Powell and P. DiMaggio (eds), *The New Institutionalism in Organizational Analysis*. Chicago, IL: University of Chicago Press.

Gamson, W. (1988). "Political Discourse and Collective Action." *International Social Movement Research*, 1/2: 219–44.

—— (1992). *Talking Politics*. New York: Cambridge University Press.

Garud, R., Hardy, C., and Maguire, S. (2007). "Institutional Entrepreneurship as Embedded Agency: An Introduction to the Special Issue." *Organization Studies*, 28/7: 957–69.

Geertz, C. (1966). *The Interpretation of Cultures*. New York: Basic Books.

Gioia, D., Schultz, M., and Corley, K. (2000). "Organizational Identity, Image, and Adaptive Instability." *Academy of Management Review*, 25/1: 63–81.

—— Thomas, J. (1996). "Identity, Image, and Issue Interpretation: Sensemaking during Strategic Change in Academia." *Administrative Science Quarterly*, 41/3: 370–403.

Glynn, M. A. (2000). "When Cymbals Become Symbols: Conflict Over Organizational Identity Within a Symphony Orchestra." *Organization Science*, 11/3: 285–98.

—— (2008a). "Beyond Constraint: How Institutions Enable Identities," in R. Greenwood, C. Oliver, K. Sahlin and R. Suddaby (eds), *SAGE Handbook of Organizational Institutionalism*. Thousand Oaks, CA: Sage Publications.

—— (2008b). "Configuring the Field of Play: How Hosting the Olympic Games Impacts Civic Community." *Journal of Management Studies*, 45/6: 1117–46.

—— Abzug, R. (1998). "Isomorphism and Competitive Differentiation in the Organizational Name Game." *Advances in Strategic Management*, 15: 105–28.

—— —— (2002). "Institutionalizing Identity: Symbolic Isomorphism and Organizational Names." *Academy of Management Journal*, 45/1: 267–80.

—— Marquis, C. (2005). "Fred's Bank: How Institutional Norms and Individual Preferences Legitimate Organizational Names," in A. Rafaeli and M. Pratt (eds.), *Artifacts and Organizations: Beyond Mere Symbolism*. Mahwah, NJ: Erlbaum.

—— Watkiss, L. (2011). "The Generative Potency of Cultural Symbols: Implications for Positive Organizational Scholarship," in K. Cameron and G. Spreitzer (eds), *Handbook of Positive Organizational Scholarship*. New York: Oxford University Press.

Goffman, E. (1963). *Stigma: Notes on the Management of Spoiled Identity*. Englewood Cliffs, NJ: Prentice-Hall.

Goodenough, W. (1971). *Culture, Language, and Society*. Reading, MA: Addison-Wesley.

Griswold, W. (2008). *Cultures and Societies in a Changing World*, 3rd edn. Thousand Oaks, CA: Pine Forge Press.

Gustafson, L. and Reger, R. (1995). "Using Organizational Identity to Achieve Stability and Change in High Velocity Environments." Best Paper Proceedings, Academy of Management.

Harris, S. and Sutton, R. (1986). "Functions of Parting Ceremonies in Dying Organizations." *Academy of Management Journal*, 29/1: 5–30.

Hernes, G. (1998). "Real Virtuality," in P. Hedstrom and R. Swedberg (eds), *Social Mechanisms: An Analytical Approach to Social Theory*. New York: Cambridge University Press.

Ibarra, H. and Barbulescu, R. (2010). "Identity as Narrative: Prevalence, Effectiveness, and Consequences of Narrative Identity Work in Macro Work Role Transitions." *Academy of Management Review*, 35/1: 135–54.

Kennedy, M. (2008). "Getting Counted: Markets, Media, and Reality." *American Sociological Review*, 73/2: 270–95.

Kreiner, G., Hollensbe, E., and Sheep, M. (2006). "On the Edge of Identity: Boundary Dynamics at the Interface of Individual and Organizational Identities." *Human Relations*, 59/10: 1315–41.

Kroeber, A. L. and Kluckhohn, C. (1952). *Culture: A Critical Review of Concepts and Definitions*. Cambridge, MA: The Museum.

Kunda, G. (1992). *Engineering Culture: Control and Commitment in a High-tech Corporation*. Philadelphia, PA: Temple University Press.

Lamont, M. and Fournier, M. (1992). *Cultivating Differences: Symbolic Boundaries and the Making of Inequality*. Chicago: University of Chicago Press.

—— Lareau, A. (1988). "Cultural Capital: Allusions, Gaps and Glissandos in Recent Theoretical Developments." *Sociological Theory*, 6/2: 153–68.

Langley, A. (1999). "Strategies for Theorizing from Process Data." *Academy of Management Review*, 24/4: 691–710.

—— (2007). "Process Thinking in Strategic Organization." *Strategic Organization*, 5/3: 271–82.

Livengood, R. and Reger, R. (2010). "That's our Turf! Identity Domains and Competitive Dynamics." *Academy of Management Review*, 35/1: 48–66.

Lounsbury, M. and Glynn, M. A. (2001). "Cultural Entrepreneurship: Stories, Legitimacy, and the Acquisition of Resources." *Strategic Management Journal*, 22/6/7: 545–64.

Maguire, S. and Hardy, C. (2009). "Discourse and Deinstitutionalization: The Decline of DDT." *Academy of Management Journal*, 52/1: 148–78.

—— —— Lawrence, T. (2004). "Institutional Entrepreneurship in Emerging Fields: HIV/Aids Treatment Advocacy in Canada." *Academy of Management Journal*, 47/5: 657–79.

Martens, M., Jennings, J., and Jennings, P. (2007). "Do The Stories They Tell Get Them the Money They Need? The Role of Entrepreneurial Narratives in Resource Acquisition." *Academy of Management Journal*, 50/5: 1107–32.

Navis, C. and Glynn, M. A. (2010). "How New Market Categories Emerge: Temporal Dynamics of Legitimacy, Identity, and Entrepreneurship in Satellite Radio, 1990–2005." *Administrative Science Quarterly*, 55/3: 439–71.

—— —— (2011). "Legitimate Distinctiveness and the Entrepreneurial Identity: Influence on Investor Judgments of New Venture Plausibility." *Academy of Management Review*, 36/3: 479–99.

Parsons, T. and Shils, E. A. (1951). *Toward a General Theory of Action: Theoretical Foundations for the Social Sciences*. Cambridge, MA: Harvard University Press.

Powell, W. and Colyvas, J. (2008). "Microfoundations of Institutional Theory," in R. Greenwood, C. Oliver, K. Sahlin and R. Suddaby (eds), *SAGE Handbook of Organizational Institutionalism*. Thousand Oaks, CA: Sage Publications.

Pratt, M. and Foreman, P. (2000). "Classifying Managerial Responses to Multiple Organizational Identities." *Academy of Management Review*, 25/1: 18–42.

Rao, H., Monin, P., and Durand, R. (2003). "Institutional Change in Toque Ville: Nouvelle Cuisine as an Identity Movement in French Gastronomy." *American Journal of Sociology*, 108/4: 795–843.

—— —— —— (2005). "Border Crossing: Bricolage and the Erosion of Categorical Boundaries in French Gastronomy." *American Sociological Review*, 70/6: 968.

Ravasi, D. and Schultz, M. (2006). "Responding to Organizational Identity Threats: Exploring the Role of Organizational Culture." *Academy of Management Journal*, 49/3: 433–58.

Ricoeur, P. (1991). "What is a Text? Explanation and Understanding", in M. Valdes (ed.), *A Ricoeur Reader: Reflection and Imagination*. Toronto, ON: University of Toronto Press, 43–63.

Rogers, M. F. (1999). *Barbie Culture*. Thousand Oaks, CA: Sage Publications.

Santos, F. M. and Eisenhardt, K. M. (2005). "Organizational Boundaries and Theories of Organization." *Organization Science*, 16/5: 491–508.

Scott, W. R. (2001). *Institutions and Organizations*. Thousand Oaks, CA: Sage Publications.

—— (2010). "Entrepreneurs and Professionals: The Mediating Role of Institutions," in W. Sine and R. David (eds), *Research in the Sociology of Work*. Bingley, UK: Emerald Group Publishing Limited.

Selznick, P. (1957). *Leadership in Administration: A Sociological Interpretation*. London: Harper & Row.

Shore, B. (1996). *Culture in Mind: Cognition, Culture, and the Problem of Meaning*. New York: Oxford University Press.

Small, M., Harding, D., and Lamont, M. (2010). "Reconsidering Culture and Poverty." *The Annals of the American Academy of Political and Social Science*, 629/1: 6–27.

Snow, D. A. and Benford, R. D. (1992). "Master Frames and Cycles of Protest," in A. D. Morris and C. McClurg Mueller (eds), *Frontiers in Social Movement Theory*. New Haven, CT: Yale University Press.

Sutton, R. I. (1991). "Maintaining Norms about Expressed Emotions: The Case of Bill Collectors." *Administrative Science Quarterly*, 36/2: 245–68.

Swart, W. (1995). "The League of Nations and the Irish Question." *Sociological Quarterly*, 36/3: 465–81.

Swidler, A. (1986). "Culture in Action: Symbols and Strategies." *American Sociological Review*, 51/2: 273–86.

—— (1995). "Cultural Power and Social Movements," in H. Johnston and B. Klandermans (eds.), *Social Movements and Culture*, 25–40. Minneapolis, MN: University of Minnesota Press.

Tajfel, H. and Turner, J. C. (1979). "An Integrative Theory of Intergroup Conflict," in W. G. Austin and S. Worchel (eds), *Social Psychology of Intergroup Relations*. Monterey, CA: Brooks-Cole.

Taylor, J. and Van Every, E. (2000). *The Emergent Organization: Communication as its Site and Surface*. Mahwah, NJ: Lawrence Erlbaum Associates.

Tsoukas, H. and Chia, R. (2002). "On Organizational Becoming: Rethinking Organizational Change." *Organization Science*, 13/5: 567–82.

Tylor, E. B. (1871). *Primitive Culture*. London: Murray.

Uzzi, B. (1997). "Social Structure and Competition in Interfirm Networks: The Paradox of Embeddedness." *Administrative Science Quarterly*, 42/1: 35–67.

Van Maanen, J. (1998). *Qualitative Studies of Organizations*. Thousand Oaks, CA: Sage Publications.

—— (forthcoming). *Tales of the Field: On Writing Ethnography*, 2nd edn. Chicago, IL: University of Chicago Press.

Walsh, I. and Bartunek, J. (forthcoming). "Cheating the Fates: Organizational Foundings in the Wake of Demise." *Academy of Management Journal*, 54/5.

—— Glynn, M. A. (2008). "The Way We Were: Legacy Organizational Identity and the Role of Leadership." *Corporate Reputation Review*, 11/3: 262–76.

Weick, K. (1995). *Sensemaking in Organizations*. Thousand Oaks, CA: Sage Publications.

Weick, K., Sutcliffe, K., and Obstfeld, D. (2005). "Organizing and the Process of Sensemaking." *Organization Science*, 16/4: 409–21.

Zilber, T. (2002). "Institutionalization as an Interplay Between Actions, Meanings, and Actors: The Case of a Rape Crisis Center in Israel." *Academy of Management Journal*, 45/1: 234–54.

Zott, C. and Huy, Q. N. (2007). "How Entrepreneurs Use Symbolic Management to Acquire Resources." *Administrative Science Quarterly*, 52/1: 70–105.

Zuckerman, E. (1999). "The Categorical Imperative: Securities Analysts and the Illegitimacy Discount." *American Journal of Sociology*, 104/5: 1398–1438.

—— (2004). "Structural Incoherence and Stock Market Activity." *American Sociological Review*, 69/3: 405–32.

5

Organizational Identity Formation: Processes of Identity Imprinting and Enactment in the Dutch Microbrewing Landscape[1]

Jochem J. Kroezen and
Pursey P. M. A. R. Heugens

Abstract: On the basis of a qualitative study of fifty-nine recently founded Dutch microbreweries, we develop a conceptual model of organizational identity formation. We employ old institutionalism as a theoretical lens to integrate several prior findings concerning the potential sources of organizational identity, such as (a) the identities of authoritative organizational insiders, (b) the preferences and judgments of organizational audiences, and (c) the identities of organizational peers. Each of these sources is shown to critically influence the two most central identity formation processes: the initial imprinting of potential identity attributes upon organizations, and the subsequent enactment of a selection of these by organizational insiders.

5.1 Introduction

Over the past two decades, academic research has highlighted how organizational identity functions as a pivotal organizational resource (Rindova and Fombrun, 1999; Fiol, 2001; Eisenhardt and Santos, 2002; Whetten and Mackey, 2002). Empirical studies on organizational identity conducted to date have provided us with a thorough comprehension of the ongoing (re-)construction processes related to this resource in mature organizations

(Dutton and Dukerich, 1991; Corley and Gioia, 2004; Ravasi and Schultz, 2006). Recently, a new line of organizational identity research has started to develop that contributes to our understanding of how organizational identities are formed from inception (see Clegg et al., 2007; Gioia et al., 2010, for pioneering studies). As research on this topic is still in a nascent stage, it is unclear to what extent existing theories derived from the broader administrative sciences can be fruitfully deployed to explain this phenomenon.

Eligible theories must meet at least three criteria. First, admissible theories must be process theories (Van de Ven and Poole, 1995; Pentland, 1999), as organizational identities do not emerge instantaneously but unfold slowly over time. Second, any appropriate theory must be a multi-level theory (Klein et al., 1994; Johns, 1999). Whereas identities are a macro-level property of organizations, they are nonetheless grounded in micro-level processes like the construction and enactment of organizational stories, myths, and symbols by individual members. Third, qualifying theories must be amicable to and accommodative of the duality between organizational symbolism and substance (Pfeffer, 1981; Westphal and Zajac, 1994). Even though identities are symbolic properties of organizations, they are nonetheless grounded in and bounded by substantive organizational properties, which can either support or undermine the authenticity of their organizational identity.

In this chapter, we demonstrate that the process of identity formation can successfully be elucidated by a preexisting body of administrative science work that has become known as "old institutionalism" (DiMaggio and Powell, 1991; Selznick, 1996) under the influence of rapid developments in the field of institutional theory (see Greenwood et al., 2008). Old institutional theory meets the aforementioned selection criteria, as it is processual in kind (Selznick, 1949), open to micro-level explanations of macro-level organizational phenomena (Blau, 1964), and accustomed to analyzing both organizational substance and symbolism (Gouldner, 1954). The use of old institutional theory opens up promising pathways for the analysis of organizational identity formation, such as likening it to related processes like "value infusion" (Selznick, 1957) and (organization-level) "institutionalization" (Stinchcombe, 1997).

However, old institutional theory offers no ready-made template for the analysis of organizational identity formation. Instead, it is best seen as a theoretical stepping-stone, which offers researchers conceptual building blocks, theoretical analogies, and a dedicated vocabulary that they can use for the formation of conceptually more specific and empirically more grounded explanatory frameworks for analysis. It is in fact our ambition to use old institutional theory in this manner in this chapter, and to use it as a source of inspiration for the development of a new theoretical model of identity formation, which we simultaneously seek to refine by grounding it in a detailed qualitative study of nascent Dutch microbreweries.

The beer brewing sector in the Netherlands—the focus of our empirical work—has experienced a true boom in organizational foundings since 1985, following decades of industry concentration and associated high levels of organizational mortality. Because of this demographic pattern (which in organizational ecology terms resembles a resource partitioning process; Carroll and Hannan, 1989; Carroll and Swaminathan, 2000), we were able to observe organizational identity formation processes for numerous organizations in situ and in vivo over the course of a five-year study. We primarily collected qualitative data, complementing our core interview-based data with on-site observations and archival document analysis.

The upshot of our qualitative analyses is a novel model of organizational identity formation, rooted simultaneously in old institutional theory and in detailed empirical research. Apart from its solid theoretical and empirical foundations, the strength of the model primarily lies in its ability to integrate various prior insights into the nature of the identity formation process. While previous research has identified a variety of sources of organizational identity—such as founders and/or top-management (e.g., Scott and Lane, 2000), audiences (Ginzel et al., 1993), and peer organizations (Clegg et al., 2007)—to date no integrative account of these sources has been presented. Our aim in this chapter is therefore to amalgamate these dispersed insights about the identity formation process into a single integrative model.

Apart from integrating dispersed findings from past research, this chapter contributes to process research on organizational identity by substantiating processes of identity formation. Linking organizational identities to substantive identity sources extends our understanding of how organizations come to develop similar (or different) identities. This is an important question as past research has shown that organizational identities play an important role in individual- (e.g., Ashforth and Mael, 1989), organizational- (e.g., Rowley and Moldoveanu, 2003; Hannan et al., 2006), as well as field-level outcomes (e.g., Carroll and Swaminathan, 2000; Hannan et al., 2007).

5.2 Theoretical background

5.2.1 Organizational identity

Organizational identity is typically defined as those aspects of the organization that are most core, enduring, and, distinctive (Albert and Whetten, 1985). The original definition, however, provided room for multiple ontological interpretations and two competing perspectives developed: organizational identity as shared understandings (the social constructivist perspective) versus organizational identity as institutionalized claims (the social actor perspective) (Whetten and Mackey, 2002; Ravasi and Schultz, 2006). Recent work has shown how both perspectives can be regarded as mutually constitutive (Ravasi and Schultz, 2006; Gioia et al., 2010), suggesting that organizational identity should be conceptualized as *both* shared understandings and institutionalized claims.

Previous research on organizational identity formation has demonstrated how new identities are developed through a recurring sequence of collective sensemaking and sensegiving processes by organizational insiders while also ascribing an influential role to the organizational environment (Czarniawska and Wolff, 1998; Clegg et al., 2007; Gioia et al., 2010). Together these studies suggest identity formation is about the construction and enactment of an identity that is considered as legitimate by other actors in the organizational field but at the same time provides the organization with distinctive character in order to survive. Eventhough Gioia et al. (2010) captured these notions in a theoretical process model of identity formation, these studies are largely silent or remain implicit with regard to how the actual substance of organizational identities is shaped by multiple identity sources (cf. Gioia et al., 2010: 6). In other words, we know through which collective sensemaking stages insiders form new identities for their organizations, but we lack knowledge about the material with which new identities are formed and how this affects their substance.

Conceptual and empirical studies on organizational culture and its relation with organizational identity provide examples of how (new) identities might be substantiated (Hatch and Schultz, 1997; Hatch and Schultz, 2002; Ravasi and Schultz, 2006). This line of work suggests that insiders employ symbolic material such as shared history, characteristic attributes, and unique practices to collectively construct and revise their organizational self-definitions (Ravasi and Schultz, 2006). Similar ideas were further grounded in an empirical study by Rindova et al. (2010), who showed how culture functions as a "toolkit" for the construction of new organizational strategies. There appears to be room for cross-fertilization between these two streams of research in order to extend our understanding of organizational identity formation and more explicitly link identity process research to identity substance and outcomes.

We found that old institutional theory provides a useful lens to integrate these ideas and accomplish the aims of our study. In the section below, we discuss the commonalities between old institutionalism and organizational identity theory and the implications for the study of organizational identity formation.

5.2.2 Old institutionalism and organizational identity theory

"Old" institutionalism as a genre in the administrative sciences (DiMaggio and Powell, 1991; Selznick, 1996; Stinchcombe, 1997) developed from "theoretical tensions" in the work of Max Weber (Gouldner, 1954), and observations in the field that conflicted with many of the ideas put forth by organizational theorists at the time. Through several detailed field studies (e.g., Selznick, 1949; Gouldner, 1954; Blau, 1964), old institutional scholars discovered that in addition to the formal structure of organizations—as described by Weber (1968) in his extensive analysis of "modern bureaucracy"—several informal elements and social processes are pertinent to their success and survival. These studies provided an opposing perspective to the "pessimistic portrayal of administrative systems" as structures of "disembodied forces," "stripped of people" (Gouldner, 1954: 16). They focused in turn on the agentic power of individuals, and on the effect of their actions on social structures.[2]

To support the main assumption of this chapter—that old institutional theory can fruitfully be employed as a theoretical stepping-stone for investigations of organizational identity formation processes—we now proceed to discuss eight areas of conceptual continuity between old institutional theory and organizational identity theory. These eight areas of continuity can be assembled into three broader categories: the informal organization, human agency, and environmental adaptation (see Table 5.1).

5.2.2.1 THE INFORMAL ORGANIZATION

A core element in both old institutionalism and organizational identity theory is the notion of "the informal organization." It covers the ideas that (*a*) an organization has a "normative core" that exists besides its "formal core" (Barnard, 1938; Gouldner, 1954), which (*b*) contributes to the

Table 5.1 Common themes between old institutionalism literature and organizational identity literature, and implications for the identity formation process

Common themes	Old institutionalism literature	Organizational identity literature	Implications for the identity formation process
Informal organization: Normative core	Organizations contain informal elements besides the formal structure—they are made up of informal relations, and sets of norms and values that are necessary for their operation (Barnard, 1938).	Organizational identity as a normative decision cue underlying all organizational attributes and practices (Albert and Whetten, 1985)	Study the normative motivations behind the adoption of particular attributes. Study the origins of these motivations through the identification of the origins of particular attributes.
Informal organization: Distinctiveness	Each organization has a distinctive character due to the "infusion of value beyond the technical requirements" (Selznick, 1957). Distinctive character enables differentiation of organizations that perform similar technical tasks.	Identity as distinctive elements (Albert and Whetten, 1985), relational identity, self-other categories (Clegg et al., 2007)	Focus on attributes that are unique to the organization.
Informal organization: Internal dynamics	Organizations are continuously "in flux." Underlying organizational changes are processes of social development and informal organization (Blau, 1972).	Identity dynamics (Hatch and Schultz, 2002; Ravasi and Schultz, 2006); adaptive instability (Gioia et al., 2000)	Organizational identity construction is a social process that is always ongoing. Thus, studying the formation of an organizational identity requires a focus on internal social processes and events, and data covering a long period of time.
Human agency: People	Institutionalization takes place through the actions of individuals, who are the "guts" of institutions (Stinchcombe, 1997).	Focus on sensemaking and sensegiving activities of individual members (e.g., Dutton and Dukerich, 1991; Ravasi and Schultz, 2006)	Examining organizational identity formation requires a focus on the individuals that influence organizational decision-making during the early stages of its life cycle.
Human agency: Work	Institutionalization takes place through the "work that must be done to	Identity regulation and identity work (Alvesson and Wilmott, 2002; Clegg	An organizational identity is formed through the intentional and

	create viable organizations, maintain them in steady states, and prepare them for change" (Selznick, 1996).	et al., 2007), reducing identity ambiguity (Corley and Gioia, 2004; Gioia et al., 2010), organizational disidentification (Elsbach and Bhattacharya, 2001)	purposeful work done by individual members.
Human agency: Politics	Institutionalization takes place through "collective bargaining" and is dependent on individuals with the most authority and the actions of organizational elites (Gouldner, 1954; Selznick, 1957).	Identity politics (e.g., "negotiating identity claims" in Gioia et al., 2010), influential role of organizational leadership in identity construction (e.g., Corley and Gioia, 2004)	Organizational identities are influenced by the individuals that had the most authority over the organization during its founding stages.
Environmental adaptation: Substance	Aspects of the organization's environment become imprinted into the organization's character as the organization adapts to its environment in natural and unplanned ways (Selznick, 1957; Stinchcombe, 1965).	Identity threats, identity–image dynamics (Dutton and Dukerich, 1991; Elsbach and Kramer, 1996; Ravasi and Schultz, 2006), audiences (Ginzel et al., 1993; Scott and Lane, 2000)	Distinctive character/identity is formed through the adaptation to a dynamic environment, where the environment has the strongest influence over the organization around the time of inception.
Environmental adaptation: Flexibility	Organizations internal structures display varying degrees of flexibility depending on the nature of their environment and on their age. Organizations in more complex environments are likely to adapt more flexible structures (Burns and Stalker, 1961). The influence is stronger near the organization's point of origin (Stinchcombe, 1965; Blau and Meyer, 1987).	Adaptive instability (Gioia et al., 2000), identity plasticity (Fox-Wolfgramm et al., 1998)	Organizational identities are ambiguous. Different individuals might provide different interpretations of the identity of their organization. Studying identity formation requires a focus on multiple sources of data and organizations of different ages.

"distinctive character" of the organization (Selznick, 1957), and which (c) makes clear that organizations are not rigid "machines" but rather flexible "organisms" that are continuously "in flux" (Blau, 1972). Table 5.1 shows how these old institutionalist notions come back in various works on organizational identity.

We observe that the ideas about the normative core and organization-level distinctiveness are apparent in all studies on organizational identity. Albert and Whetten's seminal piece (1985) clearly reflects these underlying principles. Additionally, the concept of distinctiveness is central in a number of recent empirical studies on organizational identity (Clegg et al., 2007; Gioia et al., 2010). Additionally, we observe that old institutionalism and organizational identity theory are united in their emphasis on dynamics. Studies on identity–image dynamics (Dutton and Dukerich, 1991; Hatch and Schultz, 2002; Ravasi and Schultz, 2006) and adaptive instability (Gioia et al., 2000) reflect Blau's notion of organizations (1972) as being continuously "in flux."

5.2.2.2 HUMAN AGENCY

The second category of common themes relates to the agentic power of individuals in the shaping of organizations. We see that both old institutionalism and organizational identity theory attribute importance to (a) people, (b) the work these people do to construct and maintain their organization, and (c) the politics of competing groups of people for influence over the organization.

Old institutionalism regards people as the "guts" of organizations through which institutionalization takes place (Stinchcombe, 1997). In organizational identity theory, the attention to the actions of individuals is especially apparent in social constructivist studies of organizational identity (e.g., Dutton and Dukerich, 1991; Ravasi and Schultz, 2006). Additionally, there are a variety of studies on organizational identity that show how identity is shaped through the deliberate and purposeful actions of these individuals, where the most powerful individuals end up having the most significant impact (e.g., Elsbach and Bhattacharya, 2001; Alvesson and Willmott, 2002; Corley and Gioia, 2004; Clegg et al., 2007; Gioia et al., 2010).

5.2.2.3 ENVIRONMENTAL ADAPTATION

At its core, old institutional theory is an approach to organizational–environmental adaptation, which emphasizes in particular how organizations adjust to altering conditions in their task and institutional environments. Scholars working in this tradition remind us that organizations continuously morph the substance of their work activities to align them better with their environments, most dramatically around the time of their inception (see Stinchcombe, 1965). Complex and uncertain environments typically require a more flexible and organic structure to facilitate adaptation, while organizations can suffice with more rigid structures in simpler environments with lower levels of uncertainty (Burns and Stalker, 1961).

Organizational identity theory has likewise shown that identities are constructed and reconstructed through ad hoc adaptations to environmental changes and events (e.g., Dutton and Dukerich, 1991; Elsbach and Kramer, 1996; Ravasi and Schultz, 2006), and in anticipation of and response to audience expectations (Ginzel et al., 1993; Scott and Lane, 2000). Additionally, we find parallels to the ideas about the varying degrees of organizational rigidity and flexibility in the notions of "adaptive instability" (Gioia et al., 2000) and "identity plasticity" (Fox-Wolfgramm et al., 1998) that capture the need for a certain amount of flexibility in the organization's identity and the differing degrees with which this can be found in different organizations.

5.2.3 Implications for the study of identity formation

The common themes that we have highlighted here between old institutionalism and organizational identity theory show that these theoretical genres share similar underlying assumptions and address similar phenomena (cf. Okhuysen and Bonardi, 2011). Where these genres differ, however, is in the attention paid to substance in the research of social processes. Organizational identity theorists have predominantly focused on the patterns in collective sensemaking processes, which has led to a variety of (recurrent) stage models of organizational identity (re)construction while employing (change in) identity substance as a descriptive or field-experimental background (e.g., Dutton and Dukerich, 1991; Corley and Gioia, 2004; Ravasi and Schultz, 2006; Gioia et al., 2010). The origins of the actual substance of the organizational identities under examination, however, have never been at the central point of investigation. Old institutionalism teaches us that the substance of social structures is shaped by the organizational environment and the purposeful actions of a variety of actors with vested interests. We employ the literatures and the common themes described above to define our core concepts, and ultimately reveal the sources of identity and the specific processes through which identities of the organizations in our sample were formed.

5.2.3.1 DEFINITIONS OF CORE CONCEPTS

Following recent studies, we define organizational identity as a set of multiple *identity claims* that are developed through processes of collective sensemaking and sensegiving against an institutional background (see Whetten and Mackey, 2002; Ravasi and Schultz, 2006). Identity claims are statements about organizations core, enduring, and distinctive attributes that signal membership in institutionally standardized categories (Whetten and Mackey, 2002). We label the attributes that are used to substantiate these identity claims as *proto-identity attributes*. As organizational identities are likely to be observed in all aspects of the organization, these attributes can be both symbolic in nature, for example, when they are artifacts or practices representing the organization's culture (see Ravasi and Schultz, 2006), and formal in nature, for example, the organization's business model or strategy (Baden-Fuller and Morgan, 2010). On the basis of these definitions, we can now define organizational identity formation as the collection of processes that determine the organization-specific set of proto-identity attributes and that influence the selection of identity claims.

On the basis of our review of the literature and our observations in the Dutch microbrewery field, we found that the concept of organizational identity could be divided into two intertwined parts: the *enacted organizational identity* and the *identity reservoir*. The former consists of the claims employed by an organization in social interaction. This set of claims can vary over time and differ depending on the organizational insider or the organizational audience. This conceptualization of organizational identity is compatible with a social constructionist perspective on organizational identity as apparent in the work by Gioia et al. (2000) and other researchers who have focused on the emergent and dynamic collective understandings of central features of the organization (e.g., Dutton and Dukerich, 1991; Fiol, 2002; Corley and Gioia, 2004). However, our findings indicated that identity claims are not enacted by making random draws from all available identity claims in an organizational field but by making *bounded* draws from an organization-specific set of identity claims. This organization-specific set follows from the organization's proto-identity attributes, the (material and symbolic) fundamentals of the organization and the (formal and informal) organizational practices. We call this organization-specific set the identity reservoir. This part of our conceptualization of organizational identity is more compatible not only with Albert and Whetten's initial definition (1985) of organizational identity, the social actor perspective on organizational identity (Whetten and Mackey, 2002; King et al., 2010) but also with the "culture as toolkit" analogy in organizational identity research (cf. Hatch and Schultz, 2002; Ravasi and Schultz, 2006; Rindova et al., 2010). The organizational fundamentals are the attributes (e.g., brand names, equipment, personnel, etc.) and the aims (e.g., mission statement, sales target) of the organization, which together provide the physical and strategic resources for the operation of the organization (i.e., the organizational practices).

In the rest of this chapter, we further develop these concepts and show how they are supported by our data. We demonstrate how these two concepts facilitate the study of identity formation by allowing us to distinguish between two different identity formation processes, namely *identity imprinting* processes and *identity enactment* processes.

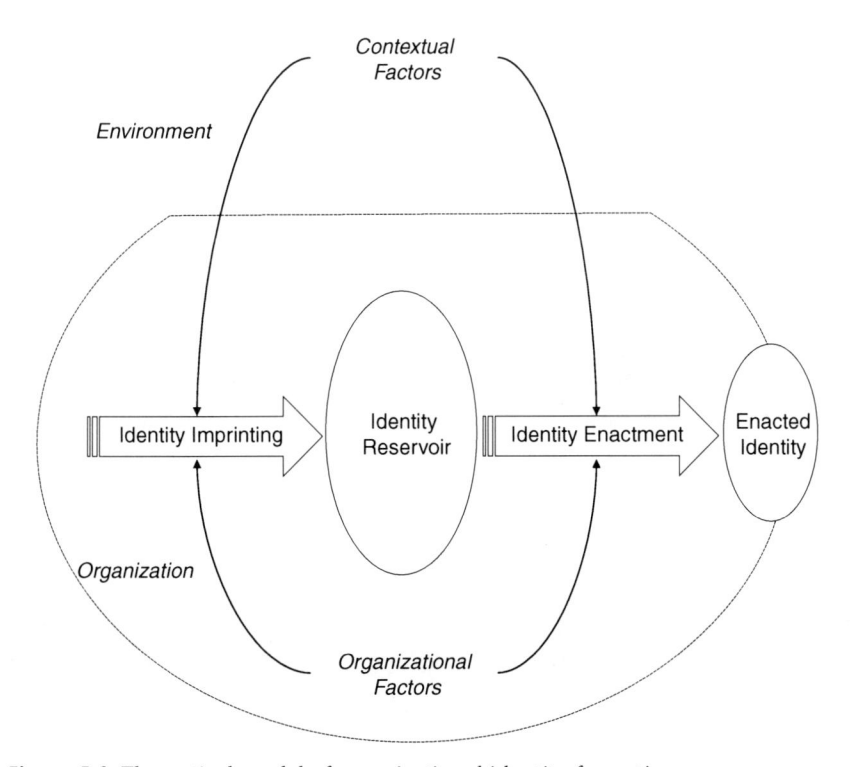

Figure 5.1 Theoretical model of organizational identity formation

Identity imprinting processes are the processes through which proto-identity attributes flow into the organization and shape the identity reservoir. Identity enactment processes are the processes through which identity claims are subsequently selected from the identity reservoir.

The aim of our study was to link these processes to the actual origins of organizational identity substance—the ultimate sources of identity. We define identity sources as those organizational and contextual factors yielding proto-identity attributes and affecting identity claim selection. Figure 5.1 shows the theoretical model that we advance based on our review of the literature that depicts the relationships between the concepts that we have defined here and forms the backbone of our empirical analysis.

5.3 Methods

5.3.1 Research strategy

To objectively reconstruct histories of multiple organizations *ex post* and uncover generic identity sources and processes, we had to systematically analyze data from a wide variety of data sources. In light of this, we chose to structure our study as a naturalistic inquiry in which we gathered insights from our data through iterative interpretation cycles (Glaser and Strauss, 1967; Lincoln and Guba, 1985) and by comparing our preliminary definitions of core concepts and hypotheses about relationships to old institutionalist notions. Because of the inductive character of our study, we started with broad definitions and hypotheses, allowing these to become more concrete and specific during the many iterative cycles between our data and our theoretical hunches. In order to facilitate the interpretation of our findings, we provided the final working definitions of our core concepts in the section above.

5.3.2 Research setting: The Dutch beer brewing industry

Our study is set in the Dutch beer brewing industry. We selected this industry for two reasons. First, at the time of our study, the industry was characterized by a significant number of newly founded organizations (all of which purported to be "microbreweries") in which most of the founders were still present in the organization. We found that roughly 85 percent of

Processes of Identity Imprinting and Enactment in the Dutch

the active independent breweries at the time of study entered the market after 1985. Research on these types of organizations was likely to produce the most valuable data for examining organizational identity formation as these breweries constructed their identities "from scratch." Moreover, for these organizations we were able to approach the individuals that were involved in the founding processes with relative ease and these individuals tended to have the founding stories relatively "fresh" in their minds.

Second, the beer brewing industry is an identity intensive environment characterized by significant product differentiation and strongly developed consumer niches. For example, the microbrewery movement (Carroll and Swaminathan, 2000) has led to strong differentiation of new breweries from the established industrial breweries all over the world. The social movement character of the microbrewery movement has presumably increased the importance of organizational identity in the beer brewing industry by making the question of "who we are as an organization?" even more salient. At the time of our study, the Dutch beer brewing industry produced approximately 27 million hectoliters (23 million barrels) of beer per year, or 170 liters (1.4 barrels) per capita (CBS, 2007). Of the total beer production, 99.9 percent was carried out at the eight largest Dutch beer breweries, which in numbers made-up only 15 percent of the entire population of beer brewers. This indicates that the majority of Dutch beer breweries at the time of our study could indeed be appropriately labeled as microbreweries, suggesting that the microbrewery movement was also prevalent in the Dutch beer brewing industry.[3]

5.3.3 Brewery sample

We collected our data through semi-structured interviews with members of different Dutch beer breweries, complemented by archival materials. Breweries were identified from two professionally organized databases created and maintained by Dutch beer journalists and enthusiasts.[4] These databases tended to identify new breweries at very early stages, which provided us with extremely current information about the population of breweries and allowed us to get access to breweries close around the time of their inception. In total, we were able to identify ninety-eight unique independent breweries that were active in the Dutch beer brewing industry at some point during our data collection period, which lasted from 2004 to 2009. On the basis of the known characteristics of these breweries and following Carroll and Swaminathan (1992), we were able to classify eighty-eight as microbreweries. All of the eighty-eight microbreweries were founded after

1985. The relatively small size of the population enabled data collection for a sample that approximated the entire population in terms of size and diversity. We were able to access fifty-nine microbreweries, which corresponded to a 67 percent share of the entire population of eighty-eight microbreweries.

For selection of particular members from the breweries for an interview, we developed a deliberate strategy based on assumptions about their influence over the identity formation process. Old institutional theory suggests that the individuals with the most authority will have the strongest influence over the formation of the organization's identity (Gouldner, 1954; Selznick, 1957). In a similar vein, studies on the formation of the related construct of organizational culture attribute much influence to organizational founders (see Schein, 1986). In light of this, we worked from the assumption that, for the purposes of our study, the founders of the breweries were the most important target members for an interview. If we were unable to get access to the founder, we approached the owner for an interview—in case that was a different individual than the founder. If the owner turned out to be unavailable, we approached the brew master.[5] And in case we were unable to interview the brew master, we settled for an interview with another member—preferably a manager. Additionally, our ambition was to cover for every brewery as many organizational roles as possible with our interviews.

For a significant majority of the selected beer breweries, we ended up being successful in approaching the founders for an interview (see Table 5.2). As most breweries were relatively small in size, the founders often fulfilled additional roles, like the role of brew master. Table 5.2 shows that for most breweries we were able to cover a variety of organizational roles with our interviews. As most interviewees did not exclusively fulfill the role of founder, they were able to provide multiple perspectives on the identities of their breweries during the interview. Moreover, the individuals that we

Table 5.2 Number of interviewees and participating breweries per interviewee role

Interviewee role	No. of interviewees	No. of participating breweries	% of participating breweries
Founder	51	45	76
Current owner	56	50	85
Brew master	49	42	71
Manager	60	54	92
Total	71	59	100

interviewed were often the only (fully) paid employees of their breweries, a result of the small size of the young breweries in our sample.

We approached all potential interviewees either by email or by telephone. Overall, the individuals we contacted were enthusiastic about the prospect of being interviewed, and most were willing to cooperate (we were able to interview an organizational member for about 80 percent of the contacted breweries). The minority of individuals that chose not to cooperate usually indicated either that they lacked the time to participate or that they were not convinced of the value of an academic study for their individual breweries. As a token of our goodwill, we made an agreement with a few brewery owners to purchase a small quantity of their products as a compensation for their time and effort. However, these were exceptions. Most interviewees cooperated without asking for any form of compensation besides the promise that they would receive the final research report.

5.3.4 Data collection method

The interviews with the brewery members constituted our main data source. We made audio recordings and transcriptions for all interviews to facilitate data analysis. In addition to the data from the interviews, we collected data from various archival sources such as breweries' websites and news articles in the Dutch quarterly beer magazine *Pint*. The collection and analysis of data from a variety of sources limited potential bias associated with the exclusive use of one specific data source and strengthened the grounding of theory through the "triangulation" of evidence (Eisenhardt, 1989). The data collected from the breweries' websites and from the news articles was used to verify the stories told during the interviews. We studied all the archival materials related to the brewery *before* the interview in order to be able to ask more specific questions and "dig deeper" into the organization's identity formation processes.

The questions that we employed in the interviews with brewery members were developed and refined during the course of the study. As a general starting point, we made sure to include in each interview questions pertaining to each of the common themes identified from the old institutionalism and organizational identity literatures (see Appendix I for a sample of the interview questions).[6]

In total, we conducted seventy-three interviews at fifty-nine different breweries with seventy-one different individuals—that is, fourteen breweries were visited twice during different data collection batches. The interviews were conducted during three concentrated periods of data collection and spread

Constructing Identity in and around Organizations

out over a five-year period from 2004 to 2009. The length of the interviews varied between 30 and 90 minutes, and was 70 minutes on average.

5.3.5 Data analysis

We analyzed our data in three general steps by making use of the software package NVIVO 8 and by following recommendations from Glaser and Strauss (1967), Corbin and Strauss (1990), and Miles and Huberman (1994). The overarching goal was to identify the sources of organizational identity and the relevant processes through which proto-identity attributes from these sources were imprinted into the identities of the organizations under study. First, the interview transcripts were coded openly. This process was focused on defining first-order concepts that emerged directly from the data and that seemed to be relevant for the present study. During this stage, we paid particular attention to the three predefined sources from the literature. Second, codes with similar meanings were clustered by making "constant comparisons" in order to uncover relevant higher-order constructs (Glaser and Strauss, 1967). Here, we compared the open codes from the individual cases with each other and with the literature to find relevant higher-order constructs and to formulate proper definitions. Third and finally, we used "axial coding" to examine the relationships between the constructs developed during the previous two steps (Corbin and Strauss, 1990). During this step, we compared cases and groups of cases with each other in order to map the relationships between the higher-order constructs that grounded the findings presented in the subsequent sections.

To reveal the relevant identity formation processes, we examined the causal chain in reverse order. We first inductively reconstructed each brewery's identity to be able to logically link potential sources and processes to specific identity claims. For this purpose, we made use of the identity claims developed by Lamertz et al. (2005) in their study of organizational image in the Canadian beer brewing industry.[7] To ensure that we incorporated the nuances of the Dutch beer brewing industry in our coding scheme, we started with an open coding process for first-order proto-identity attributes. At a later stage, we employed the identity claims developed by Lamertz et al. (2005) to group the proto-identity attributes into higher-order identity claims. We created new claims for proto-identity attributes that we were not able to group into the preexisting claim categories developed by Lamertz et al. (2005). Table 5.3 provides an overview of all the claims that were employed, their definitions, and information about the frequency with which they occurred in our sample.

Processes of Identity Imprinting and Enactment in the Dutch

Table 5.3 Description of employed identity claims* and number of breweries per claim

Identity claim	Description	No. of breweries[a]
Aesthete	Linking the organization with product sophistication and appreciation	22
Artisan	Expressed care and dedication to the tradition of brewing as art and craft	50
Collaborator**	Promoting traditional brewing culture and collaboration among peers	27
Ecologist**	Expressed care and dedication to the production of beer in an ecologically responsible manner	7
Entertainer	Linking the organization with entertainment and fun	19
Experienced scientist	Emphasizing the use of scientific principles to maintain high quality standards	19
Hobbyist**	Stressing the non-profit orientation of the organization	31
Hybrid commercial**	Underlining the multiplicity and complementarity of the breweries' product offerings (e.g., combination with restaurant or store)	30
Hybrid social**	Emphasizing the additional communal goals of the organization (e.g., museum, working with employees with disabilities)	9
Independent**	Challenging established orders and limited collaboration with organizational peers	12
Industrial producer	Emphasizing large-scale productive capability and focus on growth	6
Innovator	Highlighting the organization's focus on product development and process innovation	13
Local player	Expressed link to markets and communities in a particular locale	47
Marketer**	Highlighting the organization's orientation toward the selling of the key product (beer)	39
Merchandiser	Highlighting the organization's orientation toward brand and product expansion beyond the core activity of beer brewing	44
Not just a local player	Emphasizing the organization's orientation toward expansion beyond the local into wider sales markets	19
Pedigree	Connecting the organization with (beer brewing) history	30
Quality champion	Referring to accumulated knowledge of control over the production process and listing of performance accomplishments	36
Renter**	Referring to the use of excess production capacity of other breweries to brew own beers	20
Specialist producer	Emphasizing small-scale production methods and specialty products manufacture	44
Values pride	Emphasis on unique organizational and brand values as a sign of quality	8

*Source: Lamertz et al. (2005).
**Own addition.
[a] For the purpose of this table, an organization is considered to be a member of the identity claim category when at least some of all identity related interviewee text referred to the particular claim category. Membership in multiple categories is possible.

Constructing Identity in and around Organizations

5.4 Findings

While focusing on elements and processes related to the old institutionalism themes, we traced the causal chain of identity imprinting backward from organizations' manifest identity claims to the actual sources from which proto-identity attributes flow. This led to the discovery of three alternate but complementary sources from which the breweries in our sample formed new identities: (*a*) the identities of authoritative insiders,

Identity Imprinting	Identity Reservoir	Identity Enactment	Enacted Identity
Strategic Emulation	Org. Fundamentals	Disidentification	Selected Identity Claims
Value Prop. Formation	Org. Practices	Anticip. Audience Judgm.	(see Table 5.3)
Critical Decision-Making	Corr. Identity Claims	Image–Vision Allignm.	

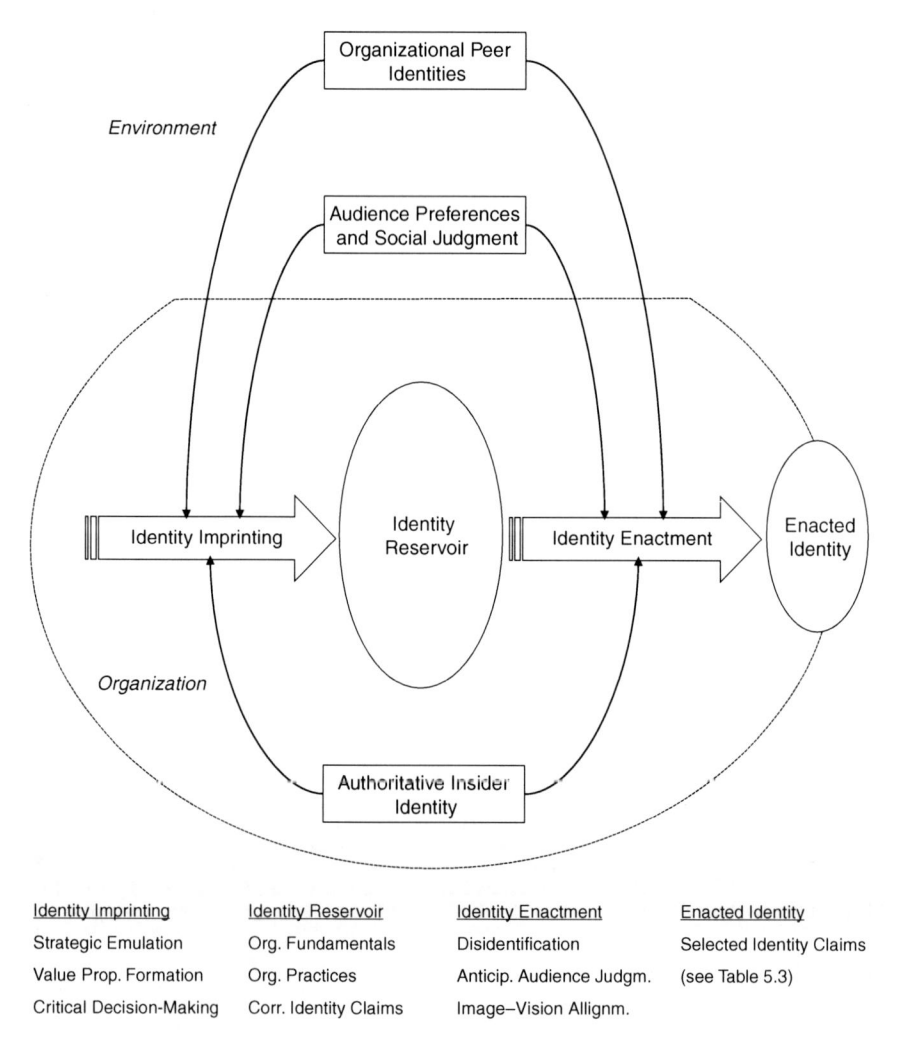

Figure 5.2 Empirical model of organizational identity formation: imprinting and enactment processes

Table 5.4 Identity formation processes per identity source and corresponding percentage scores for the empirical evidence found

Identity formation process	Type of identity formation process	Description	% of breweries[a]	% of sources[b]
Authoritative insider identity	Imprinting	The values, beliefs, and skills of an organizational insider that have significant influence over the organizational decision-making process.	95	93
Critical decision-making	Imprinting	Making decisions about core, enduring, and distinctive attributes and practices.	95	92
Image–vision alignment	Enactment	Aligning the selection of identity claims with individual vision.	34	28
Audience preferences and judgment		The organizational audience's (differing) demand for and expectations about particular products.	49	49
Value proposition formation	Imprinting	Adapting the organization's business model to the demand of consumers and the evaluative pressures from the entire audience.	22	20
Anticipating audience judgment	Enactment	Adapting selected identity claims for enactment to expected social judgment from the audience.	42	43
Organizational peer identities		Organizational identities of other organizations operating in the same industry.	97	91
Strategic emulation	Imprinting	Selecting attributes from peer organizations for the construction of own organization.	61	52
Disidentification	Enactment	Creating a distinctive enacted identity by highlighting differences between own identity and the identities of peer organizations.	92	85

[a] % of breweries reflects the number of *breweries* for which we found evidence that allowed us to causally link the particular identity formation process to the shape of the brewery's identity.
[b] % of sources reflects the number of *interviews* in which we found evidence that allowed us to causally link the particular identity formation process to the shape of the brewery's identity.

Constructing Identity in and around Organizations

(*b*) the preferences and social judgments of audiences, and (*c*) the identities of organizational peers. We found that organizational identities are shaped through a combination of imprinting and enactment processes associated with these three different sources. In this section, we discuss our findings for each identity source.[8]

Figure 5.2 is the empirical model we constructed from our findings. Our findings reveal three important identity sources: (*a*) authoritative insider identity, (*b*) audience preferences and social judgment, and (*c*) organizational peer identities. Together, these three sources affect both the imprinting of proto-identity attributes into the organizational identity reservoir and the enactment of organizational identity through the selection of identity claims from the reservoir. For each source, we define the most relevant identity imprinting and identity enactment processes. Table 5.4 provides an overview of the different identity formation processes per identity source and information about the empirical evidence found for each of these processes. In the remainder of this section, we relate our findings to the common themes we identified between old institutionalism and organizational identity theory and provide empirical support by the inclusion of selected quotations from the interview transcripts.

5.4.1 Human agency: The role of authoritative organizational insiders in identity formation

Brewery insiders had significant influence over the shape of the identities of their breweries. We found that for almost every brewery the authoritative insiders we interviewed had considerable agentic power that allowed them to incorporate elements of their individual identities into the brewery's organizational identity. This agentic power was particularly visible in one identity imprinting process (critical decision-making) and one identity enactment process (image–vision alignment).

5.4.1.1 IDENTITY IMPRINTING THROUGH CRITICAL DECISION-MAKING

One of the most apparent ways in which the authoritative insiders invoked their agentic power to shape the identity reservoirs of the beer breweries in our sample was through critical decision-making. We observed how our interviewees made decisions with particular intentions in mind. Their individual identities guided them in formulating a vision of what their breweries should look like and in taking action accordingly. We observed that the individuals with the most authority (generally the founders or the

Processes of Identity Imprinting and Enactment in the Dutch

owners) had been most able to significantly imprint elements of their individual identities into the identity reservoirs of their breweries.

One type of critical decision through which brewery insiders imprinted their individual identities into the brewery was through the deliberate construction of organizational aims (such as the brewery's mission statement). The quote below, from one of the founders of *Bierbrouwerij Grandcafé Emelisse* in Kamperland, is an example of this.

> One of the core elements of this organization is its focus on brewing beer and promoting the island 'Noord-Beveland'. I think that accurately describes the aim with which we founded this organization. Our focus is not just on the brewing of beer alone, but on its use as a vehicle for the promotion of the island. (Tom ter Horst, Founder and Manager of "Bierbrouwerij Grandcafé Emelisse" in Kamperland)

This quote includes statements about the current identity of the brewery and provides a hint about one of the sources of this identity. We regarded the interviewee's claim that an important element of the brewery was the promotion of the local region as evidence for the identity claim Local Player. We found that this claim was further supported by references to related attributes and practices, such as the brewery name and the brewery's target markets. Additionally, the interviewee claimed that the statement corresponded with the organizational aims that were set by the founders at the time of the brewery's inception. This was evidenced by the fact that the founders had first created a foundation that had as a general goal the promotion of the local region. The brewery was a vehicle that they began using to achieve this goal. Altogether, this indicates that the identity of this brewery's founders was imprinted into the brewery's identity through an agentic decision-making process about the organizational aims. In this case, the formulation of organizational aims was guided by the identities of the founders leading to the incorporation of Local Player proto-identity attributes into the brewery's identity reservoir.

5.4.1.2 IDENTITY ENACTMENT THROUGH IMAGE–VISION ALIGNMENT

Brewery insiders did not only exert their agentic power over the composition of the identity reservoir but also shaped the enacted identity of their brewery. In our interviews, members provided examples of how they highlighted or embellished preferred identity claims of their brewery that were in line with their individual visions about their breweries and their environment. In this way, members managed the brewery's image as perceived by their audiences.

We identified a good example of the influence of image–vision alignment by organizational insiders in the case of *De Haagse Bierbrouwerij* in Den Haag. In the interview, the brew master of this brewery was highlighting and embellishing the Experienced Scientist claim in favor of the Artisan claim. In this way, he differentiated his brewery from many of its microbrewery peers. What was initially unclear, however, was why he chose to enact the brewery's identity in this particular way. For instance, we also found evidence for proto-identity attributes that substantiated Hybrid Commercial or Specialist Producer claims. After further analysis of the interview, we concluded that the Experienced Scientist versus Artisan analogy was in line with the brew master's individual identity. Here, we observed how an individual's identity moderated the selection process of identity claims from the identity reservoir. The following quote illustrates this process for this particular case:

> The idea that everything has to be produced according to traditional, artisanal methods is something that I don't believe in. That is exactly the image I don't want to have. There is nothing artisanal about producing beer—it is an industrial process. And you can only control an industrial process 100% when everything is mechanized. (Anton Schults, Brew Master, and Manager of brewery "De Haagse Bierbrouwerij" in Den Haag)

This enacted identity was supported by proto-identity attributes that were imprinted by the brew manager himself such as computerized brewing equipment. This brew master had thus shaped his brewery's identity through identity imprinting processes, the outcomes of which he consequently employed to substantiate enacted identity claims.

5.4.2 Environmental adaptation: The role of organizational audiences in identity formation

Brewery identities in our sample were not just a direct representation of the individual identities of brewery founders and other insiders but they also contained important elements that were sourced from the environments of the breweries. These elements were incorporated into the breweries through processes of adaptation. One environmental source of identity was the type of organizational audiences that the brewery was confronted with. We show that audiences function as an identity source in two important ways: through their preferences that are incorporated into the breweries' value proposition and through the social judgment of brewery activities.

5.4.2.1 IDENTITY IMPRINTING THROUGH VALUE PROPOSITION FORMATION

Audience preferences were imprinted into the breweries' identities through the formation of value propositions. A value proposition appeared in our interviews as a statement about the types of products the brewery aspired to produce and the types of consumers the brewery was aiming for with these products. In other words, these were statements about how the brewery was creating value for itself and for the consumer. The formation of a value proposition can be seen as a critical decision and an indication of the agentic power of organizational insiders over the identity formation process. However, we found that the value proposition formation process was also a clear example of a problem-solving activity through which environmental elements became imprinted into the breweries' identities. We observed how brewery insiders entered into a (virtual) negotiation with their audiences to create adequate matches between product offerings and audience demands. Through this environmental adaptation process, the preferences of audience groups located in the brewery's environment were imprinted into the identity of the brewery.

The identity of brewery *De Halve Maan* was clearly shaped by the demands of audience groups in the brewery's surrounding environment. We observed that this brewery's identity reservoir contained, in addition to proto-identity attributes pertaining to the Artisan and Pedigree claims, attributes that signaled Merchandiser and Hybrid Commercial claims. The Artisan and Pedigree attributes were clearly imprinted by the brewery's founder, but the founder's identity did not explain why the brewery would develop Merchandiser and Hybrid Commercial attributes. We found that these attributes became incorporated into the brewery through processes of environmental adaptation and in particular through the formation of a value proposition. One quote from the founder about the building of the brewery illustrates this:

> The building was in a very bad state; the roof was about to collapse and it was littered with very old materials, like broken draft beer equipment. At a certain point we asked ourselves, why don't we refurbish the whole place? Initially, we had a very simple idea to just put in a bunch of new windows and doors without too much hodgepodge. Gradually we had so many people who were interested in our brewery saying: "If you open this space up we would like to rent it to throw a party." Then we started to scratch our heads. There turned out to be such a demand that we said to ourselves: "Let's revamp this place properly." At the start we just rented out for parties and tours during evenings occasionally...

But at a certain stage we took the step to open during the days as well and recently we opened a restaurant for the days that the location is not rented out where people can taste a variety of dishes in which beer is used for the preparation. (John Vermeersen, Founder, Owner, Brew Master, and Manager of brewery 'De Halve Maan' in Hulst)

5.4.2.2 IDENTITY ENACTMENT THROUGH ANTICIPATING AUDIENCE JUDGMENT

Apart from affecting the identity reservoirs of the breweries in our sample, audiences also affected the enacted identities of the breweries. We found that audiences were not mere passive consumers of the breweries' products, but that they in fact subjected the breweries to scrutiny of all their activities. In our interviews, we found that brewery insiders were aware of these evaluative pressures and that they constrained the identity enactment process. Insiders seemed to enact *those* identity claims that were likely to be evaluated favorably by their respective audiences. This indicates that the above-described image–vision alignment activities are generally driven not exclusively by the identities of organizational insiders but also by the expectations of organizational outsiders.

Brewery *De Hoeksche Waard* in Oud-Beijerland, for example, had different enacted identities for different audience groups. Their identity reservoir contained elements that supported claims such as those of Local Player, Marketer, and Quality Champion among others. We observed, however, that the Local Player attributes were highlighted and embellished in interaction with the local audience group, but downplayed in interaction with audience groups in other geographical areas. For these audience groups, the professional attributes of the brewery's identity, which we classified as Marketer and Quality Champion attributes, were embellished. The quote below further illustrates this:

> In the first place we focus on the regional character of our brewery. We would like to create an association with "de Hoeksche Waard" area *[a locality in South-Western Holland]*. You notice that it is working. People's identities are tied to the Hoeksche Waard. For example, people who used to live in the Hoeksche Waard area like to receive our product as a present. On the one hand, this provides a foundation for growth. On the other hand, we notice that if you go further away from this area people don't identify as strongly with the region. For those people it is more important how professional our products are and, not in the least, how our products taste. (Rob van der Agt, Founder, Owner, Brew Master, and Manager of 'De Hoeksche Waard' in Oud-Beijerland)

5.4.3 Environmental adaptation: The role of organizational peers in identity formation

The identities of organizational peers constitute our final source of identity. The founders and owners of the breweries in our sample worked to construct an identity that distinguished their brewery from those of their peers. They accomplished this through processes of strategic emulation and disidentification.

5.4.3.1 IDENTITY IMPRINTING THROUGH STRATEGIC EMULATION

We found that the founders and owners of the breweries in our sample were inspired by the identities of the other breweries in the industry in the formation of a distinctive identity for their own brewery. This was a process of strategic emulation, where the founders or owners performed "identity work" to construct a distinctive character (see Alvesson and Willmott, 2002; Clegg et al., 2007). They first evaluated proto-identity attributes from other breweries, then selected attributes that matched with their individual identities, and finally made slight adaptations to these attributes to create distinctive identities for their own breweries.

An example of strategic emulation and the identity-imprinting role of organizational peers can be found in the case of brewery *De Graaf van Heumen*. This brewery, which was founded in 2009 in a small village close to Nijmegen, was unique in that the brewing installation was made of glass and placed in the middle of their pub, allowing visitors to actually observe the entire brewing process. One of the founders had extensive experience in the brewing industry and this experience was used to strategically emulate a group of brewpubs. This emulation process led to the adoption of proto-identity attributes that aided the brewery in becoming a Hybrid Commercial and Entertainer, which is illustrated by the following quote.

> The brewery in Den Bosch gave us ideas about how not to run a brewery. I have many years of experience in the brewing business. I owned a brewpub in Scheveningen, for which I also designed the brewing installation. I also helped with the construction of the new brewing house of Bavaria—"Brouwhuis 3." Additionally, I worked for Heineken, and Oudaen in Utrecht. So it is safe to say that I know almost all breweries inside out. Then you know certain things about the breweries; like that they brew a very nice beer, but their installation is hidden away somewhere. Then you ask yourself: Do we want that? Well, maybe that is exactly what we don't want. (Constant Keinemans, Founder and Brew Master of 'De Graaf van Heumen' in Heumen)

5.4.3.2 IDENTITY ENACTMENT THROUGH DISIDENTIFICATION

Apart from the imprinting effect that brewery peers had on the identity reservoir, we also observed an effect on the enacted identity. Brewery members tended to highlight the distinctive character of their own brewery by disidentifying with peer breweries. This was often done through the discrediting of certain fundamentals or practices of these breweries.

Brewery *De Drie Horne*, for instance, had a range of proto-identity attributes that supported the claims Hobbyist, Quality Champion, and Marketer among others. To distinguish the brewery from certain peer breweries, the founder highlighted the non-profit nature of the brewery (an attribute supporting the Hobbyist claim) and argued how this bolstered the Quality Champion claim. At the same time, he downplayed the Marketer proto-identity attributes of the brewery, in order to differentiate the organization from marketing-driven organizations. The quote below illustrates this:

> In response to the question: "What attributes of other breweries would you rather not see back in your own brewery?"
>
> "Well, the purely commercial—pretending to produce quality and always wanting to attract the attention. I saw that, for example, (this does not necessarily have anything to do with the brewery) when Erica Terpstra [a former Dutch State Secretary of Health and Sport] visited Apeldoorn. Being a local beer brewer, they wanted me in a picture with Erica. But you should have seen how other people were trying to push others out of the way to get into the picture. That is exactly how some breweries behave. There are people who always want to just stand a bit in front of the other to get attention. But it is much better to get attention by producing good quality. The attention will come naturally—it might take a couple of years, but it will come." (Sjef Groothuis, Founder, Owner, Brew Master, and Manager of brewery "De Drie Horne" in Kaatsheuvel).

5.5 Discussion

Previous research on organizational identity formation has been predominantly geared toward identifying the micro-processes and generic stages through which identities are constructed (e.g., Corley and Gioia, 2004; Gioia et al., 2010). As this line of research is focused on improving our understanding of how identities emerge from the actions of individuals and collectives, the literature currently remains silent with respect to the issue of what shapes the actual substance of organizational identities, particularly around the time of organizational inception. In this chapter, we took

Processes of Identity Imprinting and Enactment in the Dutch

up the challenge of developing new theoretical insights concerning the processes through which the substance of organizational identity takes form during organizational nascency.

In our study of the Dutch beer brewing industry, we showed how identity elements of authoritative organizational insiders and the organizational environment were imprinted into the identities of nascent breweries. Our findings reveal a range of processes through which an organization-specific identity reservoir is formed (a process we labeled identity imprinting) and through which identity claims are selected from this reservoir and woven into strategic self-presentations and ceremonial rehearsals of field-level rationalized myths (a process we referred to as identity enactment). Together, these two processes provide building blocks for a new theory that (*a*) explains how identities of nascent organizations are formed and substantiated, and (*b*) integrates related literatures (old-institutionalism) and different theoretical perspectives (social constructionist and social actor perspectives).

5.5.1 Identity sources

Previous research on organizational identity formation suggests that organizational identities are shaped by different stakeholders such as founders and top-management (e.g., Scott and Lane, 2000), audiences (Ginzel et al., 1993), and peer organizations (Clegg et al., 2007). One of the chief contributions of our study is that we provide an integrative conceptualization of the identity formation process, through which causal linkages are established between various identity sources on the one hand and the substance of the identities of the individual organizations in our sample on the other. Specifically, we identified three different identity sources that shaped the identities of the fifty-nine breweries in our sample around the time of inception. In doing so, we have integrated findings from previous studies on organizational identity formation and construction.

A first source consists of the identities of authoritative organizational insiders, who imprint their identities into the organization through critical decision-making. Most previous studies have shown how insiders have agentic power over the shape of their organizational identities through processes of sensemaking and sensegiving (Ravasi and Schultz, 2006; Gioia et al., 2010). These studies have highlighted that insiders with high levels of organizational authority (e.g., founders or top-management) have a more influential role in shaping their organization's identity than insiders with low levels of authority (Scott and Lane, 2000; Ravasi and Schultz, 2006; Gioia et al., 2010). Our findings provide further support for these notions.

Two additional identity sources, notably, audience preferences and social judgments, and organizational peer identities, jointly constitute the identity-relevant organizational environment. We have shown that the beer breweries in our sample continuously adapt to dynamic pressures in their local environments. While these adaptations are often substantive problem solving activities by organizational insiders, these activities also produce symbolic sediment that trickles down into the organizational identity reservoir.

Our study integrates and confirms insights from studies about the influencing role of organizational audiences (Ginzel et al., 1993). Audience preferences influence the initial setup of the organization such as the business model (identity imprinting). Additionally, social judgment of the organization by its audience influences the ongoing insider interpretations about the organization's actions and performance (identity enactment) (cf. Bitekine, 2011). Finally, our study integrates findings from previous studies that have shown how identities are always constructed against the background of the identities of others (i.e., peer organizations) (Clegg et al., 2007; Ybema et al., 2009). Organizations form distinctive identities through strategic emulation of identity elements from peer organizations (identity imprinting) and through deliberate disidentification with the identities and practices of particular organizational peers (identity enactment).

Future research could provide additional evidence for our findings about the sources of organizational identity by adopting a more theory-testing approach. Subsequent quantitative studies could explore the extent to which organizations are immersed in the identity sources we identified more systematically, and assess whether this exposure has predictive power with respect to the substance of their identities.

5.5.2 The identity reservoir

We believe that another important contribution of our study is that it reveals how identity imprinting and identity enactment processes are facilitated by an identity reservoir.[9] Imprinting processes are facilitated through the reservoir's function as a "storage bin" (cf. Walsh and Ungson, 1991) for fundamentals and practices that represent the formal and symbolic core of the organization. Over time, these attributes accumulate because of the mutually constitutive and interactive imprinting roles of the different identity sources.

Additionally, the identity reservoir functions as a "toolkit" for identity enactment (cf. Rindova et al., 2010) working both forward (sensemaking of identity) and backward (legitimating identity). First, proto-identity attributes were referred to during brewery insiders' attempts to interpret and construct the identity of their breweries. Here, proto-identity attributes aided during the work done by organizational insiders to make sense of their collective identity. A second function of the identity reservoir was in legitimating enacted identity claims. For example, when brewery insiders would claim that their brewery was "artisanal" and were asked to substantiate this claim, they would refer to proto-identity attributes such as those related to their production methods in an effort to legitimate the initial identity claim employed.

What is perhaps more surprising however, was that brewery insiders did not only employ proto-identity attributes to *substantiate* institutionalized identity claims but also that they also employed them to *replace* institutionalized identity claims. For example, instead of claiming that their brewery was "artisanal" (one of the institutionalized identity claims we defined), certain interviewees made direct reference to a proto-identity attribute by stating something like: "we are a brewery that produces beer from honest ingredients." Our data suggested that whether or not an individual employs a proto-identity attribute instead of an identity claim depends on the level of institutionalization of the particular identity claim and the age of the brewery. Identity claims that were more institutionalized at the field level were more readily available to individuals when interpreting their brewery's identity. Insiders from younger breweries were less equipped to interpret and construct their identities than insiders from older breweries. As a result, insiders from younger breweries were more likely to use proto-identity attributes instead of identity claims. This supports the time-varying distinction we have drawn between identity imprinting and identity enactment. As an organization grows older, and identity formation processes take on a more performative character, its members gain a better understanding of what the organization's identity is, and how it relates to other identities in the field.

5.5.3 The dynamics of identity formation

Although we have shown that the breweries did not enact their identities by making random draws from a wide pool of industry-specific identity claims, some randomness and dynamism were introduced in the organizational identity formation process through the transpiring of unanticipated events affecting the identity sources and, subsequently, the brewery-specific identity reservoirs. These events varied in the degree to which they occurred externally to the brewery. Some events were completely external to the brewery (e.g., an unexpected change in audience preferences), others were largely internal (e.g., the infection of a large beer batch leading to the threat of negative audience evaluations). Many breweries in our sample were confronted with critical events that had altered their relation with constitutive identity sources. We found that indeed these events had led to changes in their organizational identities, replicating findings of previous studies (Dutton and Dukerich, 1991; Ravasi and Schultz, 2006) and confirming our findings related to the three identity sources.

The events that had the most impact on the shapes of the identities of the breweries in our sample were changes related to the insiders that controlled the breweries. In fact, we found evidence for fifteen breweries that suggested that these kinds of events had shaped their identities. Specifically, we found that changes in the ownership and or management of these breweries had led to the addition of new proto-identity attributes and destruction of others, leading to differences in the available identity claims for enactment. Additionally, there were six cases in which unexpected changes in audience preferences had significantly affected the breweries' identities.

We did not find any cases where changes in the composition of organizational peer identities had affected the identities of individual breweries in our sample. However, it is likely that these kinds of effects *do* play a role during identity formation, but that they were not visible for us because of our specific research design and theoretical focus. Changes in the composition of organizational peer identities are likely to depend on field-level structures and processes, such as organizational form dynamics (Hannan et al., 2007). Future research is needed to examine to what extent identities of individual organizations are constrained or enabled by field-level structures (cf. Glynn, 2008).

5.5.4 Social constructionist and social actor perspectives

Organizational identity scholars have recently begun to integrate two different ontological perspectives that used to divide the field into one coherent theory of organizational identity (Ravasi and Schultz, 2006; Gioia et al., 2010). We believe our study contributes to these efforts by offering additional theoretical building blocks that can foster further integration.

On the one hand, our findings highlight important social actor elements in the formation of new organizational identities. By comparing the identity formation process for almost an entire industry, we have shown that organizational identities can be arranged in a broader system of institutionalized identity claims, representing the symbolic structuration of an organizational field (Porac et al., 1989; Lamertz et al., 2005). We found that in interpreting and constructing their collective identities, individuals employ similar labels with institutionalized meanings. Additionally, we found that although interpretations of individual claims might change over time or differ slightly per individual, as a system these identity claims are relatively stable. In particular, we observed that the oppositional structure of this system, in which one claim or a set of claims always seems to have an oppositional (set of) claim(s), is stable over time (cf. Clegg et al., 2007). These pressures toward (relative) similarity appear to stem from the imprinting processes related to environmental adaptation. The breweries in our sample are to a large extent faced with similar environmental pressures, which seemed to have led to the adoption of similar proto-identity attributes and identity claims. However, as our study was predominantly focused on the distinctiveness of identities because of our old institutionalist theoretical lens these observations are only indirectly supported by our findings.

On the other hand, we observe that identities are strongly influenced by social constructionist and human agentic forces as apparent in the ongoing imprinting and enactment activities of organizational insiders (cf. Ravasi and Schultz, 2006). Through these processes, organizational insiders infuse the organization with distinctive character elements. We observed the way in which brewery founders deliberately made distinctive combinations of identity claims supported by unique proto-identity attributes to locate themselves in uninhabited identity positions. In contrast with the social actor elements of identity that seemed to shape the identities of the breweries beyond the actions of the individuals involved, these elements often emerged through the work done by brewery insiders to construct the pivotal elements of their organizations and ensure short-term feasibility and survival.

Where Ravasi and Schultz (2006) make a distinction between sensegiving and sensemaking in organizational identity formation, we deliberately distinguish between similar processes of identity imprinting and identity enactment. On the basis of our observations during our study of the Dutch beer brewing industry, and by narrowing our scope to the agentic power of individuals, we made an inference about the importance of these processes in identity formation over time. During the early stages of the organization's life cycle, we observed that the agentic power of individuals seemed to be mainly related to processes of identity imprinting. Actors are concerned with constructing a viable organization and creating a sense of collective identity. Over time, as the organization matures, identity enactment processes (which can also be sensegiving in nature) become more important. As the organization grows, its environment becomes more demanding and survival becomes more dependent upon the portrayal of a positive image (see Elsbach and Kramer, 1996; Elsbach and Bhattacharya, 2001). In this sense, the organizational identity formation activities will be moved away from substance to image (Alvesson, 1990).

5.5.5 Process research

Process theories generally focus on activities, interactions, and change within and of organizations, rather than structures and states of organizations (Langley and Tsoukas, 2010). Research on organizational identity formation has provided multiple exemplary studies that are demonstrative of the way in which process research can inform theories of transformational change in and of organizations (e.g., Corley and Gioia, 2004; Gioia et al., 2010). We believe that our study contributes to this line of research by identifying specific imprinting and enactment processes through which organizational identities are shaped.

However, our study is markedly different from most process studies in a number of ways. Instead of closely examining transformational change processes within one organization, we examine these processes across a wide range of organizations that almost covers an entire industry. Additionally, we did not study organizational processes in complete isolation but have causally linked them to (temporal) organizational structures—that is, organizational identity. Future research should examine the extent to which a similar process perspective (linking process to substance) could be fruitfully applied to other symbolic aspects of organization, such as organizational reputation, status, and culture.

Additionally, our study contributes to organizational identity process research, by deliberately linking process to substance. Our theoretical model integrates previous findings about organizational identity formation and offers important theoretical extensions that provide new alleys for future research on organizational identity. The distinction we have drawn between identity imprinting and identity enactment based on our findings shows how materiality plays an important role in processes of organizational identity (re)construction by facilitating and constraining enactment.

5.6 Conclusion

Our study introduced a new theoretical model explaining how elements from a variety of identity sources become imprinted into the identity of nascent organizations around inception. Although previous research has uncovered the micro-processes and generic stages through which identities are formed and constructed, our findings reveal the sources of identity and processes through which they shape organizational identities.

On the basis of the analysis of the identity formation process in fifty-nine Dutch microbreweries through an old institutionalist theoretical lens, we introduced the concept of "identity reservoir" to demonstrate how organizational identities are substantiated by proto-identity attributes and how these attributes can be traced back to their ultimate sources. By additionally distinguishing between identity imprinting and identity enactment processes, we extend theory on organizational identity formation and expand recent initiatives to integrate different ontological perspectives.

Appendix I: Sample of Interview Questions

1. General questions: The brewery

- Can you tell us something about the history of the brewery?
- Which beer styles does the brewery produce?

2. Informal organization: Central, enduring, distinctive, and dynamic organizational elements

- What are the most central characteristics of the brewery?
- Which of these characteristics are the most enduring and distinctive?
- Have there been any major shifts in the importance of these characteristics over the past few years?

3. Environmental adaptation: Audience groups and important events

- What are the brewery's target groups and what value does your product offer them?
- What were the most important events during the history of the brewery?
- How did these events influence the brewery's identity?

4. Agency: The role of founders and owners, identity work, and image management

- How were the CED elements incorporated into the brewery?
- Who is (are) the most influential individual(s) in the brewery?
- What were important actions that had to be undertaken during the founding of the brewery?
- To what organizational peers do you compare your brewery?

Notes

1. A previous version of this chapter was presented at the 2010 PROS symposium (June 13, 2010, Rhodes, Greece). We thank volume editor Majken Schultz and two anonymous reviewers for their insightful comments. Will Felps, Tony Hak, Kai Lamertz, and Vanessa Strike gave useful feedback on earlier drafts of this manuscript. Marc van Essen provided valuable research assistance during the earlier phases of data collection. Naturally, any remaining mistakes are our own.
2. Old institutionalism is different from "new" institutionalism. Although both share the underlying assumptions about the instrumentally arational elements that organizations adopt to increase their chances of survival, old institutionalism is different in that its analytical focus is on the organizational level of analysis and views organizations as distinctively embedded in their local communities (DiMaggio andPowell, 1991; Selznick, 1996; Stinchcombe, 1997). New institutionalism, on the other hand, is focused on the field or societal level of analysis and views organizations as loosely coupled structures of field-level elements, emphasizing their homogeneity (DiMaggio andPowell, 1991: 14).
3. Microbreweries are small breweries with specialized products that are generally focused on craftsmanship and taste (Carroll andSwaminathan, 1992, 2000: 2).
4. These databases were extracted from the websites of Cambrinus (www.cambrinus.nl) and Pint (www.pint.nl/nedbier/brouwerij.htm).
5. Brew masters are the individuals responsible for the development of beer recipes, for the setup and maintenance of the beer production equipment, and for the actual day-to-day production batches of beer. Because of their influence over the production process we assumed that, after the founders and owners, they were likely to be the most influential individuals in the breweries.
6. It is important to note, however, that every interview was unique in that we allowed the interview to progress in a conversational manner and asked questions in no particular order. We only ensured that the general themes were discussed and made sure the discussion remained on topic. We asked more specific questions when relevant topics were discussed related to the identity formation process to get more detailed accounts about the relevant sources and

attribute selection processes. We found that most of our interviewees had never explicitly thought about their identities and, therefore, did not seem to have any boilerplate stories ready when confronted with questions about their brewery's identity.
7. Although they refer to distinct concepts, for the purposes of this chapter we assume that organizational identity and organizational image can be constructed from the same identity claim categories.
8. As our study was limited to one specific population, questions of transferability of our findings to other domains may arise. We feel that our findings are likely to apply to other domains as well because we focused on processes of organizational construction that are not unique to our population but, we believe, are salient in every mature organizational field. It is likely that identities can be reconstructed in a similar manner for organizations in other domains. Additionally, the adoption of a specific theoretical lens and observation scheme might have obscured particular identity sources and imprinting processes. As a result of the old institutionalist lens with which we collected and analyzed our data, it is possible that we downplayed particular field-level effects on the organizational identity formation process requiring a "new" institutionalist theoretical lens (cf. Glynn, 2008). Future research from this perspective is needed in order to uncover identity sources and identity formation processes at this particular level of analysis.
9. Recent research has shown how organizational identities and identity formation processes are substantiated and facilitated by organizational culture (Ravasi and Schultz, 2006). Whereas there are clear parallels between our conception of the identity reservoir and the set of symbolic attributes and practices constituting an organizational culture, our conception is different in that it also includes—or allows for the inclusion of—more substantive elements that might not be a reflection of organizational culture but still play an important role in identity formation. For example, we found that the brewery's geographical location, the brewery's product line, and the brewery's target market were important proto-identity attributes that substantiated the identities of the breweries in our study.

References

Albert, Stuart and Whetten, David A. (1985). "Organizational Identity," in L. L. Cummings and B. M. Staw (eds), *Research in Organizational Behavior*. Greenwich, CT: JAI Press, pp. 263–95.

Alvesson, Mats (1990). "Organization: From Substance to Image?" *Organization Studies*, 11: 373–94.

—— Willmott, Hugh (2002). "Identity Regulation as Organizational Control: Producing the Appropriate Individual." *Journal of Management Studies*, 39: 619–44.

Ashforth, Blake E. and Mael, Fred (1989). "Social Identity Theory and the Organization." *Academy of Management Review*, 14: 20–39.

Baden-Fuller, Charles and Morgan, Mary S. (2010). "Business Models as Models." *Long Range Planning*, 43: 156–71.

Barnard, Chester I. (1938). *The Functions of the Executive*. Cambridge, MA: Harvard University Press.

Bitekine, Alex (2011). "Toward a Theory of Social Judgments of Organizations: The Case of Legitimacy, Reputation, and Status." *Academy of Management Review*, 36: 151–79.

Blau, Peter M. (1964). *Exchange and Power in Social Life*. New York: J. Wiley & Sons.

—— (1972). *The Dynamics of Bureaucracy: A Study of Interpersonal Relationships in Two Government Agencies*. Chicago, IL: University of Chicago Press.

Blau, Peter M. and Meyer, Marshall W. (1987). *Bureaucracy in Modern Society*, 3rd edn. New York: Random House.

Burns, Tom and Stalker, G. M. (1961). *The Management of Innovation*. London: Tavistock.

Carroll, Glenn R. and Hannan, Michael T. (1989). "Density Delay in the Evolution of Organizational Populations: A Model and Five Empirical Tests." *Administrative Science Quarterly*, 34: 411–30.

—— Swaminathan, Anand (1992). "The Organizational Ecology of Strategic Groups in the American Brewing Industry from 1975 to 1990." *Industrial Corporate Change*, 1: 65–97.

—— —— (2000). "Why the Microbrewery Movement? Organizational Dynamics of Resource Partitioning in the US Brewing Industry." *American Journal of Sociology*, 106: 715–62.

CBS (Centraal Bureau voor de Statistiek) (2007). "Bier: meer productie en export, minder consumptie." Webmagazine, November 14, 2007: http://www.cbs.nl/nl-NL/menu/themas/inkomen-bestedingen/publicaties/artikelen/archief/2007/2007-2294-wm.htm

Clegg, Stewart R., Rhodes, Carl, and Kornberger, Martin (2007). "Desperately Seeking Legitimacy: Organizational Identity and Emerging Industries." *Organization Studies*, 28: 495–513.

Corbin, Juliet and Strauss, Anselm (1990). "Grounded Theory Research: Procedures, Canons, and Evaluative Criteria." *Qualitative Sociology*, 13: 3–21.

Corley, Kevin G. and Gioia, Dennis A. (2004). "Identity Ambiguity and Change in the Wake of a Corporate Spin-off." *Administrative Science Quarterly*, 49: 173–208.

Czarniawska, Barbara and Wolff, Rolf (1998). "Constructing New Identities in Established Organizational Fields." *International Studies of Management and Organization*, 28: 32–56.

DiMaggio, Paul J. and Powell, Walter W. (1991). "Introduction," in W. W. Powell and P. J. DiMaggio (eds), *The New Institutionalism in Organizational Analysis*. Chicago, IL: University of Chicago Press, pp. 1–40.

Dutton, Jane E. and Dukerich, Janet M. (1991). "Keeping an Eye on the Mirror: Image and Identity in Organizational Adaptation." *Academy of Management Journal*, 34: 517–54.

Eisenhardt, Kathleen M. (1989). "Building Theories from Case Study Research." *Academy of Management Review*, 14: 532–50.
—— Santos, Filipe M. (2002). "Knowledge-based View: A New Theory of Strategy?," in A. M. Pettigrew, H. Thomas, and R. Whittington (eds), *Handbook of Strategy and Management*. London: Sage, pp. 139–63.
Elsbach, Kimberley D. and Bhattacharya, C. B. (2001). "Defining Who you are by Who you're not: Organizational Disidentification and the National Rifle Association." *Organization Science*, 12: 393–413.
—— Kramer, Roderick M. (1996). "Members' Responses to Organizational Identity Threats: Encountering and Countering the *Business Week* rankings." *Administrative Science Quarterly*, 41: 442–76.
Fiol, C. Marlene (2001). "Revisiting an Identity-based View of Sustainable Competitive Advantage." *Journal of Management*, 27: 691–9.
—— (2002). "Capitalizing on Paradox: The Role of Language in Transforming Organizational Identities." *Organization Science*, 13: 653–66.
Fox-Wolfgramm, Susan. J., Boal, Kimberley B., and Hunt, James G. (Jerry) (1998). "Organizational Adaptation to Institutional Change: A Comparative Study of First-Order Change in Prospector and Defender Banks." *Administrative Science Quarterly*, 43: 87–126.
Ginzel, Linda E., Kramer, Roderick M., and Sutton, Robert I. (1993). "Organizational Impression Management as a Reciprocal Influence Process: The Neglected Role of the Organizational Audience," in L. L. Cummings and B. M. Staw (eds), *Research in Organizational Behavior* (vol. 15). Greenwich, CT: JAI Press, pp. 227–66.
Gioia, Dennis A., Schultz, Majken, and Corley, Kevin G. (2000). "Organizational Identity, Image, and Adaptive Instability." *Academy of Management Review*, 25: 63–81.
—— Price, Kristin N., Hamilton, Aimee L., and Thomas, James B. (2010). "Forging an Identity: An Insider-Outsider Study of the Processes Involved in the Formation of Organizational Identity." *Administrative Science Quarterly*, 55: 1–46.
Glaser, Barney G. and Strauss, Anselm L. (1967). *The Discovery of Grounded Theory: Strategies of Qualitative Research*. London: Weidenfeld and Nicholson.
Glynn, Mary Ann (2008). "Beyond Constraint: How Institutions Enable Identities," in R. Greenwood, C. Oliver, K. Sahlin-Andersson, and R. Suddaby (eds), *The SAGE Handbook of Organizational Institutionalism*. London: Sage, pp. 413–30.
Gouldner, Alvin M. (1954). *Patterns of Industrial Bureaucracy*. Glencoe, IL.: Free Press.
Greenwood, Royston, Oliver, Christine, Sahlin-Andersson, Kerstin, and Suddaby, Roy (2008). *The SAGE Handbook of Organizational Institutionalism*. London: Sage.
Hannan, Michael T., Baron, James N., Kocak, Özgecan, and Hsu, Greta (2006). "Organizational Identities and the Hazard of Change." *Industrial Corporate Change*, 15: 755–84.
—— László Pólos and Carroll, Glenn R. (2007). *The Logics of Organization Theory: Audiences, Codes and Ecologies*. Princeton, NJ: Princeton University Press.
Hatch, Mary Jo and Schultz, Majken (1997). "Relations between Organizational Culture, Identity and Image." *European Journal of Marketing*, 31: 356–65.

Hatch, Mary J. and Schultz, Majken (2002). "The Dynamics of Organizational Identity." *Human Relations*, 55: 989–1018.

Johns, Gary (1999). "A Multi-level Theory of Self-serving Behavior in and by Organizations," in R. I. Sutton and B. M. Staw (eds), *Research in Organizational Behavior* (vol. 21). Stamford, CT: JAI Press, pp. 1–38.

King, Brayden G., Felin, Teppo, and Whetten, David A. (2010). "Finding the Organization in Organization Theory: A Meta-Theory of the Organization as a Social Actor." *Organization Science*, 21: 290–305.

Klein, Katherine, J., Dansereau, Fred, and Hall, Rosalie J. (1994). "Levels Issues in Theory Development, Data Collection, and Analysis." *Academy of Management Review*, 19: 195–229.

Lamertz, Kai, Heugens, Pursey P. M. A. R., and Calmet, Loïs (2005). "The Configuration of Organizational Images among Firms in the Canadian Beer Brewing Industry." *Journal of Management Studies*, 42: 817–43.

Langley, Ann and Tsoukas, Haridimos (2010). "Introducing Perspectives on Process Organization Studies," in T. Hernes and S. Maitlis (eds), *Process, Sensemaking, and Organizing*. Oxford: Oxford University Press.

Lincoln, Yvonna S. and Guba, Egon G. (1985). *Naturalistic Inquiry*. New York: Sage.

Miles, Matthew B. and Huberman, A. Michael (1994). *Qualitative Data Analysis: An Expanded Sourcebook*, 2nd edn. Newbury Park, CA: Sage.

Okhuysen, Gerardo and Bonardi, Jean-Phillipe (2011). "Editors' Comments: The Challenges of Building Theory by Combining Lenses." *Academy of Management Review*, 36: 6–11.

Pentland, Brian T. (1999). "Building Process Theory with Narrative: From Description to Explanation." *Academy of Management Review*, 24: 711–24.

Pfeffer, Jeffrey (1981). "Management as Symbolic Action: The Creation and Maintenance of Organizational Paradigms," in L. L. Cummings and B. M. Staw (eds.), *Research in Organizational Behavior* (vol. 3). Greenwich, CT: JAI Press, pp. 1–52.

Porac, Joseph F., Thomas, Howard, and Baden-Fuller, Charles (1989). "Competitive Groups as Cognitive Communities: The Case of Scottish Knitwear Manufacturers." *Journal of Management Studies*, 26: 397–416.

Ravasi, Davide and Schultz, Majken (2006). "Responding to Organizational Identity Threats: Exploring the Role of Organizational Culture." *Academy of Management Journal*, 49: 433–58.

Rindova, Violina P. and Fombrun, Charles J. (1999). "Constructing Competitive Advantage: The Role of Firm-Constituent Interactions." *Strategic Management Journal*, 20: 691–710.

—— Dalpiaz, Elena, and Ravasi, Davide (2011). "A Cultural Quest: A Study of Organizational Use of New Cultural Resources in Strategy Formation." *Organization Science* 22: 413–31.

Rowley, Timothy J. and Moldoveanu, Mihnea (2003). "When will Stakeholder Groups Act? An Interest- and Identity-based Model of Stakeholder Group Mobilization." *Academy of Management Review*, 28: 204–19.

Schein, Edgar H. (1986). *Organizational Culture and Leadership*. San Francisco, CA: Jossey-Bass.

Scott, Susanne G. and Lane, Vicki R. (2000). "A Stakeholder Approach to Organizational Identity." *Academy of Management Review*, 25: 43–62.

Selznick, Philip (1949). *The TVA and the Grassroots*. Berkeley, CA: University of California Press.

—— (1957). *Leadership in Administration*. New York: Harper & Row.

—— (1996). "Institutionalism 'Old' and 'New.'" *Administrative Science Quarterly*, 41: 270–7.

Stinchcombe, Arthur. L. (1965). "Social Structure and Organizations," in J. March (ed.), *Handbook of Organizations*. Chicago, IL: Rand-McNally, pp. 142–93.

—— (1997). "On the Virtues of the Old Institutionalism." *Annual Review of Sociology*, 23: 1–18.

Van de Ven, Andrew H. and Poole, Marshall Scott (1995). "Explaining Development and Change in Organizations." *Academy of Management Review*, 20: 510–40.

Walsh, James P. and Ungson, Gerardo Rivera (1991). "Organizational Memory." *Academy of Management Review*, 16: 57–91.

Weber, Max (1968). *Economy and Society: An Outline of Interpretive Sociology* (3 vols). New York: Bedminster.

Westphal, James D. and Zajac, Edward (1994). "Substance and Symbolism in CEOs' Long-term Incentive Plans." *Administrative Science Quarterly*, 39: 367–90.

Whetten, David A. and Mackey, Alison (2002). "A Social Actor Conception of Organizational Identity and its Implications for the Study of Organizational Reputation." *Business and Society*, 41: 393–414.

Ybema, Sierk, Keenoy, Tom, Oswick, Clif, Beverungen, Armin, Ellis, Nick, and Sabelis, Ida (2009). "Articulating Identities" *Human Relations*, 62: 299–322.

6

Narrative Tools and the Construction of Identity

James V. Wertsch

Abstract: Building on the observation that humans are fundamentally "story-telling animals," this chapter explores the ways in which narrative tools provide the mediational means for "mnemonic communities" to be imagined and reproduced. Focusing on national narrative tools in general, the chapter takes a specific clash between the Estonian and Russian mnemonic communities as a particular example. In outlining this case, the notion of a "narrative template" is introduced in order to help understand the underlying cognitive and emotional forces involved in national clashes over "what really happened" in the past.

In his classic volume *After Virtue*, the moral philosopher Alisdair MacIntyre (1984) argues that narrative is the key to understanding human action and identity. The social psychologist Dan McAdams takes a similar tack in his analysis of how people interpret their lives through the "stories we live by" (1993). And drawing on a range of disciplines to lay the foundations for a new cultural psychology, Jerome Bruner (1990) argues for the need to understand the "storied realities" that shape humans across history, society, and the lifespan. These authors' claims reflect a general concern in the humanities and social sciences with what narrative can tell us about individual and social identity, and as identity becomes more of an issue in Process Organization Studies (PROS) one can expect it to move front and center in this field as well.

This concern with narrative has been part of the human sciences since Aristotle and is reflected in contemporary statements such as MacIntyre's that "man is in his actions and practice, as well as in his fictions, essentially

Narrative Tools and the Construction of Identity

a story-telling animal" (1984: 216). In MacIntyre's case, this leads to the conclusion that:

> I can only answer the question 'What am I to do?' if I can answer the prior question 'Of what story or stories do I find myself a part?' We enter human society, that is, with one or more imputed characters—roles into which we have been drafted—and we have to learn what they are in order to be able to understand how others respond to us and how our responses to them are apt to be construed. (1984: 216)

MacIntyre's comments are interesting not only for what they say about the importance of narratives but also about their source. Rather than taking individuals to be the creators of their own stories, he emphasizes that the stories of which "I find myself a part" exist before our appearance in human society. Similarly, Bruner argues that culture is "already out there" before each of us arrives on the scene. It is worth highlighting such observations because they stand in opposition to Northrup Frye's image (1957) of the "copyright age" of modern individualism in which the stories that are used to make sense of the world are taken to be products of our individual creative imagination—and hence deserving of special status as intellectual property. It is precisely in order to counter such assumptions that MacIntyre, Bruner, and others emphasize the power of existing cultural resources, especially narratives, to shape our thinking and speaking.

To be sure, we customize the stories provided by our sociocultural setting for our own purposes, but as MacIntyre see it "the key question for men is not about their own authorship." Instead:

> It is through hearing stories about wicked stepmothers, lost children, good but misguided kings, wolves that suckle twin boys, youngest sons who receive no inheritance but must make their own way in the world and eldest sons who waste their inheritance on riotous living and go into exile to live with the swine, that children learn or mislearn both what a child and what a parent is, what the cast of characters may be in the drama into which they have been born and what the ways of the world are... Hence there is no way to give us an understanding of any society, including our own, except through the stock of stories which constitute its initial dramatic resources. (1984: 216)

Turning to collective identity, this focus on narrative raises questions about how stories can be shared by members of a group. Rather than focusing on how an individual employs narratives, the emphasis switches to how members of a group use a shared cultural resource. In addition to serving as "cultural tools" (Wertsch, 1998) for interpreting the world in such cases, the use of narratives by members of a group serves to create and reinforce collective identity. Just as we become members of a language community by sharing a natural language such as Russian, English, or Thai, we become members of what Eviatar Zerubavel (2003) calls "mnemonic communities" by using shared narrative tools to talk about a common past.

Mnemonic communities may be associated with corporations, professional organizations (e.g., the mnemonic community that has emerged around PROS International Symposium meetings), families, and other groups. In many cases, these are what Benedict Anderson (1991) has called "imagined communities" whose boundaries extend beyond the range of personal acquaintance and exist because they are imagined, and not because a group actually meets in one place or is based on personal ties. The most significant project in imagined and mnemonic community building in the modern era has been the nation-state. Every modern state devotes massive resources to promulgating an official national narrative in an effort to ensure national identity and loyalty, and this provides an ideal setting for the study of narrative tools and their impact on identity. To pursue these issues I turn to an illustration from Russia.

6.1 The Russian national narrative and mnemonic community

As is the case with other countries, Russia's national narrative comes into especially sharp focus when juxtaposed with that of other mnemonic communities, and in this vein I shall outline a mnemonic conflict between Russia and one of its neighbors, Estonia. With the breakup of the Soviet Union in 1991, Estonia regained its independence, but the ensuing two decades have not liberated it fully from an ongoing struggle with Russia over how the past should be remembered. Indeed, Russia and Estonia sometimes appear to be caught in a long-term "mnemonic standoff" (Wertsch, 2008*b*).

During the years that Estonia was a republic of the USSR, Soviet authorities exerted heavy-handed control over memory and history. Public differences over accounts of the past were suppressed as part of the attempt to forge a homogeneous Soviet citizenry and encourage people to forget that they were members of Ukrainian, Estonian, or other national groups. From this Soviet perspective, national identity was, or at least should have been, melting away as the socialist project created the "new Soviet man," or even the new species satirically known as "*Homo Sovieticus*" (Zinovyev, 1986). In contrast, the post-Soviet period has seen the reemergence of strong national identity projects, which are precisely what have given rise to today's mnemonic standoff between Russia and Estonia.

Narrative Tools and the Construction of Identity

The dispute in this case has taken many forms, but came into particularly sharp focus in events surrounding the "Bronze Soldier" statue in Tallinn, the capital city of Estonia. Erected in 1947 to commemorate the Red Army's arrival in 1944, the Bronze Soldier is something of a sacred site for Russians because it points to the most glorious chapter of their twentieth century history: the victory over German fascism. The official name of the Bronze Soldier statue is "Monument to the Liberators of Tallinn" (Monument osvoboditelyam Tallinna), and for Russians it reflected the larger story of how the Soviet army saved the USSR—indeed the entire world from fascism by expelling the German invaders from its homeland and liberating the countries of Europe. In contrast to this Russian interpretation, many ethnic Estonians view the Bronze Soldier as a symbol of Soviet occupation and oppression. While Russians sometimes use the affectionate nickname "Sasha" when speaking of the statue, its underground name for many Estonians during the Soviet period was the "unknown rapist," suggesting the depth of the mnemonic standoff in this case.

The Bronze Soldier stood in a small park in the center of Tallinn and was a site of Russian–Estonian tensions, especially on May 9th of each year, the "Day of Victory" (Den' Pobedy) that marks the end of the "Great Fatherland War" in 1945. For Russians, this remains the most important national holiday of the year, celebrated not only in Moscow but also in other former Soviet republics. In 1998, I was visiting Estonia on the Day of Victory and went to the park of the Bronze Soldier, where I found a crowd of people milling about on an otherwise very quiet Saturday morning. They had decorated the grounds with hundreds of freshly cut flowers placed in the earth with the help of a small hand tool. The crowd was made up of people of all ages, including families, and virtually everyone was an ethnic Russian, something that was not representative of the population of Estonia more generally with its one million ethnic Estonians and about 300,000 Russians. I was later told by Estonians that "no Estonian would go to the park on that day,"[1] calling further attention to the gulf separating the Russian and Estonian mnemonic communities.

When I arrived at the park, no organized ceremony going on, and I had the opportunity to speak with several individuals and groups about what was happening and why they were there. Their mood ranged from reflective and somber, even emotional in some cases, to the more celebratory tone I found among a few men who had started their day with vodka. The people gathered around the statue recognized me as an outsider, not so much because of my appearance, but because of my accented Russian, and in some cases this gave rise to curiosity and appreciation for my taking an interest in the event, but in others it led to suspicion and even the suggestion by a group surrounding one talkative man that he should cut short his conversation with me and leave because I might be a spy.

There were two basic interpretations of the event at the memorial site that I encountered that day, both of which reflected the mnemonic stand-off between the Russian and Estonian communities. The first was overtly nationalist and spoke of Russian resentment toward ethnic Estonians. In this vein, a middle-aged Russian man told me, "We liberated them [the Estonians] from fascism, but they never appreciated the sacrifices we made. Why do they want to oppress us now? What right do they have to tell us that we are not citizens of this country?" In the same vein, a Russian woman at the park with her ten-year-old daughter said, "I am here to teach her about the sacrifice her grandfather made. This is important to us because they refuse to recognize it here in Estonia." Such comments reflected broader concerns of the time by Russians about newly imposed requirements to pass an Estonian language test and take other steps to gain full citizenship in the country, requirements that were the object of a great deal of resentment on their part but defended by Estonian authorities as standard procedures followed in other countries like the United States.

The second interpretation I heard in the park that day was a strong denial that the Bronze Solider had anything to do with nationalism or national identity, coupled with an insistence that people were there instead to reflect on the universal human values involved in the victory over fascism. In this vein, a middle-aged man named Volodya approached me and told me that what I was observing "is about universal human suffering and a victory for *all* the people of the world over the evil of fascism." He went on to assert—quite forcefully—that "People everywhere in the world should join us in commemorating those who suffered and those who died in smashing the hitlerite fascist forces. This is a purely humanist concern, not a nationalist one. Who can be against such a commemoration?"

Judging from the vigorous nodding of people who had surrounded us, Volodya's interpretation had a great deal of support in this group. What was perhaps most striking was the vehemence with which he made his assertion, something that clearly reflected a strongly felt need to respond to what he and the others saw as a misinterpretation—and a distasteful one at that. In this sense, Volodya's statement was a "dialogic" utterance of the sort one often finds in discussions of national narratives (Wertsch, 2002). Along with using language in its referential function to identify and describe events from the past, discussions of national identity such as his often include statements designed to respond to what other mnemonic communities have said or might be anticipated to say. Indeed, in some cases it seems that speakers are more intent on asserting that what others say was *not* the case as they are concerned with reporting what happened. As a result, utterances such as Volodya's can be fully understood only by knowing the alternative accounts of the past that provide the foil or the other voice in what Mikhail Mikhailovich Bakhtin (1984) called the "hidden dialogiality" that shapes what is said. The account to which Volodya was responding in this case was a story of Soviet and Russian occupation that stood in stark contrast to the Russian account of liberating Estonia.

This story of occupation, which is an essential item in the stock of stories of the Estonian mnemonic community, focused on the violence and oppression that came in the wake of the Soviet occupation. These stories guided perceptions to such a degree that members of the Estonian mnemonic community were able to find evidence for their beliefs in the Bronze Soldier itself, a monument designed and constructed under Soviet supervision (shown in Figure 6.1). Instead of an image of triumph over fascism and a site of memory for the Soviet soldiers who liberated Estonia, in their view the sculptor produced a figure who was pensive, if not depressed about the fate of his nation. This stands in opposition to the Russian mnemonic community, which was able to look at the same statue and see the reflection of suffering and sacrifice of the liberators of Estonia in 1944.

The tension between the two mnemonic communities that I witnessed on May 9, 1998, continued to simmer over the next several years and exploded in April 2007 when open confrontation broke out over the Bronze Soldier. This was sparked by the decision of Estonian authorities to move the statue from a small park in the center of Tallinn to a military cemetery on the city's edge, and it took the form of two nights of rioting. These riots resulted in the death of one young man (an ethnic Russian), 100 injured, including 13 police officers, and 1000 arrests. As reported in the Estonian media, almost all of the rioters were "Russian speaking youth," that is, members of the Russian mnemonic community. Disturbances of this sort are unheard of in Estonia's quiet and orderly society, and most observers, both inside and outside the country, were surprised by the scale and passion of the outburst.

In months leading up to April 2007, the memorial setting had become the site of a growing number of commemorative events such as field trips for children from Russian regions of Estonia. On some occasions, these children carried red flags and portraits of Stalin, acts viewed by Estonians as provocative displays of Russian nationalism and nostalgia for the days of great power status. In this context, Estonian politicians and authorities

Figure 6.1 The Bronze Soldier in the Tallinn Military Cemetery

decided to move the statue out of the center of the city, and the riots broke out when work on this project began. In addition to dismantling and moving the statue, workers disinterred the remains of the thirteen soldiers buried in the surrounding park and either re-interred them in the Tallinn Military Cemetery or turned them over to families in Russia who requested that they be buried elsewhere.

The response by Russians to moving the Bronze Soldier was pronounced and occurred not only within, but beyond the boundaries of Estonia. In a speech in Moscow's Red Square on May 9th following the April turmoil, Russian president Vladimir Putin (2007) pointedly referred to the Tallinn events as he intoned, "Those...who desecrate monuments to war heroes offend their own people and sow discord and new distrust between states

Narrative Tools and the Construction of Identity

and people." And on that same day a massive cyber attack from computers in Russia reached its peak and almost shut down government and banking services in "E-stonia," one of the most highly wired countries in the world. Russian anger continued in the months that followed. In July, the nationalist youth group "Nashi" (Ours) held a large rally in Moscow to commemorate the death of the twenty-year-old Russian who had been killed in the April riots in Tallinn. And an even more extremist Russian religious group, Union of Orthodox Citizens, called this young man "a hero of Russia" who died defending the memorial in Tallinn "in a war between the Orthodox 'Third Rome' [Moscow] and the occult Nazi 'Third Reich.'"[2]

And the gulf between Russian and Estonian communities continued to linger long after the April disturbances. The riots appear to have reinforced the mnemonic standoff between these communities as they went about their everyday life. In December of 2007, for example, I was walking down the street in Tallinn with a young Estonian friend, and he told me it was hard not to look at people differently than he had earlier and wonder whether they shared his or the Russian perspective on the Bronze Soldier. An email he wrote a few weeks later included additional reflections.

> After the "April events" that took place here in Tallinn and other places in Estonia, a number of changes have occurred in the behavior and perception of people, both on an individual level as well as in the society at large. For instance, I have caught myself looking at people in the street and trying to guess the person's nationality. Since the majority of those involved in the events of April were Russian-speakers, in many cases even carrying a Russian passport, such guessing ultimately boils down to deciding whether the person is Russian or not. No doubt, these phenomena, as well as their timing, are intimately associated with guessing the person's potential for participating in a street riot, for committing a criminal act, or smashing a window, under the "right" circumstances as those in April.
>
> The act of guessing the nationality of people in an everyday context might be a sign of increased social and nationalistic tensions in the population. Although the accuracy of a guess is by definition imperfect, by noticing and reading certain signs and details e.g. clothing, make-up, facial characteristics, stature, and language, and when triggered by recent riots and acts of street violence performed by a homogenous group of people, even a decent person might be led to arrive at a state of mind that gives rise to an unwelcome thought when someone passes you on the street. You might think: "I'm sure that guy was Russian. Someone should arrest him before next April..."

In reflecting on the April riots, one of the most striking facts is how quickly and forcefully the Russian and Estonian mnemonic communities surfaced

Constructing Identity in and around Organizations

and "circled the wagons" and how heated the face-off became. People who had been functioning as undifferentiated citizens as they went about their everyday life suddenly became passionately committed to being members of one or the other distinct group. To be sure, precipitating events were an impetus, but in order for these events to have their incendiary impact they had to occur within a setting defined by a preexisting set of narratives. This is not to say that the narrative tools involved mechanistically determined the thoughts and actions of the groups involved. There were many individuals on both sides of this mnemonic standoff who did not actively participate in the events of 2007; indeed, most ethnic Russians and almost no ethnic Estonians were involved in the public protests at all. But the narrative resources in this case clearly laid the groundwork for mobilizing large segments of the two mnemonic communities and for shaping the views of others.

Before turning to how these narrative tools had their impact at a time of conflict, it is worth reflecting on how they function in more normal and peaceful times, and the first point to make in that regard is that they do not operate at the forefront of consciousness in everyday life. People do not normally wake up in the morning reflecting on their national narrative. Instead, a version of what Michael Billig (1995) has termed "banal nationalism" seems to be the rule. In Billig's account, we usually live in settings where national flags go unnoticed as they adorn government buildings, children mindlessly recite the Pledge of Allegiance at the beginning of their school day in US classrooms, and people in other settings go about their daily lives largely unmindful of national narratives and identity.

However, contexts do exist in which national narratives and identities emerge as sites of active reflection, two of the most important being educational settings, broadly defined (e.g., history instruction, national holidays, museums), and episodes of political mobilization such as the one surrounding the Bronze Soldier. History textbooks, for example, appear at first glance to be part of banal nationalism if one considers claims about how boring history instruction can be. But as Nash et al. (1997) have outlined in their account of the debate over setting national standards for instruction, "history wars" can occasionally erupt on this front—and not only in the United States. Indeed, one of the major undertakings in all the states that emerged with the breakup of the USSR was the revision of history textbooks used in schools, and these efforts also gave rise to major controversy, not least in Russia (Wertsch, 2002).

New history museums also sprang up with the collapse of the Soviet Union, and old ones were closed or drastically revamped around strikingly new narrative lines. In Tallinn, the Museum of Occupations was built in a strategic location right across the small park that housed the Bronze Soldier during its last years of being located there. This museum presented a narrative that begins with the independence Estonia enjoyed for two decades before being illegally and forcibly annexed by Stalin in 1940 under the secret protocols of the Molotov–Ribbentrop Pact. Technically, the museum was dedicated to "occupations" rather than a single occupation as it covers German as well as Soviet occupation, but the latter (where "Soviet" is often a code word for Russian) is the focus of the vast majority of the exhibit.

Not surprisingly, the Russian mnemonic community objected to the construction and placement of this museum. For members of this community, it is simply wrong—indeed repugnant—to suggest that 1944 was the beginning of oppression directed at Estonians. While many Russians might agree that oppression had been part of Soviet life, they also argue that this was not directed toward—or perpetrated by—any national group in particular. In this view, *all* citizens of the USSR had been victims of Soviet authorities; Estonians suffered, but so did Russians and members of all other groups in the USSR. Furthermore, from this perspective, Estonians should be grateful for having been liberated in 1944 from the much more brutal Nazi oppressors. More generally, the Russian mnemonic community often complained that the accomplishments of the Soviet period were being downplayed or dismissed in order to make room for what they viewed as overstated and sometimes bogus claims about the suffering and heroism of Estonia.

In sum, the events surrounding the Bronze Soldier in 2007 provide a good example of how national narratives become objects of active reflection in the context of political mobilization. Narrative resources that had provided the underpinnings of banal nationalism quickly became powerful sites of unification around which disparate groups could be mobilized in emotional forms of collective action. Such cases raise more general questions about the narrative tools that are involved, and answering them requires a consideration of both cognitive and emotional dimensions of these tools. From a cognitive perspective, they must be sufficiently simple and general that they are accessible to a wide range of people who otherwise share little in the way of detailed knowledge about specific events from the past. And from an emotional perspective, narrative tools must provide a way for members of a mnemonic community not just to know a common story line but to identify with it and be emotionally committed to it. This commitment is often reflected in the fact that a challenge to the truth of one's national narrative is taken to be a personal challenge or even an affront to oneself.

6.2 Cognitive dimensions of national narratives: Specific narratives and narrative templates

Claims about the role of narratives in the construction of national identity beg the question of what we have in mind when speaking of narratives, narrative tools, and the like. Of particular interest is how much concrete information is included in the narratives, an issue related to what Daniel Schacter and his colleagues have called "specificity" in memory. Was the mnemonic standoff over the Bronze Soldier about specific details of the events in 1944 or did it concern something more general? Given that most Russians knew very little about what happened when the Red Army arrived in Tallinn in 1944, it was almost certainly not the former. Was the dispute over concrete details of the Soviet victory over fascism in World War II? This is also unlikely as young Russians often demonstrate a surprising lack of knowledge of the details of the central role that the USSR played in this global conflict (Wertsch, 2002).

On balance, there is little to suggest that the Russian reaction to moving the Bronze Soldier was based on knowledge of a detailed a story about events some half century earlier. And yet large numbers of people both within and outside of Estonia were able to mobilize around some kind of common representation about what happened. It is a commonplace that mass movements rely on simple ideas or images, but how does this apply to national narratives? In cases like the Bronze Solider dispute, what kind of narrative could operate in such a "big tent" way that allows people with different levels of knowledge and from different backgrounds to coalesce so forcefully into a single mnemonic community?

In order to address such questions, it is useful to distinguish between two levels of narrative analysis, one having to do with "specific narratives" and the other with "narrative templates" (Wertsch, 2002). Specific narratives include information about particular characters, settings, and actions such as the arrival of the Red Army in Tallinn on September 22, 1944, or the Battle of the Kursk salient in the summer of 1943. In contrast, narrative templates are more generalized and schematic structures that do not include information about concrete settings, actors, and dates. They are a sort of cookie cutter plots that can be used as cognitive resources for generating multiple specific narratives about settings, actors, and events.

The notion of a narrative template grows out of ideas that have long been part of the humanities and social sciences. Among its predecessors are the ideas of Vladimir Propp (1968) on the textual "functions" that he culled out of an analysis of hundreds of folk tales and the notion of "schema" in the

Narrative Tools and the Construction of Identity

psychology of remembering as outlined by Frederic Bartlett (1932). Narrative templates are the cultural tools that mediate what can be termed "deep collective memory." This form of memory is deep both in the sense that it is largely inaccessible to conscious reflection and in the sense that members of a collective tend to have deep emotional attachment to the narrative templates that mediate it.

The very notion of a template entails that multiple copies in the form of specific narratives are involved and suggests that a general story line is used repeatedly to interpret or emplot events. In some cases, the working of a narrative template is suggested by the very appellation of events. In the Russian mnemonic community, for example, it is striking that name of the massive conflict of 1941–5, the "Great Fatherland War" (Velikaya Otechestvennaya voina), echoes the "Fatherland War" (Otechestvennaya voina) of a century and a half earlier, or what is called the Napoleonic War of 1812 in the West. The parallels between the two events become all the more apparent when one considers that the expression "Hitler as a second Napoleon" has long enjoyed widespread usage in the Russian mnemonic community. All this suggests that same basic story line or template is harnessed to talk about different specific events.

The narrative template at issue in the Russian case underlies specific narratives about a much longer list of events than these two invasions of the country. Consider, for example, the classic 1938 film "Alexander Nevsky" in which the Soviet director Sergei Eisenstein suggested that the looming danger from fascist Germany could be viewed through a lens from the thirteenth century. In his movie, invading Teutonic knights were referred to as "the German" (nemets) and depicted as wearing helmets that came straight from the uniform of the invaders in the impending conflagration in 1941. The list of parallels goes on, with Russians sometimes speaking of the conquests and invasions by numerous foreign enemies, including Tatars, Germans, Swedes, Poles, Turks, and Germans again.

What the specific narratives of these events have in common for the Russian mnemonic community is what can be called the "Expulsion of Alien Enemies" narrative template, which includes the following elements:

1. An "initial situation" in which Russia is peaceful and not interfering with others;
2. "Trouble," in which an alien enemy viciously attacks Russia without provocation;
3. Russia nearly loses everything in total defeat as it suffers from the enemy's attempts to destroy it as a civilization;

4. Through heroism and exceptionalism, against all odds, and acting largely alone, Russia triumphs and succeeds in expelling the alien enemy.

This narrative template provides a particular cognitive pattern of what Bartlett called the "effort after meaning" (1932: 44), a pattern that is widely understood and employed by Russians when making sense of events, both past and present. It provides a plot line for specific narratives such that they take the shape of the same story told again and again with different characters, something strongly suggested by expressions like "Hitler as the second Napoleon."

All this is not to say that the specific narratives associated with this template are simply fabricated or figments of the imagination of this mnemonic community. Russia obviously *has* suffered at the hands of foreign enemies on numerous occasions. But it is to say that the Expulsion of Alien Enemies narrative template provides a powerful interpretive framework that guides the thinking and speaking of the members of this community. It does so to such an extent that their interpretations of some events are quite surprising to those coming from other mnemonic communities. For example, it often astonishes members of other communities to hear Soviet communism described as an alien enemy, this time in the form of Western ideas that Russian people finally managed to defeat and expel. But this is precisely the line of reasoning used by Aleksandr Solzhenitsyn (1978), the Nobel prize winning author and critic of the USSR—and also the West, a man whose views have great credibility among many in the Russian mnemonic community.

The very general form of cognitive representation of the Expulsion-of-Alien-Enemies narrative template makes it a good cultural tool for creating a mnemonic community for at least two reasons. First, its simple and general plot structure makes it accessible to a wide range of people in the Russian community who might have in common little in the way of specific knowledge. For this reason, it provides a good basis for mobilizing large numbers of people. And second, because this narrative template includes so little in the way of concrete information, it is hard to challenge it on the basis of factual information. This property of nonfalsifiability means that when confronted with detailed and well-documented information that would seem to refute a narrative account of the past, members of the mnemonic community are often able to ignore or otherwise overcome such challenges (Wertsch, 2008*a*). As Rogers Smith has argued in his study of "stories of peoplehood," it seems to take massive, even traumatic counter evidence to move communities to change the basic story line about their past.

6.3 Emotional dimensions of national narratives: The "we-ness" of collective memory

Up to this point, I have emphasized the cognitive dimension of narrative templates, their generalized, schematic nature that underlies the capacity to generate multiple specific narratives. This breadth of application is sometimes so great that it would seem to extend across mnemonic communities. For example, with references to "Russia" taken out, the Expulsion-of-Alien-Enemies narrative template might appear to apply to other societies. But this is something that would strike Russians as ridiculous, if not offensive. There is obviously something that limits the possibilities for generalization, something that makes it impossible for most Russians to agree that their mnemonic community is based on the same general story as someone else's. This comes from a tendency of narrative templates that operates in opposition to their proclivity for wide applicability, a tendency toward ethnocentric particularity.

This ethnocentric particularity stems from assumptions by members of a mnemonic community that (*a*) their national narrative template applies exclusively to themselves and not to anyone else, and (*b*) the template is the one true story of their group, with no competing narrative template imaginable. These are assumptions that can obviously distinguish one mnemonic community from another, even when they seem to share general cognitive patterns for making sense of the past.

The general picture, then, is one in which narrative templates are organized around a tension between two opposing poles: a proclivity for cognitive schematization and generality, on the one hand, and a tendency toward ethnocentric particularity, indeed "ethnocentric narcissism" (Assmann, 2007), on the other. The latter is what lies behind oft encountered claims about how "Our nation's history is unlike that of any other country" and results in many nations' assertions that they are not only unique, but somehow "more unique" than anyone else. It also often lies behind claims about having a special, even messianic mission for humankind, claims that often are associated with a tendency to reject the legitimacy of others' perspectives and national narratives. Given this context, the idea that there might be legitimate alternatives to a group's story, especially alternatives suggested by someone outside the group, is likely to be dismissed as heresy.

The tendency toward ethnocentric narcissism and the emotional commitments that come with it is obviously powerful, and sometimes quite dangerous, yet we have little understanding of how it operates. What is it about national narratives and the collective memory they support that give rise to this? One source of insight can be found by considering the "me-ness" of individual memory (Kihlstrom, 1997) and the parallels that might be found in the "we-ness" of collective memory. The roots of "me-ness" go back more than a century to an argument William James (1890) made in *The Principles of Psychology* about how an act of memory "requires more than mere dating of a fact in the past. It must be dated in *my* past... I must think that I directly experienced its occurrence" (650). The kind of complex dual representation that takes into account both the past and the individual's relation to the past was such that James concluded that memory is not a single psychological faculty like attention or conception. Instead:

> A general feeling of the past direction in time, ... a particular date conceived as lying along that direction, and defined by its name or phenomenal contents, an event imagined as located therein, and owned as part of my experience—such are the elements of every act of memory... What memory goes with is... a very complex representation, that of the fact to be recalled *plus* its associates, the whole forming one 'object'... known in one integral pulse of consciousness. (James, 1890: 650–1)

The importance of what James termed the peculiar "feeling relation" between self and past event is one that continues to surface in the psychology of memory today. Perhaps the most important contemporary reflection of the insight raised by James is in Endel Tulving's classic idea (1984) of "episodic memory," which presupposes a notion of self. Tulving's description of episodic memory as mental time travel entails the notion that this travel is undertaken by one and the same self, thereby putting me-ness squarely in the picture.

Insights by figures such as James, Tulving, and Kihlstrom play a central role in the study of memory in the individual, but invoking them in an analysis of collective phenomena seems to break one of the cardinal rules of memory studies against drawing unmotivated parallels between individual and collective processes. Such loose metaphors are precisely what Bartlett warned against when he resisted the idea of memory *of* the group, a vague notion pointing to some sort of ephemeral group mind or consciousness. This suggests the need for great caution when thinking about how observations by psychologists about me-ness might apply to mnemonic communities.

But there is reason for making such a connection in this case, stemming from a sort of projection employed by members of a collective when remembering their group's past. Indeed, it may be difficult to account for the highly emotional nature of collective memory without recognizing this projection. To some extent the gulf that separated the Russian and Estonian mnemonic communities over the Bronze Soldier derives from the nonfalsifiability of narrative templates outlined earlier. This can make it difficult for members of a mnemonic community to accept that what others take to be conflicting evidence presents a fundamental challenge to a national narrative they have long accepted. But the depth of such differences over national narratives often suggests emotional defensiveness that goes further and includes an involvement of self and a deep emotional attachment to a national narrative.

What seems to be particularly difficult to account for in such cases is that the emotions are tied to events that occurred well before people's lived experience. The young Russians who were so upset with Estonian revision of the account of the 1940s were not born until decades after the events actually occurred, raising questions such as the following: In what sense is it *their* past that haunts the present? How is *their* self involved? This is not to doubt the strong feelings that emerge when the group's account of the past was called into question. In this case, Estonians were suggesting that the arrival of Soviet forces in 1944 was an act of occupation rather than liberation, and this was taken to be deeply insulting by the young Russians who came out in the streets in 2007—as well as by the larger Russian community in Estonia and Russia. They took the Estonian questions to be an attack on their group or even on them personally.

The spontaneous and incendiary emotions involved in such cases point again to the idea that something beyond the cognitive limitations of narrative templates or instrumentally calculated self-interest is involved. That is, it suggests that a version of James's me-ness of memory lies at the heart of the feeling of personal outrage when others question the account of the past held by one's group. Specifically, it seems to be based on the moral authority and commitment associated with personal experience of a past event. In James's account, remembering involves the feeling that "I must think that I directly experienced [an event's] occurrence" (1890: 650), the implication being that to question a memory is to question one's trustworthiness in some way. Doing so in the case of an event that happened before one's lifetime may indeed involve the kind of conflation of individual and collective memory that is highly suspect in memory studies (Wertsch, 2002), but it appears to be a conflation that we have a hard time avoiding when acting as members of mnemonic communities. It involves a projection of the me-ness that is a natural and inherent part of individual memory onto the collective plane to create a sort of "we-ness."

In his account of memory in the individual, James did not go into details on the origins of me-ness or how it might be influenced by efforts of remembering. His argument was that individual memory presupposes some such notion. At the collective level, what appears to be the case is that rather than simply presupposing the existence of a well-formed community, remembering plays a role in constituting and recreating it. Remembering what "we" did or what others did to "us," is a sort of invitation to create an image of who "we" are in the first place. In contrast to analytic history, which aspires to keep the identity of the narrator distanced from narratives about the past (Wertsch, 2002), what William James called the "integral pulse of consciousness," when applied to collective memory, may not only assume but also help create and reinforce an imagined group, with all the ideas of continuity and agency that go along with it.

6.4 Conclusion

Discussions of the role of narratives in human action and identity touch on what it is to be human in the first place, and for this reason they have a timeless quality and will continue to be part of philosophy, literary analysis, psychology, history, and other disciplines in the future. With the emergence of interest in identity in PROS, it is reasonable to expect narrative to take on an increasingly important role in this field as well, and for that reason it will be useful to reflect on narrative tools in greater depth.

In doing this it will be helpful to keep a few key points in mind. First, it is important to think of narratives as cultural tools, as instruments provided by the broader sociocultural setting that are taken over by individuals to make sense of themselves and the world around them. Instead of succumbing to the temptations of the copyright age to think of narratives as products of individual imagination, it is important to keep in mind that they are a kind of off-the-shelf technology that ties us to our institutional, historical, and cultural context. Among other things, taking this stance makes it possible to occupy the kind of interdisciplinary space preferred in PROS, a space that allows the study of individual psychological forces while not losing sight of insights from other areas of the social sciences and humanities. Second, by focusing on how narratives are shared by members of a social group, it is possible to examine not only differences in collectives' interpretations of the world but also how the collectives are constituted in the first place. And third, the differences between collectives, especially mnemonic communities that emerge in this process, can be profound enough to give rise to conflict, including violent conflict.

I have outlined a case of conflict between two mnemonic communities in an attempt to understand these issues. The key to understanding the cognitive and emotional power of the national narratives at play in this case is to recognize a distinction between two levels of narrative analysis, one concerned with specific narratives and the other with narrative templates. It is only by positing the narrative templates as an underlying level of representation that we can begin to understand how mnemonic communities can be formed out of groups that otherwise appear to be quite disparate. This involves claims about simple, quite general cognitive representations that allow for such mobilization. At the same time, there is something very particularistic, if not narcissistic, about narrative templates that gives them their emotional power, and in this respect I have outlined the notion of the "we-ness" of collective memory.

The concrete case I have outlined to illustrate these claims comes from the most committed and sustained effort at creating mnemonic communities in human history, namely that associated with nations and national narratives. The lessons to be drawn from my exercise, however, are not limited to national narratives and identities. Many of the same principles and processes are involved in other groups; it seems that everyone from corporations, universities, and professional organizations to families is concerned with the narrative tools at its disposal for creating collective identity. In the years ahead, it will be up to purveyors of PROS (a collective that has its own identity narrative tools) to spell out the applications of these ideas in this field.

Notes

1. This and other quotes from this visit come from field notes I took at the time.
2. http://www.directionstoorthodoxy.org/mod/news/print.php?article_id=434

References

Anderson, B. (1991). *Imagined Communities: Reflections on the Origin and Spread of Nationalism.* London: Verso.

Assmann, J. (2007). "Cultural Memories and National Narratives: With Some Relation to the Case of Georgia," *Caucasus Context*, 3/1: 40–3.

Bakhtin, M. M. (1984). *Problems of Dostoevsky's Poetics*. Minneapolis, MN: University of Minnesota Press (ed. and trans. C. Emerson).

Bartlett, F. C. (1932). *Remembering: A Study in Experimental and Social Psychology*. Cambridge: Cambridge University Press.

Billig, M. (1995). *Banal Nationalism*. London: Sage Publications.

Bruner, J. (1990). *Acts of Meaning*. Cambridge, MA: Harvard University Press.

Frye, N. (1957). *Anatomy of Criticism: Four Essays*. Princeton, NJ: Princeton University Press.

James, W. (1890). *The Principles of Psychology*. New York: Dover.

Kihlstrom, J. F. (1997). "Consciousness and Me-ness," in J. D. Cohen and J. W. Schooler (ed), *Scientific Approaches to Consciousness*. Mahwah, NJ: Lawrence Erlbaum Associates, pp. 451–68.

MacIntyre, A. (1984). *After Virtue: A Study in Moral Philosophy*, 2nd edn. Notre Dame, IN: University of Notre Dame Press.

McAdams, D. P. (1993). *The Stories we Live by: Personal Myths and the Making of the Self*. New York, NY: W. Morrow.

Nash, G. B., Crabtree, C., and Dunn, R. E. (1997). *History on Trial: Culture Wars and the Teaching of the Past*. New York: Alfred A. Knopf.

Propp, V. (1968). *Morphology of the Folktale*. Austin, TX: University of Texas Press (translated by Laurence Scott).

Putin, V. (2007). *International Herald Tribune*. http://www.iht.com/articles/2007/05/09/news/russia.php

Schacter, D. L., Gutchess, A. H., and Kensinger, E. A. (2009). "Specificity of Memory: Implications for Individual and Collective Remembering," in P. Boyer and J. V. Wertsch (eds), *Memory in Mind and Culture*. New York: Cambridge University Press, pp. 83–111.

Smith, R. (2003). *Stories of Peoplehood: The Politics and Morals of Political Membership*. New York: Cambridge University Press.

Solzhenitsyn, A. (1978). "Text of an Address at Harvard Class Day Afternoon Exercises," Thursday, June 8, 1978. http://www.columbia.edu/cu/augustine/arch/solzhenitsyn/harvard1978.html

Tulving E (1984). "Precis of Elements of Episodic Memory." *Behavioural and Brain Sciences*, 7: 223–68.

Wertsch, J. V. (1998). *Mind as Action*. New York: Oxford University Press.

—— (2002). *Voices of Collective Remembering*. New York: Cambridge University Press.

—— (2008a). "Blank Spots in Collective Memory: A Case Study of Russia." *The Annals of the American Academy of Political and Social Science*, 617: 58–71.

—— (2008b). *A Clash of Deep Memories. Profession 2008*. New York: Modern Language Association, pp. 46–53.

Zerubavel, E. (2003). *Time Maps: Collective Memory and the Social Shape of the Past*. Chicago, IL: University of Chicago Press.

Zinovyev, A. (1986). *Homo Sovieticus*. New York: Grove/Atlantic.

7
Villains, Victims, and the Financial Crisis: Positioning Identities through Descriptions

Frank Mueller and Andrea Whittle

Abstract: This chapter draws insights from the field of Discursive Psychology (DP) to examine the identity positioning employed in the narratives surrounding the financial crisis. Existing narrative, discursive, and communicative approaches to studying identity have tended to focus on more or less explicit identity-talk, where participants produce direct accounts of themselves or others. What is less well understood is how descriptions of objects, actions, and events perform identity work. This chapter contributes by showing how DP enables us to understand how apparently "neutral" and "factual" descriptive accounts act as a form of identity positioning. We focus our analysis on the identity positions constructed during a public hearing involving senior banking executives in the United Kingdom. The analysis suggests that two competing identities, victim and villain, were constructed for the bankers in the dialogue between the witnesses (bankers) and the questioners (politicians). We argue that apparently neutral descriptions of events, such as accounts of what happened and why, can represent methods of positioning identity. We propose that a "discursive devices" approach, inspired by DP, contributes to the understanding of identity positioning by highlighting the power of micro-linguistic tools in laying out the moral landscape of the characters involved in the description. We conclude by arguing that the characters and stories surrounding the financial crisis are important because they acted to shape how the crisis was made sense of and acted upon.

7.1 Introduction

In this chapter, we examine the role of identity positioning in the process of making sense of the recent financial crisis. We examine the identity positions crafted during a public hearing in the United Kingdom that was designed to uncover "what (or who) went wrong." Our central contribution lies in showing how "discursive devices" (DDs) (Whittle et al., 2008; Mueller and Whittle, 2011)—a term drawn from the field of Discursive Psychology (DP) but also used elsewhere (e.g., Watson, 1995)—are used as linguistic building blocks in the construction of identity positions. DP views the "inner world," "psychology," and "identity" of the speaker and others (their thoughts, feelings, goals, foibles, charms, defects) as a key component of the very *business* of talk itself (Edwards, 1997: 93–5), as people try to construct a version of "what I am like" and "what they are like" in their accounts. For us, DDs are linguistic tools that are employed as part of interactional business. A DD can be a single word, such as the collective pronoun "we," or a more complex set of words, linguistic styles, metaphors, or phrases, such as the use of footing positions or rhetorical contrast. We argue that DDs are commonplace linguistic tools that people use to construct accounts of themselves and others. We use DDs analysis to examine the identity positions constructed in the cross-examination of four senior executives of banks that received state support ("bail-outs") from the UK Treasury. We show how DDs are used to portray key characters as "villains" and "victims" in the competing narratives produced by the bankers and politicians.

The chapter is structured as follows. In the next section, we substantiate our central theoretical perspective on identity positioning, focussing in particular on the role of descriptions and moral positioning. The chapter then moves on to illustrate our argument through analysis of the identity positions extracted from a publicly available transcript[1] of the Treasury Select Committee cross-examination. We frame our analysis in terms of the two different identity positions put forward by the questioners (MPs) and witnesses (bankers). The final section discusses our conclusions and the wider implications of our analysis.

7.2 Identity from a discursive psychology perspective

The idea that identity is socially constructed is now widely accepted in *Organization Studies* (Thomas and Davies, 2005; Alvesson et al., 2008; Beech, 2008). This argument has a long pedigree in sociology from the classical statements by Cooley (1902) and Goffman (1959, 1967). The field of DP has emerged in recent years as an important body of work that seeks to radically rethink the traditional categories of analysis used in psychology, including cognition and identity (te Molder and Potter, 2005). DP has been described as "one of the major contemporary theories of human action" (Harré and Stearns, 1995: 1). DP draws inspiration from, and contributes to, a wide range of fields, including socio-linguistics, social psychology, post-structuralism, the sociology of scientific knowledge, and conversational analysis (Wiggins and Potter, 2008: 74). DP is part of a wider social constructionist school of thought on identity, which views "who we are" not as something that we simply "have," as a predefined, unified, and self-contained entity (Shotter, 2010). Rather, the social constructionist tradition views identity as something that we do: something we develop through our interaction with the social world around us. Hence, we need to study this inter-subjective, relational, back-and-forth nature of social interaction (Shotter, 2010): what Gergen (2010) calls "confluence." Identity is therefore a fragmented, fluid and fragile construct that we continually have to *work upon* in the flow of social interaction.

The concept of identity *work* helps us to understand how people engage in ongoing processes of "forming, repairing, maintaining, strengthening or revising the [identity] constructions that are productive of a precarious sense of coherence and distinctiveness" (Alvesson and Willmott, 2002: 626). According to Langley and Tsoukas (2010: 14), the word *work* is important because it brings a more dynamic processual lens on apparently static concepts. Kenneth Gergen has made ongoing contributions toward a relational, processual, and discursive understanding of identity (e.g., Gergen, 2010). For us, DP is a way to *practice* a process orientation (Shotter, 2010). DP's value, we propose, lies in its ability to map the micro-linguistic moves through which this identity work is undertaken. Hence, DP is compatible with, and contributes to, a wider body of social constructionist research that includes communication research (e.g., Cooren, 2000; Putnam and Nicotera, 2009), discourse analysis (e.g., Phillips and Hardy, 2002), and (some) identity research (e.g., Alvesson and Willmott, 2002). However, DP differs in subtle but important ways from some approaches in these fields— we explore these differences in more detail in the conclusion. In this section, we focus on laying out the central tenets of the DP perspective on identity.

First, DP states that identity should be studied *situationally* and *socially*. This means that the analyst should pay attention to the identity-claims and counterclaims that are employed in everyday talk. For example, in the case of the cross-examination of bankers in this study, their class background, or even the fact that they are bankers is a relevant identity only *if it is made relevant* (either explicitly or implicitly) in talk and/or interaction. DP therefore rejects the "essentialist" or "realist" approaches to identity (Widdicombe, 1998b: 194) typical of structuralist–functionalist (Parsons, 1964) or class-based (Goldthorpe, 1980) approaches. Our focus is in line with Conversation Analysis and Discursive Psychology on "whether, when, and how identities are used" (Widdicombe, 1998b: 195). From this perspective, identity can be treated as a "membership category" (Widdicombe, 1998a: 52): it is a category that can be used in talk for differentiating oneself from others.

Second, DP rejects the idea that social identity categories—such as race, gender, or class—should be used by social scientists to *explain* social behavior. The focus is upon how identity is deployed by members themselves, and not on how identity can be deployed as an explanatory variable used by social scientists (e.g., Greatbatch and Dingwall, 1998: 121–2). DP rejects the idea that analysts should try to establish "whether someone truly "had" this or that identity category, or what "having" that identity made them do or feel" (Antaki and Widdicombe, 1998: 2). For example, DP asks: how identity categories (such as "being a woman" or "being a man") are used by members of a social group (Benwell and Stokoe, 2006: 57)? What sort of social meaning, action, or order does this usage (i.e., identifying oneself using a gender category) achieve? For DP, identities such as age, parental and marital status, nationality, gender, and so on are not necessarily and always a defining aspect of one's identity but instead depend on what is deemed situationally relevant by members themselves. "Indeed, rather than starting with a predefined or conventional list of such items, what we need to do is find whatever it is that participants do invoke, and how they use it" (Edwards, 1998: 20). DP therefore rejects approaches that are concerned with identity as a central and enduring characteristic (e.g., Pratt and Foreman, 2000). Instead, DP focuses on "how identity categories crop up, how they are "oriented to" or noticed by speakers, and what the consequences are for the unfolding interaction" (Benwell and Stokoe, 2006: 8). Hence, DP focuses on the "fluidity, flexibility and variability" of identity positions (Wetherell and Potter, 1992: 79), as they are used in different situations to perform different actions.

Third, DP is sensitive to the *unfolding* and *ongoing* process through which identities are negotiated within interaction. Talk-in-interaction is a primary site for the construction of identities, making identity a distributed and fragmented process (Gergen, 1992; Alvesson and Sveningsson, 2003).

Positioning Identities through Descriptions

"Who we are" is understood as "accomplished, disputed, ascribed, resisted, managed and negotiated in discourse" (Benwell and Stokoe, 2006: 4). Identity claims and positions can always be altered or refined during the interaction process (Goffman, 1967). As a result, the identities of the characters involved can be contested and recast over time (Czarniawska, 1997). For example, Hutchby and Wooffitt (1998: 179–85) argue that identity labels such as "punk," "skinhead," "goth," and "rocker" can be met with a response that questions the very category itself (e.g., "Just because I dress like this does not make me any different to anyone else"). Whether or not a person identifies oneself (or allows others to identify him or her) according to these labels is not an outcome of any kind of cognitive correlation between the category itself and the person's own self-concept (Antaki and Widdicombe, 1998: 17). Rather, identity positions are created as part of interactional methods for displaying identity to others that is relevant to a specific interaction in hand (ibid.).

Fourth, DP emphasizes the *social actions* that can be performed by enacting certain identity positions. DP enables us to appreciate "the great range of jobs that identities are used for: they may be invoked as footings for the conduct of business, to allocate blame and responsibility, to accuse and defend, to mobilize other identities, and so on" (Widdicombe, 1998b: 191). Hence, DP is often referred to as an *action-oriented* perspective (Edwards and Potter, 1992: 2). Wetherell and Potter's study (1992) offers a good example of the kind of social (and ideological) actions performed by identity positions. The interviewees in their study of racist discourse in New Zealand differentiated between "average Māoris," "Māoris who are friends," "Māoris who can be invited into the house," "Europeans," "the Māori people," and "extremists" (p. 77). These identity positions, Wetherell and Potter suggest, are not simply the outcome of cognitive patterns of in-group and out-group categorization. Rather, they are used in flexible and variable ways to perform certain social actions, such as justifying racist government policies while also presenting oneself as not racist.

Fifth, DP enables the analyst to focus on potential inconsistencies in a person's identity positioning. For DP, viewing identity as always "in process" means that it is always precarious and therefore has the potential for inconsistency and contradiction. Contradiction is not problematic for DP because it rejects the idea of an essential, humanistic self. For example, Reynolds and Wetherell's study (2003) of what "being single" meant for middle-aged women found that accounts were "highly variable," "distributed and multiple" and littered with "contradictions and inconsistencies" (p. 493). They point to the ongoing and situation-specific

Constructing Identity in and around Organizations

Table 7.1 Core tenets of the DP perspective on identity

Central tenet of DP perspective	Implications for studying identity in (and of) organizations
Identity should be studied as part of social situations.	Identity is not something that we simply "bring to" interactions, it is something that we build and refine during social interaction. For example, what type of person we are seen as could change when we are faced with counter-narratives about "who we are" told during organizational storytelling.
Identity categories should not be used to *explain* behavior or outcomes—the focus should instead be on how, when, and to what effect identity categories are invoked.	Identity is not something that analysts need to know about because it explains something else. For example, knowing whether a speaker is a "woman" or "man," or "manager," or "employee," is not used to explain why they are behaving a particular way, in a cause-and-effect manner. Instead, the analyst focuses on which identities are being made relevant *by the participants themselves*. For example, if two people orient toward each other as "managers" or as "mates," it is likely to make a difference to the interaction and meaning-making.
Identity should be understood as an ongoing, unfolding process.	Identity is not a fixed "essence," rather it changes as we interact with others. For example, we may need to refine or defend our presentation of self if it comes up against challenges or counter-constructions in workplace conversations.
Identity-talk acts as a form of social action—it *does* things.	Claims to having a particular identity make a difference because they perform social actions. For example, if someone says "As your manager I would like you to do this," the identity category "manager" performs the action of *instructing* through appealing to higher authority, whereas "As your friend . . . ." acts as a form of *persuasion* through appeal to the obligations of friendship.
Identity positions or claims can be flexible, varying according to the social and interactional context, including the possibility of contradiction.	Identity is not a fixed entity that we bring to situations, but can vary according to different situations. For example, a speaker could emphasize being a woman in one context, but emphasize her role as a manager in another encounter. Within the same stretch of interaction (e.g., research interview) contradictory identity positions could be claimed, as participants use different repertoires to present themselves.
Apparently "factual" descriptions can also perform identity work.	Descriptions of the "world out there" are material for studying identity because they act to present the speaker in particular ways. For example, a speaker who appeals to descriptions of the economic context or changing customer preferences to justify the need for organizational change also presents oneself as someone who is neutral and rational, without a personal "axe to grind" or vested interest in the change (Mueller and Whittle, 2011).

challenge of combining or switching between two identity positions, such as "lonely spinster" (as per the interpretative repertoire of singleness involving a personal deficit) and the position of "having chosen to be single" (as per the interpretative repertoire of independence and choice) (Reynolds et al., 2007: 348). Other studies have highlighted how agents navigate potential inconsistencies. McKinlay and Dunnett (1998) analyzed how gunowners negotiated between two potentially contradictory identity positions: being an average citizen who is like everyone else but also being a gunowner who, in principle, is willing to use deadly force against a potential threat (ibid.: 42, 44, 46). According to Van Den Berg (2003), contradiction is an essential part of constructing a convincing argument, including arguments about the person's identity. Thus, DP focuses on how potential inconsistencies are managed in specific situations and interactions.

Sixth and finally, DP expands the remit of identity research by examining how apparently "neutral" descriptions of events bring about certain identity positions for the speaker and those spoken about. Given the importance of this final aspect for the purposes of this chapter, we discuss it in more detail in the following section. For summary purposes, we have outlined the six core tenets of the DP perspective on identity in Table 7.1.

7.2.1 Descriptions as identity discourse

In this section, we focus in more detail on the role of factual discourse because it is the central focus of our chapter. The way in which the "facts of the matter" get worked up in discourse does not serve only to establish "what happened." To "describe events" does not just mean recalling certain memories, making certain connections, and putting forward certain explanations. Descriptions are also implicated in the work of establishing *identities*: including the dispositions, attitudes, motives, temperament, and values of those involved. For example, in one of Sacks' cases cited by Edwards (1997: 96–7), a man's call to a helpline is analyzed with regard to suspicion of violence having been used against his wife (the wife's sister had called the police). The husband uses descriptions like "moved her out of the way" and "shoved her" but denies "smacking her" (Edwards, 1997: 96–7), in order to position himself as a "non-violent" person.

Public hearings, such as the one analyzed in this chapter, are classic situations for eliciting the production of identity positions through descriptions. When witnesses are asked "what happened?," they attend not only to the events themselves but also to their role (or lack thereof) in the events described (Lynch and Bogen, 1996). John Dean's testimony to the

Watergate inquiry (Edwards and Potter, 1992: chs. 2 and 3) demonstrates the way discourse is used by Dean to present himself as a *modest, honest,* and *reliable* character, not seeking to take credit for the work of others, or seeking to deflect blame onto others. The "truthfulness" of his account was carefully worked up with reference to the *type of person* he is: his traits, attributes, attitudes, judgments, and so on (Edwards and Potter, 1992: 42). Oliver North's testimony to the Iran-Contra hearings presents himself as the type of person who is *modest* enough to concede the fallibility of his memories, *concerned* with producing an accurate account, and a *cooperative* witness who is trying hard to provide reliable information (Lynch and Bogen, 1996: ch. 1). These identity positions matter not only for "face saving" (cf. Goffman, 1959) on the part of the speaker. More than this, identity positioning is also crucial for establishing the perceived *integrity* of the witness and the perceived *reliability* of the testimony. These in turn constitute what is regarded as "the facts of the matter" and "the truth about what really happened." We are likely to "accept or reject the witness's testimony on the basis of surface or face-value assessments of credibility and plausibility" (Lynch and Bogen, 1996: 26). How, then, did North accomplish his "stunning role reversal from the accused to the accuser" (p. 31)? One answer is to point to his "justificatory counter-narrative" (p. 50) where values (or imperatives) of "system and accountability" implying respect for the Committee's work are trumped by *higher imperatives* of "secrecy, sovereignty, and adventurism" (e.g., p. 55, 89). The integrity of North's character and the reliability of his testimony rested upon his positioning himself as a man of higher values, driven by higher goals of protecting lives and protecting the president from political damage.

Gephart's study (1993) focussed on the sensemaking processes during a public hearing conducted in 1985 by the Canadian federal government energy board following a 1985 pipeline accident. Gephart found that "blaming was not an institutionally appropriate process in the focal inquiry, and this may also be the case in other institutional settings." He argues that different and even contradictory interpretations of the same event can coexist, which serve to criticize reified perspectives on organizations as ontologically stable and predefined entities. Our study takes this perspective further by showing how the study of competing descriptions of events can enable us to question the idea of identity as a stable entity or personal possession.

In the case of the financial crisis, the term "tsunami" is a good case in point; as used during cross-examination by former CEO of Lehman Brothers, Richard Fuld (Sorkin, 2009: 505). "Tsunami" is not only a powerful metaphor for describing the "butterfly effect" when complex, interconnected, global products like securities go wrong. It also implies an *identity position* for the speaker: a person who was a "victim" of events beyond their control, swept up in a wave of events that were not implicative of their own psychological characteristics, such as greed or arrogance. Thus, accounts of self and accounts of events are *mutually constitutive*. Edwards (1997: 40) refers to the "mutually implicative relations between (constructions of) reality and (constructions of) the minds, motives, and personalities of whoever might be perceiving, understanding or making claims about the nature of the world." People can refer to aspects of *themselves* (the "inner world") to bolster their account of events, making the account seem more accurate, reliable, factual, and so on. They can also refer to aspects of *events* (the world "out there") to bolster their account of themselves, making their character seem more unbiased, reliable, honest, or well-intentioned. Hence, "world-making" and "self-making" are interlinked processes (Edwards and Potter, 1992: 127).

Descriptions of events attend not only to the character of the speaker, of course, but also to that of those spoken about. For example, Thatcher's account of Nigel Lawson's resignation from Cabinet presents him as a *selfless* and *admirable* individual, willing to sacrifice his own career for the good of the country (Edwards and Potter, 1992: 134). Character can also be contested or discounted in other texts and accounts. Newspaper reports and cabinet discussions both recast the character of Lawson in different terms: as a *petty* and *vindictive* man with more concern for professional rivalry than public duty (Edwards and Potter, 1992: 141). Hence, multiple and contradictory identities can be constructed both within and between accounts. In this chapter, we focus on the contradictory *moral* positions constructed by witnesses (bankers) and questioners (politicians). We turn to the question of moral character next.

7.3 Identity and moral positioning

Moral integrity is a key concern for identity positioning. Not surprisingly, people often attempt to portray themselves in a positive moral light as virtuous, honorable, courageous, caring, committed, competent, and so on (van Langenhove and Harré, 1999: 26). From a DP perspective, the question is not about whether people can be judged to have acted in an ethical way (or not), but rather how people draw on notions of morality in positioning their identity or the identity of others. In fact, Kornberger and Brown (2007) argue that "ethics" can operate as a key discursive resource

Constructing Identity in and around Organizations

through which actors individually and collectively build their identities and legitimate certain decisions and behaviors. In the not-for-profit innovation network organization they studied, the idea of an "ethical person" was used to actually *do* things, such as make recruitment decisions (by selecting people based on their trustworthiness), train new recruits (by ensuring employees did not exploit information from clients for personal gain), and establish trust with clients (by assuring clients that information would be treated confidentially). The notion of being "ethical people" and an "ethical organization" was a powerful ordering device for constructing their sense of "who I am" individually and "who we are" collectively.

Questions of moral character are often dealt with indirectly. In most cases, issues of right and wrong are dealt with implicitly as part of an unfolding narrative. We argue that moral character is often built up in these delicate acts of positioning vis-à-vis alternative counterclaims, where identity is often dealt with *indirectly* through supposedly "factual" descriptions (i.e., talk about events and actions) rather than through *explicit* identity-claims (e.g., "I am a competent person," "I am a good person," etc.). Let us examine two examples to explain how descriptions can act as methods of identity positioning. The first example is Wetherell's study (1998) of masculinity and youth identity. Wetherell shows how an apparently "trivial" detail in a description of a night out with friends performs important identity work for the speaker. The interviewee is asked about his experience of "pulling" (i.e., having intimate sexual contact with) several girls in the same night. In his description of the event in question, the interviewee emphasizes that he was "just out with his mates" and just out for a "laugh." This description enables the interviewee to avoid the actual or potential intimation that he had an ulterior sexual motive to his night out, or is the type of person to exploit women. Factual descriptions of who he was with (his "mates") and what they were doing (having a "laugh") act to maintain his presentation of self as a person who is respectful to women, not a "lad" or a "womanizer."

The second example is Lynch and Bogen's analysis (1996) of the Iran-Contra hearings. They show how the apparently "neutral" and "factual" statement "[General] North shredded documents on November 21" can be used to construct two very different identity narratives. One narrative put forward by the "Report of the Congressional Committee" casts North as a dishonest and devious character: "North is told that Justice Department officials will inspect his files the next day, and he begins shredding documents" (Lynch and Bogen, 1996: 80). In this narrative, a "bad," "improper" motive is clearly imputed into North's shredding activity. However, North employs a different narrative in his testimony, where the improper motive is rejected by creating a *background of shredding as an "ordinary" activity*: "the reason the Government of the United States gave me a shredder, I mean I didn't buy it myself, was to destroy documents that were no longer relevant." He goes on to claim: "I engaged in shredding almost every day that I had a shredder" (Lynch and Bogen, 1996: 22). By describing shredding as an "everyday" and "normal" occurrence, North protects himself from the accusation that he was a *strategic* and *deceitful* person, who deliberately sought to destroy evidence. These are clearly different narratives with widely diverging implications for the projected identity of North. Identity positioning is central to our analysis because we focus on a situation where bankers are held to account (and to blame) for their part in the recent financial crisis. Moral positioning can be used to portray oneself in a positive light and avoid damage to one's social status.

7.4 Methodology

The DP perspective we employ involves a particular approach to data collection and analysis. People contributing to the DP agenda typically like to "work with direct records of interaction from various institutional and everyday settings" (Hepburn and Wiggins, 2007: 1). We follow on from Taylor's argument (2006: 96) that "talk is understood as the site in which identity is instantiated and negotiated, so the "identity work" of speakers is investigated through the analysis of their talk." Thus, DP's commitment to studying talk-in-interaction means that we focus on naturally occurring data because it enables us to examine the stories constructed in situ by those involved in the sensemaking following the financial crisis. "Naturally occurring" simply means that they are part of the normal social order rather than staged for purposes of research (as in interviews): "naturally occurring social interactions" are those "that happen irrespective of the researcher's need for data" (Edwards, 1997: 130). While discursive practices are best studied in the context of "everyday rational accountability," DP has also been used to study situations where people are formally called upon to justify themselves (Edwards, 2007: 46). We include the latter scenario under the label of "naturally occurring accounts" as the cross-examination did not take place as part of research but as part of being held professionally and occupationally accountable. Following Brown's analysis (2005) of the reports following the collapse of Barings Bank, we view the Treasury Committee Hearings as constituting an "important discursive contribution to people's understanding of a significant episode in UK and global banking" (Brown, 2005: 1584).

One limitation of this publicly available data source is that detailed Jeffersonian transcription, the established method of DP, is not always possible. The official Treasury Committee transcription was available to us, and we also got access to the video which enabled us, if necessary, to check for complex interactional features such as pauses and overlapping talk that could then be added to the standard transcription. For the present chapter, we have not made systematic use of the video and instead use the publicly available transcript. We acknowledge this methodological limitation, but remain convinced of the overall value of analyzing public texts because they show how discourse is used in "creating, clarifying, sustaining and modifying" a particular "version of "reality" (Brown, 2005: 1584).

Second, our DP approach brings with it certain methodological commitments. DP views talk as a medium of social action, rather than a reflection of inner cognitive entities, such as thoughts, memories, emotions, or attitudes. Hence, the job of the analyst is not to delineate the "true" or "correct" account among the competing versions produced by the bankers and questioners in our study. Rather, our analysis focuses on *how these versions are constructed* to present themselves as an authentic, genuine, factual, plausible, or "objective" version of events. This leads us to examine the "range of styles, linguistic resources and rhetorical devices" (Edwards and Potter, 1992: 28) used in this process: what we term "discursive devices."

The transcript we analyze was part of a series of meetings and reports announced by the UK Treasury Committee on November 25, 2008, as part of its Banking Crisis inquiry. The inquiry involved a series of seventeen oral evidence sessions, which we term "hearings," involving banking executives, senior politicians, regulators, and experts. This chapter focuses specifically on the hearing held on Tuesday February 10, 2009, when four former bank executives were questioned by a range of MPs from across the political parties. The questions asked during the hearing were numbered in the publicly available transcript and are referenced accordingly (e.g., Q1570) in our discussion. A list of the participants in the hearing quoted in this chapter is given in Table 7.2.

We focus on this single hearing for two reasons. First, an analysis of the entire range of seventeen hearings would not be compatible with the detailed analysis of DDs we pursue in this chapter: the data-set is simply too large to enable this micro-focus. Second, we chose this single hearing because issues of identity positioning would be likely to be foregrounded

Positioning Identities through Descriptions

Table 7.2 Participants in Treasury Select Committee meeting February 10, 2009

Role	Name	Position
Questioners	John McFall	Chair of Treasury Committee, MP (Labour, West Dunbartonshire)
	John Mann	MP (*Labour, Bassetlaw*)
	Michael Fallon	MP (*Conservative, Sevenoaks*) (Chairman, Sub-Committee)
	Jim Cousins	MP (*Labour, Newcastle upon Tyne Central*)
	Andrew Love	MP (*Labour, Edmonton*)
	Mark Todd	MP (*Labour, South Derbyshire*)
	Graham Brady	MP (*Conservative, Altrincham, and Sale West*)
Witnesses	Sir Tom McKillop	Former Chairman of RBS Group plc
	Sir Fred Goodwin	Former Chief Executive of RBS Group plc
	Lord Stevenson of Coddenham	Member of the House of Lords, Former Chairman of HBOS plc
	Mr Andy Hornby	Former Chief Executive of HBOS plc

here: bankers were widely reported in the press as a major cause of the crisis, due primarily to their greed and excessive bonus payments and hence warped incentives. Hence, we anticipated that contrasting identity positionings would be most likely to appear in this particular hearing, not excluding the possibility that others would exhibit similar patterns of conflicting identity positionings. We are intent on showing "that analytically relevant characterizations of social interactants are grounded in empirical observations that show that the participants themselves are demonstrably oriented to the identities or attributes in question" (Drew and Heritage, 1992: 20).

7.5 Identity positioning: Victims and villains

In what follows, we will examine three extracts from the Banking Crisis meeting on February 10, 2009. Our aim is to illustrate the way in which the characters of the politicians and bankers were constructed in the descriptions of events given by both parties. The first extract given below is an edited version (for space considerations) of an exchange between MP John Mann, one of the politicians questioning the bankers during the hearing, and Andy Hornby, former Chief Executive of HBOS plc—one of the banks that was "bailed out" with British taxpayers money. Mann starts by referring to letters he has received from staff of Halifax, part of the HBOS group.

Q1714 John Mann: Is not the thing that really annoys them—I know from letters I have seen—that you are still being paid, are you not? Is it £60,000 a month?

Mr Hornby: Mr Mann, I have a short-term consultancy arrangement with Lloyds TSB which, can I just stress, Lloyds TSB asked me to do.

Q1715 John Mann: £60,000 a month—

Mr Hornby: That is correct.

Q1716 John Mann: —which would be 36 of the lower paid staff jobs in the Bank. 36 of them could be paid each year out of that money. The question they are asking is: considering the failure, why is failure being rewarded? Why are you still getting this money? Is it to cut their jobs?

Mr Hornby: ...can I just please reiterate in terms of your impression about rewards for failure what I outlined earlier; that I have invested early single penny of my bonuses in my time with HBOS into shares; I have lost considerably more money over the last two years for the period I have been Chief Executive than I have earned; and I share all your concerns for staff morale; and I really do hope and believe that the future under Lloyds TSB will allow that morale to get back to where it was 18 months ago. It will take time and I accept there is job insecurity.

(Extract 1)

Mann's question sets up not only a description of events (bankers getting paid bonuses while staff lose their jobs) but also a description of Hornby's character and his own character. By stating that senior executives are still being paid hefty salaries/bonuses while employees are being made redundant, Mann implies that Hornby is a *greedy* and *selfish* character who is happy to line his own pockets while staff lose their jobs—a character of questionable moral standards. Mann uses a particular type of *footing* to achieve this "character assassination." Footing refers to the basis on which an account is offered, such as from personal experience or opinion, based on the testimony of a reliable other, or a disinterested statement of fact (Potter, 1996: 142–8). By referring to the "letters" he has received, Mann employs the footing position of *spokesperson* or *animator* of the views of others, many of whom are the residents of the constituency he represents in parliament. Speaking as an animator enables the speaker to deflect responsibility for an action or viewpoint "away from themselves and (commonly) onto some other party" (Clayman, 1992: 165). The attack on Hornby's character is thereby depersonalized, simply being a faithful representative of the view of others ("The question they are asking is..."). This helps to make the character description appear more justified, valid, and unbiased. Mann thereby attends to *his own character* in the process: he is not an "aggressive" individual who takes pleasure from "attacking" others; he is simply "doing his job" by representing the views of the British public. As we mentioned earlier, DP analyzes how event descriptions allow inferences regarding the character of the person making the description as well as those being described (Edwards, 1997: 40).

Hornby's reply carefully attends to the character (greedy, selfish) attributed to him by Mann. By referring to his current position in Lloyds TSB as something "[they] asked me to do," Hornby presents himself as a type of person who has simply accepted offers from others, not purposefully seeking money out of selfish greed. In addition, by claiming to have "lost" more money than he had "earned," he presents himself as a *victim* of the crisis, rather than a perpetrator. In fact, Goodwin later refers to great distress to see "what my colleagues are going through." This claim also presents him as "in the same boat" as everyone else, sharing the same losses, feeling the same pain: a form of empathy device. Hornby constructs a common group with a common identity: "we are all in this together." This can be seen as an example of *membership categorization* (Edwards and Potter, 1992: 51, 160), meaning the group categories used to describe yourself and others, including what responsibilities, expectations, rights, and obligations are involved. In combination with the empathy device he also employs ("I share all of your concerns for staff morale"), Hornby presents himself as a caring, compassionate character—someone with honorable moral thoughts and feelings.

Hornby also attends implicitly to the character constructed by Mann for himself. If we follow Clayman's suggestion (1992: 167) to focus in particular on how recipients respond to footing stances "by either ratifying it, contesting it, or ignoring it," we can see here that Hornby ignores the animator stance taken by Mann and refers instead to "your impression about rewards for failure." The viewpoint that Mann attributes to those who wrote him letters (anger and annoyance at the hypocrisy and unfairness of Hornby's pay) is repositioned by Hornby and attributed to Mann personally, as the author or principal of this viewpoint. Hornby suggests that Mann uses the letters in order to formulate something that he believes in himself, which itself casts him as an angry and vengeful character who is intent on destroying Hornby's image and reputation. This acts as a form of motive ascription. Subtly highlighting the potential motives, attitudes, and intentions of the questioner can thereby serve to defend against the moral attack on the character of the witness.

The second extract is an exchange between Mann and Fred Goodwin, former Chief Executive of RBS Group, plc., another one of the "bailed out" banks:

Q1718 John Mann: Sir Fred, in the public eye, in the media, you are perhaps taking a much harder hit than anyone on this. This is not actually to get to you—I am interested in the culture. Is it that you are an aberration? Is it that you are someone with a different moral compass in terms of what motivates you; or, in your view, are your integrity and ethics representative of the trade and profession of bankers?

Sir Fred Goodwin: I think, reflecting on everything that has happened, there is certainly cause to question some of the judgements that we have made, and that is reflected in how things have turned out. I am not aware of a basis for questioning my integrity as a result of it all. I could not be more sorry about what has happened. I am not going to go back through all of that again; but I have invested a lot in RBS, and I do not mean financially, over a very long period of time and it is of great distress to me to see what particularly my colleagues are going through and I do not diminish customers and shareholders as well.

(Extract 2)

Footing (Goffman, 1981: 128; Potter, 1996: 142–8) is again important in the way Mann sets up his own character. He presents himself as representing the views of "the public" and repeating the views of "the media." He positions his own character by stating that his intention is not to "get to" Goodwin, perhaps out of spite, malice, or anger. His question does not make an explicit attack on Goodwin's character. Rather, he invites Goodwin to assess his own character, by asking him whether he is an unusually "bad" person ("different moral compass") or is typical of the "culture" of the profession as a whole ("are your integrity and ethics representative"). Goodwin is thereby invited to publicly *display* and *assess* his own moral character. Posing the accusation as a *question* enables Mann to present himself as a fair questioner who is allowing the witness to respond before forming a judgment. However, the question remains framed as an *accusation* that Goodwin is an immoral character.

Goodwin employs a "rhetorical contrast" (Edwards, 1997: 187) in response: namely the contrast between "some of the judgments that we have made" that perhaps were wrong and his overall "integrity," which should not be questioned. Implicitly, the shortcoming is deemed to lie around the technical dimension (i.e., we got our calculations and forecasts wrong) not the moral (i.e., we acted unethically) dimension of the actions being described. The collective pronoun "we" is significant because it diffuses blame and responsibility to others, avoiding shadows being cast on his own personal character. In contrast, when the individual pronouns "I" and "my" are used, Goodwin notably concedes far less, thus defending

Positioning Identities through Descriptions

his character. Nonetheless, rather than explicitly state that "I am not a bad person" or "I do not have a different 'moral compass' to others," Goodwin couches his statement in more modest, reflective terms. Rather than state categorically that he *is* a "good" person, he states that he does not know of any grounds for him being a "bad" person ("I am not aware of a basis for questioning my integrity..."). The question of moral values and integrity gets subtly reframed as a question of lack of evidence to the contrary: indeed, certain things can only be said indirectly.[2] The kind of analysis informed by DP is highly tuned to the importance of such subtle and delicate shifts in framing of questions that are important in identity positioning.

Finally, Goodwin employs the recurring device of empathy, as described earlier. Goodwin displays himself as an *apologetic*, *humble*, and *compassionate* character, who is "sorry" about what has happened and who is personally "distressed" by the suffering of others. The qualification he offers to "having invested a lot in RBS" is significant. Against the back-drop of the previous turns, which characterized the bankers as greedy and selfish, Goodwin qualified the term "invested" as "I do not mean financially." This qualification achieves two things. First, it rebukes the characterization of himself, as his fellow bankers, as solely concerned with money. Second, it presents him as someone who invested himself in the bank, suggesting a sense of *attachment*, *care*, and *dedication*. What Goodwin achieves in his turn is a so-called "*disentangling*" shift from a *discourse of anger* from the moral outrage implied in Mann's question (a transgression–retribution plot) to a *discourse of sadness* from Goodwin's display of concern and regret (a plot about sorrow, reconciliation, and community solidarity) (Edwards, 1997: 186): "by engaging in disentangling, speakers tacitly acknowledge the prior value of community solidarity, ritually closing the conflict episode as a source of disruptive thoughts and actions" (White, 1990: 53). Emotion is employed rhetorically to narrate a moralistic story and construct a moral character for the protagonist.

The final extract has been chosen for analysis because it addresses a central aspect of character construction: the sincerity with which a person's character is being performed. It is also important because it shows how identity positions can be later *challenged* by others in an ongoing *process* of identity construction and reconstruction. In the extract that follows, the Chairman of the inquiry (a Labour MP) addresses his question to Andy Hornby, former Chief Executive of HBOS, plc., regarding an apology previously given in response to an earlier question.

> **Q1719 Chairman**: Could I just pick up a point Andy Hornby made to John Mann. You said, "I don't feel I am particularly personally culpable." What exactly are you apologising for? We have been told that you have been coached extensively, meticulously by PR people and lots of money has been spent. The papers tell us that, Sir Tom. Are you expressing sympathy because your PR advisers advise you to do so?
> *Mr Hornby*: No, let me just stress, I have already apologised several times on behalf of myself and the whole Board for what has happened. The precise question I was asked is whether I felt purely personally culpable, I think we all take responsibility for what has happened in the two years I have been running the company. I fully accept my own role within all of that and I repeat the apology.

(Extract 3)

The Chairman's question raises skepticism about the sincerity of Hornby's previous apology, given earlier in the proceedings. The Chairman invokes the idea of "PR advisers" being reported in "the papers." Footing is again important here for handling the character of the questioner, with "the papers" and others who have "told" the Chairman this information being placed in the role of *principal*, rendering the Chairman simply the *animator* (Goffman, 1981: 128). At the heart of the Chairman's accusation is that Hornby's display of sympathy and regret is simply a "PR stunt" and does not reflect his *true* character or *genuine* sentiment. The unspoken implication is that Hornby is thereby presented as a potentially *insincere* and *manipulative* character. Of course, if the accusation is justified, that is, they have been coached, then they will also have been coached in what to say in response to a coaching accusation. The questioner seems to be attempting to take Hornby onto the backstage, as in "ok we've heard the official version, tell us now what you really think." However, this attempt to create a micro pocket of a "backstage" (as in "come on, just between you and me...") is unlikely to succeed in a public, recorded hearing such as this. Implicitly, the chairman is perhaps pointing at a paradox in Hornby's past and present statements: if he does not actually feel culpable, then how could the apology have been sincere? This is a variation (notwithstanding certain differences) of the "Liar's paradox" that was used to analyze Ollie North's performance: "(*a*) Lying is justified to prevent our adversaries from knowing our secrets. (*b*) Our adversaries have access to this very testimony. (*c*) I am not now lying. *And I really mean it, honest!*" (Lynch and Bogen, 1996: 43).

Hornby immediately and swiftly denies the Chairman's characterization of himself (as someone lacking sincerity) with a simple "no," before

Positioning Identities through Descriptions

Table 7.3 Comparison of identity positions attributed to bankers in Treasury Select Committee meeting, February 10, 2009

	Character of bankers constructed by MPs	Character of bankers constructed by bankers
Character traits implied in talk	Greedy, selfish, unethical, false, insincere	Empathetic, caring, compassionate, humble, remorseful, dedicated, sincere
Overarching identity constructed in talk	Villain	Victim
Plot of story	Transgression–retribution	Sorrow, solidarity, and reconciliation

attending to the more subtle business of qualifying his earlier apology. He mixes his apology "on behalf of myself" with an apology "[on behalf of] the whole Board." He also mixes his admission of responsibility between himself ("I fully accept my own role") and a broader collective ("we all take responsibility"). Combining the personal and the collective in this way helps to make Hornby appear sorry for what he has done (i.e., a humble and remorseful person), while also presenting himself as one of many who did the same things, therefore avoiding singling himself out as a "bad apple" (i.e., a person with especially repugnant values and ethics). In a way, Hornby is playing on the many shades of meanings of the word "culpable," including the collective sense in which he accepts a share of "what has happened." This is reminiscent of North's defense in response to being accused of lying to the American people, when he invokes a whole list of scenarios where lying *can* be justified (Lynch and Bogen, 1996: 115–16). What becomes clear in such situations is that words like "blame" or "lie" contain a whole range of possible meanings, meanings which only have a "family resemblance" with each other (Wittgenstein, 1953: para. 67, 77, 108). Communication may run empty where the assumption is made that they have a *precise* meaning (Holt and Mueller, 2011).

In Table 7.3, we summarize the types of character traits that are implicitly invoked in order to build the overarching identities of "victim" and "villain," along with the plots they are associated with.

7.6 Conclusions and implications

In this section, we first discuss the conclusions that derive from our analysis, including how they help us understand processes of identity positioning in other (more mundane) organizational settings. Second, we outline the main contributions that DP makes to the study of identity. The third section looks at how DP relates to other approaches to studying discourse and identity. The fourth and final section discusses the wider implications of our analysis for sensemaking and policy responses to the financial crisis.

7.6.1 What conclusions can be drawn from this analysis?

Organizations are abound with moral tales of heroes and villains, victims and innocent bystanders, as well as corruption and temptation (Czarniawska, 1997; Gabriel, 2000). We have argued that people can use discourse to make themselves appear as the victim or describe someone else as the villain. Upon entering the hearing, the protagonists were already aware of societal perceptions of them; indeed, "Fred the Shred was perfectly cast as a villain" (Rawnsley, 2010: 610). Hence, identity positioning often involves forms of *moral positioning*. Allocating blame, or offering an excuse, only makes sense within a moral order, that is, where the people involved attempt to construct a particular moral position (van Langenhove and Harré, 1999: 26), for example, as decent, honest, honorable, innocent, victims of world-events, and so on. Some characters easily exceeded the "high" standards set for basic villain status and became elevated to "monster" status in the retelling of stories, in particular Cassano who headed up AIG's London Financial Products operations (Lewis, 2010: 87)—he was basically insuring the CDOs held by the world's banks, at one point insuring up to 1tn dollars (Brown, 2010: 88)! The DDs we have analyzed performed a particular social action for the bankers, namely "recasting" the moral status of their character. In the institutional setting of a public hearing, it is clear that many of the questions of the MPs also contain character assessments, which in turn occasioned contestations from the bankers. The bankers sought to discredit the picture painted of the greedy, arrogant, negligent villain, and instead framing themselves in positive moral terms as caring, compassionate, and competent types of people.

In our analysis of how bankers were questioned during a public hearing, descriptions of apparently "factual" elements—how much a banker is paid, whether bad judgments were made, whether or not they have hired PR advisors—were central to the construction of two rival identity positions for the bankers. The bankers were cast as both *villains* (by the politicians questioning them) and *victims* (by the bankers themselves), depending on the description of "what happened" told by the two parties. These identity positions were not constructed using simple ascriptions or labels, such as "You are a villain" or "I am a victim." Rather, they were carefully "worked up" in the descriptions of actions and events, through the use of DDs—the micro-linguistic tools—such as footing, empathy, and collective pronouns ("we") for instance.

While our analysis is on the basis of a rather unique highly charged public setting, similar processes are likely to be found in other organizational settings where identities are implicated. While few of us are likely to be subject to a Government enquiry during our working lives, we are certainly more likely to encounter situations where competing narratives cast us in less-than-favorable identity positions. Certainly, for those who work in dirty, deviant, or degrading occupations, workers face constant challenges to the legitimacy or value of their identity, which require linguistic strategies (perhaps even similar DDs used by the bankers) to maintain/repair their dignity and worth (e.g., Ashforth and Kreiner, 1999). In other workplaces, new discourses may come into conflict with existing, entrenched occupational or professional identities, such as the introduction of neoliberal agendas into professions (e.g., Mueller et al., 2004; Thomas and Davies, 2005; Mueller and Carter, 2007), promoting intensive *identity work* (Alvesson and Willmott, 2002) to repair and defend established identities. Identity work is not exclusive to such major challenges, though, and is part and parcel of the everyday "scepticism or inconsistencies faced in encounters with others" (ibid.: 626).

Challenges to desired identity positions can also emerge during routine workplace storytelling situations. Stories about "what happened" and "who is to blame" occur in mundane organizational interaction, such as lunchtime conversations, besides the type of public hearing that we have analyzed. According to Boje (1991: 107), there are always "alternative stories with alternative motives and implications" that can be told about every event. Existing research has shown that divergent stories often emerge following periods of organizational change and turmoil. For example, Brown and Humphreys (2003) found that senior managers and staff constructed very different stories about the merger they had just experienced, with senior managers presenting themselves as "heroic leaders" whereas staff presented themselves as the "victims" of incompetent managers. A simple phrase such as "[it was] very much a rescue operation" (ibid.: 129) does not only describe *events* but also position the *identity* of the speaker by presenting senior management as "heroes" who were rescuing a "sinking ship." DP's contribution lies in its ability to understand the subtle linguistic tools through which these competing identities (e.g., heroic leader vs. incompetent manager) are established, contested, and reinterpreted in descriptive discourse.

While our analysis, and much of DP, focuses on *individual* identity, the principles of DP analysis are also applicable to the study of *organizational* identity. The DDs we have discussed in this chapter are also relevant to understanding collective identity claims. For instance, Brown and Humphreys' study (2003) of an organizational merger of two Further Education colleges reveals competing collective identity claims—about the new collective "[we are] business" (p. 29), the merged college "[they are] cushion-stuffers and egg-painters" (p. 132), and the old identity that has been lost in the merger "[we *were* based] on cooperation, and taking care of each another" (p. 133). Factual descriptions—the focus of this chapter—also played a role in identity construction: for instance, descriptions of the book bought by the new principal (p. 132) worked to paint a picture of the new leadership as aggressive, macho, and commercially driven. DP is therefore a valuable approach for studying identity at both an individual and organizational level.

7.6.2 How does DP contribute to the study of identity and process theory?

We propose that DP contributes to the study of identity and process in three ways. First, DP adds to the growing body of work that proposes a *dialogical* approach to studying identity, which focuses on the "back-and-forth" nature of social interaction (Shotter and Cunliffe, 2003; Beech, 2008). As Shotter (2010) argues, our sense of ourselves as a person is fundamentally social: "our entire vocabulary of the individual—who thinks, feels, wants, hopes, and so on—is granted meaning only by virtue of coordinated activities among people. Their birth of "myself" lies within the relationship" (p. 62). DP contributes to this body of literature by drawing attention to the importance of, among other things, the *immediate interactional context*—how versions of the self are worked up in response to prior turns at talk. Thanks to the intellectual inspiration gained from Conversational Analysis (CA) and ethnomethodology, DP is sensitive to "how the orderliness of mundane social life is a moment-by-moment concerted accomplishment" (Edwards, 1997: 80). In terms of identity, therefore, DP focuses on how the process of unfolding dialogue with others shapes the identities that are enacted and invoked (Antaki and Widdicombe, 1998). Instead of viewing identity as a relatively stable and coherent self-concept, it is understood as a variable and flexible resource for self-positioning, which is occasioned by the immediate interactional context (e.g., what was immediately just said, what claims were being made in previous turns). Thus, identity is not something we "possess." Rather, identity has to be actively worked up and *achieved*, particularly in the face of counterclaims. In the case of our study, being a "good" (ethical) person was at the heart of the claims and counter-claims of the MPs and bankers. As such, DP is a processual perspective because it views identity not as a "thing" but as a process of discursive construction that we continually engage in, which shifts over time as we engage in processes of interacting with others. What our version of DP can specifically contribute to process theory is a better understanding of the detailed, often small, actions that make up processes of identity positioning. We saw, for example, how a single utterance can achieve a form of disentangling that can attempt to close a conflict episode: in this case, a conflict between competing descriptions of "what happened." For us to better understand how temporal bracketing is actually accomplished in specific settings is a long-standing ambition of process theorizing (Langley, 1999, 2009). Gergen (2010: 58) emphasizes the room for cross-fertilization between process studies on the one hand, and "organizational discourse, conventional processes, ethnomethods, dramaturgical scenarios, rituals" on the other hand—this is what we have attempted in this chapter.

Second, DP draws our attention to the *social actions* performed by identity-talk. Identity claims (and counterclaims) are viewed as a *tool* for doing something (Antaki and Widdicombe, 1998). DP's central argument is that discourse, including identity-talk, is *consequential* (Antaki and Widdicombe, 1998: 14): that is, it makes a difference. Identity claims can enable certain actions or ideas to come across as more justified, neutral, or reasonable. Characterizing bankers as "villains" or "victims," we argue, makes a difference not only to the bankers themselves but also to how we make sense of the financial crisis as a whole. For example, taxes on bankers' bonuses make more sense within a moral framework within which bankers are cast as greedy villains that deserve retribution (Brown, 2010: 103–5).

Third, DP makes an important contribution to identity research by viewing descriptions—a type of "factual discourse" (Edwards and Potter, 1992: 128)—as forms of identity-talk. The intellectual heritage of DP from the sociology of scientific knowledge, such as the seminal work of Gilbert and Mulkay (1984) for instance, gives us a sophisticated understanding of the processes by which accounts *are rendered into* "fact" and "truth." Identity-work, according to DP, is done not only through explicit identity-talk ("I am an honest person," "He is upper class," etc.) but also implicitly through descriptions of "what happened" (memories of events) and "why" (attributions of cause). DP enables us to examine how "versions of self and identity...are integrally related to the construction of factual versions of events," where processes of world-making and self-making interconnect (Edwards and Potter, 1992: 127).

Fourth and finally, our analysis has highlighted the importance of *self-positioning* for the process of attributing identities to *others*. Ascribing identities to others relies upon, among other things, a credible identity position on the part of the speaker. Identity attributions, we suggest, require a delicate positioning of the speaker's own footing: their relationship to the ideas and opinions they express. Footing is crucial, we argue, for presenting identity attributions (e.g., "You are an immoral person") as fair, unbiased, and representative of the views of others, for instance. Our study supports Clayman's argument (1992: 168) that questioners such as journalists and news presenters "commonly shift footings during their (i.e., utterances', the Authors) production, thereby placing some degree of distance between themselves and their more overtly opinionated remarks." For example, in Extract 1, MP Mann cites "letters" from "lower paid staff" in order to *author* a view that could otherwise be seen as very aggressive and opinionated. Atkinson's research (1992) in a London small claims court is relevant here: the arbitrator is, unlike much in the Anglo-American justice system, *not* supposed to work in the adversarial tradition, but will nevertheless need to pass judgment: "If he is to be seen as acting fairly in this latter capacity, it is therefore essential that he should not be seen to be taking sides while questioning either plaintiff or defendant" (p. 210). The author G. Brown points out that he now recognizes that new financial instruments might diversify but still *increase* risk—a realization that the politician, G. Brown, did not have, which the author now describes as a "far-reaching mistake" (2010: 19). We propose that footing is crucial for authoring compelling or credible identities. While the MPs in our study could hardly be called "neutral," the use of footing to reduce perceived bias and hostility is crucial for making their character attributions of the bankers seem like a fair and representative judgment as opposed to a personal, politically motivated attack.

7.6.3 How does DP compare to existing approaches?

How, then, does DP differ from other approaches to studying discourse and identity? Work inspired by Foucault and Fairclough represent two influential strands of research in discourse analysis. Foucauldian approaches tend to adopt a "muscular" view of discourse—defined as prevalent systems of thought and often referred to with a capital "D"—emphasizing its power to define subject positions and focusing on what discourse *does to* people

(Alvesson and Karreman, 2000). DP, on the other hand, focuses on the variability and flexibility of how people use discourse—understood as actual language use—in practical settings, emphasizing what people *do with* discourse. DP has been subject to many criticisms, including being criticized for having an individualistic emphasis on the rhetorical strategies of the speaker, the assumption that persuasion is the main driver of human conduct, bringing in psychosocial features through the "back door," problems of generalization from a single data extract, failure to deconstruct the analyst's own writing as a rhetorical construction, inability to explain anything beyond the talk and text, and failure to provide a coherent theory beyond methodological prescription (Fairclough, 1992: 23–5; Hammersley, 2003).

Notwithstanding these criticisms, we view DP's emphasis on detailed analysis of actually situated language use as a major contribution to existing post-structuralist approaches, such as the Foucauldian literature. As Wetherell (1998) argues, DP's inspiration from CA enables it to focus on how actors orient toward broader discourses in variable and flexible ways, without assuming a priori the power effects of any discourse or overemphasizing the fragility of subjects: two major criticisms of Foucauldian analyses (Newton, 1998; Fournier and Grey, 1999). However, it is important not to overstate the contrast between DP and the Foucauldian tradition to the point where they are positioned as incompatible. Instead, we view DP and Foucaudian approaches as operating at different levels of analysis, but with a shared interest in issues of power and social construction. In fact, the work of Margaret Wetherell and colleagues has shown the value of bringing together the more CA-inspired level of analysis of DP with post-structuralism to address wider issues of power and inequality (e.g., Reynolds and Wetherell, 2003; Dixon and Wetherell, 2004).

The differences between DP and discourse analysis inspired by the critical realist approach of Norman Fairclough and colleagues, under the rubric of Critical Discourse Analysis (CDA), are also subtle but important in our view. DP offers a more thoroughly constructionist approach that maintains a healthy scepticism toward claims about the "real" (Fairclough, 1992: 66), "extra-discursive" (p. 79), or "non-discursive" (p. 48). For instance, CDA maintains that elements such as "interests" remain outside the realm of discourse and social construction: a position that DP contests (Whittle and Mueller, 2011). This distinction is important for identity research because it helps us understand the process through which identities are constructed, contested, and maintained, without viewing them as fixed "essences" that lie outside of discourse. In fact, as we have shown elsewhere (Whittle and Mueller, 2011), the process of handling actual or potential imputations of stake ("having a stake in a situation"), motive ("having a reason for doing something"), and interest ("having something to gain from an event or action") can be ways of presenting ones' identity in a particular way: as an altruistic, unbiased, or compassionate person, for instance. DP enables us to focus on the linguistic processes through which identity is constructed, without making more speculative assumptions about underlying "real" entities (e.g., motives, interests, etc.) that supposedly drive it.

DP contributes to the broader literature on the social construction of identity by illuminating the micro-linguistic "moves" that are undertaken during the process of defining, constructing, and refining our sense of "who we are" during social interaction. As such, it is positioned within the broad "church" of approaches that view identity as a narrative process (e.g., Brown and Humphreys, 2003; Beech, 2008), or as a communicative process (e.g., Ashforth and Kriener, 1999), and those approaches that focus on identity work and identity regulation (e.g., Alvesson and Willmott, 2002; Thomas and Davies, 2005). DP is more critical of approaches that adopt a more narrow psychological framework, such as Social Identity Theory (SIT), on the grounds that it "psychologizes" the underlying forces behind processes of group identification, ignoring issues of power and discourse (for a more detailed critique of SIT from a DP perspective, see Wetherell and Potter, 1992: ch. 2). DP is also critical of psycho-analytical approaches for making assumptions about cognitive processes that lie behind language use. DP's strength lies in studying how psychological processes, such as attitudes, emotions, memories and so on, are *handled in discourse*, rather than simply viewing language as a neutral medium through which these cognitive entities are expressed.

As a discursive approach, DP focuses primarily on language as the "primary arena for action, understanding and intersubjectivity" (Wiggins and Potter, 2008: 73)—including the construction of identity. However, this does not dogmatically exclude nonverbal or material elements. Indeed, the transcription notation drawn from CA allows for the inclusion of nonverbal gestures and material elements, including the presence of certain objects made relevant within the interaction. For instance, a single cough or raised eyebrow can be demonstrably relevant to the participants in terms of the emergent meaning-making, and is therefore taken seriously during the process of analysis. However, while DP draws on some of the methods and concept of CA and ethnomethodology, the key distinction is that DP foregrounds processes of social construction through language (Wiggins and Potter, 2008). Moreover, DP shares much in common with Goffman's work (1959, 1967) looking at the presentation of self in everyday life, through its focus on how people use language (and other things like gestures) to present themselves to others. Nevertheless, some subtle but important difference between DP and Goffman have been articulated, such as criticisms of the concepts such as "face" as an explanation of conduct on the grounds that it presumes underlying psychological processes (such as state of mind or personal motives) that are not warranted by analysis of the talk itself (see Antaki and Horowitz, 2000: 165).

We also contribute to the ethnomethodologically informed literature on public hearings and testimonies (e.g., Gephart, 1993; Gephart and Zhang, 2010; Gephart et al., 2010). Our focus in the present chapter was on how protagonists used DDs in order to position themselves as a certain type of person (competent, caring, humble, and remorseful) and *not* as another type of person (incompetent, greedy, selfish, and insincere). Thus, our focus is different but complementary to Gephart and Zhang's focus (2010: 29) on how "professionals use different linguistic resources and make different identity claims than do non-professionals." We instead focus on how questioners and respondents in a public inquiry differentially positioned a certain occupational group, namely bankers.

7.6.4 Wider implications

The question often leveled at DP and other "micro" approaches to studying identity-in-interaction is "so what?" What difference does this apparently "minor" detail of interaction make to the world? DP views detailed analysis of actual interaction as a vital step in the process of finding out how, for instance, facts become established, proposals gain legitimacy, and blame and responsibility get allocated in everyday talk. In this regard, we build on established work on how telling stories forms part of handling responsibility and blame in the context of disaster sensemaking (Gephart, 1993). DP's central contribution to studying identity lies in its proposition that "the detailed language of describing persons is a resource for action" (Edwards and Potter, 1992: 129). In other words, identity-talk matters not only for the protagonists themselves, in terms of "saving face" for instance, but also for the *events* being talked about because it makes certain courses of action seem more plausible, justified, or acceptable. For example, in the case of Wetherell and Potter's (1992) study of racist discourse in New Zealand, an interviewee described herself as having "Māori friends" (see p. 77). This identity-talk presents the interviewee as someone who is not bigoted or racist (her projected identity), which in turns helps to present her arguments (such as being against the compulsory teaching of Māoris language) as more balanced, fair, and rational (a social action). This in turn helps to justify (or legitimate) certain practices, such as keeping Māori issues off the political agenda. Thus, DP views identity not as an individual cognitive process of deciding "who I am," "who I am like" and "who I am not," but as part of the "collective domain of negotiation, debate, argumentation and ideological struggle" (p. 77). Hence, the detailed micro-level study of DDs does not constitute "navel gazing" in our view. On the contrary, we think studying DDs is important because it enables us to see precisely how answers to the questions "what happened?" and "what should be done about it?" are debated and decided.

The positioning of bankers as villains was not exclusive to the public hearing we analyzed here. In the United Kingdom and beyond, media reports were dominated by "character assassinations" of the bankers involved, particularly those from banks that were "bailed out" with taxpayers money. "Bankers already competed with paedophiles for the lowest position on the league table of public esteem." (Rawnsley, 2010: 607). The need for someone to blame and the desire to exact vengeance on those responsible were keenly felt across the world (Brown, 2010: 103–5; Rawnsley, 2010: 633). Thus, the *villain* character was clearly a relevant identity position for the bankers, in spite of their claims to being "innocent victims" in the hearing we analyzed. However, it is important to note that DP does not adjudicate about who was right or wrong in a technical (i.e., whose version of events is correct) or ethical (i.e., who is morally correct) sense. Rather, DP focuses on the role of discourse in working up these identity positions. DDs, we suggest, play an important role in presenting both a factual version of the world and a *moral version of the self*.

Since 2008, there has been a lively debate (e.g., Johnson and Kwak, 2010: ch. 7) about whether responses by governments and regulators have followed (or *should* follow) the same transgression–retribution plot structure (Edwards, 1997: 168). The logic behind many policies follows the same moral framework: If the *greed* of bankers is to blame, their bonuses should be capped or taxed in some way to mediate this inherent (incentive) character flaw. Indeed, many countries around the world, including the United Kingdom, have since considered special "super taxes" on banks and measures to publicize the bonus payments given to staff. While it is beyond the scope of this chapter to comment on the measures that could (or should) be taken to avoid a repeat of the recent financial crisis, we have shown how identity positioning contributes to the construction of a "moral landscape" in which certain kinds of policy responses may gain legitimacy and support.

Notes

1. http://www.publications.parliament.uk/pa/cm200809/cmselect/cmtreasy/144/09021002.htm
2. "In the seventeenth century it was accepted that honesty and sincerity could not be communicated. Anyone claiming to be honest would at the same time give off the impression that there might be doubts about it" (Luhmann, 1994: 27).

References

Alvesson, M. and Sveningsson, S. (2003). "Managing Managerial Identities: Organizational Fragmentation, Discourse and Identity Struggle." *Human Relations*, 56/10: 1163–93.

—— Kärreman, D. (2000). "Varieties of Discourse: On the Study of Organizations through Discourse Analysis." *Human Relations*, 53/9: 1125–49.

—— Willmott, H. (2002). "Identity Regulation as Organizational Control: Producing the Appropriate Individual." *Journal of Management Studies*, 39/5: 619–44.

—— Ashcraft, K. L., and Thomas, R. (2008). "Identity Matters: Reflections on the Construction of Identity Scholarship in Organization Studies." *Organization*, 15: 5–28.

Antaki, C. and Horowitz, A. (2000). "Using Identity Ascription to Disqualify a Rival Version of events as 'Interested.'" *Research on Language and Social Interaction*, 33: 155–77.

—— Widdicombe, S. (1998). "Identity as an Achievement and as a Tool," in C. Antaki and S. Widdicombe (eds), *Identities in Talk*. London: Sage, pp. 1–14.

Ashforth, B. and Kreiner, G. E. (1999). "'How can you Do it?' Dirty Work and the Challenge of Constructing Positive Identity." *Academy of Management Review*, 24: 413–34.

Atkinson, J. M. (1992). "Displaying Neutrality: Formal Aspects of Informal Court Proceedings," in P. Drew and J. Heritage (eds), *Talk at Work: Interaction in Institutional Settings*. Cambridge: Cambridge University Press, pp. 199–211.

Beech, N. (2008). "On the Nature of Dialogic Identity Work." *Organization*, 15/1: 51–74.

Benwell, B. and Stokoe, E. (2006). *Discourse and Identity*. Edinburgh, UK: Edinburgh University Press.

Boje, D. M. (1991). "The Storytelling Organization: A Study of Storytelling Performance in an Office Supply Firm." *Administrative Science Quarterly*, 36: 106–26.

Brown, A. D. (2005). "Making Sense of the Collapse of Barings Bank." *Human Relations*, 58/12: 1579–604.

——Humphreys, M. (2003). "Epic and Tragic Tales: Making Sense of Change." *Journal of Applied Behavioral Science*, 39/2: 121–44.

Brown, G. (2010). *Beyond the Crash: Overcoming the First Crisis of Globalization*. London: Simon & Schuster.

Clayman, S. E. (1992). "Footing in the Achievement of Neutrality: The Case of News-Interview Discourse," in P. Drew and J. Heritage (eds), *Talk at Work: Interaction in Institutional Settings*. Cambridge: Cambridge University Press, pp. 163-98.

Cooley, C. (1902). *Human Nature and the Social Order*. New York: Charles Scribner's Sons (revised edn 1922).

Cooren, F. (2000). *The Organizing Property of Communication*. Amsterdam: John Benjamins.

Czarniawska, B. (1997). *Narrating the Organization: Dramas of Institutional Identity*. Chicago, IL: University of Chicago Press.

Dixon, J. and Wetherell, M. (2004). "On Discourse and Dirty Nappies: Gender, the Division of Labour and the Social Psychology of Distributive Justice." *Theory and Psychology*, 14: 167-89.

Drew, P. and Heritage, J. (1992). "Analyzing Talk at Work: An Introduction," in P. Drew and J. Heritage (eds), *Talk at Work: Interaction in Institutional Settings*. Cambridge: Cambridge University Press, pp. 3-65.

Edwards, D. (1997). *Discourse and Cognition*. London: Sage.

—— (1998). "The Relevant Thing About Her: Social Identity Categories in Use," in C. Antaki and S. Widdicombe (eds), *Identities in Talk*. London: Sage, pp. 15-33.

—— (2007). "Managing Subjectivity in Talk," in A. Hepburn and S. Wiggins (eds), *Discursive Research in Practice: New Approaches to Psychology and Interaction*. Cambridge: Cambridge University Press, pp. 31-49.

—— Potter, J. (1992). *Discursive Psychology*. London: Sage.

Fairclough, N. (1992). *Discourse and Social Change*. Cambridge: Polity Press.

Fournier, V. and Grey, C. (1999). "Too Much, Too Little, and Too Often: A Critique of du Gay's Analysis of Enterprise." *Organization*, 6/1: 107-28.

Gabriel, Y. (2000). *Storytelling in Organizations: Facts, Fictions, and Fantasies*. Oxford: Oxford University Press.

Gephart, R. P. (1993). The Textual Approach: Risk and Blame in Disaster Sensemaking." *Academy of Management Journal*, 36: 1465-514.

—— Zhang, Z. (2010). "Identity Construction with Numbers." Prepared for presentation to the *Second Annual Process Organization Studies Conference*, Rhodes, Greece, June.

—— Topal, C., and Zhang, Z. (2010). "Future-Oriented Sensemaking: Temporalities and Institutional Legitimation," in A. Langley and H. Tsoukas (eds), *Perspectives on Process Organization Studies* (vol. 1). Oxford: Oxford University Press, pp. 275-311.

Gergen, K. J. (1992). *The Saturated Self: Dilemmas of Identity in Contemporary Life*. New York: Basic Books.

—— (2010). "Co-Constitution, Causality, and Confluence: Organizing in a World without Entities," in T. Hernes and S. Maitlis (eds), *Process, Sensemaking, and Organizing*. Oxford: Oxford University Press, pp. 55-69.

Gilbert, N. and Mulkay, M. (1984). *Opening Pandora's Box: A Sociological Analysis of Scientists' Discourse*. Cambridge: Cambridge University Press.

Goffman, E. (1959). *The Presentation of Self in Everyday Life*. Harmondsworth: Penguin (1990 Reprint).

—— (1967). *Interaction Ritual*. New York: Anchor.

—— (1981). *Forms of Talk*. Oxford: Blackwell.

Goldthorpe, J. H. (1980). *Social Mobility and Class Structure in Modern Britain*. Oxford: Clarendon Press.

Greatbatch, D. and Dingwall, R. (1998). "Talk and Identity in Divorce Mediation," in Antaki, C. and Widdicombe, S. (eds), *Identities in Talk*. London: Sage Publications, pp. 121–32.

Hammersley, M. (2003). "Conversation Analysis and Discourse Analysis: Methods or Paradigms?" *Discourse & Society*, 14/6: 751–81.

Harré, R. (1979/1993). *Social Being*. Oxford: Blackwell.

—— (1995). "Agentive Discourse," in R. Harré and P. Stearns (eds), *Discursive Psychology in Practice*. London: Sage, pp. 120–36.

—— Stearns, P. (1995). "Introduction: Psychology as Discourse Analysis," in R. Harré and P. Stearns (eds), *Discursive Psychology in Practice*. London: Sage, pp. 1–8.

Hepburn, A. and Wiggins, S. (2007). "Discursive Research: Themes and Debates," in A. Hepburn and S. Wiggins (eds), *Discursive Research in Practice: New Approaches to Psychology and Interaction*. Cambridge: Cambridge University Press, pp. 1–28.

Holt, R. and Mueller, F. (2011). "Wittgenstein, Heidegger and Drawing Lines in Organization Studies." *Organization Studies*, 321: 67–84.

Hutchby, I., Wooffitt, R. (1998). *Conversation Analysis*. Cambridge, UK: Polity Press.

Johnson, S. and Kwak, J. (2010). *13 Bankers: The Wall Street Take over and the Next Financial Meltdown*. New York: Pantheon.

Kornberger, M. and Brown, A. D. (2007). "'Ethics' as a Discursive Resource for Identity Work." *Human Relations*, 60/3: 497–518.

Langley, A. (1999): "Strategies for Theorizing from Process Data." *Academy of Management Review*, 24/4: 691–710.

—— (2009). "Temporal Bracketing," in A. Mills, G. Durepos, and E. Wiebe (eds), *Sage Encyclopaedia of Case Study Research* (vol. 2). Thousand Oaks, CA: Sage, pp. 919–21.

—— Tsoukas, H. (2010). "Introducing 'Perspectives on Process Organization Studies'," in T. Hernes and S. Maitlis (eds), *Process, Sensemaking, and Organizing*. Oxford: Oxford University Press, pp. 1–26.

Lewis, M. (2010). *The Big Short: Inside the Doomsday Machine*. London: Allen Lane.

Luhmann, N. (1994). "Politicians, Honesty and the Higher Amorality of Politics." *Theory, Culture & Society*, 11: 25–36.

Lynch, M. and Bogen, D. (1996). *The Spectacle of History: Speech, Text, and Memory at the Iran-Contra Hearings*. Durham, NC: Duke University Press.

McKinlay, A. and Dunnett, A. (1998). "How Gun-owners Accomplish Being Deadly Average," in C. Antaki and S. Widdicombe (eds), *Identities in Talk*. London: Sage Publications, pp. 34–51.

Mueller, F. and Carter, C. (2007). "'We are All Managers Now': Managerialism and Professional Engineering in U.K. Electricity Utilities." *Accounting, Organizations & Society*, 32/1–2: 181–95.

—— and Whittle, A. (2011). "Translating Management Ideas: A Discursive Devices Perspective." *Organization Studies*, 32/2: 187–210.

—— Sillince, J., Harvey, C., and Howorth, C. (2004). "'A Rounded Picture is What We Need': Rhetorical Strategies, Arguments and the Negotiation of Change in a U.K. Hospital Trust." *Organization Studies*, 25/1: 85–103.

Newton, T. J. (1998). "Theorizing Subjectivity in Organizations: The Failure of Foucauldian Studies." *Organization Studies*, 19: 415–47.

Parsons, T. (1964). *Social Structure and Personality*. New York: The Free Press.

Phillips, N. and Hardy, C. (2002). *Discourse Analysis: Investigating Processes of Social Construction*. London: Sage.

Potter, J. (1996). *Representing Reality: Discourse, Rhetoric and Social Construction*. London: Sage.

Pratt, M. G. and Foreman, P. O. (2000). "Classifying Managerial Responses to Multiple Organizational Identities." *Academy Management Review*, 25: 18–42.

Putnam, L. L. and Nicotera, A. M. (eds) (2009). *Building Theories of Organization: The Constitutive Role of Communication*. New York: Routledge.

Rawnsley, A. (2010). *The End of the Party*. London: Penguin (updated edition).

Reynolds, J. and Wetherell, M. (2003). "The Discursive Climate of Singleness: The Consequences for Women's Negotiation of a Single Identity." *Feminism & Psychology*, 13/4: 489–510.

—— —— Taylor, S. (2007). "Choice and Chance: Negotiating Agency in Narratives of Singleness." *Sociological Review*, 55/2: 331–51.

Shotter, J. (2010). "Adopting a Process Orientation.... in Practice: Chiasmic Relations, Language, and Embodiment in a Living World," in T. Hernes and S. Maitlis (eds), *Process, Sensemaking, and Organizing*. Oxford: Oxford University Press, pp. 70–101.

Shotter, J., Cunliffe, A. I. (2003). "Managers as Practical Authors," in D. Holman and R. Thorpe (eds), *Management and Language: The Manager as a Practical Author*. London: Sage, pp. 15–37.

Sorkin, A. R. (2009). *Too Big To Fail: Inside the Battle to Save Wall Street*. London: Allen Lane.

Taylor, S. (2006). "Narrative as Construction and Discursive Resource." *Narrative Inquiry*, 16/1: 94–102.

te Molder, H. and Potter, J. (eds) (2005). *Conversation and Cognition*. Cambridge: Cambridge University Press.

Thomas, R. and Davies, A. (2005). "Theorising the Micro-politics of Resistance: Discourses of Change and Professional Identities in the UK Public Services." Organization Studies, 26/5: 683–706.

Van den Berg, H. (2003). "Contradictions in Interview Discourse," in H. van den Berg, M. Wetherell, and H. Houtkoop-Steenstra (eds), *Analyzing Race Talk:*

Multidisciplinary Approaches to the Interview. Cambridge: Cambridge University Press, pp. 119–38.

van Langenhove, L. and Harré, R. (1999). "Introducing Positioning Theory," in R. Harre and L. van Langenhove (eds), *Positioning Theory*. Oxford: Blackwell, pp. 14–31.

Watson, T. J. (1995). "Rhetoric, Discourse and Argument in Organisational Sense-Making: A Reflexive Tale." *Organization Studies*, 16/5: 805–21.

Wetherell, M. (1998). "Positioning and Interpretative Repertoires: Conversation Analysis and Post-Structuralism in Dialogue." *Discourse & Society*, 9/3: 387–412.

—— Potter, J. (1992). *Mapping the Language of Racism: Discourse and the Legitimation of Exploitation*. London: Harvester Wheatsheaf.

White, G. M. (1990). "Moral Discourse and the Rhetoric of Emotions," in C. A. Lutz and L. Abu-Lughod (eds), *Language and the Politics of Emotion*. New York: Cambridge University Press, pp. 46–68.

Whittle, A. and Mueller, F. (2011). "The Language of Interests: The Contribution of Discursive Psychology." *Human Relations*, 64/3: 415–35.

—— —— Mangan, A. (2008). "In Search of Subtlety: Discursive Devices and Rhetorical Competence." *Management Communication Quarterly*, 22/1: 99–122.

Widdicombe, S. (1998a). "'But You Don't Class Yourself': The Interactional Management of Category Membership and Non-membership," in C. Antaki and S. Widdicombe (eds), *Identities in Talk*. London: Sage Publications, pp. 52–70.

—— (1998b). "Uses of Identity as an Analysts' and a Participants' Tool," in C. Antaki and S. Widdicombe (eds), *Identities in Talk*. London: Sage Publications, pp. 191–206.

Wiggins, S. and Potter, J. (2008). "Discursive Psychology," in C. Willig and W. Stainton Rogers (eds), *The Sage Handbook of Qualitative Research in Psychology*. London: Sage, pp. 72–89.

Wittgenstein, L. (1953). Philosophical Investigations (trans. and ed. G. E. M. Anscombe and R. Rhees). Oxford: Blackwell.

8

Identity and Time in Gilles Deleuze's Process Philosophy

James Williams

Abstract: This chapter presents Gilles Deleuze's process philosophy of time. It argues that times are multiple and that his philosophy has a ninefold grid of times, where times take others as dimensions. In order to show the potential of this philosophy for process organization, the grid is applied to an example from the organization and management of time around objective-setting and review. Three criticisms are raised on the division, multiplicity, and selection of times. These are answered by closer studies of Deleuze's understanding of the present and past. The chapter concludes with a study of his account of the future.

Long after the young and unworldly might judge that they should have in all decency ended, the secret of H's seductions could be found on the small balcony of an apartment with no other outside space. The secret of the "terrace" with its attached "orangerie" could be found in its herb garden. Though the flavorings, potions, and drugs certainly bewitched the victim's senses, the deepest secret of all, the prelude to complete and sublime abandonment, was the novel tale told to each visitor. In truth, the story was always about the same small cultivation. This stable reference, with its spatial organization as rigid and detailed as any formal garden, was steadily to be undone. Unforeseeable and singular changes in the seasons, reflections of the sun on neighbors' windows, hybrid and smuggled seeds, dastardly shadows from construction sites, streetlights, city smoke and dust, newfound tastes and dislikes, small illnesses and great health, and the vagaries of watering and wind were set to work then recounted. All stable certainties faded and the fortunate victim's buttresses of order, identity, and

Identity and Time in Gilles Deleuze's Process Philosophy

propriety dissolved into the new tale of becoming and eternally reborn desire.

For Gilles Deleuze, identity always comes after process. Even when it has arrived, through multiple geneses, identity is never free of process. Identity as such, identity as being, identity as stable, and identity as complete representation are therefore mere illusions. There is no identity as such independent of the processes making and unmaking it. No identified organization has a final and determined being; it is always a multiplicity of becoming. There is no stability escaping movements that give birth to it, then topple it, make it tremble, and dissolve it into novel processes, in rhythm with a multitude of open and ongoing transformations. A photograph of a garden, its identity as a scattering of colors and shade, of horticultural labels and tools, is then always an illusion abstracted from the biological processes drawing it to different patterns and names. This order of priority of becoming and identity, where identity is always secondary, dependent and illusory in any claim to permanence, bequeaths a value system to Deleuze's philosophy. Life is led to the full when it maximizes its expression of the multiplicity of becoming giving rise to fleeting identities. There has to be identity for the expression of difference, but its task is to test how far it can stretch itself without destroying its power to bring becoming into life.

In order to explain and defend these wide claims about identity and difference, this chapter will discuss the genesis and disruption of identity in Deleuze's philosophy of time. This philosophy is developed in his 1968 and 1969 masterworks *Difference and Repetition* (Deleuze, 1968; see Williams, 2003 for full commentary) and *Logic of Sense* (Deleuze, 1969; see Williams, 2008 for commentary). The explanation is difficult and necessary, as his philosophy of time is the latest and most radical philosophy of time departing from common sense assumptions about time and raising difficult paradoxes about time and identity. As such, his work joins the line of great philosophical works on time stretching back to Heraclitus, through Aristotle, Augustine, Kant, Nietzsche, Bergson, and Whitehead—to name but some (for a helpful situation of Deleuze in relation to other figures in the philosophy of time, see Turetzky, 1998; for a full account of Deleuze's philosophy of time, see Williams, 2011). These wide historical roots and contrasts will be narrowed down here to serve a more restricted yet socially urgent purpose. The aim will be to show how this philosophy of time relates critically to techniques in the management and organization of time. Such technologies are often quite simple, such as the setting of successive common deadlines by a project manager, yet they are designed to tame great complexity. Deleuze's philosophy can show the costs and omissions of this enterprise. It can also offer suggestions for approaches more in tune with life as prior process and as multiple becoming.

A sense of the radical nature of Deleuze's ideas can be grasped from the application of his main theses on identity and becoming to the definition of time. Time has no single identity, for instance as a line of time or as a single space–time continuum. Instead, Deleuze's philosophy of time gives us a multiplicity of times. "Time" is an irreducible network of processes making many times. These many times are related, but only according to numerous asymmetrical transformations. The concept of asymmetry is important here because it underpins the irreversibility and hence direction of time. In Deleuze's work, however, this asymmetry does not imply that time only flows irreversibly from past to future. It is rather that no process is reversible back to its original state, so for instance we can also say that time flows irreversibly from present to past. Even the well-worn metaphor of the flow of time is superseded by this new philosophy and its radical commitment to time as process.

There is a sense of continuity afforded by the image of a river flowing before us, as if we change but the river flows forever. For Deleuze, there is instead a mutual transformation such that a more appropriate metaphor might be of the series of intertwined and ever-shifting arms of a river delta, where broken banks on one arm imply changes in flow in others. Time as process does not so much flow as divide and transform according to a multiplicity of interrelated upheavals and tensions. This image of a succession of disjunctions and ongoing transformations is used by Deleuze toward the beginning of *Difference and Repetition*. It supports his claim that we never inhabit the same world because of the universality of singular processes: "We therefore set generality, as generality of the particular, in opposition to repetition as universality of the singular" (Deleuze, 1968: 8). Rather than a repetition of similar instances, history gives us a repetition of singular events, where the connection is not between identities but differences. Time as process is not about the continuity of the same, but rather about the continuous return of difference, of different singular processes.

This distinction explains a puzzle in Deleuze's work concerning the necessity for continuity and its place in his metaphysics. We could assume that when time flows continuously it provides an unchanging reference point to judge the changes in things. We can judge upon a difference between A at t1 and A' at t2 because we can relate t1 and t2 according to a well-ordered time line. This reliance on a fixed identity, on the equivalence of instants and intervals in time, runs contrary to Deleuze's response to one of Plato's paradoxes of knowledge from the *Theaetetus*. Against

Identity and Time in Gilles Deleuze's Process Philosophy

affirmations of ubiquitous flux drawn from Heraclitus, Socrates draws Theodorus into a nonsensical position. If all is flux, nothing can be known, not even flux itself: "But now, since not even white continues to flow white, and whiteness itself is a flux or change which is passing into another colour, and is never to be caught standing still, can the name of any colour be rightly used at all?" (Plato, 1987: 36) Instead, according to Deleuze's account, such knowledge is only a secondary illusion dependent on prior differences between differences. With time as pure becoming all we have are ongoing transformations. Identity then only comes into consideration when we need to fix such processes as actual. This provides us with an important lesson about Deleuze's method in his works from the late 1960s. Paradoxes do not present us with problems to be resolved. They are instead a matrix generating series of creative responses, such as the idea of relations between multiple differences, rather than the Platonic securing of differences upon a fixed reference point. Such responses never finally dismiss the paradox, but instead take it as revealing reality as essentially paradoxical. Reality is a mutating challenge to be sparred with because its transformations are an essential part of our lives.

The concept of asymmetry resists any reduction of the overall multiplicity in Deleuze's metaphysics, because whenever we try to coordinate states of the system to each other they have moved on according to asymmetrical processes (for discussions of the concept of multiplicity on Deleuze's work, see DeLanda, 2002: 71–3; de Beistegui, 2004: 248–9). They cannot be traced back according to a single uniform set of rules or model of transformation (Deleuze, 1968: 105–6). It is not unusual for thinkers to assign an arrow to time—to claim that it cannot be reversed—but Deleuze takes the challenge much further by positing many times, each with its arrows (for related discussion of arrows of time, see Hawking, 1988: 169; Prigogine and Stengers, 1988: 120–1; Savitt, 1995: 12). These arrows are determined by relations to other times. More importantly, for our arguments here, every one of these relations is a process of reciprocal transformation, rather than a single function from one state to another. A and B are both changing according to a process going from A to B. But then they are also both changing according to a process running in the other direction. Deep down we have a subtle and perhaps repressed affinity to such reciprocal and asymmetrical processes through our experiences of communication. The asymmetry explains the ubiquity of human misunderstandings. Whenever we try to fix the meaning of statement in a dialogue by returning to it from a later point, the way the statement works within a continuing process will have changed it in a multiple way according to the asymmetrical processes of time.

This does not mean that it is futile to attempt to clarify a statement. It means that the return to its original and secure sense is impossible. Though it is beyond the scope of this chapter, it is still worth noting that this commitment to asymmetry also underpins Deleuze's opposition to a symmetrical concept of causality where we can reverse time and process by tracing back to the cause from the effect. His model is instead that we have asymmetrical relations between causes, where a cause is defined by its power as cause, and asymmetrical relations between effects, where an effect is defined as an intensity of relations to other effects (Deleuze, 1969: 115–17; see Simont, 2003, for a discussion of intensity in relation to events). A cause changes the power of another cause, but this change cannot be reversed and is not subject to any form of regularity. An effect alters with this change in power in terms of its relations to all other effects, again with no implication that the relation can be reversed. A quick way of grasping these odd views about causality and regularity comes from Deleuze's claims on singularity and repetition quoted above. As we never have repetition of the same, but only a series of singular events, we cannot view such events under a causal law. Critically, this raises the objection to Deleuze that his model leads to a radical scepticism about the relation of past events to future ones and about natural laws as causal and regular.

Thus, for Deleuze, times are made by reciprocal yet asymmetrical processes. These processes and attendant times are then played out in transformations of identities. An initial understanding of the multiplicity of times and their relations through processes of transformation comes from an important novel use by Deleuze of the concept of dimension in relation to times rather than spaces. Past, present, and future are not separate. Instead, they can take each other as dimensions according to which time is taken as prior in terms of process. The question of how priority is determined is a difficult one. A simple and preliminary answer depends on the concept of asymmetry. A process is primary when it determines another process but this secondary process does not determine it in return. The secondary process is then a dimension. There is therefore a time where the present is the prior process (Deleuze, 1968: 105). Past and future then becomes different dimensions of the present. In *Difference and Repetition*, Deleuze calls this set of relations the first synthesis of time. However, there is also a time where the present is a dimension of the past, in the second synthesis of time. There is a time where the past is a dimension of the future, in the third synthesis of time (Deleuze, 1968: 125). The present as prior process is not equivalent to the present as dimension of the past. No

Identity and Time in Gilles Deleuze's Process Philosophy

	First synthesis of time (synthesis in the present)	Second synthesis of time (synthesis of the past)	Third synthesis of time (synthesis for the future)
Present	As prior contraction	As made to pass as the most contracted state of the pure past	As incapable of returning and as caesura
Past	As dimension contracted into the present through a singular selection	As pure past	As returning as pure difference and as symbolic process
Future	As dimension contracted into the present as a range of possibilities and probabilities	As freedom and destiny	As the only process remaining the same and as the new as assembly and seriation

Figure 8.1 Manifold of the syntheses of time

time is equivalent as prior and as dimension. This means that the multiplicity of times forms a nine square manifold (Figure 8.1).

Each of the columns shows one of Deleuze's syntheses of time with its characteristic dimensions in each line. The first synthesis takes the present as prior such that the past and future become its dimensions. The process at work on each of these dimensions is contraction (Deleuze, 1968: 103). The past becomes contracted into the present, for example, in the way years of practice are tested and shown to be worthwhile or wasted in a test in the present—*all those hours of revision lost by not reading the question properly* . . . . The future, on the other hand, becomes contracted because selections in the present alter the probabilities to be ascribed to future outcomes, for example, in the way an irreversible decision can make some future events extremely unlikely—*he handed himself into the police and saw his life as a free man disappear* . . . . In the first synthesis of time, everything is drawn into and decided in the present (Deleuze, 1968: 104). In contrast, in the second synthesis the present becomes a dimension as that which must pass into the past. This can seem be difficult to grasp, but one way of thinking about it is in terms of an experience of powerlessness in the present in relation to the place our actions will take as past. For example, the past "makes the present pass" when we realize that our reputation is becoming tarnished and that there is nothing we can do to redeem it—*she realized their disapproval would always define her* . . . . (Deleuze, 1968: 105). The synthesis of the past also gives it a hold on the future by determining it as both destiny and freedom.

According to Deleuze's account, the past determines the future, but it also gives it a marker to affirm its freedom against. We can understand this apparent contradiction better in light of his approach to causality discussed briefly above. We can be determined by past events yet nonetheless retain a freedom to shape the future—*the destiny of his class was to remain at the bottom of society but he resolved to break with it*. This also explains why Deleuze prefers to speak of destiny rather than causal determination, as destiny allows for a degree of freedom that rigid accounts of causality do not (though there are compatibilist versions of causality that allow for freedom in conjunction with determination) (Deleuze, 1969: 13). Freedom, however, is not given its full grounding in Deleuze's philosophy of time until the third synthesis of time. There, the present and past are broken with in a radical manner. The present as dimension of the future is defined as cut or caesura and impossibility of return. The past is defined as a reserve of pure differences and symbolic processes rather than as representations that can return as the same. The future is therefore freed from present and past by severing time in the present and disallowing any return of the same. We will investigate this complex third synthesis more deeply in the third section below. At this stage, it is important to note that its main source comes from Deleuze's original interpretation of Nietzsche's doctrine of eternal return (Nietzsche, 1969: 179), where Deleuze does not see the return as an infinite return of the same events, but on the contrary of pure differences, that is of variations in value or intensity as conditions for events differing from one another despite superficial similarities (Deleuze, 1968: 384) (for detailed background to this important area of Deleuze and Nietzsche research, see Heidegger, 1991: 212; Badiou, 1997: 113; Klossowski, 1997: 69; Ansell Pearson, 2002: 197–205; Grosz, 2004: 141; Bryant, 2008: 221–2; Widder, 2008: 98–9).

These syntheses of time can seem very abstract and demanding, but in fact they are highly practical and provide very powerful analytical and explanatory tools. Perhaps, the best source for grasping this practical element can be drawn from Deleuze's cinema books (Deleuze, 1983; Deleuze, 1985). These were published more than fifteen years after *Difference and Repetition*, but they return to many of the ideas and sources of the earlier book, such as the notion of a multiplicity of dimensions of times, discussed in relation to Augustine (Deleuze, 1985: 132), and the concept of the pure past, discussed through a lengthy study of Bergson (Deleuze, 1985: 109; see Rodowick, 1997, for a discussion of time and Deleuze's work on cinema). Unfortunately, in connection with process organization, the film books can seem specialized in their vast cinema references and detailed analyses of films and *auteurs*. Yet one of the main insights of the cinema books is still a very useful tool for the explanation of the revolutionary and eminently applicable approach to time in Deleuze. Film shows us how common sense ideas about time and unreflective approaches to perceptions of movement and time hide much more complex relations, for instance, in the way a flashback scene unlocks the work of the past in the present by drawing the past more immediately and more vividly into present perception. So, by observing and then following the lead of how a film-maker reveals deeper processes of time, we can release our understanding of organization in relation to process. Thereby, we can free ourselves from the hold of common sense assumptions about identity in space and time.

8.1 Applying Deleuze's philosophy of time

In this section, I will apply Deleuze's philosophy of time and some aspects of the ninefold grid of dimensions of time to a simplified example from the management of time. The example of yearly objective-setting and review has been chosen because it is a common technique for the management, organization, and taming of time (Armstrong, 1998: 151; 2006: 505–6). In this case, the stretch of a year and the multiple processes unfolding within it are organized thanks to a technique involving the projection of the stretch and processes on to two dates separated by a year and on to a list of recorded objectives to be reviewed once the year has passed. The point of this study of this review process is, first, to indicate the critical potential of Deleuze's philosophy, albeit in simplified and speculative terms. Second, it is to begin to show the alternative approaches suggested for the process organization of time by Deleuze's more complex grid of dimensions and processes of time.

Let W and G be in a small overheated meeting room, away from their usual workspace. W, the line manager, is reviewing G's performance against a set of agreed objectives. The objectives were set a year earlier. There are high stakes for the review in terms of pay, promotion, and future in the company for G. There are other important factors for W too, in the opportunity to use the meeting as a management tool and to achieve W's own set of objectives. The training and human resources manual are clear about the dialogical nature of the review and about the need to be flexible in relation to changing circumstances. The review process is meant to be reasonable and progressive. Nonetheless, three documents and a simplified power relation dominate the exchange. The documents are last year's objectives statement, this year's report on the attainment of those objectives, written by G, and a joint review to be drafted at the meeting and agreed by both parties. This last report will form the basis for remuneration discussions.

The documents are signs of the reduction of the complexity of time, from multiple stretches and many lines of time and tasks, to the date of the original setting and the date of the review, and to the list of objectives and attainments. Further signs of this reduction can be found in the funneling of a year's relationship between colleagues into a short meeting and on to thin documents. A year's worth of resentments and debts, joint successes and failures, as well as slights and generous acts come to bear on the meeting, but they are also transformed and intensified at it. The meeting is a peak of stress not only because of its high stakes but also because of the pressure of years of emotions and experiences crushed into it. This also explains the superstructure of reassurances, checks, and balances around the review process, such as claims that the review documents are to remain confidential, that they do not have a direct bearing on remuneration, that reviewers go through training in rights legislation, and that reviews should be two-way, allowing reviewed staff to report on their reviewers.

The power relations around objective setting and review are of course highly complex as they run the full range of interpersonal, intracompany, and society-wide relations. However, the dominant relations are that the reports must be filed. They will form some part of pay and promotion. W, as line manager, has control over the process. I have drawn attention to power

	First synthesis of time	Second synthesis of time	Third synthesis of time
Present	All work is concentrated on the present of the objective-setting and review meetings	The present moment of the meeting is also passing away into the past in a way that renders the actors passive	Once the meeting has passed, it is irretrievably lost. Its relation to the future is as a radical break with what came before.
Past	Past actions are selected and contracted into the review documents and the discussion about successful or failed attainment	There is no limit in principle as to which events in the past call to and transform the present as it is made to pass	For future actions, the past is a set of symbols to be reinterpreted and intense values to be selected within and reaffirmed
Future	Future possibilities are opened and closed according to the flow of the discussion about success or failure in relation to objectives	The past year's activities and last year's objectives are a destiny for the actors, yet the actors are also free to debate over them and try to rearrange this destiny	The future, as creativity, will reassemble all of the past and the present meeting, it will set them into new series, but it will never do so as the same events, only as different ones

Figure 8.2 Deleuze's manifold of time dimensions

here to underline the artificiality of the reduction of time. The two points selected a year apart are not a reflection of a natural order and quality of time. Nor is the limited set of objectives. They have to be imposed and time is subject to techniques of control themselves guided by economic and management imperatives. Figure 8.2 translates the meeting and process into Deleuze's manifold of time dimensions.

The first synthesis captures the priority given to the present. Deleuze analyzes its relation to the past, which it takes as a dimension, through Hume's accounts of habit and synthesis in the imagination (Deleuze, 1968: 97; Hume, 2009: 68). Habits are formed by past repetitions such that the past becomes active in the present and present acts are passive to those repetitions. Deleuze broadens Hume's analysis by moving beyond human and animal habits to the concept of repetition in series (Bell, 2009: 26–9). In the first synthesis, past repetitions are played out in present events. However, though there is a passive synthesis of past repetitions in the present, present events decide upon the sense and value of those repetitions. We can imagine this concentration of the past under the direction of a film-maker's take on the business meeting. Past scenes come to mind for the participants and can be shown to an audience as reduced, expanded, transformed, and selected by present events in a number of flashbacks inserted into the filmed meeting. Though repetitions in the past have made the present, events in the present decide on the significance of those of the past. For instance, in an attempt to devalue some of G's efforts, W might state that though they have led to achieved objectives, they are now outside the new set of priorities given to the business by a new CEO. Many past repetitions and acts then slip away through their subservience to the present. The key lesson from the first synthesis of time as priority for the present is that there is a time where all past efforts are replayed and transformed in critical present events. The past is always in play. It cannot be appealed to as a settled and reliable reserve of facts or commitments—*but you promised that if I fulfilled these objectives I'd get promotion . . . Sorry, things have changed . . .* .

For the future, the operation of the first synthesis is not one of concentration through selection of actual repetitions, but rather through changes in the probability of future ones. The future is in play in the present as a changing array of probabilities for possible future events. Again, we can visualize this through imagination or film. As a critical promotion meeting goes badly a set of possible futures becomes less and less likely, while more negative ones increase. So when the line manager suggests ticking the "Unsatisfactory" box for "Attainment of Stated Objectives" it is not merely a series of past efforts that turn out to have been irrelevant or misplaced.

A film comedy might flash forward and show an imagined future at the helm of the company dissolve like a mirage. The participants go through this changing array of probabilities viscerally, as their physical states and moods shift according to the flow of positive and negative signs. A feeling of sickness and confusion might accompany the fading of the dreamed of future, or a rising sense of elation might run parallel with the increased probability of promotion. With this flow of signs and physical manifestations, a set of future plans and projects is also rearranged and assigned different probabilities. The important feature to retain from this synthesis of the future in the present is that nothing in the future retains an independence from the present and the present thereby gains in urgency and weight. So the objective-setting meeting is not only onerous because it can decide upon a cherished and hard-earned past but also vital because all futures are touched by it.

Whether it is for the past or for the future, the important factor to retain in the first synthesis is the subjection to the present. Time is concentrated and contracted on the present as a time of struggle between activity and passivity (Deleuze, 1968: 104–5). This present is a drama determining paths through fading efforts and shifting dreams. However, three surprising and difficult factors should be taken into account here. They all concern the division of time into multiple presents. As the first synthesis is a process concentrating time on particular present events, we are not given a single present for all events, but instead many different presents with different ways of concentrating the past and the future. Thus, in our example, W and G have different times determined by the ways in which their present passions and actions determine the past and the future in the present. There could be a time concentrated around W's sense of a meeting that went well, where the future became more settled in terms of G's work patterns within the company. This time, though, might well run alongside another where G's sense of a disastrous meeting accompanies a determination to leave the company because of its failure to recognize worth and effort in a flexible manner. The first problem therefore concerns the relation of different presents and their accompanying pasts and futures. Deleuze calls this the problem of the communication of events. How do different times communicate yet also retain their individuality as processes?

The second problem can be traced to the nature of the processes in the present. The example we have taken is a human one and up to now the synthesis has been organized around human passions and actions, that is, the events we are passive to and those we shape. However, there is no necessity to this anthropocentrism in Deleuze's philosophy. It is quite the contrary. Any transformation determining process as individual can serve as a passive synthesis around a living present. This includes not only individual animals but also groups of beings (human and animal) and even inanimate objects. All that is required is a singular change concentrating the past and the present within it. Instances of this could be growth in an individual animal, a mutation in a species or an alteration in a physical state, a fissure due to an earthquake, or the reflection of the sun on to a specific position in a room. The multiplicity of presents is infinite in line with the infinity of differences that can occupy a given space. Therefore, the second problem is not about the communication of presents but about the arbitrariness of their selection within this communication. How do we decide which presents to include and which to exclude? Should we focus on changes in individuals or in a workforce? Is the novel form of light in a meeting room significant? Should we take account of the heat of uncommonly dry summer?

Third, these problems of selection, profusion, and communication do not only arise for different presents, but in a single one. This is because the process of concentration does not have necessary limits in time. Any individual synthesis in the present is a synthesis of all the past and all possible futures under its singular selections. When we come to describe this synthesis or act upon it we inevitably make another selection and lose something or the former one. I have highlighted these difficulties because they demonstrate a powerful objection to Deleuze's philosophy of time in practical context. It appears to lead us into a profusion of separate times and hence into a lack of legitimacy in terms of the selection of any one of them. The selection thereby becomes radically contingent. However, I have also discussed these problems because Deleuze's response to them provides us with a number of methodologies and examples not only concerning practical applications of the first synthesis of time but also for the second and third syntheses. In turn, this allows for a narrow focus on the very large amount of material covered by those syntheses.

Two ideas allow us to grasp the methods that can be used to work with the problems of the multiplicity and infinite extension of presents. These ideas bring precise distinctions and manageable entities to a field that appears beset by insurmountable complexity and randomness. First, though no present can be reduced to another, every present includes all the others. Inclusion or "folding in" is a process of transformation. It means that though two presents are different, they also transform each other. This transformation, however, is asymmetrical. In the case of our example, it means that

W and G transform each other but do so such that the transformations cannot be taken as part of a wider common system without losing something of the singularity of each. In turn, this leads to a methodology where we seek to present both transformations rather than privilege one or the other or bring them under a third term. Instead of fusing them together we have to set each process alongside the other as an inequality to be worked with rather than as a unity. In very practical terms this means that a review document should not erase different perspectives in an agreed version. Instead, richer narratives should be included. Though these need not be long, they should seek to express the multiple processes surrounding the search to attain objectives. They should also be told from different points of view.

The methodological emphasis is then twofold: a focus on the presentation of differences and an understanding of these differences as processes of concentration of the past and of the future on the present. Critics, however, will claim that such a method can only be a step toward a later resolution or elimination of the differences. This critical angle will emphasize the need for comparability between different reviews. It will also insist that a review has to have a quantitative aspect. How does this review compare to that one? Has this member of staff achieved as many objectives as that one? As we have seen, there is a counterargument based on Deleuze's philosophy of time. Comparability and quantification are based on fictions denying a much more complex network of processes. Irrespective of whether the reduction is necessary or not, there is value in drawing attention to it through techniques placing multiple documents and narratives alongside the objectives and reports that elide them (for a discussion of Deleuze's philosophy of time in relation to narrative in the work of Paul Ricoeur, see Williams, 1996). This has an analytical merit as it permits us to become aware of the background to crises and tensions emerging because of restrictive processes. It also has a creative value in allowing a more sensitive account of the unfolding of effort. This in turn has the merit of drawing on a richer set of capabilities and of information for organization and planning. The understanding of time and process in Deleuze's first synthesis of time contributes to a healing of the wounds inflicted by a violent reduction of the complexity of time and life. That understanding also leads to a creative response to the complexity. It is at the same time more true to life and sensitive to its inherent dislocations and conflicts.

These more sensitive narratives and objectives need to take account of a more varied set of past events and of a larger set of imagined futures (and the different weights different protagonists assign to both of them). They are necessarily creative not only in the selections they have to make, but

Identity and Time in Gilles Deleuze's Process Philosophy

also in their format and content. Why, though, is this not a sufficient account of time? What is the role and necessity of Deleuze's second and third syntheses of time? How can accounts of time that do not give priority to the present but instead make it a dimension of the past, or of the future, inform organizational practices and processes? A good way to grasp the necessity and function of these additional syntheses can be detected through the difference they bring to the present. In both cases, these differences introduce positive and negative elements to our practice, where positive indicates principles for the creative construction of novel practices and negative implies limits ascribed to that creativity.

In the second synthesis of time, the prior process is the synthesis of the pure past (Deleuze, 1968: 108–9). This is not the past as a set of representations of events, for instance, an unchanging archive of images and texts. Instead, the pure past is a changing set of intensities of relations of value and significance. It is not a record of actual presents that become past, but rather all the changeable relations of value that accompany the passing of any present. This can seem very strange and abstract, so here is an example. Let G be a very reliable employee such that all G's past actions are connected with high intensities ascribed to a set of values such as "to depend," "to trust," and "to rely." When present events pass away, these intensities change. G wins the lottery and the next day systematically sabotages the firm's computer systems, leaks trade secrets to competitors, and irreversibly poisons colleagues' relationships by reporting what they have said about one another in confidence. With the new present, the set of relations of values changes dramatically. The intensities of relations of trust, reliability, and dependence diminish and become attached much more strongly to values around wealth and independence, mistrust, and vengefulness. This change in the intensity of values takes place in a virtual realm Deleuze calls the pure past. Any actual realm is incomplete without its parallel virtual realm of intensity and value.

The way the present is made to pass by the pure past is therefore counterintuitive and laden with unusual but important consequences. We could think that the passivity and inevitability implied by the passage of the present into the past should be understood as a passing into fixed record: a passage from a changeable and lived present within our power into fixed unchangeable representations. In Deleuze's philosophy of time, the past never takes this form. Instead, the past is always in flux and cannot contain representations (Deleuze, 1968: 110). Every version of the past is process-like. The passage from living present to passing present must therefore be understood as the passage from a present contracting the past and the future into a present contracted by the past. The present then passes away from a selection in the past made by the present into all of the pure past as transforming the present passing into it. This passage from living present to passing present can be understood in terms of a distinction drawn in terms of legacy. Our actions and living present have a double legacy. On the one hand, each present can be included in contractions of another present, as described above in terms of the first synthesis of time. On the other hand, each present passes into the pure past into which all living presents must pass. For the former, each present grasps the other directly as singular event and in terms of asymmetrical selections and transformations. For the latter, every present connects to every other but only through the mediation of the pure past. In terms of our guiding example, the difference is between the asymmetry of a dialogue between reviewer and reviewed, an asymmetry of singular perspectives, and a communication of reviewer and reviewed through all the values and intensities that have been and will be but that they pass into in a singular manner.

The pure past and the second synthesis of time therefore introduce a different kind of passivity and, paradoxically, a wider yet less concrete responsibility into the present. This is because when the present becomes a dimension of the pure past as the most concentrated state of its shifting set of relations, it only does so through a changing series of intensities, rather than actual events. In behaving badly toward a colleague, we are reviewing we leave a concrete legacy, but we also express and fall away into all of the past now connected to the intensity and significance of our behavior. Here, responsibility is not to a concrete individual but to all individuals and events that would have passed away. They become connected to our singular legacy into the whole of the past. The difference is then between a direct call to behave well toward another being and a legacy we leave as a destiny for all beings, past, present, and future. For instance, an infamous act is then divided into its direct relations to the other causes it touches upon and its indirect relations mediated through the pure past.

In terms of guidelines for a practice such as yearly review, the second synthesis of time implies that we must not limit care to the multiple asymmetrical narratives at play in any dialogue about, say, objectives. It means that within any given narrative and the acts around them we must pay heed to the unseen and indirect legacies of those acts, to which values we have intensified and which drawn energy away from. This care will not be a science, or even a clear practice (Massumi, 2002, and Protevi, 2009, have explored this practical side of Deleuze's work at length). It is rather a creative art where we try to connect to as many positive values as possible as intensely as possible. This is not a good life not for our sake, or even for those in our direct ambit, but a good life as impersonal legacy.

8.2 Conclusion: The place of the future in Deleuze's process philosophy of time

There is a risk in the order we have treated Deleuze's syntheses of time. The same risk is also implied by their numbering. It could be thought that present and past take precedence over the future in his philosophy of time. This order of priority has important practical consequences inviting a serious critical point. The first two syntheses emphasize passivity, a living present answerable to the past and to the future, and the weight of the pure past that draws every present into the whole of the past (for a discussion of Deleuze in relation to the weight of the past, see Williams, 2009). Does this mean that in practice Deleuze's philosophy must be reactionary, held in sway by all the ongoing processes concentrated in the present and caught in the strictures of destiny and of the demand to express as many values as possible, as intensely as possible? Is there a danger of paralysis due to too great demands? Is there an antiprogressive program based on the call of the past?

There are two answers to these questions. The first is technical and concerns the order and dimensions of time. It involves deep philosophical problems at the heart of contemporary debates in Deleuze scholarship, notably phrased in critical terms by two of the most influential negative readers of Deleuze, Alain Badiou (1997), and Peter Hallward (2006). The second answer is more practical and helps us to understand how the past and the present can become progressive when taken as dimensions of the future. I will discuss the first answer briefly, to give a sense of the wider stakes in Deleuze interpretation. Then I will pass to the more practical approach in the context of the ongoing theme of the organization of time in terms of process.

For Deleuze, the numbering of the syntheses does not indicate a priority. On the contrary, each synthesis and the dimensions of time it defines respond to paradoxes and problems in the others. This means that instead of a hierarchy of times and syntheses, we have a system of interdependence. In accordance with this system, no account of time or of a process in time is complete until it includes all the syntheses of time. When the future takes the past and future as dimensions, it frees them from reactionary and retrograde pressures by introducing a necessity for creativity and freedom. For the present, this means that any present must be seen as a caesura in time, a break where time is dramatically cut, reassembled differently, and set into new series (Deleuze, 1968: 120). This responds to the problem of the passivity of the first synthesis and to the paradox that, although the present contracts the past and the future, it seems to lack a source and explanation of its freedom to do so. The principle of the future taken as prior in time is derived from a novel interpretation of Nietzsche's doctrine of eternal return: only difference returns and never the same. In its singularity, any present must therefore be a cut in time; it cannot have any continuity of being, or sameness.

This cut is also an assembly and a setting into series of time, a seriation, but this continuity cannot be based on continuous identities. Instead, it is based on a variation of the past; it is a continuity of transformation of the pure past as expressed in new actual creations. This is what Deleuze means by the eternal return of difference. It is the eternally renewed expression of values and intensities in the new actual beings that express them. These beings will necessarily pass and cannot return, but they leave a trace in the pure past: a virtual reserve to be expressed anew in future works. This turn to the virtual and to abstractions from actuality then leads to a critique of Deleuze on the basis of a mystical detachment and a turn away from the real. The counter to this critical reading lies in the complete version of his philosophy of time. We never have only the future, or the pure past, but rather a multiplicity of times. Any reading of Deleuze that emphasizes one above the other distorts that multiplicity and misses the dependencies between times.

Once the future takes the present and the past as dimensions, Deleuze's practical philosophy takes on its most progressive tenor (Deleuze, 1968: 125). Any act in the present is confronted by the dual challenge of having to live up to its situation as a break with the past and as an identity that must necessarily pass, never to return. The present is then a decision and an action in relation to its difference with the past. There is a freedom and a necessity to do things differently. Therefore, though we have to give a narrative based on the past within any organization of the past, we also have to create a novel event. When these injunctions are combined, we have the association of destiny and free creation characteristic of Deleuze's philosophy (Deleuze, 1968: 113). The protagonists in a review meeting are caught by the past and must give their different versions of it, but they must do so through a creation not only of that past, through a novel narration, but also of the present as break with that past. What guides this creation? What values can it realize?

In creating a novel event, the first guide given by Deleuze's account of the future is that the same never returns. We can never preserve the past or the present as the same, in any given identity. Every aim of maintaining a state is doomed. However, something does return: difference as variation of intensity in the values we associate with novel actual identities. Our actions should then seek to express the strongest, the most intense, connections between events. This means that any action that divides and opposes beings or fixes them into well-defined identities consigns them to a past that they can never return from. We should then seek to express those relations of collective transformation against division and separate existence. We have to do so with actual beings, but the vehicle must not be confused with the values it can express. The highest challenge Deleuze's philosophy sets us is then not how to connect with the past as we have come to represent it, but rather how to introduce maximum transformation into beings without destroying their power to express as many values from the past as they can, but in new situations and through new ways of living, individually and collectively.

References

Ansell Pearson, Keith (2002). *Philosophy and the Adventure of the Virtual: Bergson and the Time of Life*. London: Routledge.

Armstrong, Michael (1998). *Managing People a Practical Guide for Line Managers*. London: Kogan Page.

—— (2006). *A Handbook of Human Resource Management Practice*. London: Kogan Page.

Badiou, Alain (1997). *Deleuze: la clameur de l'être*. Paris: Hachette.

de Beistegui, Miguel (2004). *Truth and Genesis: Philosophy as Differential Ontology*. Bloomington, IN: Indiana University Press.

Bell, Jeffrey (2009). *Deleuze's Hume: Philosophy, Culture and the Scottish Enlightenment*. Edinburgh: Edinburgh University Press.

Bryant, Levi R. (2008). *Difference and Givenness: Deleuze's Transcendental Empiricism and the Ontology of Immanence*. Evanston, IL: Northwestern University Press.

DeLanda, Manuel (2002). *Intensive Science and Virtual Philosophy*. London: Continuum.

Deleuze, Gilles (1968). *Différence et répétition*. Paris: Presses Universitaires de France. (Trans. Patton P. (1994). *Difference and Repetition*. New York: Columbia University Press).

—— (1969). *Logique du sens*. Paris: Éditions de Minuit. (Trans. M. Lester, and C. Stivale. *The Logic of Sense* (1990) New York: Columbia University Press.)

—— (1983). *Cinema-1: L'Image-mouvement*. Paris: Éditions de Minuit. (Trans. H. Tomlinson and B. Habberjam (1986). *Cinema 1: The Movement-Image*. Minneapolis, MN: University of Minnesota Press.)

Deleuze, Gilles (1985). *Cinéma-2: L'Image-temps*. Paris: Éditions de Minuit. (Trans. H. Tomlinson and R. Galeta. *Cinema 2: The Time-Image* (1989). Minneapolis, MN: University of Minnesota Press.)

Grosz, Elizabeth (2004). *The Nick of Time: Politics, Evolution and the Untimely*. Durham, NC: Duke University Press.

Hallward, Peter (2006). *Out of this World: Deleuze and the Philosophy of Creation*. London: Verso.

Hawking, Stephen (1988). *A Brief History of Time: From the Big Bang to Black Holes*. London: Bantam.

Heidegger, Martin (1991). *Nietzsche* (vols. 3 and 4; ed. D. F. Krell). San Francisco, CA: Harper Collins.

Hume, David (2009). *A Treatise of Human Nature* (ed. D. F. Norton and M. J. Norton). Oxford: Oxford University Press.

Khalfa, Jean (2003). *An Introduction to the Philosophy of Gilles Deleuze*. London: Continuum.

Klossowski, Pierre (1997). *Nietzsche and the Vicious Circle* (trans. D. Smith). London: Athlone.

Massumi, Brian (2002). *Parables for the Virtual: Movement, Affect, Sensation*. Durham, NC: Duke University Press.

Nietzsche, Friedrich (1969). *Thus Spoke Zarathustra*. Trans. R. J. Hollingdale. London: Pengain.

Plato (1987). *Theaetetus* (trans. R. Waterfield). London: Penguin.

Prigogine, Ilya and Stengers, Isabelle (1992, originally 1988). *Entre le temps et l'éternité*. Paris: Flammarion.

Protevi, John (2009). *Political Affect: Connecting the Social and the Somatic*. Minneapolis, MN: University of Minnesota Press.

Rodowick, D. N. (1997). *Gilles Deleuze's Time Machine*. Durham, NC: Duke University Press.

Savitt, Steven F. (1995). *Time's Arrows Today: Recent Physical and Philosophical Work on the Direction of Time*. Cambridge: Cambridge University Press.

Simont, Juliette (2003). "Intensity, or: The 'Encounter,'" in Khalfa, pp. 26–49.

Turetzky, Philip (1998). *Time*. London: Routledge.

Widder, Nathan (2008). *Reflections on Time and Politics*. University Park, PA: Pennsylvania State University Press.

Williams, James (1996). "Narrative and Time." *Proceedings of the Aristotelian Society*, Supplementary volume, Spring, pp. 47–61.

—— (2003). *Gilles Deleuze's Difference and Repetition: A Critical Introduction and Guide*. Edinburgh: Edinburgh University Press.

—— (2008). *Gilles Deleuze's logic of Sense: A Critical Introduction and Guide*. Edinburgh: Edinburgh University Press.

—— (2009). "Ageing, Perpetual Perishing and the Event as Pure Novelty: Péguy, Whitehead and Deleuze on Time and History," in C. Colebrook and J. Bell (eds), *Deleuze and History*. Edinburgh: Edinburgh University Press.

—— (2011). *Gilles Deleuze's Philosophy of Time: A Critical Introduction and Guide*. Edinburgh: Edinburgh University Press.

Part II

General Process Perspectives

9

The Bakhtinian Theory of Chronotope (Time–Space Frame) Applied to the Organizing Process

Philippe Lorino and Benoît Tricard

Abstract: Adopting a process view of organizations (Tsoukas and Chia, 2002), what kind of process is the organizing process? This chapter begins by arguing that the organizing process is an inherently narrative abductive inquiry. Taking a praxeological (purposeful activity-focused) rather than discursive (language and discourse-focused) view of narrativity, it concentrates on the narrativity of organizing processes per se, rather than specific narrative objects (texts) or practices (storytelling) within organizations. The second part of the chapter studies the presupposed, tacit, often invisible, and generic narrative frames ("architextures") by which narrative practices must abide to make sense in a given cultural environment. A key "architexture" is the chronotope, or time–space frame of narratives, theorized by Bakhtin (1981), who viewed the close integration of time and space as the basis of narrative social intelligibility. This concept is applied here to organizing inquiries. Referring to Deleuze's extended view of chronotope (Deleuze, 1984/2006) and Genette's theory of narrative levels (Genette, 1972), the chapter analyzes situations in which the organizational chronotope is destabilized by actions that transgress narrative boundaries ("metalepsis"). Some organizational actors may then "scream" to reaffirm and defend the normal time–space frame, defying rational discourse. We then present two case studies showing the connections between time–space structures, meaning-making schemes, and professional identities: (*a*) a historical analysis of the computer industry move from manufacturing to services in the 1990s and its time–space dimension; and (*b*) the disruption, for work safety reasons, of the traditional building industry's "project design," "project preparation," and "on-site building" sequence. In both cases, metalepsis situations drew "screams" from key organizational actors. Finally, we explore the theoretical, methodological, and practical perspectives the chronotope concept offers to organization studies.

Mainstream of organization studies have long conceptualized organizations as structures imposing order on individual and collective practices. But, following Karl Weick's theory of "organizing" as a collective sensemaking process (Weick, 1979, 1995, 2001), a growing number of scholars (Chia, 1996; Tsoukas and Chia, 2002; Tsoukas, 2005; Shotter, 2006, 2008; Yoo et al., 2006; Cooper, 2007; Nayak, 2008) have opted to view organizing as an ongoing process, given the ceaseless learning experience of organizations adapting to their changing environment. However, "process" remains a fuzzy concept. An object falling under Newton's law of gravity and the writing of a poem are both processes. A key question for organization research is therefore: What kind of process is the organizing process?

As a human and social process, it differs from biological and physical processes insofar as it involves (a) a specific type of agency: not the "dyadic" action–reaction agency of physical laws, but a "triadic" agency involving sensemaking and the semiotic mediation of signs such as texts, images, tools, and rules (Peirce, 1958/1931: 8/328, 220) and (b) not an isolated subject, but multiple sensemaking agents, who must continuously build the meaning of situations through dialogical interactions (Tsoukas, 2009), with a range of interpretive perspectives resulting, for example, from the functional division of labor (Carlile, 2002; Bechky, 2003). This type of process, which intertwines acting and thinking, transforming the world, and making sense of that transformation, is an *inquiry* in the pragmatist sense (Dewey, 1980/1938). The question: "What kind of process is the organizing process?" thus becomes the more precise: "What kind of inquiry is the organizing inquiry?"

According to Peirce, 1958/1931: V.145), meaning-making inquiries combine three modes of reasoning: deduction, which develops a hypothesis into more focused, testable propositions; induction, which designs the protocols of empirical validation; and abduction, which builds a new hypothesis when confronted with an unstructured, unintelligible situation. Abduction is the cornerstone of the inquiry. Whereas induction and deduction move between generic and specific manifestations of the same explanatory model, abduction is the only type of inference that creates new classes of meaning. Peirce stresses the narrative nature of abduction and inquiries: Abduction is about building a plausible narrative account of a situation, and the inquiry aims at formulating, developing, and testing this plausible story. Adopting this view, we can translate the question: "What kind of inquiry is the organizing inquiry?" into: "What kind of narrative is the organizing inquiry?."

Organization research has already benefitted from excellent narrative studies, but they do not precisely address the above question. There are two dominant trends. One focuses on specific narrative practices (storytelling) *within* organizations, which aim at building the credibility of strategic discourses (Barry and Elmes, 1997), legitimating the organization toward its stakeholders as an "independent social actor" (Golant and Sillince, 2007: 1152), completing the employees' "individual memories" with "institutional memory" (Boje, 1991: 106), or imposing political domination (Boje, 1995). The other trend focuses on the methodological contribution of narratives. Specific narrative objects (stories) are a major, at times unique, source of information about organizational processes (Czarniawska, 1998). They provide access to organizational features that are inaccessible to rational observation (Tsoukas and Hatch, 2001). Narratives can also be a convenient form to communicate research results (Czarniawska, 1999). With a few exceptions (Cunliffe et al., 2004; Tsoukas, 2009), narrative studies rarely address the intrinsic narrativity of organizing processes per se.

On the side of sensemaking theory, Weick and Browning (1986) get close to characterizing organizing as a narrative process, with such assertions as: "stories are everything" (p. 249) or "facts need some narrative to bind them together to enhance their intelligibility" (pp. 250–1), but they finally keep the communication theory framework, viewing narration as "communication *in* organizations" (p. 251, our emphasis) and narratives as information-processing "devices that store complexity in a compact, retrievable manner" (p. 254). There remains then a gap between the theory of organizing as a process (Weick, 1979, 1995, 2001) and narrative studies.

This chapter attempts to bridge this gap by suggesting in its first part that organizing processes are narrative in nature, taking a praxeological rather than discursive view of narrativity (narrativity in acts, including speech acts, rather than in words). It is concerned with the narrative characteristics of the organizing process per se rather than specific narrative objects (texts, discourses) or specific narrative practices (storytelling) *within* organizations.

The second part of the chapter turns from narrative organizing processes to the existence of presupposed, implicit generic frames ("architextures") (Genette, 1979) to which narratives must conform to make sense in a given social and cultural environment. It analyzes one particularly important architexture for organizational studies: the time–space frame of the narrative, Bakhtin's "chronotope" (Bakhtin, 1981). After a survey of the academic literature about time–space in organizations, the chronotope theory is applied to analyze the close integration and fundamental role of time and space in organizing processes.

The third part of the chapter analyzes how the organizational chronotope, normally taken for granted and invisible, manifests itself. In "metalepsis" situations (Genette, 1972), the time–space of organizing is disrupted by the intrusion of extraneous time–space frames. Key organizational characters may then reaffirm "their" time–space universe defensively, suddenly "screaming" their belief in defiance of rational argument. Such situations offer organizational research and change management opportunities to unveil tacit time–space frames and associated values.

Finally, the chapter presents two case studies. A historical study, drawn from one author's direct experience, describes one such "chronotopic scream" in the context of the computer industry's strategic transformation from manufacturing to services in the 1990s. In the second case study, a "chronotopic scream" occurs at the end of a research project about work safety in the building industry. Finally, the theoretical, methodological, and practical contribution of the "chronotopic view" is discussed.

9.1 Organizing processes are narrative

9.1.1 The features of narrativity

The concept of "narrative process" here is more than simply "telling a story." It is a social, purposeful process, intended to produce meaning in a situation, with four basic characteristics. First, mediation: it uses systems of signs, for example, words, images, gestures, and interpretable acts. Second, emplotment: narrative processes impose some form of temporal order ("before–after" sequences, beginning–end, pacing) and logical order (cause–effect relationships, objectives and obstacles) on a collection of events and acts. Third, character definition: the narrative process assigns behaviors to characters who may, to a variable extent, represent generic social roles. Fourth, dialogicality: the narrative process involves authors addressing an actual or virtual audience. The distribution of roles is not fixed. The audience takes an active part in the narrative process; what is narrated, and how it is narrated, depends on the audience's action. Narrative forms are diverse. A text, but also a painting, a photograph, or an organizational action, can be considered as distinctly narrative.

Narrative processes are inherently mimetic (Ricœur, 1984), that is, they are *processes about processes*, or narrating processes about narrated processes.

The Bakhtinian Theory of Chronotope Applied to the Organizing Process

They involve at least two distinct levels of meaning-making, two "diegetic" levels (Genette, 1972): the meaning of the narrated story, and the meaning of the narrating action in its particular context. As a result, narrative processes display double temporality (narrated story and narrating process temporality), double spatiality (physical and social context of the story and of the narrating process), and a double dialogical configuration (dialogues between characters within the story and dialogues between narrators and narratees). Narrative mimesis is a key way of assigning events rational structures—to demonstrate—and aesthetical shapes—to attract or repel, in short, to *prove and move*. It transforms the flow of events into meaningful human experience: "time becomes human to the extent that it is articulated through a narrative mode" (Ricœur, 1984: 52, quoted by Cunliffe et al., 2004: 271). Narration projects past, fictional, or foreseeable "experience one"—the narrated events—into "experience two"—the present living experience, by ordering events in a plot that makes sense in the present context of the narrating situation.

9.1.2 Organizing processes are inherently narrative

Historically, organizations emerged to perform tasks requiring coordinated intervention by different classes of actors because of division of labor (Chandler, 1977). Collective activities such as designing, producing, or managing flows involve heterogeneous competences, complex cooperation schemes, and shared work objects and tools, to accomplish transactions with the world. Coordination and cooperation require permanent interaction to adapt to the evolving environment, maintain compatible understandings of work situations, ensure mutual intelligibility and predictability, and keep activity going. "Only through a relation with other people does man relate to nature itself" (Leontyev, 1981). Researchers thus seek "an account of the interactional work" (Button, 1993, quoted by Orlikowski and Barley, 2001) through which the meaning of work situations is permanently renegotiated.

Through this continuous process, actors simultaneously (*a*) act together to transform the world (e.g., produce, design, transport, etc.), and (*b*) interpret the work situations they face to make continuation of collective activity feasible. This type of social process, intertwining acting and interpreting, transforming the world, and making sense of that transformation, is an *inquiry* in the pragmatist sense (Dewey, 1980/1938). One key step in inquiries is abduction, that is, construction of hypotheses about the situation. As Peirce noted (1998/1903: 2–287; 1997/1903: 282–3), abduction has a clear narrative nature as it aims at building a plausible story that can account for the situation in meaningful and workable ways. Abductive inquiries are triggered by disruptive events (e.g., a quality or safety problem), which require organizational responses. They make "comprehensible a deviation from a canonical cultural pattern" (Bruner, 1990: 49–50, quoted by Czarniawska, 1998: 6).

Organizing narrations are polyphonic. They involve not isolated subjects, but multiple agents with a diversity of interpretive perspectives, caused, for example, by the functional division of labor, which can hinder mutual intelligibility and effective cooperation (Carlile, 2002; Bechky, 2003). As Boje (1995: 2001) observes, "organizations cannot be registered as one story, but instead are a plurality of stories and story interpretations in struggle with one another." Inquiring agents must continuously negotiate the meaning of situations through dialogical interactions (Boje, 1991; Cunliffe et al., 2004; Tsoukas, 2009), "ongoing dialogues among various subcultures" (Boje, 1995: 1029). Barry and Elmes (1997: 444) observe that strategic narratives are "increasingly polyphonic (Bakhtin, 1984)... Different logics not only coexist, but inform and shape one another." Therefore, organizing processes are collective, not in the static and holistic sense of a "common" central narrative "shared" by organization members (Boyce, 1995), but in the dynamic sense of meaning emerging from the friction between distinct interpretive perspectives, as stressed by Weick and Roberts' concept (1993) of the "collective mind": "not a given property of a collectivity, but the pattern whereby individuals heedfully interrelate their actions" (Tsoukas and Hatch, 2001: 1006).

9.1.3 A praxeological view of organizing

This view of narrativity in organizing processes is praxeological—that is, focused on purposeful action—rather than discursive. It is not assumed here that "language and discourse do the work of organizing" (Boje et al., 2004: 576). This research focuses neither on discursive superstructures (texts, speeches) built *about* organizing, to manage organizational change (Goodall and Kellet, 2004) or impose political domination (Boje, 1995; Humphreys and Brown, 2002), nor on discursive practices such as storytelling (Boje, 1995). Discursive productions are just one particular form of action, performative "speech acts" (Searle, 1969). Many other nondiscursive types of action are required to perform collective activity and make meaning of it (Lorino, 2007). Organizing inquiries are dialogues *in acts*, which per se have the basic features of narrativity.

The praxeological view of organizing processes converges with philosophical reflections that suggest extending Ricœur's concepts of narrativity

The Bakhtinian Theory of Chronotope Applied to the Organizing Process

and mimesis (Ricœur, 1984), focused on the individual subject's inner personal experience, to an ontology of action (Mink, 1978; Carr, 1991*a*, 1991*b*, 1991*c*; Michel, 2003). "In planning our lives we are composing the stories we will act out (. . .) We are constantly explaining ourselves to others (. . .) We want things to come out right in the end, with all the threads of the plot neatly tied up" (Carr, 1991*b*: 265–6). Furthermore, as some philosophers and organization scholars (Cunliffe et al., 2004: 268) suggest, this ontological role of mimetic narrative can be extended from the individual subject's living experience to the construction of social entities and the narrative organizing experience (Carr, 1991*a*: 210, our translation): "It can be said that communities have a 'narrated existence', that they only exist insofar they establish themselves as narrative units, as subjects of a story," which shapes collective action.

9.1.4 Epistemological and methodological implications

These views on organizing processes have epistemological and methodological implications. Researchers are embedded in the organizing narratives in two ways. First, they share, at least partly, the narrative archetypes, culturally taken-for-granted, of organizational actors. Second, researchers can be considered as "readers" of the organizing inquiries, but active readers, in the sense of Eco's theory of the reader who co-constructs meaning (Eco, 1984; Yanow, 1994: 2; Barry and Elmes, 1997: 432). There is no such thing as passive reading or neutral observation. To access and understand organizing inquiries, researchers must enter into dialogical interactions with organizational members. Narratives are in essence fields of meaning, where "parts of the plot are left to the hearer's imagination" (Boje, 1991: 115), rather than strictly determined paths of meaning.

Therefore, research about organizing narratives can hardly follow a representational epistemology and attempt to *accurately* describe organizing processes. Cunliffe et al. (2004: 281) ask the key epistemological question: "If we accept that we are not all-knowing researchers-narrators, that we cannot explain precisely 'original' events, nor tell others how to construct their worlds, then what can we do?" In the pragmatist perspective (Lorino et al., 2011), researchers can dialog with organizational actors to co-construct the meaning and workability of organizational situations (Cunliffe et al., 2004: 268). Narrativity, then, qualifies the research object rather than a precise research method. The methodological issue here is: "What kind of method should be used to study organizing processes, taking into account their narrative nature?" rather than: "Is it relevant to use narrative methods for organizational research?" This is "an important distinction between research taking a narrative mode of analysis, where stories are an epistemological tool for analyzing reality, and the radically reflexive approach, where we (organizational members, researchers, ordinary people...) create and make sense of experience *in our narrative discourse with others*" (Cunliffe et al., 2004: 263, our emphasis), or, in accordance with our praxeological view: "*in our narrative interaction with others.*"

As a result, research evaluation can hardly be based on its capacity to deliver the *true* interpretation of organizational narratives. Yet the issue of evaluation cannot be altogether disregarded, in a relativist, deconstructionist stance that views all coherent, seductive narratives as equivalent (Czarniawska, 1999). In a pragmatist framework (Dewey, 1980/1938), narrative inquiries should be evaluated on the basis of their practical implications: to what kind of action do they lead narrators and narratees? Some narrative inquiries induce disasters, because they prompt actors into forms of action that threaten the organization's physical or moral survival. While there is no final end to the organizing narrative, "since dialogues construct plurivocal meanings" (Boje, 1995: 1029), there are at least strong punctuations that start and end narrative episodes, when irreversible actions are undertaken and evaluation issues are raised.

9.2 The chronotope, "architexture" of narrative organizing processes

9.2.1 The architexture of narratives

To make sense, any narrative process requires authors and audiences to share a common intersubjective world of cultural meanings (Cassirer, 1961/1942), for example, shared language or narrative conventions. In a given social environment, narrative archetypes delineate the boundary between intelligible and unintelligible narratives. Partly natural and partly cultural, they can be metaphorically compared with the architecture of a building. To be physically stable, practically appropriate to its planned utilization, and socially recognizable, a building must conform to predetermined architectural rules, partly natural (physical laws) and partly cultural (functional forms such as lecture theatres in a university, or symbolic attributes such as church spires). The narratologist Gérard Genette named those metanarrative structures "architextures" (Genette, 1979), defining them as "the set of general or transcendent categories—discourse types, utterance modes, literary genres etc.—to which each singular text belongs" (Genette, 1982: 7).

The Bakhtinian Theory of Chronotope Applied to the Organizing Process

The architexture of a narrative is close to Ricœur's M1 mimesis as summarized by Cunliffe et al. (2004: 270): "Narratives are embedded with an implicit 'pre-understanding' of a society's meaningful structures, symbolic systems, and temporal nature (...) There are taken-for-granted cultural plots, themes, characters, values, and sequencing of events." The architextures shape the interpretation of narrative processes by their social environment. They are presupposed and tacit, "what is not said, and yet is shared" (Boje, 1991: 107), taken-for-granted, and often unconscious.

The need for architextual frames is even more compelling in the case of organizing processes, because they conjoin narrative diversity (division of labor, cultural complexity) and coherence imperatives, because of the practical coordination requirements of collective activity. There is no "grand narrative" (including all organizing processes as subnarratives) (Boje, 1995: 1030), but there are presupposed common schemes, rules, and frames (e.g., accounting and legal norms, functional division of labor) that enable internal and external understanding of organizing processes. One key architextual element is the "time–space universe of the narrative," named "diegesis" by narratology (Genette, 1972: 280).

9.2.2 Time–space in organization studies: A survey

The organizing inquiry takes place in space and time: "we interpret and construct our social realities in and through narratives enacted in many moments of time (duration) and across many contexts (spaces)" (Cunliffe et al., 2004: 268). The very notion of "process" involves the development of some phenomenon over time. Organizational time has specific characteristics: it is, to some degree, irreversible; nonlinear (Butler, 1995; Lee and Liebenau, 1999; Hassard, 2002; Hatch, 2002), with speeding-up and slowing-down phases; socially constructed (Elchardus, 1988; Butler, 1995; Sahay, 1997); three-dimensional: "initial social conditions of action (structure), process of interaction (agency), and projected outcomes" (Toyoki et al., 2006: 110); and it is the locus of individual and collective emotions linked with memory and expectations.

The organizing process also involves space. It entails movement (Hatch, 2002), that is, the modification of some spatial data (positions, shapes, quantities). The time of the process is filled with nonlinear, irreversible, spatial transformations. Like organizational time, organizational space has specific characteristics: it is not smooth and plane but "hilly," that is, there are slopes and obstacles; and some trajectories, better experimented than others, form the "cognitive trails" of the organization (Cussins, 1992).

Organizational space can be physical or virtual: the nodes of a network may be physically distant but in informational vicinity. It is socially constructed (Kornberger and Clegg, 2004). It is the locus of individual and collective emotions linked with cultural symbols and rituals.

9.2.3 The rational time–space view

Time and space, important in organization studies for more than a century, have generally been analyzed through dualist frameworks that separate them and often link them with other dichotomies, for example, space with body and time with mind, or space with information and time with learning. The rational or Cartesian view of time–space, developed by management pioneers like Frederick Taylor (1972/1911), remains influential. It considers both time and space as homogeneous variables and measurable magnitudes. The cornerstone of Taylorism is the establishment of *an equivalence between time and space*, in the form of an equivalence between actual and standard time. Standard "time" is actually a form of *space*: standard "hours," similar to "produced tons" or "produced square meters," are simply a universal scale to measure, add, and compare production volumes. Actual time, on the contrary, is *time*: the time spent by the worker on the machine, linked with his effort and fatigue. Space and time are both measured in hours (standard and actual hours), through the standardization of operations: a "normal" worker produces a certain volume (standard time) in a certain period (actual time). The basic equation of the Taylorian model:

one standard hour = one actual hour

reflects 100 percent productivity, a target for the manufacturing organization. It expresses an *essential isomorphism between space and time*, materialized in time by a clocking system, and in space by the functional layout of machines in the factory.

9.2.4 Bergson and intuitionist critiques of the rationalist view of time–space

Rationalism's reduction of time to geometric space was criticized by the philosopher Bergson in the early twentieth century (Bergson, 1997/1896). Bergson contrasted the duration of inner life, with its irregularities, accelerations, and decelerations, with clock time, which does not in fact express duration but a spatial simultaneity, for example, the geometric movement of the clock. Bergson's analysis inspired organization scholars (Chia, 1996;

The Bakhtinian Theory of Chronotope Applied to the Organizing Process

Cooper, 2007; Nayak, 2008), who advocate the rediscovery of life experience in the heart of organizational processes. They contrast authentic time experience with its spatial reduction; continuous flow (Chia, 1996) or cyclical movement (Hassard, 2002; Hatch, 2002) with the discrete segmentation of physical time scales; spontaneous inner life with the "readymade" use of language, viewed as a spatial segmentation of meaning; indivisible time with divided space (Cooper, 2007; Nayak, 2008); and learning "from within" with learning "about" (Shotter, 2006).

This criticism makes an important contribution to the study of organizing processes as continuous "organizational becoming" (Tsoukas and Chia, 2002). Organizational time consisting of learning cycles, exploration, and exploitation phases (March, 1991) hardly corresponds to the geometric metaphor. But the extreme subjectivism of some authors, who trust only individual intuition to reunify conscience with the world, sometimes leads to a mirror image of Cartesian body–mind dualism. Intuition, seen as the unmediated flow of time, is separated from the intentional structure of conscience, seen as the mental geography of reflection, with its origins, destinations, and paths. While Merleau-Ponty reproached Bergson for his "blindness to the intentional structure of conscience" (Merleau-Ponty, 1945), Nayak, for example, pleads for a phenomenological return to "the introspective reality in its immediate, epistemologically *unmediated and pure* state," to avoid "our introspection [becoming] *stained by* admixtures unconsciously borrowed from our sensory experience" (2008: 177, our emphasis). This spiritualist dualism that promotes time as the "true" dimension of living experience leads to dichotomous views, for example in art and literature: "Picasso, Braque, and Duchamp *stopped painting space and began painting time*" (Kramer, 2004: IV, our emphasis).

9.2.5 Toward an integrated time–space framework

If, unlike philosophers focusing on the individual subject (Habermas, 1970), we see human beings as inherently social and dialogical (Mead, 1934; Vygotsky, 1978, 1986), then intuition and intention are not only projection toward the future (time) but also projection to an "elsewhere" (space) where others stand and pay attention. Reflexivity, too often identified with subjective reflexivity, is closely linked with sociality and interaction. In dialogical views of reflexivity, human beings build their reflexive capacity within and through social interactions (Tsoukas, 2009). Systematic historicism ultimately forgot that space too is a vital and creative experience, as Michel Foucault (1980: 70, quoted by Czarniawska, 1998: 28) observes, up to the 1960s, "space was treated as the dead, the fixed, the undialectical.... Time, on the contrary, was fecundity, life, dialectical."

The key issue is not defending space against time, but observing the deep integration of time and space into one unified "time–space" framework of experience and meaning: "the unique circumstances of each moment, the context of performance and interpretation, and the specific interrelationships and connections that occur in the moment, all interweave to create a unique discursive time–space" (Cunliffe et al., 2004: 273), and, beyond "discursive," a unique *living/acting* time–space. Time experience is embedded in space experience, and vice versa. Time confers orientation and irreversibility to space. "Plotting" (Ricœur, 1984) relates places and objects to events, paths to processes, and spatial sets to temporal sequences. There is a social and spatial "scope of temporal structures: how broadly they are recognized and enacted within communities" (Orlikowski and Yates, 2002: 695). Symmetrically, spatial structures are continuously evolving. Their degree of mutability is a key feature of the organization. "Time use in organizations is closely connected to space use. Time and space should be taken into account altogether" (Lee and Liebenau, 1999: 1053). Many organizational stories analyzed from a temporal angle can equally be read from the complementary spatial angle. For example, Staudenmayer et al. (2002) tell three stories where "changes in a collective's experience of time help to facilitate organizational change" (p. 583). All the described temporal shifts are also spatial shifts. In one of these stories, "at BBA, events that halted normal production activities, such as new product introductions, process revisions, or equipment changes, created temporal shifts. By halting the production line, such rhythm changes provided a sense of *'found time'* to workers... Individuals undertook special projects while the line was down" (p. 589). Through breaks in production, workers leave the production line for other working spaces corresponding to different activities, for example, offices for quality analysis, or training rooms. Even the space around machines becomes another space when the machines stop running. The integrated time–space is a basic ecological characteristic of human society, as suggested by Lefebvre (1991/1974: 95, quoted by Ming Lim, 2006: 126): "In nature, time is apprehended within space—the hour of the day, the season, the elevation of the sun above the horizon... *Time was thus inscribed in space.*"

Scholars investigating time in organizations sometimes use the ancient Greeks' distinction between two concepts of time: *Kairos* and *Chronos*. *Chronos* is physical linear time, characterized by regular periodicity (day and night, seasons). *Kairos* qualifies the irregular time of favorable occasions: "now is the right time to act." But it is worth noting that the Greek word "*kairos*" originally has a spatial meaning: a particular point of discontinuity in a structure, an opening, or a cut. It is striking to observe that organization scholars who use "kairos" as a temporal concept often rediscover its spatial implications, unconsciously returning to the root. Orlikowski and Yates (2002: 686) link the chronos–kairos dichotomy with the dichotomy between "objective temporal structuring" and "subjective temporal structuring," but their field study shows that all temporal circumstances are in fact *time–space* structuring episodes, with a permanent interplay between copresence and distance: project contributors collaborating through a virtual network take the opportunity of a conference to meet in person; after a while, they use the communication network to hold votes remotely.

Chia's definition (2002: 867) of the integrated time–space framework is quite close to Bakhtin's concept of chronotope: "All societies organize their lives by firstly establishing rhythms that eventually, through the ages, become the spatio-temporal frameworks for regulating interactions, social activities and modes of thought. [They] inevitably influence how the flux and flow of our life-worlds are structured and conceptualized into events and situations; how identity is established and social entities created, how causal relations are imputed, and how symbols and representations are used to substitute for reality."

9.2.6 Bakhtin's chronotope theory

To conceptualize the integrated time–space framework of organizing and its close links with identities highlighted by Chia, we shall use the "chronotope" concept, defined by Bakhtin (Bakhtin, 1981; Todorov, 1981) to study literary narratives. This concept has been extensively applied to literary, cinema, and art criticism, ethnology, and social studies, but is still seldom used in organization studies. Bakhtin does not oppose static space to the dynamic flow of time. Instead, he calls "chronotope" (literally: "time–space") the deep correspondence between space and time, not in the geometric way criticized by Bergson, but as the "intrinsic connectedness of spatial and temporal relationships" in sensory experience. "In the literary chronotope, spatial and temporal indicators are fused into one carefully thought-out, concrete whole. Time thickens, takes on flesh, becomes artistically visible; likewise, space becomes charged and responsive to the movements of time, plot and history. The chronotope in literature has an intrinsic generic significance... It can even be said that it is precisely the chronotope that defines genre and generic distinctions... The chronotope as a formally constitutive category determines to a significant degree the image of man in literature, always intrinsically chronotopic" (Bakhtin, 1981: 84–5). In narratives, space is a trace of time, time is a marker of space, and the time–space framework is the matrix of meaning: "the place where the knots of narrative are tied and untied (...). The chronotope, functioning as the primary means for materializing time in space, emerges as a center for concretizing representation" (Bakhtin, 1981: 250). Bakhtin analyzes certain generic literary chronotopes (e.g., the encounter, the road, the salons) and links them with narrative genres and generic characters: shepherds and maidens in the chronotope of the pastoral idyll, knights and ladies in the novel of chivalry, etc. These typical characters are provided with time–space attributes, generic identities, and competences.

Bakhtin stresses that each generic chronotope is linked with certain emotions and values: "In literature, temporal and spatial determinations are inseparable and always colored by emotions and values. Abstract thought can conceive time and space as separate entities and things apart from the emotions and values that attach to them. But *living* artistic perception makes no such divisions" (Bakhtin, 1981: 243). The chronotope provides not only the internal structure of the narrative but also a link between the narrative and the social and cultural context of the narrating performance: "out of the actual chronotopes of our world emerge the reflected and *created* chronotopes of the world represented in the work" (Bakhtin, 1981: 253, in the text).

While it first appears as a set of physical characteristics (where? when?), the chronotope actually frees the meaning-making process from physical constraints and presence. Each generic chronotope involves specific signs that point toward an unseen background, "off-screen" characters and objects, which can be taken for granted. In the product development chronotope, for example, marketers and development engineers spend much time and energy analyzing the "future customer's" requirements and reactions, even though she/he does not yet exist. That is why Gregory criticizes Giddens' dichotomic "conceptualization of space in terms of presence and absence because it does not adequately account for the production of space in both its material *and symbolic* representations" (Gregory, 1989, quoted by Sahay, 1997: 243, our emphasis): what is absent can be made present, through semiotic mediations. The same can be said about temporal contemporaneity and past/future instantiation in the narrative through symbols. The chronotope draws boundaries, not so much between absence and presence, but between what is relevant and irrelevant for the meaning of the situation, and between what is imaginable and potentially meaningful and what is not.

The Bakhtinian Theory of Chronotope Applied to the Organizing Process

9.2.7 Chronotope and organizing processes

Like any narrative process, organizing processes conform to a presupposed chronotope. The division of labor and the organizational rules assign places and timings to activities. Paraphrasing Bakhtin, there is an "intrinsic connectedness of spatial and temporal relationships that are actively expressed in organizations. It can be said that it is precisely the chronotope that defines generic types of organization..." Similar to generic literary chronotopes (Bakhtin, 1981), there are generic organizational chronotopes such as the manufacturing chronotope, the service chronotope, or the supply chain chronotope; they characterize organizational genres and "shape, but do not determine how community members engage in everyday social interaction" (Orlikowski and Yates, 1998). Like literary chronotopes, they involve generic characters, with their identities, which sometimes correspond to functional roles (e.g., the manufacturing engineer, the design engineer, the accountant) and, in the wider institutional context, to professions. As the chronotope links organizations to their social/institutional environment, in particular to professional categories, the organizing inquiry involves professional characters with generic roles to accomplish cross-functional actions (selling, producing, etc.). The functional boundaries which segment collective activity often appear "naturalized" to actors, as if they were objective characteristics of the collective activity, taken for granted in the same way as the chronotope itself. For example, engineers who design a product and manufacturers who make it seem to belong to "naturally" separate spatial, temporal, and social worlds (Bechky, 2003), whereas the traditional craftsman simultaneously designs and produces.

By defining the boundary between imaginable and unimaginable forms of organizational activity, organizational chronotopes delineate the scope of conceivable futures, activities which are not carried out today, but might emerge as part of organizational change. What the chronotope leaves out is the unthinkable forms of activity that defy imagination and cannot make sense for actors.

The literary chronotope frames the readers' reading of a narrative and the narrator's perception of the readers. Likewise, the organizational chronotope frames the organization's reading of its social environment and, reciprocally, the social, historical, and institutional intelligibility/acceptability of the organization. Toyoki et al. (2006: 111) observe how temporal rhythms link organizations and their social environment: "Certain instances of social reproduction" in the organization's environment "may favor certain rhythmic dispositions over others." Butler (1995) and Forray and Woodilla (2002: 902) show how "temporal frames provide meaning-making structures that frame both individual and institutional experience, linking past, present and future through the codification of knowledge as a social memory." The time of accounting, budgeting, and reporting unifies the company's internal space (divisions worldwide report their financial results and are consolidated simultaneously), and moulds the image of the organization for external observers such as financial markets, tax inspectors, or banks (Sahay, 1997: 255).

9.3 Scream and metalepsis

9.3.1 Deleuze's extended view of chronotope

Gilles Deleuze applies the chronotope concept to analysis of philosophical thought as a process framed by a tacit temporal/spatial order. Bakhtin had already alluded to this extension of the chronotope concept to thought: "without such temporal-spatial expression, even abstract thought is impossible" (Bakhtin, 1981: 258). In a lecture on the cinema, Deleuze (2006/1984) explains that any philosophical thought conforms to an implicit "image it builds of itself," with a tacit temporal frame and a geographic mapping (our translation and emphasis):

> Philosophy can be defined as the methodology of thought. A method has two aspects. A temporal aspect: the order of ideas, the organization of thought order. The method has another aspect: a spatial aspect; namely the determination of the aims and means of thought and the obstacles it faces. Those are the two aspects of method, temporal and spatial. The *presupposed image* of thought must not be confused with the *method* of thought, it is presupposed by the method. The method does not tell us *how thought pictures itself. It presupposes an implicit image of thought*, assumed by every method. What could we call it as simply as possible? I borrow a word from the great literary critic Bakhtin: *chronotope*. He uses "chronotope" in a simple sense: it is a time-space, a spatiotemporal continuum. For example he tells us that answering the question "what is the novel?" requires us to determine the specific chronotope of the novel, i.e. a type of time-space presupposed by the novel. In the same way, there is a chronotope of thought, and every method refers to a chronotope from its dual point of view: first, the temporal order of thoughts; second, the spatial distribution of ends, means and obstacles. This chronotope ... *is never given* ... What may be given is a method, but not its presupposed frame. It takes specific efforts to determine it.

For Deleuze (2006/1984), the chronotope is not set in stone, and may change in specific situations. "This presupposed chronotope of thought

The Bakhtinian Theory of Chronotope Applied to the Organizing Process

can undergo transformations (...) How can we recognize it? It is not itself an object of philosophical discourse. *The chronotope itself can only be punctuated.* It is not punctuated by concepts like elements of the philosophical discourse; it is principally punctuated and signaled by something stranger: by *screams*. In other words, there are philosophical screams which bound the implicit image of thought. Then the discourse, the method, covers the screams and the chronotope. But that time–space image, its places and moments, are marked by screams." Deleuze mentions examples of such "screams" which suddenly reveal the presupposed, almost subterranean, chronotopic framework: Descartes' "I think, therefore I am" or Aristotle's "there must be a limit somewhere." These are screams that express the underlying thought of boundaries. For example, for Descartes, the method of doubt must be applied to all beliefs, except one belief which for him is beyond doubt: "if I think, I exist." This is not a rational demonstration, but a "scream": "there can be no doubt that a thinking being exists." Modern literature may later imagine thoughtful beings who realize they do not exist and are dreamers' dreams (Borges, 1974); this is beyond the frontiers of Descartes' philosophical narration. Deleuze compares such philosophical screams with birds' alarm screams in forests, which suddenly replace birdsong when there is an intrusion in their territory. The chronotope of thought utters alarm screams when thought arrives at the edge of its territory.

In organizational life, the chronotope of organizing processes is the presupposed time–space framework of organizing, which delineates the frontier between thinkable and unthinkable, and meaningful and meaningless practices. Strategic boundaries may evolve, following "the dialogicality of realities and potential realities, which constantly shift their boundaries" (Marková, 2003: 165). However those variations take place within tacit, impassable, and often unconscious limits. Organizational actors can suddenly "scream," in words or in acts, when deeply rooted time–space schemes of meaning and identities are challenged.

Such screams result from situations that destabilize the tacit time–space frame, analyzed by narratology scholars as *"metalepsis"* situations. An invisible but normally impassable frontier separates the universe of the narrated from the universe of narrating. The narrator cannot be at the same narrative level as the characters and events narrated. For example, a film character should not step out of the film and meet the audience in the cinema, or vice versa—as in Woody Allen's *The Purple Rose of Cairo*. Metalepsis is defined as the existential breaking of the boundaries that separate distinct narrative levels, any narrator's or narratee's intrusion into the narrated universe or vice versa, or any intrusion by a narrative character into the narrator's world (Genette, 1972). This forced "frame-breaking" irruption of one time–space into another can also happen when characters from other narrative genres are suddenly enrolled—as if a cowboy appeared in a salon novel!

Metalepses can be found in logic, mathematics, cognitive psychology, arts, etc. Examples include the liar paradox in logic (the sentence "this sentence is false" can neither be true nor false), Gödel incompleteness theorems in mathematics (a single discourse cannot develop a mathematical theory and the axiomatics of that theory) or Magritte's picture "this is not a pipe": all raise the paradox of "strange loops" (Hofstadter, 1979), in which logical impossibility is generated by the confusion between distinct narrative levels. Logically incoherent, metalepsis is always experienced as a transgression and often triggers a defensive scream: "you cannot be there, now; this is unthinkable," reaffirming the existing chronotope as the boundary of the conceivable world.

9.3.2 Methodological implications

The organization scholar is neither an all-seeing "extradiegetic" listener, nor a narrator positioned outside the narrated situation to tell *the* story of the organization (Boje, 1995). Situatedness is not an obstacle to knowing "how decisions are *really* made" (Czarniawska, 1998: 30, in the text), but a requirement to access narrative intelligibility. However, there is a price to pay for the researcher's diegetic participation within the organizational narrative: in ordinary circumstances, the chronotope partly escapes researchers' understanding. There is a strange loop here: it is impossible to simultaneously understand the "text," here the organizing narrative, and its architexture, here the organizational chronotope. The deeper the narrative understanding, the less accessible the chronotope is. The history of research in organization and management provides examples of insider's myopia. Management accounting research took decades to realize that product cost is largely predetermined by product design. For researchers and practitioners, product design concerned product engineers rather than cost control, which focused on operations. Product design and cost control were two alien chronotopes. Instead of hopelessly looking for the "true" story of the organization, managers and researchers had often better design time–space breaking inquiries to trigger revealing screams. The curtain may fall away and new fields of knowledge and action emerge.

Two empirical examples of such metalepsis situations are presented in the next part of the chapter. They are not field studies designed to explore the chronotope framework. In both situations, the inquirers were rather surprised by the "scream." Their analysis through the lens of the chronotope is therefore an ex post reinterpretation, the chronotopic framework offering new possibilities to understand such apparent organizational deadlocks. The two examples have different methodological status. The first episode was directly experienced by one of the authors twenty years ago. The retrospective account of lived experience is completed by analysis of documents. It was repeatedly discussed with other actors of the situation in the three following years, and with other researchers at seminars and conferences later, making the narrated events an object of controversy. This study is a hybrid between management case studies and historians' inquiries based on testimonies. The second example, focused on the definition of generic chronotopic roles, is a brief, but meaningful episode from a longitudinal action-research project about work safety on building sites. The two cases also focus on distinct issues. Bull case stresses the importance of "chronotopic" performance indicators as symbols of a given time–space identity, in the context of a fundamental strategic move that upsets an entire industry. The building case stresses the cultural definition of professional roles linked with time–space characteristics, in a situation characterized by continuous safety improvement rather than a strategic revolution.

9.4 The Bull case: "You can tell a man's a manufacturer because he gets his hands dirty with machine grease"

9.4.1 The strategic transformation of the computer industry in the late 1980s

Till the late 1980s, the manufacturing cost and value added of computers were very high, particularly because of the expensive machines for sophisticated product testing. Computer technology was R&D intensive, but the average life cycle of a product was still fairly long at around seven years. R&D expenses could thus be absorbed by a high volume of products over a long period. The economic balance of each product primarily depended on its production cost, selling price, and market share, last two parameters linked with product quality. The manufacturing function controlled two major parameters: product cost and quality.

There were deep-seated transformations in the computer industry at the turn of the decade. It moved from proprietary operating systems to standard systems common to all manufacturers, such as UNIX and Windows.

Constructing Identity in and around Organizations

The development of standard components gradually reduced computer manufacturing to assembling purchased components. As the market migrated from information systems to complete turnkey solutions (e.g., accounting solutions), software and services gained commercial importance to the detriment of hardware. Product standardization made product testing much less expensive. With the quick progress in component technology, the average life cycle of a computer model fell from seven years to less than one year, leading to frequent inventory obsolescence.

As a result, manufacturing value added decreased dramatically. The relative share of purchased components in the computer's final value became dominant. The cost of inventories increased because of obsolescence. Manufacturing value added (less than 8 percent of sales value) fell below the cost of carrying inventories (around 10 percent of sales value). The computer industry began to look more like a logistics activity, moving high value objects without adding value to them, than a manufacturing activity, adding value to objects by transforming them.

9.4.2 A metalepsis episode: "You can tell a manufacturer by the way his hands are dirty with machine grease"

During a meeting in 1990, the production manager, who was redesigning the factories' performance reporting system, asked the controller—one of the authors of this chapter—to review the first draft of a new factory scorecard. The controller was surprised to find the draft put "overhead cost to direct production cost" ratio (O/DC) as the head indicator, to be minimized by factory managers. Overheads (O) reflected time spent on support activities such as quality analysis, predictive machine maintenance, and scheduling. Direct costs (DC: direct labor and machine use) reflected time actually spent on working machines. Minimizing O/DC seemed counterproductive, as it prompted factory actors to maximize production rates but sacrifice just-in-time and quality management, which were strategic priorities.

At their next meeting, the controller raised the drawbacks of the O/DC ratio. The production manager proposed to revise the draft. But in his revised version, the head measurement was...the O/DC ratio! The controller, amazed, repeated his views. The production manager answered: "I expect you're right. But *I'm a manufacturer*, and I supervise *manufacturing people*. Our job is to produce. *When* do we produce? When we're *on running machines*. When a machine stops, I can't tell them: that's good! If I drop this ratio, there's a risk they will lose their morale and values. *You can tell a man's a manufacturer because he gets his hands dirty with machine grease.*"

The Bakhtinian Theory of Chronotope Applied to the Organizing Process

The interaction between the controller and the production manager can be analyzed as the gradual emergence of a metaleptic situation. O/DC, the ratio between *time* spent by operators *on the machine* (DC), the "raison d'être" of manufacturing heroes, and *time* spent by operators *away from the machine* (O), is a typical "chronotopic" indicator. When he criticizes O/DC as contrary to corporate strategy, the controller actually means that manufacturing actors should spend a large amount of time away from running machines, which condemns the manufacturing chronotope. Formally, the production manager can only agree, but he cannot actively adhere to a narrative frame that eliminates manufacturing stories. He finally "screams" in defense of "his" chronotope which links Bull organization with manufacturing culture: in deeds (keeping the O/DC indicator) and in words: "*You can tell a man's a manufacturer because he gets his hands dirty with machine grease.*" For production engineers and technicians, trained to produce as much as possible, as well as possible, the manufacturing chronotope, symbolized by O/DC, was the foundation of their professional identity.

9.4.3 The traditional manufacturing chronotope

This industry, like most manufacturing industries, conformed to a sequence of three chronotopes: "product developing," "product manufacturing," and "product selling." The boundaries between chronotopes were materialized by "buffers" (see Figure 9.1 and Table 9.1):

- Between manufacturing and selling, a material buffer inventory of finished products; before entering it, products underwent continuous physical metamorphoses through the "manufacturing story." Once products entered the inventory, they became commercial objects with no further physical modifications.
- Between engineering and manufacturing, an informational buffer data base of technical product data; before entering it, the technical product data underwent continuous informational metamorphoses through the

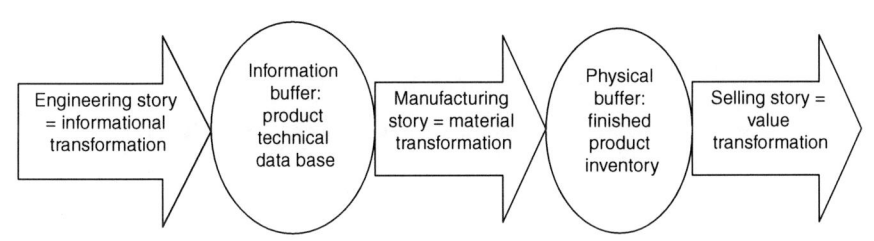

Figure 9.1 The chronotopes of manufacturing

Constructing Identity in and around Organizations

Table 9.1 The chronotope of manufacturing

	Sequential articulation		
	The engineering chronotope	The manufacturing chronotope	The selling chronotope
Time–space frame	Development cycle (one year) in central engineering offices. Long life cycles (seven years). Sequential time.	Shopfloor in factories. Production cycle (three months). Sequential time.	Offices in scattered local branches. Short selling process (days or weeks).
Roles and characters. A "crossing character": the product	Product engineers, marketers, and controllers. The product is a concept and undergoes conceptual metamorphoses.	Production engineers, workers, foremen, and quality and cost controllers. The product is an object and undergoes physical metamorphoses.	Sales managers, sellers, distributors, and customers. The product is a set of functions.

"engineering story." Once data entered the data base, they became stable production guidelines, with no further significant modification.

- The central position was occupied by manufacturing operations.

Manufacturing came down to merely assembling purchased standard components, while customer service moved from computer after-sales to the engineering of customized solutions. A system of three new chronotopes, not sequential but concurrent, emerged, as a completely new way of

Product life cycle management:
analyzing future market, designing, midlife redesigning, phasing out the product

Supply chain:
forecasting sales, managing customer orders, scheduling, managing inventory

Customer service:
customer need analysis, contracting, solution engineering, installing, after sale service

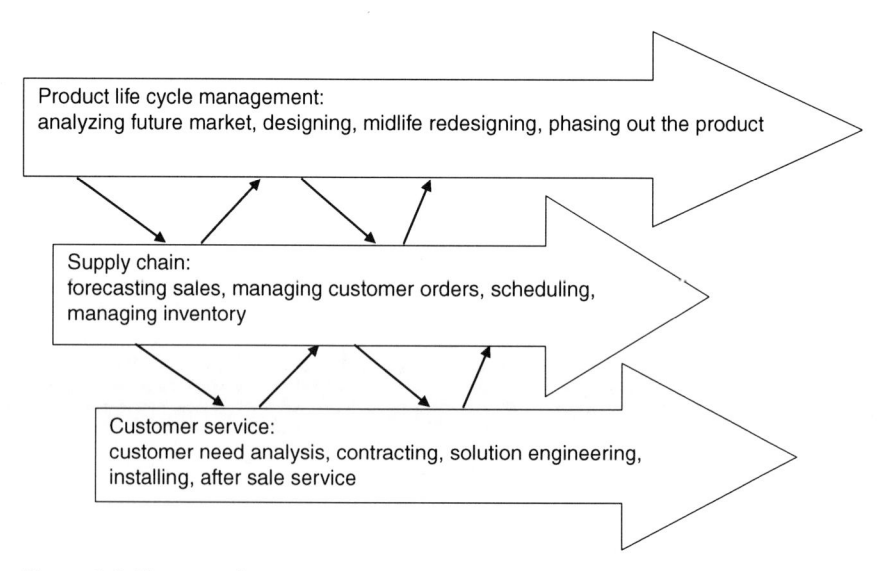

Figure 9.2 The new chronotopes

The Bakhtinian Theory of Chronotope Applied to the Organizing Process

Table 9.2 The new chronotopes

	Concurrent articulation		
	System life cycle chronotope	Supply chain chronotope	Customer service chronotope
Spatial and temporal frame	Offices in central headquarters. Short life cycles (ten months). Overlapping time.	Warehouses, factories, logistic centers, and planning offices. Short logistic cycle (two to three weeks). Concurrent time.	Service branches and customer sites. Geographic mobility and dispersion. Long projects for major customers.
Roles and characters. No more "crossing character"	Product engineers, strategic marketers, purchasers, and planners. Products are kits of components.	Logistic engineers, purchasers. Products are parcels to move quickly.	Expert consultants, customers, and project managers. The concept of product is replaced by customized *solutions*.

narrating the business: life-cycle management (managing dematerialized product information), supply chain (moving objects with little transformation), and customer service (designing solutions to respond to customized requirements). This transformation involved a radical loss of importance for manufacturing, which could now be viewed as an optional segment of logistics, depending on make-or-buy decisions (see Figure 9.2 and Table 9.2).

9.4.4 An alternative story

Most computer manufacturers could not manage the strategic move from manufacturing to services effectively and collapsed in the 1990s. This case suggests that dramatic environmental changes require not only explicit changes in organizing narratives but also more difficult architextural transformations. Bull leaders considered modification of chronotopic indicators such as O/DC a technical issue, whereas it might have been a key strategic channel to transform meaning-making schemes and values.

In the same period, Hewlett-Packard (HP) offers one example of successful joint transformation of chronotope and chronotopic indicator. Till the late 1980s, one key performance measurement in the product engineering department was "Time to market" (TTM): how long does it take to develop a new product, from initial studies to commercial launch? This indicator measures time spent by engineers in one place, the engineering laboratories. It no longer satisfied managers, because engineers were increasingly asked to help manufacturing and sales departments in the early months of the new product's commercial life, solving technical problems in the factories or in the after-sales services. In TTM perspective, this was a waste of their time, as the product had already been launched on the market. The engineering department then invented another indicator, "Break Even Time" (BET), adding to TTM the time necessary for a product to reach break-even point, that is, for product revenues to cover the original investment. This points to another type of story, in which engineers are not only people who design products in laboratories but also experts who make products profitable by handling manufacturing and sales problems, spending part of their time in factories and commercial branches. BET was gradually rolled out to the group: "Marketing, manufacturing, and R&D at HP are becoming more aware that they jointly manage a cross-functional process. Their improvement efforts rely on concepts such as break-even time (BET)" (Graves et al., 1991). The chronotope and the key indicator had been modified in unison.

9.5 The building safety case: "You can tell a man's a bricklayer because he lays bricks"

In late 2004, a large building firm engaged the authors of this chapter for a three-year research project (Tricard, 2009) about the organizational factors of work safety on building sites. The researchers adopted a dialogical inquiry method, close to action-research (Lorino et al., 2011). They interacted with organizational actors in various forms: (*a*) twenty-six interviews; (*b*) field immersion: twelve days with pricing teams and method engineers (project design), 100 days on building sites; (*c*) fifteen cross-functional workshop meetings to analyze activities and propose organizational changes to improve safety; and (*d*) every two months, the executive in charge of R&D and safety and the manager in charge of safety (here named Mr Grey and Mr Pink) convened the project's steering committee involving managers and researchers (see Figure 9.3).

This building company has a clear-cut separation between the "office world" and the "building site world." Method engineers and sales managers literally "invent" new projects; site managers, foremen, and workers transform what they tend to consider as "dreams" into tangible realities. The two worlds' values are fundamentally different, with distinct missions and personal profiles, but they generally seem complementary. Project management follows a sequential model (see Figure 9.4 and Table 9.3).

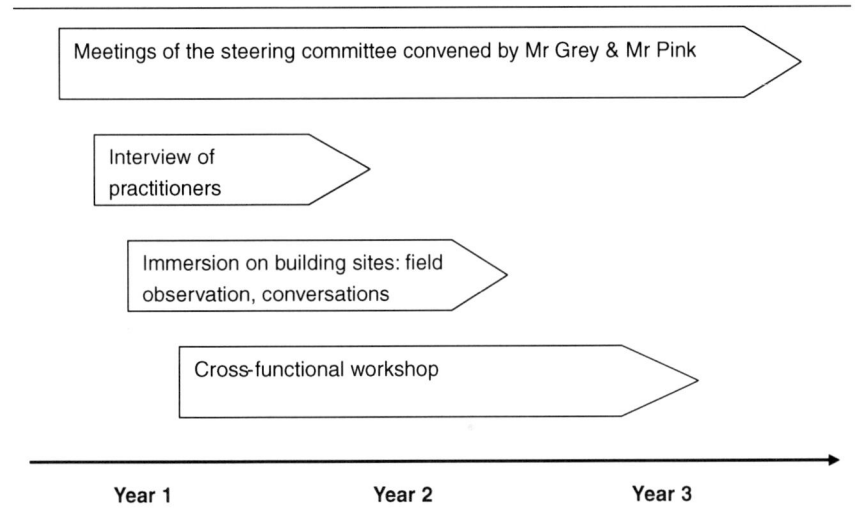

The Bakhtinian Theory of Chronotope Applied to the Organizing Process

Figure 9.3 The time schedule of the research project

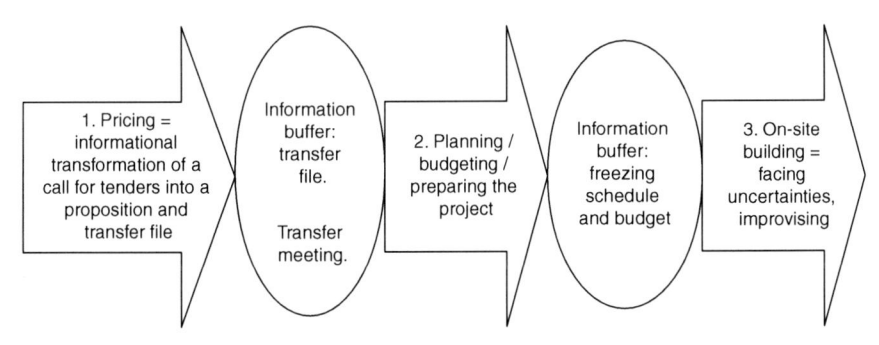

The diagram shows overlapping activities across Year 1 to Year 3:
- Meetings of the steering committee convened by Mr Grey & Mr Pink
- Interview of practitioners
- Immersion on building sites: field observation, conversations
- Cross-functional workshop

Figure 9.4 The traditional chronotope of the building industry

The diagram shows the sequence:
1. Pricing = informational transformation of a call for tenders into a proposition and transfer file
— Information buffer: transfer file. Transfer meeting.
2. Planning / budgeting / preparing the project
— Information buffer: freezing schedule and budget
3. On-site building = facing uncertainties, improvising

The time–space boundaries between activities were often discussed at steering committee meetings. Although dangerous situations occur during on-site operations, most of them are rooted in designing and planning activities, which are located in off-site offices, and take place before actual building starts. Deficiencies include resource planning problems (e.g., changing the crane for a critical phase was not budgeted), time scheduling problems (because of over-tight schedules, some critical tasks are left to hazardous on-site improvisation; or the building team suspends normal safety measures to work faster), inadequate technological choices, training deficiencies, and poor selection of suppliers and subcontractors.

Reciprocally, when problems appear on site, the risk may be worsened by hasty changes to work methods and insufficient technical support from

Table 9.3 The traditional chronotopes of the building industry

	Sequential articulation		
	The pricing chronotope (project design)	The planning/budgeting chronotope	The on-site building chronotope
Spatial–temporal frame	Offices. Two-month horizon to write a proposition. Location physically stable. Time planned.	Offices and meeting rooms whose walls are covered with architect's drawings. Two-month horizon for the planning of a site. Location physically stable. Time planned.	Six months to two years. High time uncertainty due to weather, ground, the permanent 3D spatial transformation of the workplace (building site).
Roles and characters	Quantity surveyors for raw material estimates, method engineers, sales managers, key roles of customer specs, and architect's drawings to optimize the project and get the contract.	A site manager and a chief engineer. Budget and schedule are the objects.	Site manager, chief engineer, foremen, and workers. The building—the daily flow of concrete—is the object.

method engineers. Mr Grey, Mr Pink, the researchers, and other managers involved in the project agreed that the clear-cut separation between "pricing," "planning–budgeting," and "on-site building" chronotopes had become a major impediment to safety improvements. Pricing (designing), budgeting, and scheduling activities often lacked on-site skills and, reciprocally, building site operations often lacked designing expertise. Therefore, pricing and planning actors should become actors on the building site, and on-site building actors should become actors of project design.

Yet at the end of the three-year project, Mr Grey uttered a "scream" that contradicted the analyses he had consistently shared before, as shown in the following quotations from steering committee meetings, ordered chronologically.

The French expression used by Mr Grey: "c'est au pied du mur qu'on reconnaît le maçon" has a double meaning; first: "You can tell a man is a bricklayer because he lays bricks!"; but "au pied du mur" also means "confronting a difficult and urgent task, with his back to the wall." Mr Grey's contradiction can be better understood in the light of the managers' general hesitations about safety, and their apparent "one step forward and two steps back." The cross-functional workshop clearly showed this to-ing and fro-ing at the frontier of the chronotope. The following discussion took place during the fifteenth and final workshop meeting. Action proposals

The Bakhtinian Theory of Chronotope Applied to the Organizing Process

July 15, 2005
Mr Grey: Safety should be given high priority in all processes of the project, during the whole project, from the very beginning, as soon as project design starts.

October 13, 2006
Mr Pink to researchers: Giving workers safety instructions is useless if work conditions are already too bad. What you suggest [analyzing risk as soon as projects are priced] is more promising than sanctions, because it is inappropriate only to judge the workers taking risks.

Mr Grey: [talking as a former site manager] I agree with you, on site, the only thing workers can do is comply with our instructions!

Mr Pink and Mr Grey agree that on-site risk concerns more people than workers and safety controllers and is often rooted far beyond the temporal and spatial boundaries of the building site.

May 14, 2008 (last meeting of the steering committee) Mr Grey to researchers: The purpose of this research is to promote safety in operations.
One of the researchers: OK, but the project analysis showed that many obstacles to safety are deeply rooted in the activities which design and plan building projects.
Mr Grey: I know, I know, but after all, *you can only tell a man's a bricklayer because he lays bricks!*

Mr Grey's final "scream" reveals the chronotope to which ultimately he metaphorically returns: in his profession (he is a former site manager), risk belongs to the temporal/spatial frame of building sites, when/where workers find themselves "with their backs to the wall" and have bricks to lay.

had been selected, detailed, and would soon be presented to the steering committee, to launch experimentation. The aim was to break the compartmentalization of projects between pricing, budgeting, and building and transform the time–space boundaries that frame professional identities. For example, it was suggested that foremen should be involved in the pricing and budgeting phases, which meant that they should be appointed earlier, trained to read architectural drawings, and be assigned new objectives. It was also suggested that method engineers should spend part of their time on the sites they had designed, after the transfer meeting, which meant redefining their mission statements. Mr Brown, a foreman; Mr Black, a safety manager; and the two researchers participated in the final workshop meeting convened by Mr Red, a process engineer.

Constructing Identity in and around Organizations

Quotations	Comments
Researcher 1: We concluded that building schedules should be established in the pricing phase, with input from the foreman.	Involving a foreman before/outside building sites is culturally challenging, because the temporal–spatial boundary of the building site mirrors the foreman's mission and self-perceived professional identity. The foreman strongly states that offices are not part of the foremen's world.
Mr Red: To do that, foremen should be appointed for projects already in the design phase, well before on-site building starts, much earlier than they are today.	
Mr Brown: Don't forget, foremen don't like sharing responsibility on abstract issues, we need concrete stuff, we like to touch things! *When we go to the offices, we see it as a punishment!*	
Mr Red: OK but what about method engineers moving to meet foremen on their current building site to consult them?	This would extend pricing engineers' chronotope significantly, since today they seldom go on-site.
Mr Brown: Yes, that would make us feel more confident.	
Mr Black: OK, but meeting the foreman on his present building site to embark him on the design of his next project is awkward from a managerial point of view. It could be regarded as bypassing his present bosses!	The present chronotopes involve basic managerial prerogatives.
Researcher 2: If foremen aren't involved in projects before the transfer meeting, they discover the project late in the process.	So far Mr Red had defended chronotope transformation. Suddenly, he makes a U-turn: functional hierarchy—that is, the present chronotope—is reasserted as an impassable boundary.
Mr Red: The site manager can present the project to the foreman later, after the transfer meeting. *The issue is between the foreman and his boss!*	

In this conversation, there is a permanent subterranean fight between two chronotopes: "safety should be designed-in" versus "safety should be managed on-site." Beyond rational argument, the "old" chronotope periodically surfaces in sentences like: *"when we go to the offices, we see it as a punishment!"* or *"the issue is between the foreman and his boss!,"* which echo

Mr Grey's "*You can only tell a man's a bricklayer because he lays bricks!*" What is at stake here is a deep change in professional and organizational values, identified with space (offices versus building sites), time (pretransfer versus posttransfer phases), and rules (hierarchical prerogatives).

9.6 Conclusion

This chapter studies organizing processes as narrative inquiries. It develops a praxeological rather than discursive approach to organizing inquiries (narratives in acts rather than in discourses). It stresses the importance of presupposed tacit frames, the "architextures," to relate narratives to their social and cultural environment and make them intelligible. It focuses on one of the most important "architextures" of organizing inquiries: their chronotope (time–space frame). Questioning the basic organizational chronotopes triggers "screams" to defend the time–space boundaries that are culturally acceptable in a given context. Through "chronotope-breaking," that is, the destabilization of time–space narrative structures, researchers and managers can explore and possibly transform the deep, invisible meaning-making frames linked with professional and organizational identities.

Chronotope analysis makes theoretical, methodological, and practical contributions:

1. In *theoretical* terms, it bridges the process-oriented and the narrative approaches of organizing, by conceptualizing organizing processes per se as narrative inquiries, rather than considering specific storytelling practices. The chronotope perspective questions epistemological dichotomies like time–space, intuition–reasoning, situated–generic, real–symbolic, and text–context (Barry et al., 2006) and stresses the deep integration of time and space, the living experience and its context, action, and thought in organizational inquiries.
2. In *methodological* terms, the chronotope approach can be used, as it is in ethnological studies, to decipher organizing processes through their time–space frames and get access to deep, partly invisible values and representations. It then allows *critical* inquiries, making the tacit, presupposed and taken-for-granted chronotopes of organizing processes explicit and debatable.
3. In *practical* terms, the chronotope concept can provide pointers for managing organizational change; it may be an effective path to explore organizational change, starting the "organizational journey" by

questioning the time–space frames of activity in concrete ways, rather than trying to impose preestablished models of future organizations.

The two cases presented in this chapter were focused on situations characterized by a sudden chronotopic "scream" in defense of the existing time–space frame, linked with professional identities, roles, and management tools. As they were not specifically designed *ex ante* to explore the potential of chronotopic analysis, they did not allow tracing time–space in microsituations, daily practices, emotions, and behaviors to "give flesh" to the chronotope. In future research, field studies specifically designed to analyze organizational chronotopes should more closely look for time–space archetypes in actors' activity, speeches, and habits. It could also more systematically explore the methodological potential of "chronotopic inquiries."

References

Bakhtin, M. M. (1981). "Forms of Time and the Chronotope in the Novel," in M. Holquist (ed.), *The Dialogic Imagination: Four Essays*. Austin University of Texas Press, Slavic Series, pp. 84–258.

—— (1984). *Problems of Dostoevsky's Poetics*. Ed. and trans. C. Emerson. Manchester: Manchester University Press.

Barry, D. and Elmes, M. (1997). "Strategy Retold: Toward a Narrative View of Strategic Discourse." *Academy of Management Review*, 22/2: 429–52.

—— Carroll, B., and Hansen, H. (2006). "To Text or Context? Endotextual, Exotextual, and Multi-textual Approaches to Narrative and Discursive Organizational Studies." *Organization Studies*, 27/8: 1091–110.

Bechky, B. A. (2003). "Sharing Meaning Across Occupational Communities: The Transformation of Understanding on a Production Floor." *Organization Science*, 14/3: 312–30.

Bergson, H. (1997/1896). *Matière et mémoire: Essai sur la relation du corps à l'esprit*. Paris: Presses Universitaires de France.

Boje, D. M. (1991). "The Storytelling Organization: A Study of Story Performance in an Office-Supply Firm." *Administrative Science Quarterly*, 36: 106–26.

—— (1995). "Stories of the Storytelling Organization: A Postmodern Analysis of Disney as '*Tamara*-Land.'" *Academy of Management Journal*, 38/4: 997–1035.

—— Oswick, C., and Ford, J. D. (2004). "Introduction to Special Topic Forum. Language and Organization: The Doing of Discourse." *Academy of Management Review*, 29/4: 571–7.

Borges, J. L. (1974). *Obras completas I*. Buenos Aires: Emecé Editores.

Boyce, M. E. (1995). "Collective Centring and Collective Sense-Making in the Stories and Storytelling of One Organization." *Organization Studies*, 16/1: 116–37.

Bruner, J. (1990). *Acts of Meaning.* Cambridge, MA: Harvard University Press.
Butler, R. (1995). "Time in Organizations: Its Experience, Explanations and Effects." *Organization Studies*, 16/6: 925–50.
Button, G. (1993). "The Curious Case of the Vanishing Technology," in G. Button (ed.), *Technology in Working Order: Studies of Work, Interaction and Technology.* London: Routledge, pp. 10–28.
Carlile, P. R. (2002). "A Pragmatic View of Knowledge and Boundaries: Boundary Objects in New Product Development." *Organization Science*, 13/4: 442–55.
Carr, D. (1991a). "Epistémologie et ontologie du récit," in J. Greisch and R. Kearney (eds), *Paul Ricœur: Les métamorphoses de la raison herméneutique.* Paris: Éditions du Cerf, pp. 205–14.
—— (1991b). "Contribution to the Round Table Discussion 'Ricoeur on Narrative,'" in D. Wood (ed.), *On Paul Ricœur: Narrative and Interpretation.* London: Routledge, pp. 160–87.
—— (1991c). *Time, Narrative and History (Studies in Phenomonelogy and Existential Philosophy).* Bloomington, IN: Indiana University Press.
Cassirer, E. (1942). *Zur Logik der Kulturwissenschaften.* Göteborg: Göteborgs Högskolas Årsskrift 47 (1961: translated as *The Logic of the Humanities*). New Haven, CT: Yale University Press.
Chandler, A. D. Jr. (1977). *The Visible Hand. The Managerial Revolution in American Business.* Cambridge, MA: Belknap Press of Harvard University Press.
Chia, R. (1996). *Organizational Analysis as Deconstructive Practice.* Berlin: Walter de Gruyter.
—— (2002). "Essai: Time, Duration and Simultaneity. Rethinking Process and Change in Organizational Analysis." *Organization Studies*, 23/6: 863–8.
Cooper, R. (2007). "Organs of Process: Rethinking Human Organization." *Organization Studies*, 28/10: 1547–73.
Cunliffe, A. L., Luhman, J. T., and Boje, D. M. (2004). "Narrative Temporality: Implications for Organization Research." *Organization Studies*, 25/2: 261–86.
Cussins, A. (1992). "Content, Embodiment and Objectivity: The Theory of Cognitive Trails." *Mind*, 101/404: 651–88.
Czarniawska, B. (1998). *A Narrative Approach to Organization Studies.* Thousand Oaks, CA: Sage.
—— (1999). "Management She Wrote: Organization Studies and Detective Stories." *Culture and Organization*, 5/1: 13–41.
Deleuze, G. (2006/1984). Cinéma et pensée, course 67 taught on October 30, 1984, online access: http://www.univ-paris8.fr/deleuze/article.php3?id_article=4 (G. Deleuze (2006). *Gilles Deleuze: Cinéma.* Paris: Gallimard, collection "A voix haute.")
Dewey, J. (1980/1938). *Logic: The Theory of Inquiry.* New York: Henry Holt (reprinted 1980 in New York: Irvington Publishers).
Eco, U. (1984). *The Role of the Reader: Explorations in the Semiotics of Texts (Advances in Semiotics).* Bloomington, IN: Indiana University Press.

Elchardus, M. (1988). "The Rediscovery of Chronos: The New Role of Time in Sociological Theory." *International Sociology*, 3/1: 35–9.

Forray, J. M. and Woodilla, J. (2002). "Temporal Spans in Talk: Doing Consistency to Construct Fair Organization." *Organization Studies*, 23/6: 899–916.

Foucault, M. (1980). *Power/Knowledge: Selected Interviews and Other Writings, 1972–1977*. New York: Pantheon.

Genette, G. (1972). *Figures III*. Paris: Editions du Seuil.

—— (1979). *Introduction à l'architexte*. Paris: Editions du Seuil.

—— (1982). *Palimpsestes*. Paris: Editions du Seuil.

Golant, B. D. and Sillince, J. A. (2007). "The Constitution of Organizational Legitimacy: A Narrative Perspective." *Organization Studies*, 28/8: 1149–67.

Goodall, H. L. and Kellet, P. M. (2004). "Dialectical Tensions and Dialectic Moments as Pathways to Peak Experiences," in R. Anderson, L. A. Baxter, and K. N. Cissna (eds), *Dialogue: Theorizing Difference in Communication Studies*. Thousand Oaks, CA: Sage, pp. 159–74.

Graves, S. B., Carmichael, W. P., Daetz, D., and Wilson, E. (1991). "Improving the Product Development Process." *Hewlett Packard Journal*, 24/3: 71–6.

Gregory, D. (1989). "Areal Differentiation and Post-Modern Human Geography," in D. Gregory and R. Walford (eds.), *Horizons in Human Geography*. Ottawa: Barnes & Noble, pp. 67–95.

Habermas, J. (1970). "Toward a Theory of Communicative Competence," in H. P. Dreitzel (ed.), *Recent Sociology*. London: MacMillan.

Hassard, J. (2002). "Essai: Organizational Time: Modern, Symbolic and Postmodern Reflections." *Organization Studies*, 23/6: 885–92.

Hatch, M. J. (2002). "Essai: Doing Time in Organization Theory." *Organization Studies*, 23/6: 869–75.

Hofstadter, D. R. (1979). *Gödel, Escher, Bach: An Eternal Golden Braid*. New York: Basic Books.

Humphreys, M. and Brown, A. D. (2002). "Narratives of Organizational Identity and Identification: A Case Study of Hegemony and Resistance." *Organization Studies*, 23/3: 421–47.

Kornberger, M. and Clegg, S. R. (2004). "Bringing Space Back in: Organizing the Generative Building." *Organization Studies*, 25/7: 1095–114.

Kramer, E. M. (2004). "Guest Editor's Introduction: Narrative and Time." *Tamara Journal of Critical Postmodern Organization Science*, 3/1: IV–V.

Lee, H. and Liebenau, J. (1999). "Time in Organizational Studies: Towards a New Research Direction." *Organization Studies*, 20/6: 1035–58.

Lefebvre, H. (1991). *The Production of Space*. Oxford: Blackwell. (Trans. Donald Nicholson-Smith from (1974) *La production de l'espace*. Paris: Anthropos.)

Leontyev, A. N. (1981). *Problems of the Development of the Mind*. Moscow: Progress Publishers.

Lorino, P. (2007). *The Instrumental Genesis of Collective Activity: The Case of an ERP Implementation in a Large Electricity Producer*. Paris: Essec Research Center, DR-07014.

—— Tricard, B. and Clot, Y. (2011). "Research Methods for Non-Representational Approaches to Organizational Complexity: The Dialogical Mediated Inquiry." *Organization Studies*, 32/6: 769–801.

March, J. G. (1991). "Exploration and Exploitation in Organizational Learning." *Organization Science*, 2/1 (special issue: Organizational Learning: Papers in Honor of (and by) James G. March): 71–87.

Marková, I. (2003). *Dialogicality and Social Representations*. Cambridge: Cambridge University Press.

Mead, G. H. (1934). *Mind, Self and Society from the Standpoint of a Social Behaviourist*. Ed. C. W. Morris. Chicago, IL: University of Chicago.

Merleau-Ponty, M. (1945). *Phénoménologie de la perception*. Paris: Gallimard.

Michel, J. (2003). "Narrativité, narration, narratologie: du concept ricœurien d'identité narrative aux sciences sociales." *Revue Européenne des Sciences Sociales*, XLI-125: 125–42.

Ming, L. (2006). "The (Re)production of Organizational Time: Reading the Feminine through Henri Lefebvre." *Tamara Journal*, 5/2: 125–37.

Mink, L. (1978). "Narrative Form as a Cognitive Instrument," in R. H. Canary and H. Kozicki (eds), *The Writing of History: Literary Form and Historical Understanding*. Madison, WI: University of Wisconsin Press, pp. 129–49.

Nayak, A. (2008). "On the Way to Theory: A Processual Approach." *Organization Studies*, 29/2: 173–90.

Orlikowski, W. J. and Barley, S. R. (2001). "Technology and Institutions: What Can Research on Information Technology and Research on Organizations Learn from Each Other?" *MIS Quarterly*, 25/2: 145–65.

—— Yates, J. A. (1998). "Genre Systems: Structuring Interaction through Communicative Norms." *MIT Sloan School of Management Working Papers*. CCS WP #205, Sloan WP #4030.

—— —— (2002). "It's about Time: Temporal Structuring in Organizations." *Organization Science*, 13/6: 684–700.

Peirce, C. S. (1958/1931). *Collected Papers*. Cambridge, MA: Harvard University Press. First published in 1931.

—— (1997/1903). *Pragmatism as a Principle and Method of Right Thinking: The 1903 Harvard Lectures on Pragmatism*. Ed. P. A. Turrisi (1997). Albany, NY: State University of New York Press.

—— (1998/1903). *The Essential Peirce. Selected Philosophical Writings*. Vol. 2 (1893–1913), ed. the Peirce Edition Project (1998). Bloomington, IN: Indiana University Press.

Ricœur, P. (1984). *Temps et récit, tome I: L'intrigue et le récit philosophique*. Paris: Le Seuil. (English trans. K. McLaughlin and D. Pellauer, *Time and Narrative, vol. I*. Chicago, IL: University of Chicago Press.)

Sahay, S. (1997). "Implementation of Information Technology: A Time–Space Perspective." *Organization Studies*, 18:2: 229–60.

Searle, J. (1969). *Speech Acts: An Essay in the Philosophy of Language*. Cambridge, MA: Cambridge University Press.

Shotter, J. (2006). "Understanding Process from Within: An Argument for 'Withness'-Thinking." *Organization Studies*, 27/4: 585–604.

—— (2008). "Dialogism and Polyphony in Organizing Theorizing in Organization Studies: Action Guiding Anticipations and the Continuous Creation of Novelty." *Organization Studies*, 29/4: 501–24.

Staudenmayer, N., Tyre, M., and Perlow, L. (2002). "Time to Change: Temporal Shifts as Enablers of Organizational Change." *Organization Science*, 13/5: 583–5.

Taylor, F. W. (1972/1911). *The Principles of Scientific Management*. Westport, CT: Greenwood Press Publishers.

Todorov, T. (1981). *Mikhail Bakhtine: Le principe dialogique*. Paris: Seuil. (English trans. (1984) *Mikhail Bakhtin: The Dialogical Principle (Theory & History of Literature)*. Minneapolis, MN: University of Minnesota Press.)

Toyoki, S., Spicer, A., and Elliott, R. (2006). "Beyond Old Horizons: Theorising the Rhythms of Social Reproduction." *Tamara Journal*, 5/2: 96–115.

Tricard, B. (2009). "La genèse organisationnelle du risque d'accidents sur les chantiers de construction: Une approche dialogique de l'activité collective organisée." Ph.D. Dissertation, ESSEC Business School.

Tsoukas, H. (2005). *Complex Knowledge: Studies in Organizational Epistemology*. Oxford: Oxford University Press.

—— (2009). "A Dialogical Approach to the Creation of New Knowledge in Organizations." *Organization Science*, 20/6: 941–57.

—— Chia, R. (2002). "On Organizational Becoming: Rethinking Organizational Change." *Organization Science*, 13/5: 567–82.

—— Hatch, M. J. (2001). "Complex Thinking, Complex Practice: The Case for a Narrative Approach to Organizational Complexity." *Human Relations*, 54/8: 979–1013.

Vygotsky, L. S. (1978). *Mind in Society: The Development of Higher Psychological Processes*. Cambridge, MA: Harvard University Press.

—— (1986). *Thought and Language*. Cambridge, MA: The MIT Press.

Weick, K. E. (1979). *The Social Psychology of Organizing*. Reading, MA: Addison-Wesley.

—— (1995). *Sensemaking in Organizations*. Thousand Oaks, CA: Sage.

—— (2001). *Making Sense of the Organization*. Oxford: Blackwell.

—— Browning, L. D. (1986). "Argument and Narration in Organizational Communication." *Journal of Management*, 12/2: 243–56.

—— Roberts, K. H. (1993). "Collective Mind in Organizations: Heedful Interrelating on Flight Docks." *Administrative Science Quarterly*, 38: 357–81.

Yanow, D. (1994). "Reader–Response Theory and Organizational Life: Action as Interpretation and Text." Paper presented in the symposium, Rhetoric, Narrative, Text: Telling Organizational Tales at the annual meeting of the Academy of Management, Dallas, TX.

Yoo, Y., Boland, R. J., and Lyytinen, K. (2006). "From Organization Design to Organization Designing." *Organization Science*, 17/2: 215–29.

10

The Momentum of Organizational Change[1]

Elden Wiebe, Roy Suddaby and William M. Foster

Abstract: The purpose of this chapter is to clarify the concept of momentum by situating momentum within the flow of time (past, present, and future), and in doing so, reconceptualize momentum as agentic. Organization scholars have typically equated momentum with inertia and hence the inability of organizations to change. Close examination of the organization literature, however, reveals that the concept of momentum is not so narrowly defined. From the literature, we identify and delineate three types of momentum—inherent, exploratory, and emergent—on the basis of their relationship to time (past, future, and present, respectively). On the basis of their temporal grounding, we then describe how momentum can be conceptualized as agentic. Finally, we describe the interaction of each temporal dimension (past, present, and future) within each type of momentum. We conclude with some considerations of the implications for organizational change.

10.1 Introduction

The conceptualization of momentum in the organization studies (OS) literature is a curiosity. For the most part, momentum is equated with inertia (e.g., Miller and Friesen, 1980; Kelly and Amburgey, 1991; Amburgey and Miner, 1992). In contrast, the more popular press has recognized a greater dynamism connoted by momentum than suggested by the term "inertia," evident in comments about the momentum of politics (e.g., elections, political unrest leading to change), the economy (e.g., recovery from recession), and sports teams (e.g., winning streaks). Sociologists have also contrasted, rather than equated, momentum and inertia (Adler, 1981), as have organization scholars writing for a more popular audience (Baden-Fuller and Stopford, 1994; Goodman, 1995; Collins, 2001).

The concept of momentum in the organization literature is also confusing. The literature is replete with definitions of and adjectives for momentum. For example, momentum has been defined as a "tendency to keep evolving in the same direction" (Miller and Friesen, 1980: 599), "sustained periods of pursuit" (of a particular goal) (Gersick, 1994: 23), "the level of effort and commitment top-level decision-makers are willing to devote to action designed to resolve an issue" (Dutton and Duncan, 1987: 286), and "the force of motion, or alternatively, the force or energy associated with a moving body" (Jansen, 2004: 277). Inherent in these definitions are several metaphors, ranging from biology to goal-setting theory to social construction to physics, all of which provide a different basis for understanding momentum. Then further, organization scholars have applied the concept of momentum to several organizational phenomena, giving rise to several types of momentum: positional momentum, contextual momentum, institutional momentum, and behavioral momentum. Jansen (2004) adds two other terms—stasis-based momentum and change-based momentum.

There have been some attempts at gaining clarity concerning momentum, and thereby increasing its potential value for understanding organizational change. For example, Goodman (1995) differentiated inertia and momentum by pointing to organizational outcomes. If negative, then the organization had experienced inertia; if positive, momentum. In this way, Goodman is able to salvage from the negative connotations of inertia the obviously positive aspects of repetitive behavior, such as learning, reliability, and accountability (1995: 100). However, the concept remains confusing as Goodman claims momentum "implies that inertia has been overcome to produce or change movement" (Goodman, 1995: 100). It is difficult to understand how momentum overcomes what is essentially momentum. Moreover, how does one discern which activity is good to reproduce (momentum) and which is bad (inertia), accept after the fact? In a more sophisticated manner, Jansen (2004) readdressed momentum as a dynamic force. Jansen differentiated between inertia and momentum by linking momentum to energy. Whereas inertia is characterized by a lack of energy and no effort, momentum is energy that can be actively directed with either small effort (minor change) or large effort (major change). The key issue in the amount of energy expended is the organization's trajectory. If remaining on the current trajectory, the organization exerts small effort (stasis-based momentum) creating incremental change. If pursuing a new trajectory, the organization must exert large effort (change-based momentum) creating frame-breaking change. But there are difficulties with this delineation as well. For example, exertion of little energy, thereby slowing down a change process (perhaps even seen as resistance to change), may be what is necessary to implement a major change well (Wiebe, 2010). Further, a series of small changes (small effort) may in fact lead to radical change (Plowman et al., 2007). Third, the repetition of the past (inertia) may be what an organization needs to change from its current trajectory (frame-breaking change). For example, O'Connor (2000) demonstrates how a high tech company in Silicon Valley reaffirmed its character as being innovative by going back to the "original" roots. This company claimed that its founding on the basis of innovation was the essential element of the organization, and this in turn formed the impetus for its reinvigoration (change in current trajectory). Going back allowed the company to go forward in a new way.

In this chapter, we also seek to clarify momentum. We do so, however, by drawing on what is implicit, and yet largely neglected, in the concept of momentum—time. This is not to say that a relationship between time and momentum has not been noticed. Previous studies recognize that momentum waxes and wanes over time (Adler, 1981; Jansen, 2004). Others have noted that the past has a strong influence over organizations (e.g., Miller and Friesen, 1980, 1982). In their study of organizational change and development, Kimberly and Bouchikhi (1995) provide a temporal description of momentum when they explicate "how the past shapes the present and constrains the future." Adler (1981) in particular noted a myriad temporal concepts associated with momentum: rhythm, pacing, tempo, ebb and flow, and synchronization. Yet, in spite of the recognition of temporality associated with momentum, time itself—that is, time as intrinsic to momentum, not just a backdrop against which momentum takes place—has remained outside of considerations of that which gives impetus to momentum.

We also draw on time because time and organizational change are intimately related (Burrell, 1992; Tsoukas and Chia, 2002; Sherover, 2003; Purser et al., 2005; Wiebe, 2010). Whether time is a necessary condition for change (see Sherover, 2003) or change is a necessary condition for time (Mead, 1932), time and change are inseparably linked. For our purposes, we draw on the classic temporal dimensions of past, present, and future to delineate three types of momentum as discerned in the OS literature. These dimensions reflect the central elements in the flow of time by which we understand that something is changing. Past, present, and future, in that order, are implicated in the change and development of phenomena. The opposite direction—future, present, and past—is implicated in human deliberation (Tsoukas and Hatch, 2001; Sherover, 2003). Both are implicated in momentum.

This last point leads to one further consideration. Human deliberation in the flow of time suggests a level of freedom that a more deterministic sense of development from past to present to future may not allow. Recently, Emirbayer and Mische (1998) have situated human freedom, or perhaps better, human agency, in the flow of time in order to better understand how humans may be agentic even in highly deterministic contexts. They reconceptualize human agency as

> a temporally embedded process of social engagement, informed by the past (in its habitual aspect), but also oriented toward the future (as a capacity to imagine alternative possibilities) and toward the present (as a capacity to contextualize past habits and future projects within the contingencies of the moment). (Emirbayer and Mische, 1998: 963)

At any one time, people may have a predominant temporal stance (e.g., past, present, or future) toward something, but they are also capable of changing that stance (e.g., from past to future), and thereby changing their relationship to that something (Emirbayer and Mische, 1998: 964). In doing so, they gain opportunity to act within a context in ways perhaps not available within the original stance. Thus, our engagement with time recognizes (*a*) time as intrinsic to, not just an envelope for, phenomena; (*b*) the opposite temporal processes of phenomena and human deliberation; and (*c*) the agency available to people as they situate themselves in the flow of time.

Time, then, forms an important basis for linking momentum, organizational change, and human agency. By drawing on time, we seek to delineate momentum as agentic and point to how the impetus of the past, present, and future may shape the momentum of organizational change. The chapter progresses as follows. We begin by delineating the concept of momentum in the OS literature on the basis of temporality (past, future, and present), identifying three types that we label inherent, exploratory, and emergent, respectively. Second, we develop these types further, reconceptualizing them as agentic from the perspective of time. Finally, recognizing that we are always in the flow of time, we offer reflection on the interaction of the three temporal dimensions within each particular temporal focus. We conclude with some implications of our typology for organizational change.

10.2 The depiction of momentum in the organization studies literature

To make sense of the definitions and uses of momentum in the literature, we begin by defining momentum anew. While several definitions already exist in the literature, as noted above, we are aware of some important problems with them. Some definitions are imbued with temporal assumptions that close down the conceptual space for other ways of understanding momentum (Miller and Friesen, 1980; Gersick, 1994). Others are laden with metaphorical baggage that again constricts how momentum can be conceptualized (Kelly and Amburgey, 1991; Amburgey and Miner, 1992; Jansen, 2004). Our definition of momentum derives from several definitions found in various dictionaries (e.g., *Oxford English Dictionary*). In particular, we sought definitions of momentum that were not related to physics either explicitly or metaphorically (see especially Tsoukas and Hatch, 2001: 990–6, who point out difficulties of the timeless and imperfect generalizations of the Newtonian style of thinking). Thus, we define momentum as an impetus for action that stems from an element considered essential for action. Three of the four definitions found in the OS literature suggest that element essential for action is temporal in nature (the fourth is timeless in the Newtonian sense)—the past inexorably intruding into the present and future (Miller and Friesen, 1980), the future goal shaping the present and breaking the strength of the past (Gersick, 1994), and the present as the contextual ground on which the past and future interact with the present in the ongoing accomplishment of momentum (Dutton and Duncan, 1987). Using these three classic dimensions of time as a heuristic, we now delineate the depiction of momentum in the OS literature (see Table 10.1).

10.2.1 Inherent momentum

The literature depicts a past-oriented momentum that we refer to as inherent; that is, it is conceptualized as an innate aspect of all organizational phenomena. Momentum is assumed to lie within organizational phenomena themselves. The exemplars for this conceptualization are Miller and Friesen (1980, 1982) and Amburgey and colleagues (Kelly and Amburgey, 1991; Amburgey and Miner, 1992; Amburgey et al., 1993). For example, in their foundational texts for momentum in the OS literature, Miller and Friesen (1980, 1982) conceptualized momentum as a "tendency to keep

Table 10.1 Depiction of momentum in the organization studies literature

Essential element for momentum	Inherent — Past	Exploratory — Future	Emergent — Present
Exemplar(s)	Miller and Friesen (1980, 1982), Amburgey and colleagues	Gersick (1994)	Dutton and Duncan (1987), Jansen (2004)
Metaphor(s)	Biology Newtonian physics	Punctuated equilibrium	Newtonian physics Social construction
Level of analysis	Organization, structures, and processes	Organization, Project	Individuals within organizational context
Managerial agency	Managers have none or very little agency	Managers have high agency initially and at temporal milestones	Managers have high levels of agency
Type of organizational change	No change or minor incremental change	No change or minor incremental change	Low level of energy leads to incremental change. High level of energy leads to radical change
How organizational change is accomplished	Episodic (unanticipated event-based)	Episodic (time-based)	Continuous change
Key question in relation to radical change	How can momentum be broken? (assumes both the presence of momentum in the organization and organization phenomena, and that once broken, it remains broken)		How can momentum be maintained and strengthened?
Temporality and the accomplishment of radical change	Temporality is broken. The past is negated by the future		Temporality is preserved from the foundation of the present

evolving in the same direction," meaning that any organizational phenomenon, as well as the organization as a whole, would continue to follow and develop along the path of its initial direction. They suggested that momentum was not limited to certain organizations or phenomena but that it was associated with many organizational designs and phenomena, and that further development in these designs and phenomena tended to follow their initial direction, whatever that direction might be. For example, momentum is not simply associated with mechanistic organizations, often characterized as slow in responding to environmental changes, and hence bound by "natural resistance to change" (Miller and Friesen, 1980: 591), but also with organic organizations, which were highly innovative (Miller and Friesen, 1982). Mechanistic organizations become more mechanistic over time, but organic organizations also become more organic over time. As Miller and Friesen (1980: 592) note, organizations "appear to be biased in their direction of evolution so that they generally extrapolate past trends." The same tendency exists at the level of organizational structure and processes: an organization's style of decision-making, job design, level of product innovation, type of control and information gathering, etc., all display a tendency to continue evolving in the same direction.

Amburgey and colleagues concur that "Inertia can mean remaining static, but it can also mean staying in uniform motion" (Amburgey and Miner, 1992: 335). In this way, they not only depicted momentum as inertia and hence adverse to change but also drew into the notion of momentum/inertia what had until then been juxtaposed with inertia, namely an organization's change processes. "When organizations repeat changes that they have experienced in the past, their change processes are said to have momentum" (Kelly and Amburgey, 1991: 596; but see Beck et al., 2008, for a contrary argument). Within this context of momentum, Amburgey and colleagues found partial support for further development (minor incremental change) in the extension of the emphasis and direction of the past. This occurred through repeated actions, the shaping power of context (structure and culture), and the further application of an organization's positional strategy.

The metaphors used to delineate this sense of inherent momentum reinforce (or give rise to) the notion of innateness. Miller and Friesen (1980) use the metaphors of biology and evolution. The tendency to evolve in the same direction is analogous to the life cycle of an organism on the one hand, and to biological evolution on the other. On the basis of the life-cycle model, the organization will follow a prescribed series of stages through its "life-time," always moving in the same basic direction. Change is "in the genes," incremental and inexorable. From the evolutionary perspective, the individual organization, like the biological organism, will face a changing environment. In biological evolution, a changing environment forces some entities to decline and disappear and provides the context for the appearance of other new and novel entities. Applying the metaphor to organizations, Miller and Friesen (1980) suggest that the radical change of the organization, in which a new direction is pursued after the incremental change of inherent momentum has run its course to excess, is such an instance of the death of an old organizational form and the birth of a new one. Amburgey and colleagues, on the other hand, draw on Newtonian physics. While in itself it does not connote innateness, their use of physics is limited to the conception of inertia, which underscores the inherent unchangeableness of organizations and organizational phenomena.

Organizational change in relation to this depiction of momentum is either nonexistent or incremental in minor ways. This notion has been variously referred to in the literature as convergent (Tushman and Romanelli, 1985) or first-order change (Bartunek, 1984), supporting an organization's particular configuration (Miller and Friesen, 1980), archetype (Greenwood and Hinings, 1993), or strategy (Amburgey and Miner, 1992). Inherent momentum and radical change, understood as a change in direction, are mutually exclusive. An instance of one precludes the concurrent existence of the other. As such, inherent momentum and radical change occur sequentially. As radical change signifies the termination of inherent momentum, these can only occur one after the other.[2]

10.2.2 Exploratory momentum

The literature also depicts a future-oriented momentum that we refer to as exploratory. It is conceptualized as a tentative pursuit of a goal because it is uncertain whether the established set of activities will in fact achieve the future time-linked goal. Gersick (1994) is the exemplar for this conceptualization of momentum. Gersick defines momentum as the persistence, perseverance, and pursuit of a particular goal. Gersick found that organizations bound to deadlines (i.e., venture capital start-ups) reassessed their progress at one or more temporal milestones, at which time they reoriented their strategies and activities if their progress was not sufficient for successful completion by the deadline. This influence of temporally linked teleology on momentum is the fundamental addition provided by Gersick (1994). It is this linkage to a firm timeframe that encourages persistence, perseverance, and pursuit of a particular goal with a specified set of activities for a specified period of time. It also allows this momentum to be reshaped or even terminated by managerial intervention if that goal is not being met by those particular actions within the specified timeframe.

Gersick (1994) draws on the metaphor of punctuated equilibrium to reconceptualize and provide additional nuances for exploratory momentum and organizational change. This metaphor is typically conceived within an evolutionary framework in which momentum continues indefinitely until the mismatch between the organization and the environment is too great and creates a crisis (Miller and Friesen, 1980; Tushman and Romanelli, 1985; Gersick, 1991). In Gersick's work (1994), however, the model of punctuated equilibrium is elaborated from the perspective of a constructed goal linked to specified timeframes that delimit the convergence (momentum) period.

Organizational change in relation to this depiction of momentum is, as with inherent momentum, either nonexistent or incremental in minor ways, but now delimited by the temporally specified period. Assessment at a temporal milestone may continue the period of convergence until another milestone is reached, or it may result in a new set of activities deemed more appropriate in the pursuit of a particular time-linked goal. The temporally specified periodicity can create regularly paced episodic change, sequentially alternating between convergence and (radical) change.

10.2.3 Emergent momentum

Finally, the literature depicts a present-oriented momentum that we refer to as emergent; that is, it is conceptualized as the product of interactions of managers with other managers as well as with animate and inanimate things, and the subsequent actions taken by those managers. Emergent momentum is the effortful accomplishment of managerial action. It must be brought into being by managers' actions, and is subject to development and attrition.

The exemplars for this conceptualization are Dutton and Duncan (1987) and Jansen (2004). Dutton and Duncan (1987: 286) define momentum as "the level of effort and commitment top-level decision-makers are willing to devote to action designed to resolve an issue." The authors theorize that organizations respond differently to environmental changes because managers are differentially alerted to and interpret those changes. Gaining energy for a particular course of action (i.e., momentum) involves numerous interpretive activities referred to as strategic issue diagnosis (SID):

activation thresholds, which must be attained for issues to capture the attention of managers; managerial assessments of urgency, which refer to the importance of taking action on those issues; managerial assessments of feasibility, which refer to the understandability of the issue and the perceived capability for dealing with it; contextual influences such as the organization's belief structure, which shapes the breadth of the organization's ability to identify and understand issues; and the organization's resources, which shape the potential urgency and capability of dealing with an issue. They suggested that the energy (low or high) that develops from these issue assessments and contextual influences then determines whether managers will favor and pursue incremental change (low energy) or radical change (high energy) in the organization's strategy.

Jansen (2004: 277) defines momentum as "the force of motion, or alternatively, the force or energy associated with a moving body," which is in contrast to inertia in which there is no movement. Jansen discerns two types of momentum: (*a*) stasis-based momentum (corresponding to momentum as constant movement, e.g., Kelly and Amburgey, 1991) to which energy may be added to expand activity along an existing trajectory (Amburgey and Miner, 1992) and (*b*) change-based momentum, which is the application of significant energy to affect and sustain activity in a new direction. Jansen's empirical study (2004) centers on change-based momentum. A high level of energy was associated with achieving significant movement along a new trajectory (i.e., radical change). Change-based momentum also displayed dynamism. It fluctuated over time, being impacted positively or negatively by social information conveyed by (change) leaders, events/actions that shifted attention away from the accomplishment of radical change, the initial positions of stakeholders vis-à-vis the change initiative, interaction (i.e., talk) about the change initiative, early wins that created progress toward the final goal, and commitment to the change initiative.

The metaphors undergirding emergent momentum are twofold. Jansen (2004) explicitly appeals to the metaphor of Newtonian physics. Using the theory more broadly than Amburgey and colleagues, Jansen utilizes the elements of inertia, movement, and velocity, which incorporates speed and direction (velocity as a vector quantity). From this foundation, Jansen (2004) highlights three key distinctions: (*a*) inertia, linked to mass, involves no effort and suggests no change and no movement; (*b*) momentum is movement that is achieved by the application of force (effort) that overcomes the resistance of inertia; and (*c*) the simultaneous existence of many forces, each with a particular quantity of speed in a particular direction, draws attention to the particular trajectory or path of the momentum of interest as a very important consideration.

Dutton and Duncan (1987) utilize social construction. Social construction highlights the meaning making that takes place through interaction. "Alternative judgements of the meaning of an event are imposed, created and legitimated in a social context" (Dutton and Duncan, 1987: 280). Strategic issues do not appear to managers labeled as such; rather, the significance of events is ascribed to those events through interpretive processes in the context of interaction between people, and animate/inanimate things. In this way, events become issues that managers must resolve in some way. Reality is socially constructed rather than given (Berger and Luckmann, 1967).

Organizational change in relation to this depiction of momentum can be either minor incremental change or major radical change, which is determined by the amount of energy engendered by interpretive processes for the change project. Moreover, both types may exist at the same time. Jansen's work (2004), as well as Ginsberg and Venkatraman's empirical test (1992, 1995) of Dutton and Duncan's theory (1987), showed the co-occurrence and influence of what we refer to as inherent momentum on emergent momentum. Jansen's study (2004) also shows this dynamic interaction over time, leading to emergent momentum waxing and waning as different forces impinge on the change initiative. Momentum conceptualized in this way does not show the same sequence of momentum/radical change/momentum/radical change and so on, central to the previous two conceptions of momentum.

10.3 Momentum and agency

Evident from our review is that momentum is much more than inertia. We have seen that momentum becomes agentic when shaped by managers with an orientation toward the future, and even more so when shaped by managers with an orientation toward the present. Perhaps this is not surprising in that both exploratory and emergent momentum are constructed through interpretive processes in social contexts. Both are the product of meanings that organizational members, through interaction, attach to issues, concepts, progress, and relationships. Dutton and Duncan (1987: 280) suggest, "the meanings formed in SID create the momentum for change through which forces for further adaptation are set into place."

Whether focused on the future or the present, momentum becomes an ongoing, effortful accomplishment by managers.

Given this insight, we suggest that inherent momentum can also be conceptualized as agentic. Rather than being highly constraining and inexorable, given tight coupling and the resulting hyperstability (Miller and Friesen, 1980; Sydow et al., 2009), we suggest that inherent momentum, like exploratory and emergent momentum, is shapeable by managerial agency as managers direct their attention not to the future or the present but to the past.

Managerial agency linked to inherent momentum is already hinted at in the literature. For example, Miller and Friesen (1980) point to enduring organizational myths and ideologies, narrow self-affirming models of creativity, successful heuristics, political coalitions, and the programs, goals and expectations that grow up around an organization's modus operandi as sources of momentum. Kelly and Amburgey (1991) suggest that momentum as repeated action at least crudely captures managerial values, learning by organizational members, and the development of implementation capabilities. Amburgey and Miner (1992) point to organizational routines and competencies, as well as managerial cognition to provide a theoretical basis for the existence of their three types of momentum. They further speculate that other sources of momentum may be found in political processes and the development of commitment. These postulated sources of momentum are very similar to those identified by authors in the emergent momentum stream. For example, Dutton and Duncan (1987) point to past success (high resources, managerial confidence), political coalitions, organizational routines and competencies, managerial values and confidence, and managerial cognition as important for gaining energy for a particular course of action. Thus, in spite of the differences in definitions and metaphors employed across the three types of momentum, the postulated sources of momentum from the past are very similar to one another.

So how might we conceive inherent momentum as agentic? Is the past not constraining and inexorable? Are we not locked into a particular set of choices and their trajectory? Drawing on the insights of Mead (1932) and Emirbayer and Mische (1998), we suggest the answer is no—rather, the past is as shapeable by managerial agency as the future and the present.

Our assertion is based on three principles. First, the temporal dimension of the present is the "seat of reality" (Mead, 1932: 32) from which the past and the future are reshaped as an emergent event is encountered. That is, "[a]s actors respond to changing environments, they must continually reconstruct their view of the past in an attempt to understand the causal conditioning of the emergent present, while using this understanding to control and shape their responses in the arising future" (Emirbayer and Mische, 1998: 968–9). In other words, the past remains as open and potential as the future; the past has happened, but the meaning of the past remains open to reconstruction in light of new, emergent events.

This is quite different than the abstract Newtonian view of time, which is, ironically, timeless (Adam, 1998; Tsoukas and Hatch, 2001; Purser et al., 2005). In this conception, time is a series of instants that march on without any context, and the present is nothing more than a fleeting instant between an infinitely extended past and future. Such a lack of explicit attention to the present has been detrimental on both a theoretical and practical level. Theoretically, it has contributed to the undertheorization and lack of empirical study of the present (Emirbayer and Mische, 1998). Yet it is here in the present that "changing" actually takes place. On a practical level, organizational change is frequently depicted as setting aside/leaving the past and moving to a future that is qualitatively different. In juxtaposing the past and future, however, the present becomes neglected, even negated; furthermore, the movement from the past to the future becomes nebulous. We have observed a manager, in describing the process of organizational change, masterfully depict this negation. In a presentation to other high level managers on how to accomplish change in the organization, this manager drew two cliffs, one labeled the past and the other labeled the future, separated by a wide, bottomless chasm. While not labeled as such, it became obvious that the chasm represented the present in the continuum of time. Other managers were dismayed at this groundless present, and nervously joked about crashing into the chasm if the change initiative was not achieved. Mead's theorizing (1932) of the present reconceptualizes the present as the vast, expansive ground on which we encounter the new and come to ascribe new meaning to the old while also prevising a different future.

Second, re-ascribing meaning to the past reconfigures our relationship to things in the past and, for that matter, the future. What was once taken-for-granted, now becomes neglected; what was once considered a strength in the organization and thus defended vociferously becomes a weakness and is discarded. As Emirbayer and Mische (1998: 963–4) note:

> the structural contexts of action are themselves temporal as well as relational fields—multiple, overlapping *ways of ordering time* toward which social actors can assume different simultaneous agentic orientations.... As actors move within and among these different unfolding contexts, they switch between

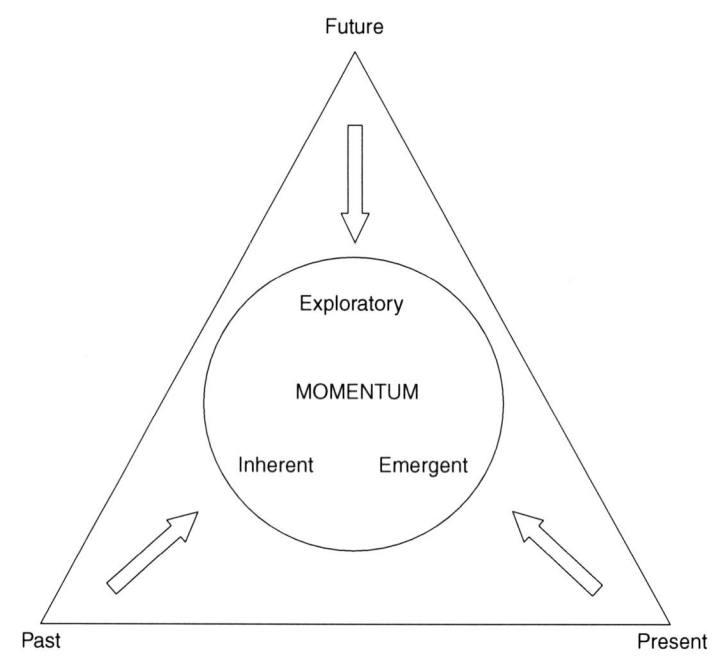

Figure 10.1 Momentum in the flow of time

(or 'recompose') their temporal orientations—as constructed within and by means of those contexts—and thus are capable of changing their relationship to structure. (Original emphasis)

Thus, not only the meaning of the past is open to change, but our relationship to things in the past is also open to change. As meaning of and relationship to the past changes, agency may be exercised where once the only option exercised was unreflective, largely unconscious repetition of past patterns.

Third, even as emergent momentum obviously retains links to all three temporal dimensions, so too inherent momentum implicates all three dimensions (see Figure 10.1). Being in the flow of time, the three dimensions are always present and act as a "chordal triad" (Emirbayer and Mische, 1998: 972), though in any given situation an actor may be more attuned to one over the others. "It is possible to speak of action that is more (or less) engaged with the past, more (or less) directed toward the future, and more (or less) responsive to the present" (Emirbayer and Mische, 1998: 972). Recognizing that momentum is not a unitary concept, but rather is shaped by all three dimensions of time even if predominantly focused on one, increases our understanding of momentum more generally as well as how inherent momentum more specifically can be conceptualized other than deterministic. For inherent momentum, though the past is dominant, the present and the future remain linked and provide for a broader scope of activity than the literature intimated as available.

At this point, a caveat is in order. Managers' conception of time shapes the degree of repetition an orientation to the past may be in practice. For those managers who conceive of time as essentially cyclical, there is less to support the idea of changing one's situation and create a different future. On the other hand, if managers conceive of time as linear, they will likely be more goal-directed and have a sense of efficacy in changing what is necessary in the pursuit of a future goal/vision. Interestingly, Zimbardo and Boyd (2008) have shown how more or less future oriented temporal orientations are linked to geography (those near the equator tend to think of time as cyclical and largely unchanging) and to religious orientation (those in Protestant countries tend to be more future oriented) (see also Weber, 1958).

10.4 Interaction of the temporal dimensions in inherent, exploratory, and emergent momentum

How might the past, present, and future within any particular temporal focus interact? Our consideration of the operation of the "minor chords" (Emirbayer and Mische, 1998) within a particular temporal focus begins with emergent momentum, which is the most well described in the OS literature in this respect. Note that this description of sensemaking in the present is somewhat representative of the deliberations undertaken within inherent and exploratory momentum, though in these cases there is a greater relative emphasis on the past and future respectively. Also, there is obvious overlap when considering, for example, the future within any particular temporal focus. What differentiates the attention on the future within each temporal focus is the relative emphasis on a particular temporal dimension. Thus, while similar, there are important differences that arise given the particular temporal focus (Table 10.2).

10.4.1 Emergent momentum and the flow of time

In emergent momentum, the past is conditioning but only to some extent. Emirbayer and Mische (1998: 998) suggest that when the present is the

Constructing Identity in and around Organizations

Table 10.2 The temporal interactions of agentic momentum

	Inherent	Exploratory	Emergent
Essential element for momentum	Focus on past	Focus on future	Focus on present
Locus of agency	Schematization	Hypothesization	Contextualization
Past	*Conditioning*: Tacit taken-for-granted corporeal, affective, and cognitive patterns	*Identifying*: Draw on what is known from the past in order to understand the future and achieve future aspirations	*Characterizing*: Things in the past are revised in various ways in relation to the present situation
Present	*Maneuvering*: Applying routines to daily contingencies in a way appropriate to those contingencies	*Experimenting*: The course of action presumed to achieve a future goal is enacted tentatively The use of deadlines and other temporal milestones removes some of the indeterminacy of the action taken	*Judging*: The influence of the revised past and the anticipation of the future come together with the interactions of people and objects Leads to judgments that may challenge the current situation in any number of ways
Future	*Expecting*: Predictability and stability on the basis of the past, and maintenance of expectation when facing disruption	*Projecting*: Imagining possible future outcomes	*Deliberating*: Considering how future goals and aspirations, possibilities and even wishes/dreams may/ should shape the present situation

Adapted from Emirbayer and Mische (1998).

focus, actors seek to characterize the past. This is akin to Mead's assertion (1932) that the past is revised when an emergent event takes place. How actors characterize the past depends on the problematic situation facing the actor. It may mean that something in the past must continue as it has continued; on the other hand, it may mean the modification of some aspect of the past or its cessation entirely. Dutton and Duncan's theoretical work (1987) provides some understanding of how this might occur. For example, the past conditions what managers perceive to be important strategic issues for the organization. Past successes, especially if they have been reinforced by subsequent success over time, exert significant pressure on managers to continue following the same path in spite of signals to the contrary from the environment. As managers engage in assessing the feasibility and urgency of a strategic issue, they seek to understand the issue by clothing it in familiar garb—that is, comparing the issue to past issues dealt with previously. Furthermore, the belief structures and the culture of the organization, established over time, shape how managers think about new issues that they are facing, conditioning them to see and to deal with them in particular ways. The past, then, produces conditioning over what is done in the present, but it does not determine what is done in the present.

The future can also provide managers with impetus to act on issues in certain ways. Emirbayer and Mische (1998: 999) suggest that within a present focus, actors respond to present contingencies by deliberating them in light of future goals or projects, seeking to determine how to best deal with those contingencies. Dutton and Duncan (1987) broaden this further by theorizing that future-looking scenario analyses can provide managers with a sense of what an issue may entail for the organization, giving them confidence that an issue can be dealt with (a hypothesized "future perfect"; Gioia et al., 2002). Deadlines associated with an issue can also shape a manager's perception: an immanent deadline increases the sense of urgency associated with an issue providing impetus for a manager to act quickly. Finally, the anticipated duration of the issue can again increase the sense of urgency of a strategic issue. If a particular event in the environment is expected to remain for a considerable time, managers will feel compelled to act. Ultimately, the future goal of a change initiative shapes activities in the present as managers align priorities and activities that are seen to support the accomplishment of that particular end state (i.e., means-end deliberation).

The present then is somewhat conditioned by the past, and partially shaped by deliberating the future, which is both "knowable" via invention through scenario analysis and goals, and unknowable in terms of emergent events and indeterminate durations (see also Purser and Petranker, 2005, for a view of the future as unconditioned). Ultimately, the present is where contextualization of past and future is undertaken and judgment is made concerning appropriate actions to take. Emergent issues appear and must be contended with, utilizing the past for sensemaking and the future for possibilities as far as one is able to determine. This process is highly contextual, multilevel, and dependent on the meanings given to emergent events, established structures and processes, and future goals and plans through an interpretive process involving cognition, emotion, negotiation, legitimation (Dutton and Duncan, 1987), timing (Dutton et al., 2001; Jansen, 2004), and embodied practices (Emirbayer and Mische, 1998). In this way, the determination of the issues and appropriate actions is accomplished, at least tentatively.

In the context of emergent momentum, it is important to highlight the significance and power of language. Suddaby and Greenwood (2005) observed that rhetoric is associated with "the deliberate manipulation of institutional logics" (p. 61), which, when changed, lead to institutional change, including the creation of new institutions. Rhetoric operates under the assumption of "a direct and dynamic relationship between rhetorical structures of speech or argument and the cognition and action of actors" (p. 40). Even more profoundly, they observed that "the fundamental elements of institutional agency, conflict, and power are embedded in the rhetoric used to create, maintain, and alter the meaning systems that underpin institutions" (p. 61). Emirbayer and Mische (1998: 994) also point to the critical nature of communication in what we call emergent momentum:

> This communicative process is what distinguishes the 'strong' situational moment of deliberative decision making from the 'weak' situatedness of, ... in the iterational dimension [what we refer to as inherent], tacit maneuver.

Shotter and Tsoukas (2011) concur: "for practitioners, the role of language can hardly be overestimated: after all, rational authority is primarily exercised through the word." The vital importance of communication and language, however, is in the realization that the "verbal discourse is indissolubly associated with the extraverbal situation within which it emerges" (Shotter and Tsoukas, 2011). As Shotter and Tsoukas point out, drawing on Bakhtin, this brings the fullness of the context into the dialogue, and thus the patterns of the past and the imaginings of the future in the context of the present are always open-ended and are always able to be further specified. The central action of judging in present-focused emergent momentum, then, is always tentative.

Wiebe (2010) noted this present focused orientation in two of five worlds of organizational change discerned in his study of temporal sensemaking by managers involved in a significant organizational change. One of these, termed "A Rocky Road," is characterized by close and full engagement with the exigencies and contingencies encountered day-to-day. The metaphors used to express this world of change—the dance, walking through mud, and paddling a boat upstream—all depict and emphasize continual involvement and judgment with the vagaries of context in order to continue to make progress in implementing change. When roadblocks, of which there were many, manifested themselves, they were dealt with in various ways. For example, government inaction, which could have been highly detrimental to the change, was redefined by managers as an opportunity to shape the government agenda (characterization). When the core group responsible for implementing change became dysfunctional, those leading the group discerned that this was important to deal with and took considerable time to sort out the numerous frustrations that had arisen and to restructure the group. Doing so was deemed critical in continuing the change process (deliberating). Rather than being stifled by problems, managers took the momentum for change upon themselves and continued to move ahead propelled by a pragmatic as well as moral imperative (judging). In this way, barriers to change were quashed, redefined, or transformed such that they did not stop the progress of change even though at times that progress was severely impeded.

10.4.2 Inherent momentum and the flow of time

Past-oriented inherent momentum draws on what Emirbayer and Mische (1998) identify as schematization. This refers to the tacit and taken-for-granted scripts that have been established and now are used by managers to get things done day-to-day. Schematization also refers to the patterns that have been developed and reinforced through use over time, including those that are corporeal and affective, as well as cognitive (Emirbayer and Mische, 1998: 975). The past is both embodied in structures (e.g., buildings, SOPs, mission statements, organizational myths) and enacted day-to-day. Enacted patterns are not truly in the past, but rather now exist in the present. In the present, enacted patterns are modified as emergent events are encountered. For example, Feldman and Pentland (2003) demonstrate that routines can be sources of change rather than simply forces for stability as day-to-day contingencies are encountered. The embodied past, while more inscribed, is also open to change via our temporal relations to those objects. Thus, a mission statement embodying a particular set of values may be reinterpreted from the perspective of new challenges and shifting organizational norms. The past is also enacted with a sense of the future—that expectation regarding what will be achieved. Known results of past actions suggest very similar outcomes again. When that predictability is not achieved, maintenance work is required (Emirbayer and Mische, 1998: 981). This may introduce new actions and new relations, thereby modifying the past. If even then the desired outcomes are not achieved, further search and modification will be required (Butler, 1995), introducing more significant change (Plowman et al., 2007).

To illustrate inherent momentum, we return to Kimberly and Bouchikhi's question (1995) of "how the past shapes the present and constrains the future." In their study of a computer and software retailer, Kimberly and Bouchikhi (1995) noted how key events in the founder's past were drawn on in shaping the computer company she eventually founded. These values represented several formative "lessons learned" in the course of gaining work experience over several years. One key organizational value was lack of bureaucracy: no formal job descriptions, no organization chart, no formal titles, and no formal budgets. While the company was relatively young and small, this value came to be taken-for-granted; it became a part of the way things were done (conditioning). However, as the company grew and as institutional pressures from banks and suppliers for signs of reliability increased, the pressure on the company to formalize increased. Internally, the founder held onto this value by maintaining personal contact with employees and creating a "family" relationship between and among her employees. Control was not achieved through bureaucracy but through relationships (maneuvering and expecting). Externally, the founder presented external stakeholders with the sort of information requested (e.g., organization charts), but would not distribute or utilize it internally (expecting). Further pressure for formalization came with dramatic growth (from eleven to ninety-two employees) and the creation of new divisions geographically dispersed. Maintenance of the old values became increasingly difficult. The founder attempted to maintain personal contact with all employees but invariably she became more distant (attempt at expecting). Also, new hires' experience was now quite different than it had been in the early days. Together, these pressures began to shift the culture away from being a family. The creation of new subsidiaries and their geographic dispersion exacerbated the problem. Interestingly, it was the loosening of a key value (not to grow beyond ten employees) in light of burgeoning success (exploratory momentum) that led to the increasing difficulty in maintaining the lack of formalization. The case concludes without revealing how the company subsequently dealt with the issue of formalizing.

10.4.3 Exploratory momentum and the flow of time

Exploratory momentum focuses on a future that is more or less hypothetical. Various ends, ranging from the whimsical to the purposefully set and sought, may be envisioned, but even where future goals and the means of achieving them are set, situations arise that may make both highly indeterminate (i.e., the emergent present (Mead, 1932), or the unconditioned dynamic future (Purser and Petranker, 2005)). As possible futures are envisaged, the past is drawn on to better understand how the envisaged future may be realized. This is always tentative as the past is never repeated without variation (Adam, 1990), and thus may not lead to expected outcomes, nor may a particular aspect of the past prove to be conducive in achieving a desired end.

> Such anticipatory identifications are never accomplished once and for all, but rather are subject to continual reevaluation in light of the shifting and multidimensional character of human motivation and social relationships. (Emirbayer and Mische, 1998: 989)

Having established a desired future and identified what seem appropriate ways of reaching that desired future, those ways are now enacted in the present in a tentative, experimental way with the anticipation of achieving the desired end.

Gersick's study (1994: 23) illustrates future-focused exploratory momentum well. The venture capital start-up in Gersick's study sought to achieve liquidity. That end was the firm goal decided upon by the company and its venture capital backers. How to get to that end, however, changed as different approaches were used. Overall, the strategy initially was to sell the company to an acquirer in the first of three markets the company would eventually have products in. After one year, the CEO concluded that no one in their initial market would purchase the company. This led to a different strategy, that being to focus on an acquirer in the second market. Only two weeks of effort in this case persuaded the CEO that this was not the right course of action. He again changed his strategy, now seeking to secure the company as an entity in their first market, at which time they would seek to go public by finding another company in their market that they could purchase. As this strategy concluded, the board of the venture capital start-up decided to strengthen their position even further by acquiring yet another company in their first market and undertaking a private stock offering in order to finance growth in the short term.

Evident in this excerpt is the imagining of a possible future (liquidity), and a series of possible ways of attaining that outcome identified from past experience in bringing venture backed organizations to liquidity (this appears to have been done serially). These were then put into action in an experimental way. After a year of effort, the first was deemed to not be the right way to move forward. Another method was undertaken, only to be abandoned quickly (two weeks). Finally, the CEO settled on a third method that proved partially successful. At its conclusion, however, the board decided it was not enough (respecifying the future goal) and undertook additional actions (drawing on the past) to strengthen what had been achieved (experimentally enacted). In this way, exploratory momentum was enacted and moved the organization forward toward the intended goal. Gersick also noted the use of temporal milestones (clock-time based pacing) to provide regular intervals for evaluating progress in attaining the company's goals. These temporal milestones created focused effort leading up to the milestone and permission to shift activities at the milestone if the action taken to that point proved inadequate in achieving the end goal. The use of time to regularly assess an experiment allows for some control of the indeterminacy of the actions taken.

10.5 Conclusion

In this chapter, we have sought to clarify the concept of momentum. To do so, we have drawn on time, which has allowed us to reconceptualize momentum as agentic. In doing so, we hope to provide room for its usefulness in analyzing and theorizing organizational change. In particular, we note that with our typology of momentum, organizational change no longer has the character of episodic alterations of momentum and change. Rather, incremental and radical change can exist side by side, as some organizational aspects are maintained (inherent momentum) and others jettisoned (exploratory momentum). Moreover, temporal continuity is preserved in each type of momentum, providing the foundation for change to be characterized as continuous.

We also suggest that our typology of momentum may be useful to those who recognize that history matters for organization (e.g., Stinchcombe, 1965). How history matters has lead to studies developing concepts such as path dependence (e.g., Garud and Karnøe, 2001; Sydow et al., 2009), imprinting (e.g., Stinchcombe, 1965; Boeker, 1989; Marquis, 2003), sunk costs, both economic and cognitive (e.g., Oliver, 1997), structural inertia (e.g., Hannan and Freeman, 1984), and institutionalization (e.g., Berger and Luckmann, 1967; Powell and DiMaggio, 1991). Momentum is pertinent to this conversation but has been largely missing, except implicitly as captured in the notion of inertia. Momentum conceptualized as inertia would suggest a highly deterministic view of the past where the present and future are not much more than the outworking of the past (Emirbayer and Mische, 1998). However, momentum conceptualized as agentic, even and especially what we have identified as inherent momentum, suggests that the past is actively replicated and appropriately applied among present contingencies and in light of future aspirations. This view of the past is neither constraining nor restricting. It does not lock us into a path or imprint on us social forms that are unbending and unchanging. Rather, in our typology history becomes a resource that can be used in replication, creating stability, consistency, identity, confidence, and trust (Emirbayer and Mische, 1998). It is a resource that can be drawn upon in creative ways to deal with daily contingencies (Feldman and Pentland, 2003). It is a resource that can be selectively utilized to reframe the logic of the organization in light of emerging events, setting the organization on a new course (O'Connor, 2000) or creating a new organizational form (Suddaby and Greenwood, 2005). It is a resource that can be reframed and denigrated to build greater contrast with a desired future (Ybema, 2004).

Finally, we are cognizant that in creating a typology of momentum we are glossing over exceptions and nuances as well as drawing sharper lines than might be warranted between the three types. Certainly, no typology is able to portray fully all empirical instances that it purports to describe (Huy, 2001). Nevertheless, we believe there is value in the typology and its delineation. It has allowed us to clarify and characterize a confusing literature, and thereby to make momentum more accessible and applicable for organizational change researchers. Foremost, however, the typology can provide another vantage point from which we are better able to analyze and theorize the accomplishment of organizational change.

Notes

1. We gratefully acknowledge the research funding provided by the Canadian Health Services Research Foundation and the Alberta Heritage Foundation for Medical Research through the Health Organization Studies research team at the University of Alberta School of Business. We also thank Karen Golden-Biddle, Trish Reay, C. R. Hinings, Judith Golec, and Connie Gersick for their encouragement and insightful comments on earlier versions of the chapter. We also thank the members of the International Network for Time in Management and Organization (INTIMO) for their support. An earlier version of this chapter won the doctoral student scholarship for the Second Improvisational Conference (July 2004) hosted by INTIMO at INSEAD. Finally, we are grateful to Haridimos Tsoukas and an anonymous reviewer whose insights and direction have greatly improved this chapter.
2. Note that this does not happen all at once. See Gersick (1991) for an explanation of the interstitial period.

References

Adam, B. (1990). *Time and Social Theory.* Cambridge: Polity Press.

—— (1998). *Timescapes of Modernity: The Environment and Invisible Hazards.* London: Routledge.

Adler, P. (1981). *Momentum: A Theory of Social Action.* Beverly Hills, CA: Sage Publishing.

Amburgey, T. L. and Miner, A. S. (1992). "Strategic Momentum: The Effects of Repetitive, Positional and Contextual Momentum on Merger Activity." *Strategic Management Journal*, 13/5: 335–48.

—— Kelly, D., and Barnett, W. P. (1993). "Resetting the Clock: The Dynamics of Organizational Change and Failure." *Administrative Science Quarterly*, 38/1: 51–73.

Baden-Fuller, C. and Stopford, J. M. (1994). "Maintaining Momentum," *Rejuvenating the Mature Business: The Competitive Challenge.* Cambridge, MA: The President and Fellows of Harvard College, pp. 231–61.

Bartunek, J. M. (1984). "Changing Interpretive Schemes and Organizational Restructuring: The Example of a Religious Order." *Administrative Science Quarterly*, 29/3: 355–72.

Beck, N., Brüderl, J., and Woywode, M. (2008). "Momentum or Deceleration? Theoretical and Methodological Reflections on the Analysis of Organizational Change." *Academy of Management Journal*, 51/3: 413–35.

Berger, P. L. and Luckmann, T. (1967). *The Social Construction of Reality: A Treatise in the Sociology of Knowledge.* Garden City, NY: Doubleday.

Boeker, W. (1989). "Strategic Change: The Effects of Founding and History." *The Academy of Management Journal*, 32/3: 489–515.

Burrell, G. (1992). "Back to the Future: Time and Organization," in M. Reed and M. Hughs (eds), *Rethinking Organizations.* London: Sage, pp. 165–83.

Butler, R. (1995). "Time in Organizations: Its Experience, Explanations, and Effects." *Organization Studies*, 16/6: 925–50.

Collins, J. (2001). *Good to Great.* New York: HarperCollins Publishers Inc.

Dutton, J. E. and Duncan, R. B. (1987). "The Creation of Momentum for Change Through the Process of Strategic Issue Diagnosis." *Strategic Management Journal*, 8/3: 279–95.

—— Ashford, S. J., O'Neill, R. M., and Lawrence, K. A. (2001). "Moves That Matter: Issue Selling and Organizational Change." *Academy of Management Journal*, 44/4: 716–36.

Emirbayer, M. and Mische, A. (1998). "What is Agency?" *American Journal of Sociology*, 103/4: 962–1023.

Feldman, M. S. and Pentland, B. T. (2003). "Reconceptualizing Organizational Routines as a Source of Flexibility and Change." *Administrative Science Quarterly*, 48: 94–118.

Garud, R. and Karnøe, P. (2001). *Path Dependence and Creation.* Mahwah, NJ: Lawrence Erlbaum Associates.

Gersick, C. J. G. (1991). "Revolutionary Change Theories: A Multilevel Exploration of the Punctuated Equilibrium Paradigm." *Academy of Management Review*, 16/1: 10–36.

—— (1994). "Pacing Strategic Change: The Case of a New Venture." *Academy of Management Journal*, 37/1: 9–45.

Ginsberg, A. and Venkatraman, N. (1992). "Investing in New Information Technology: The Role of Competitive Posture and Issue Diagnosis." *Strategic Management Journal*, 13/special issue: 37–53.

—— —— (1995). "Institutional Initiatives for Technological Change: From Issue Interpretation to Strategic Choice." *Organization Studies*, 16/3: 425–48.

Gioia, D. A., Corley, K. G., and Fabbri, T. (2002). "Revising the Past (While Thinking in the Future Perfect Tense)." *Journal of Organizational Change Management*, 15/6: 622–34.

Goodman, M. B. (1995). "Organizational Inertia or Corporate Culture Momentum," in D. P. Cushman and S. S. King (eds), *Communicating Organizational Change: A Management Perspective*. New York: SUNY Press, pp. 95–112.

Greenwood, R. and Hinings, C. R. (1993). "Understanding Strategic Change: The Contribution of Archetypes." *Academy of Management Journal*, 36/5: 1052–81.

Hannan, M. T. and Freeman, J. (1984). "Structural Inertia and Organizational Change." *American Sociological Review*, 49/2: 149–64.

Huy, Q. N. (2001). "Time, Temporal Capability, and Planned Change." *Academy of Management Review*, 26/4: 601–23.

Jansen, K. J. (2004). "From Persistence to Pursuit: A Longitudinal Examination of Momentum During the Early Stages of Strategic Change." *Organization Science*, 15/3: 276–94.

Kelly, D. and Amburgey, T. L. (1991). "Organizational Inertia and Momentum: A Dynamic Model of Strategic Change." *Academy of Management Journal*, 34/3: 591–612.

Kimberly, J. R. and Bouchikhi, H. (1995). "The Dynamics of Organizational Development and Change: How the Past Shapes the Present and Constrains the Future." *Organization Science*, 6/1: 9–18.

Marquis, C. (2003). "The Pressure of the Past: Network Imprinting in Intercorporate Communities." *Administrative Science Quarterly*, 48/4: 655–89.

Mead, G. H. (1932). *The Philosophy of the Present*. Chicago, IL: Open Court Publishing Co.

Miller, D. and Friesen, P. H. (1980). "Momentum and Revolution in Organizational Adaptation." *Academy of Management Journal*, 23/4: 591–614.

—— —— (1982). "Innovation in Conservative and Entrepreneurial Firms: Two Models of Strategic Momentum." *Strategic Management Journal*, 3/1: 1–25.

O'Connor, E. S. (2000). "Plotting the Organization: The Embedded Narrative as a Constraint for Studying Change." *The Journal of Applied Behavioral Science*, 36: 174–92.

Oliver, C. (1997). "Sustainable Competitive Advantage: Combining Institutional and Resource-Based Views." *Strategic Management Journal*, 18: 697–714.

Plowman, D. A., Baker, L. T., Beck, T. E., Kulkarni, M., Solansky, S. T., and Travis, D. V. (2007). "Radical Change Accidentally: The Emergence and Amplification of Small Change." *Academy of Management Journal*, 50/3: 515–43.

Powell, W. W. and DiMaggio, P. (1991). *The New Institutionalism in Organizational Analysis*. Chicago, IL: University of Chicago Press.

Purser, R. E. and Petranker, J. (2005). "Unfreezing the Future: Exploring the Dynamic of Time in Organizational Change." *Journal of Applied Behavioral Science*, 41/2: 182–203.

—— Bluedorn, A. C., and Petranker, J. (2005). "The Times of Cause and Flow in Organizational Change." *Research in Organizational Change and Development*, 15: 1–29.

Sherover, C. M. (2003). *Are We in Time? And Other Essays on Time and Temporality*. Evanston, IL: Northwestern University Press.

Shotter, J. and Tsoukas, H. (2011). "Complex Thought, Simple Talk: An Ecological Approach to Language-Based Change in Organizations," in P. Allen, S. Mcquire, and B. McKelvey (eds), *The Sage Handbook of Complexity and Management*. Thousand Oaks, CA: Sage Publishing,

Stinchcombe, A. L. (1965). "Social Structure and Organizations," in J. G. March (ed.), *Handbook of Organizations*. Chicago, IL: Rand McNally, pp. 142–93.

Suddaby, R. and Greenwood, R. (2005). "Rhetorical Strategies of Legitimacy." *Administrative Science Quarterly*, 50/1: 35–67.

Sydow, J. R., Schreyögg, G., and Koch, J. (2009). "Organizational Path Dependence: Opening the Black Box." *Academy of Management Review*, 34/4: 689–709.

Tsoukas, H. and Chia, R. (2002). "On Organizational Becoming: Rethinking Organizational Change." *Organization Science*, 13/5: 567–82.

—— Hatch, M. J. (2001). "Complex Thinking, Complex Practice: The Case for a Narrative Approach to Organizational Complexity." *Human Relations*, 54/8: 979–1013.

Tushman, M. L. and Romanelli, E. (1985). "Organizational Evolution: A Metamorphosis Model of Convergence and Reorientation," in L. L. Cummings and B. M. Staw (eds), *Research in Organizational Behavior*. Greenwich, CT: JAI Press, pp. 171–222.

Weber, M. (1958). *The Protestant Ethic and the Spirit of Capitalism*. Trans. T. Parsons. New York: Scribner's.

Wiebe, E. (2010). "Temporal Sensemaking: Managers' Use of Time to Frame Organizational Change," in T. Hernes and S. Maitlis (eds), *Process, Sensemaking, and Organizing*. Oxford: Oxford University Press, pp. 213–41.

Ybema, S. (2004). "Managerial Postalgia: Projecting a Golden Future." *Journal of Managerial Psychology*, 19/8: 825–41.

Zimbardo, P. and Boyd, J. (2008). *The Time Paradox*. New York: Free Press.

11
Management Knowledge: A Process View[1]

Simon Grand and Adrian Ackeret

Abstract: This chapter provides a theoretical conceptualization and a detailed empirical study of management knowledge from a process perspective. It describes the development of management knowledge after an unprecedented event—the unexpected leave of the founder-owner-CEO of an entrepreneurial software engineering company. In particular, the chapter studies how management knowledge is enacted by the new executive management, the board of directors, and other senior managers within multiple situations, interactions, and engagements; how it is justified and routinized in the face of uncertainty; and how it is shifting and changing over time, through multiple situated enactments. Drawing from convention theory, management knowledge is conceptualized as "engagement regimes"—a conceptualization that permits a description of the processual dynamic of management knowledge *and* managerial knowing in a single, coherent, theoretical framework.

11.1 Introduction

Managing implies forward-looking activities: building competencies for the future advancement of the organization (Teece et al., 1997); allocating strategic resources to projects and opportunities for building future businesses (Burgelman, 2002; Bower and Gilbert, 2005); taking decisions on the future strategic directions in dynamic contexts (Hamel and Prahalad, 1989); and integrating distributed activities (Tsoukas, 1996). Managing therefore implies enacting uncertainty with respect to these forward-looking initiatives (Spender, 1989, 1996), so firm-specific reference systems (Gomez and Jones, 2000), routines (Nelson and Winter, 1982; Feldman and Pentland, 2003), and knowledge (Grant, 1996; Tsoukas, 2005) are important. As a result, a central managerial issue is the justification of these reference systems and of knowledge as "justified true beliefs" (Nonaka, 1994; Spender, 1998).

Managing takes place in the form of multiple situated activities (Mintzberg, 1971; Watson, 1986, 1994, 2001) that are characterized by their "... pace, brevity, variety, fragmentation, interruption, orientation to action ..." (Mintzberg, 2009: 40). They require managerial knowhow, which can be understood as managers' "competence to act" (Tsoukas, 2005), emphasizing its situated, contextual, and routinized qualities. Recently, a processual conceptualization of knowledge as "knowing" (Orlikowski, 2002) has been advanced, leading to organizational knowledge being studied in its situated creation (Nonaka, 1994), as well as in the collectivization, generalization, and routinization of local experiences, transient insights, and situated knowing (Tsoukas, 2005).

Taking these views together, one confronts a key conceptual nexus of management and knowledge: management is enacting organizational knowledge in specific situations, initiatives, and events, while, at the same time, contributing to its creation, justification, and routinization (Spender, 1996; Rüegg-Stürm and Grand, 2007). In this chapter, we empirically explore how *management knowledge* is enacted within managerial practices and processes. In particular, we describe how management knowledge is justified and routinized in the face of uncertainty due to an unprecedented event. We study shifting management knowledge at an adolescent Swiss software engineering company, which we call AdNovum Informatik AG (short form: AdNovum). This case stands out because the founder-owner-CEO unexpectedly left and sold the company within a few months in 2006, and a new owner, a new management team, and a partially new board of directors had to establish their own interpretation of what management means, how management is done, and on what basis management is legitimized. We followed this process over three years, on multiple management levels, exploring how particular concepts, interpretations, activities, and images of management were enacted; and how management knowledge was thus created, justified, and routinized in managerial practices and processes in the face of uncertainty.

Our chapter makes contributions to management research in several ways. First, we know of no other empirical study dedicated to management knowledge as a particular type of knowledge, as well as its justification and routinization. Second, a conceptualization of knowledge and knowing (Cook and Brown, 1999; Tsoukas and Vladimirou, 2001) combined within a single theoretical perspective has been missing—a gap this study fills. Third, management is typically discussed in relation to implicit concepts, expectations, experiences, and practices of management (Tsoukas, 2005), and process studies such as this one, explicitly describing the interplay between managerial activities (Mintzberg, 2009), management practices (Mintzberg, 2004), and concepts of management (Tsoukas, 2005), are rare. Fourth, we contribute to empirical analyses of management succession using a process perspective (cf. Denis et al., 2000), with a particular focus on management knowledge.

11.2 Theoretical background: Management knowledge

11.2.1 Knowledge research and management knowledge

Management knowledge is at the same time an important source of orientation and a potential site of controversy in the face of uncertainty. As a consequence, it must be justified and routinized in situated managerial activities. Knowledge research has identified several qualities of organizational knowledge in the face of uncertainty: it is contextual, gaining meaning only in relation to specific situations (Spender, 1996; Tsoukas, 2005); and it is collectivized and routinized through processes of translation, turning local experiences and situated insights into justified true beliefs (Nonaka, 1994), which are—at least momentarily—accepted (Elkana, 1986) and taken-for-granted (Gomez and Jones, 2000). Taken-for-granted organizational knowledge, however, remains fragile and preliminary (Latour, 1999) because it can always be questioned. At the same time, organizational knowledge is related to situated and dispersed activities, as a potential to act, to be actualized, and interpreted in situated knowing (Orlikowski, 2002). Knowledge is therefore necessary *and* potentially problematic in the face of uncertainty (Spender, 1998; Gomez and Jones, 2000). Further, management research, as knowledge creation concerning managerial phenomena, becomes inherently reflexive when researching management knowledge (Tsoukas, 2005).

For our study of management knowledge, research on organizational knowledge, in relation to organizational knowing, is central (Cook and Brown, 1999; Tsoukas and Vladimirou, 2001). We understand organizational knowledge as "... the capability members of an organization have developed to draw distinctions in the process of carrying out their work, in particular concrete contexts, by enacting sets of generalizations whose application depends on historically evolved collective understandings and experiences" (Tsoukas and Vladimirou, 2001: 983). Therefore, management knowledge is narrower than organizational knowledge, delineated as a particular type of management-related organizational knowledge. However, at the same time, it is also broader, including management-related knowledge transcending organization-specific knowledge. Because of the "... open-endedness of the world, that gives rise to new experience and learning, and gives knowledge its not-as-yet-formed character ..." (Tsoukas and Vladimirou, 2001: 989), the situated, provisional qualities of knowledge-in-action, explored as organizational knowing in practice, become visible (Orlikowski, 2002).

Only recently, attempts have been made to integrate the concepts of knowledge and knowing into a single theoretical framework. Two perspectives are relevant: management as an established repertoire of concepts and tools, practices, and routines (Mintzberg, 2004; Birkinshaw et al., 2008); and managing as the situated management-in-action (Mintzberg, 2009). Studying management knowledge allows researchers to explore management and managing as interwoven empirically; and provides a context for advancing a conceptualization of knowledge and knowing from a single theoretical basis. We suggest convention theory (Boltanski and Thévenot, 1991; Thévenot, 2006) as a fruitful theoretical perspective in this context: convention theory traditionally describes how taken-for-granted knowledge is justified and legitimized as conventions in the face of uncertainty (Boltanski and Thévenot, 1991); more recently, it explores the importance of routinization processes for establishing taken-for-granted knowledge in the context of controversies (Gomez and Jones, 2000); and currently, it explores also how knowledge is enacted in situated engagements, while being generalized as conventions that hold beyond individual situations (Thévenot, 2006).

11.2.2 Convention theory and engagement regimes

Convention theory emphasizes the contingency of organizational knowledge, and thus management knowledge (Boltanski, 2009): whatever is justified as unquestioned knowledge, and routinized through situated practices, can potentially be questioned. As a consequence, it is important to focus on how specific controversies are enacted in situated managerial interactions (Thévenot, 2006); in addition, it is important to understand how knowledge as conventions is stabilized and changed through justification and routinization over time (Boltanski and Thévenot, 1991). More recently, convention theory has incorporated ideas from the so-called practice turn in social theory (Schatzki et al., 2001). As a result, besides studying the creation, establishment, and change of taken-for-granted, justified knowledge through controversies and debates over time, the enactment of knowledge in the face of an unprecedented event is coming into focus (Thévenot, 2001, 2006; Grand et al., 2010).

Convention theory describes, at the same time and on a single theoretical basis, how management knowledge is challenged and destabilized in controversies, and established and restabilized through justification. Its focus is on the creation and establishment of common knowledge, taken-for-granted perspectives, and unquestioned references in the face of uncertainty (Boltanski and Thévenot, 1991; Gomez, 1994, 1996). Convention theory therefore emphasizes a paradox (Ortmann, 2003, 2004): agency is impossible in the face of uncertainty without relying on unquestioned knowledge and references (Spender, 1989; Gomez and Jones, 2000; Thévenot, 2006); but these references cannot be taken-for-granted in the face of uncertainty—they must be seen as contingent and potentially and actually controversial (Boltanski, 2009). Processes of justification are therefore essential for stabilizing management knowledge under uncertainty (Boltanski and Thévenot, 1991). These processes are inherently fragile, because they work only as long as the management knowledge, to which they refer, can be taken-for-granted, and hence, as long as these references are seen "as if" they are unquestionable (Ortmann, 2004).

Recently, convention theory has built on insights from practice theory. In this vein, the situated enactment and routinization of knowledge (Tsoukas, 2005) comes into focus as much as its justification. Management knowledge holds not only because it is justified but also because it is mobilized and routinized in particular situations. Recent contributions to convention theory have suggested the concept of engagement regimes (Thévenot, 2001, 2006) to make sense of this simultaneity of justification and routinization. Over time, particular engagement regimes are routinized as firm-specific repertoires of action patterns, which are enacted by referring to particular ways of knowing, while being justified through relating to taken-for-granted references. In this perspective, management knowledge can be seen as consisting of specific engagement regimes. Convention theory therefore benefits from action theories, which emphasize the creative qualities of situated engagements (Joas, 1991; Tsoukas and Knudsen, 2002). Furthermore, convention theory draws on insights from science studies (Callon, 1986; Latour, 2005), in particular the notion that knowledge is becoming "bigger" and more general in some situations, and "smaller" and more specific in others (Boltanski and Thévenot, 1991). In this view, situated enactment (i.e., "knowing"), routinization of managerial practices (i.e., a process view on "knowing" and "knowledge"), and explicit justification (i.e., in view of "knowledge") are no longer distinguished, but seen as inherently interwoven.

11.2.3 Management knowledge as engagement regimes

Management knowledge can be conceptualized as engagement regimes (Thévenot, 2006). Engagement regimes are "... social 'devices,' which govern our way of engaging with the environment inasmuch as they articulate two notions: an orientation towards some kind of good; and a mode of access to reality ..." (Thévenot, 2001: 67). Management knowledge shapes managerial engagement with particular situations and unprecedented events, inasmuch as engagement regimes orient action toward a particular explicit or implicit preunderstanding of management (and its justification in case of controversies), as well as a related mode of enacting as management, including its routinization and de-routinization in particular situations and over time. Management knowledge, as engagement regimes, is therefore relevant only as long as it is actualized, mobilized, and modified in particular situations and managerial activities (Thévenot, 2001, 2006). Management knowledge is thus not seen as something given, tangible, and explicitly created by management but rather as an ephemeral, emerging, and shifting phenomenon, which can only be studied insofar it is enacted and shaped in specific situations.

If managerial knowledge is seen as stable and self-evident in a particular situation or in the face of a particular event, it enables efficient coordination and managerial action; if it is seen as rather fragile and controversial, it leads to a lack of orientation and alignment with respect to management-related activities. However, management knowledge can only be taken-for-granted inasmuch as it has been justified and routinized in multiple engagements. On the basis of these considerations, we ask the following research question: *How is management knowledge justified and routinized in managerial practices and processes in the face of uncertainty?* More specifically, we explore in our case how management knowledge is justified and routinized in the face of an unprecedented event and further managerial challenges over time.

11.3 Methods

11.3.1 Research approach: In-depth, longitudinal process study

To address our research question, we draw on an in-depth, longitudinal process study (Langley, 1999, 2007). Because it allows for examining how and why events, actions, practices, and processes unfold over time (Mintzberg, 1979), a process study is well suited for studying management knowledge as engagement regimes. Notions such as "following forward" processes as closely as possible, grasping emergent shifts of "destabilizing stability," and identifying how "outputs [are fed back] as inputs" into local patterns (Langley, 2007) require a degree of closeness to a particular organizational setting, which is only possible by focusing attention on a detailed empirical study. A process study allows us to explore in detail how and why management knowledge loses and regains its taken-for-granted self-evidence over time, in the face of uncertainty, and, in particular, in the face of an unprecedented event. We adopt a radical process view (Hernes, 2008)—taking into account the temporal extension and complex interaction of activities and events on various levels of analysis (Langley, 2007)—in order to focus on the contingent, controversial, and fragile qualities of knowledge in the face of uncertainty (Spender, 1989).

We conducted our in-depth, longitudinal single-case study (Eisenhardt, 1989; Yin, 1994) at AdNovum AG, an innovative and fast-growing Swiss software engineering company. We followed the company's development for almost three years from 2006 to 2009. AdNovum AG offered an ideal context to conduct an event study, which in convention theory is identified as the most appropriate approach to explore how the self-evidence of knowledge is maintained and challenged, destabilized and restabilized in particular situations (Gomez, 1994, 1996, 2003). In 2006, the founder-owner-CEO unexpectedly left the company, eighteen years after he founded it, and sold it at once. In consequence, a new management team and new management structures were put in place to oversee the company's further development. Thus, this research context allowed tracing an unprecedented event with respect to management knowledge, as an unusually high degree of change in management structure interacted with marked uncertainty regarding key assumptions about the nature and direction of the company that had previously been taken for granted.

The study presented in this chapter is part of an extensive, on-going research collaboration of almost ten years on AdNovum AG's evolution by the first author, spanning the firm's fast growth from a small

Constructing Identity in and around Organizations

entrepreneurial company to a leading provider of software solutions in Switzerland. Furthermore, it is embedded in a larger research program, studying a series of similar software companies in Switzerland and in Germany, which takes seriously reflexivity in scientific knowledge production on management knowledge (Tsoukas, 2005) by understanding the research collaboration as a reflexive process of coproduction of scientific and managerial knowledge (Grand, 2003). This is consistent with the self-referencing aspect of process research investigating knowledge and knowing, as we have discussed above (Spender, 1996; Tsoukas, 1996): while describing and understanding management knowledge as it is unfolding over time, we at the same time create scientific knowledge on management knowledge, and are thus ourselves involved in questioning taken-for-granted qualities of scientific knowledge in management research while creating new knowledge at the same time (Elkana, 1986; Tsoukas, 2005).

11.3.2 Research setting: AdNovum Informatik AG, 2006–9

AdNovum Informatik AG is a software engineering company based in Zurich, focusing on sophisticated tailor-made software solutions, especially in the context of distributed networks, often involving security and scalability themes. The company has traditionally been focusing on large software development projects for customers in the financial services industry, and, in recent years, for government and customers in other industries. The company has gone through several attempts to translate its expertise, knowledge, and technology into software products, to even better leverage the current business model. It has also developed a highly skilled workforce—the majority of employees are university graduates in software engineering and related disciplines. Substantive investment went into developing internal processes, especially the software engineering process. As of mid-2009, AdNovum AG employed around 170 people, of which 50 were in Eastern Europe (i.e., near shoring); was just over 20 years old; and had gone through a ten-year period of rapid growth (from 35 to over 150 employees in about five years).

During the time of our study, from end-2006 to mid-2009, AdNovum AG went through a period of particularly high uncertainty, as it experienced a complete makeover of its governance structure and ownership constellation. At the end of 2006, the CEO, who was a founder of the company, its sole owner, and the chairman of its board of directors, decided to leave the company at age 45, unexpectedly for most internal and external parties. He sold the company to a holding company owned by a respected Swiss industrialist family whose chairman—representing the family's third

Management Knowledge: A Process View

generation in business—was a personal friend of his. Subsequently, the chairman of the holding company became the nonexecutive chairman of the board of directors of AdNovum AG. The board was enlarged by three outside directors with industry experience, with the aim of transforming it from a "club of sparring partners" of the founder-owner-CEO into an autonomous supervisory body. In parallel, the management team was fundamentally rebuilt.

At first, the new ownership—on recommendation by the former founder-owner-CEO—decided to search for an experienced external CEO. In the meantime, an interim executive board was formed consisting of four former senior managers at AdNovum AG, who had already borne a large part of operational responsibility for project management, software development, technology management, and for the company's subsidiary in Eastern Europe. In order to smooth the transition, one of the new outside members of the board of directors worked full-time at the company for a few months, coaching and supervising the new executive management. After extensive discussions with a potential new CEO failed at an advanced stage, the board of directors opted for an internal succession, and the former head of the Eastern Europe subsidiary became CEO in mid-2007. At the same time, two additional senior managers with long-time experience were appointed as members of the executive board by the new CEO. For the first time in the history of AdNovum AG, a formal executive board was formed—this at a company that prided itself as having a nonhierarchical, informal, unconventional, unique entrepreneurial culture.

11.3.3 Data collection: Multiple data sources

We relied on four types of data: interviews and observations, as well as documents and archival data from previous research phases at AdNovum AG. Semi-structured and open interviews provided the majority of data collected and were conducted on three levels: with each member of the board of directors (five to six members, changing over time), with each member of the executive board (four to six members, changing over time), and with senior managers and senior software engineers outside the executive board. Interviews lasted between 1 and 3 hours each, and each interviewee was interviewed typically two to three times in the time window of the study. Each interview was recorded and fully transcribed. The interviews took place in mid-2007, in early 2008, and in late 2008 / early 2009. This data was supplemented by data from interviews in mid- to end-2006, to cover the period before the change in governance and ownership.

The study is also based on personal observations, in particular at board meetings and strategy workshops as well as in personal encounters, informal meetings, and interactions with employees at AdNovum AG's main office. Preliminary findings were presented to the executive board and the supervisory board twice, in 2008 and again in 2009. Individual encounters with several members of the executive board and with the owner added personal interpretations and evaluations to the data. Complementing interviews and observations, selective documents such as company presentations, project proposals, as well as Intranet and Internet page histories were analyzed. In order to gain additional historical context of the developments at AdNovum AG during the time of study, data from previous research phases at the company was drawn upon on a selective basis.

11.3.4 Data analysis: Triangulation and coproduction of knowledge

We followed an inductive theory-building approach (Eisenhardt, 1989; Miles and Huberman, 1994; Strauss and Corbin, 1998). In a first phase, the empirical data were coded separately by the two authors, remaining first on a descriptive basis, followed by a gradual convergence on central themes and categories, while staying alert to new emerging issues. The different phases and steps of the analytical process are maintained in the presentation of the findings below. After each interview round, the main insights were presented to the board of directors and the executive board of AdNovum AG separately, as well as discussed in more detail with the new owner and the new CEO of the company. The ensuing in-depth discussions provided additional perspectives and relevant feedback on the evolving analysis. Moreover, this particular format of close collaboration highlighted the idea of coproduction between researchers and practitioners, which pervaded the whole research process.

Over time, evidence emerged that confirmed the key role of two simultaneous, interacting dimensions relating to management knowledge under uncertainty at AdNovum AG: mobilizing multiple references on the one hand, to justify the engagements of the executive board and its members, as well as of the board of directors and the owner, in multiple instances, situations, and events; and enacting routinized action patterns on the other hand, characterizing the ways in which these instances, situations, and events have been shaped by the multiple managerial actors involved. The basic concept of engagement regimes, deduced from convention theory, therefore shaped data analysis. Beyond this basic conceptualization, which is interpreted as an open analytical scheme by convention theory itself

(Boltanski and Thévenot, 1991), all insights reported as research findings have emerged from the research process. On the basis of Thévenot's discussion (2001) of engagement regimes, a concept that is very open and underspecified intentionally to allow for enrichment through detailed empirical research (Thévenot, 2006), we identified a series of important events, processes, and episodes as they were unfolding over time and have been enacted by the management.

11.3.5 Research focus: Multiple managerial engagements

On the basis of our research question, theoretical perspective, and methodological approach, we focused on major engagements of management at AdNovum AG between 2006 and 2009. We observed multiple themes and issues, questions and controversies, in which management was proactively engaging, committing attention and resources. These themes were enacted by management referring to different engagement regimes, and varied in their time extension—some were brief and clear, decided and resolved within a few weeks or hours (such as defining individual responsibilities among board members), while others extended over months or years (such as creating and pursuing new large projects). The themes also varied with respect to the people directly or indirectly involved, from focused face-to-face interactions to broad, company-wide debates, involving different management layers.

Overall, we observed managerial engagements relating to diverse, controversially discussed issues, including an evaluation of the organization structure and possibilities to change it; the day-to-day management of the uncertainties, which emerged after the exit of the former founder-owner-CEO; multiple expectations concerning leadership of the new executive board, in relation to the self-understanding of the owner and the board of directors; changes in project controlling procedures; issues concerning internal and external communication, storytelling, and representation; the pressure for proactive sales activities; the need for creating and exploring new business opportunities, to ensure the mid-term development of the company; and questions concerning the content, structure, process, and format for strategy development. Table 11.1 provides an overview of these major managerial engagements. The table lists the twenty-five most significant engagements and indicates their approximate duration as well as the dimensions of the engagement regime of management, which were explicitly referenced. These engagements are separated analytically, while mutually shaping one another.

Table 11.1 Multiple managerial engagements

	Engagements	Quarter	Patterns of justification			Patterns of routinization		
			Success	Innovation	Organization	Governance	Decision-making	Resource allocation
[E1]	Establishing an interim executive board	Q4 2006			x	x		
[E2]	Allocating responsibilities among interim executive board members	Q4 2006			x	x	x	
[E3]	Interim executive board stabilizing on-going activities	Q4 2006–Q1 2007			x	x	x	
[E4]	Interim executive board establishing leadership, setting priorities	Q4 2006–Q1 2007	x				x	x
[E5]	Introducing new project controlling	Q4 2006–Q1 2007	x	x			x	x
[E6]	Introducing new project planning and staffing	Q4 2006–Q1 2007		x	x		x	x
[E7]	New owner introducing himself to board and staff	Q2 2007	x		x	x		
[E8]	New internal CEO taking up his responsibilities	Q2 2007–Q3 2007			x	x	x	
[E9]	New permanent executive board constituting itself and assuming its responsibilities	Q2 2007–Q3 2007			x	x	x	
[E10]	New board of directors assuming responsibilities	Q4 2006–Q3 2007			x	x		
[E11]	Devising new organization chart	Q1 2007			x	x	x	
[E12]	Generating and pursuing new project leads	Q2 2007–Q3 2008	x	x	x			x

272

[E13]	Discussing and abandoning idea of employee stock ownership program	Q4 2006–Q3 2007	x				x
[E14]	Clarifying role of former owner-CEO	Q4 2006–Q4 2007			x	x	
[E15]	Pursuing new opportunity in the healthcare industry (e-Health), eventually unsuccessfully	Q3 2007–Q4 2008	x	x	x	x	x
[E16]	Dealing with challenges in large government project	Q3 2007–Q1 2008	x	x	x	x	
[E17]	Establishing partnerships with major software companies	Q3 2007–Q2 2008		x	x		x
[E18]	Pursuing opportunity and acquiring large new project in the logistics industry	Q3 2007–Q2 2008	x	x			x
[E19]	Involving seniors (nonboard members) in company leadership	Q3 2007–Q1 2008			x	x	
[E20]	Driving technological and business innovation initiatives	Q3 2007–Q3 2008		x			x
[E21]	Holding strategy workshops	Q4 2007–Q1 2008	x		x	x	
[E22]	Defining and communicating four business areas	Q1 2008	x		x	x	
[E23]	Renaming "sharing experience" initiative as new business area "IT-Consulting"	Q1 2008–Q2 2008	x	x	x		x
[E24]	Establishing permanent teams for IT-Consulting and 2nd level support	Q1 2008–Q2 2008	x		x	x	
[E25]	Establishing new sponsorship and branding initiative: sailing (instead of motor racing)	Q3 2008	x	x	x	x	

A detailed coding of each engagement, and of their discussion during meetings and workshops, led to an extensive visual mapping, showing their extension in time (Langley, 1999). This mapping formed the basis for developing further insights into broader developments and interactions, and led to the identification of empirically grounded dimensions of patterns of justification (with respect to *success, innovation,* and *organization*) (see Tables 11.2a–11.2c) and patterns of routinization (with respect to *governance, decision-making,* and *resource allocation*) (see Tables 11.3a–11.3c), as discussed in section 11.4.1. In an ensuing phase, development patterns of the engagement regimes, within and between individual engagements, were identified (see Figure 11.3). We distinguished four major patterns of change (see Table 11.4), as well as several controversial issues, emerging over time (see Table 11.5), reported in section 11.4.2. This allowed us to describe not only how management knowledge was enacted in specific engagements but also how management knowledge, and related concepts of management, shifted over time (see Figure 11.4), as described in section 11.4.3.

On the basis of our conceptualization of management knowledge as engagement regimes, our focus was not on identifying management knowledge as a describable, detached entity but rather on engagement regimes enacted in individual situations, over time, and in the face of an unprecedented event. Figure 11.1 summarizes the processual relationship and dynamic interplay between concepts. A detailed description follows in Section 11.5.

Overall, we found not only that the flow of managerial activities was characterized by situated, ephemeral, fluid incidences and events but also that managerial activities, at the same time, actualized and mobilized, as well as developed and changed, managerial knowledge.

11.4 Findings

11.4.1 Engagement regimes and their dimensions

As we have seen, each managerial engagement focuses on a specific theme, issue, or controversy, spanning and integrating a range of activities across the organization and over time. Notably, each engagement implies the simultaneous mobilization of patterns of justification and routinization. For example, the engagement with a new project-controlling framework relates to both established patterns of justification (references of success and quality: in time; running from day one; sophisticated engineering;

```
                    ┌─   CONTROVERSIAL ISSUES
ENACTING UNCERTAINTY┤     ─────────↕─────────────────────
                    └─   MANAGERIAL ENGAGEMENTS              Flow of
                         Routinization    Justification      Managerial
                         ENGAGEMENT REGIMES                  Activities
                    ┌─   ─────────↕─────────────────────
MANAGEMENT KNOWLEDGE┤     CONCEPT OF MANAGEMENT
                    └─
```

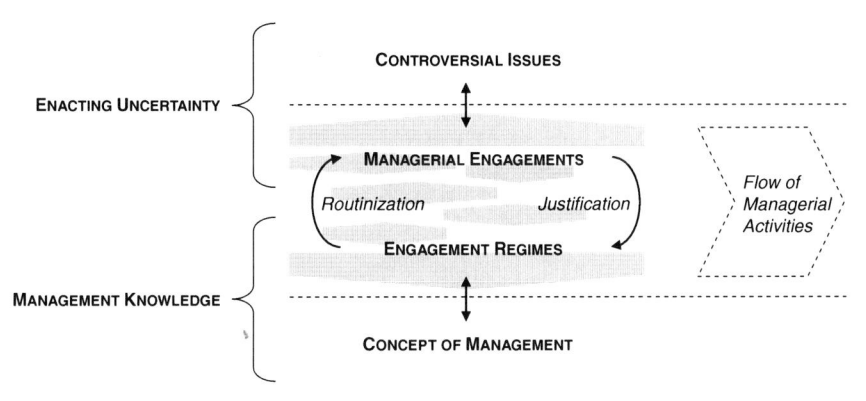

Figure 11.1 Management knowledge: a process view

and novel solution) and new, emerging ones (by integrating financial measures); and adapts patterns of routinization (decision-making from technology management). Overall, it is the sum of situations, issues, and decisions in which management is engaged that constitutes, to a large extent and indirectly, the occasions and challenges toward which management knowledge is mobilized and changed. Thus, it is through simultaneous justification and routinization that the engagement regime of management is actualized, confirmed, or changed, in a highly iterative, contingent, situated process.

Besides the specificities of situations, two key factors shape the enactment of managerial engagements. As engagements overlap in time, relating to and contextualizing each other, their distribution over time and their bundling in a particular time window have implications for the ways in which they are mobilized. However, this distribution and configuration, which is to a large extent contingent and depending on when and how certain issues and themes emerge in the company, is also shaped by the specific ways in which the engagement regimes are actualized, confirmed, and adapted. For example, the development of the new executive board setup led to the establishment of more collective modes of decision-making and resource allocation, to align, coordinate, and integrate the different perspectives and interests represented; this in turn led to a more "pluralistic" idea of organization, with separated responsibilities among the board members. It also went hand in hand with a more explicit discussion and definition of certain important business areas or with a greater openness toward external partnerships.

We identified six dimensions of firm-specific engagement regimes: three dimensions of justification, consisting of references against which managerial issues are argued, explained, justified, and legitimized; and three dimensions of routinization, consisting of shared practices, in which managerial issues are enacted in situated interactions and everyday activities. These dimensions represent analytical distinctions; in the situative enactment of the engagement regime, patterns of justification and routinization are intertwined. Figure 11.2 illustrates the dimensions of engagement regimes, shaped by their multiple enactments in the context of specific engagements over time, with reference to seven managerial engagements ([E2], [E5], [E15], [E16], [E17], [E22], and [E25]) only, rather than all, to facilitate reading.

11.4.1.1 JUSTIFICATION

Management is the justifying of multiple activities and initiatives by referencing to fundamental, collective conventions. Invoked in company-specific arguments, examples, metaphors and stories, these references serve as foci of everyday coordination in dispersed activities. They provide a common, general "hinterland" (Law, 2004) for dealing with controversial issues in a specific situation. We found three dimensions of justification, revolving around key taken-for-granted beliefs about *success*, *innovation*, and *organization*, respectively. Tables 11.2a–11.2c offer more detailed descriptions of how managerial engagements relate to the three dimensions of justification.

- *Referencing "success"*: Many activities are argued for (and against) in terms of whether they contribute (or not) to company success. The meaning of "success" is also shifting over time, from a focus on organizational growth as an indicator that the company successfully convinces the market of its unconventional approach to software engineering to operational continuity and financial performance as indicators that the company is "on track": "... *[financial performance of projects] will be more transparent to project leaders, and I want them to be responsible for and be judged by financial results as well* ..." (CEO, 08/2007). The discussion of how to ensure success has been shifting from radically focusing on basic technological and industrial transformations as the main reference point before 2006, toward an opportunistic, situated focus on business development and project generation after 2007. As a result, "strategy" turns into something that is explicitly specified, jointly developed in regular workshops, formally defined, and documented: "... *we defined certain goals, including key performance indicators, such as each of these four business areas should contribute 10 percent of sales within five years* ..." (CEO, 09/2008).

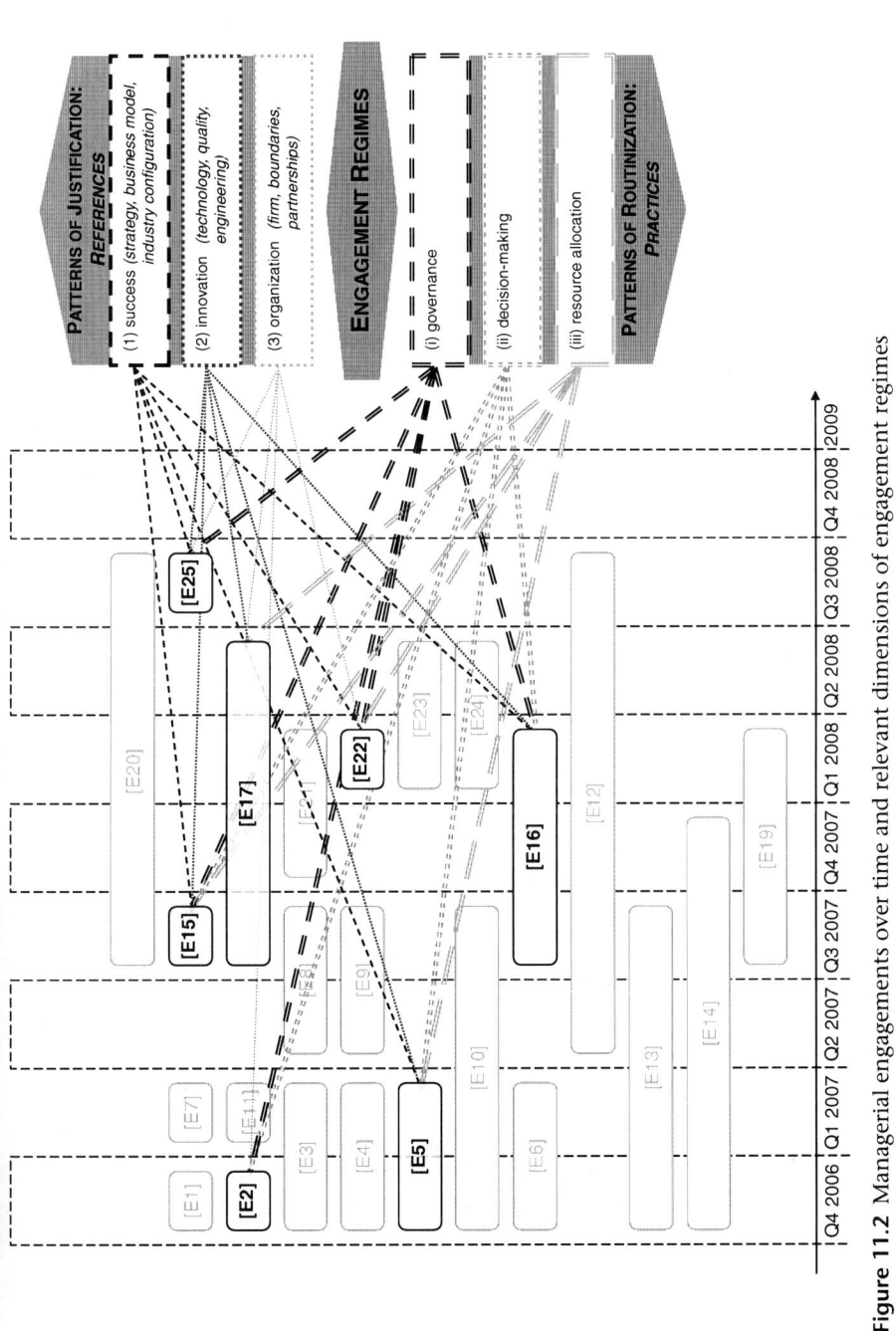

Figure 11.2 Managerial engagements over time and relevant dimensions of engagement regimes

(The relevant dimensions of only seven managerial engagements are highlighted to facilitate reading; for descriptions of the different managerial engagements, see Table 11.1)

277

Constructing Identity in and around Organizations

Table 11.2a Patterns of justification: dimensions—success

Engagement		Implication and quote
[E4]	Interim executive board establishing leadership, setting priorities	Reenacting, actualizing, and reformulating justification of fundamental decisions without being able to resort to former founder-owner-CEO's founder's legitimacy and style of argumentation "I then realized, for instance during year-end evaluation meetings with employees that there had been a number of issues that could be answered by saying, you know, that's how [the former founder-owner-CEO] wants things to be. Now, that's no longer an answer." (Executive board member, 10/2007)
[E5]	Introducing new project controlling	Making projects' performance indicators relative to budget (both internal and external) transparent, the new project controlling pushed a broader awareness for financial success within the company "... [Financial performance of projects] will be more transparent to project leaders, and I want them to be responsible for and be judged by financial results as well." (CEO, 08/2007)
[E7]	New owner introducing himself to board and staff	The new owner, chairman of a large family holding company, giving a strong message of continuity in personal meetings with employees, large customers, and project partners "One of [the new owner's] main priorities is to assure a continuous further development of the company along the path taken in the past few years." (CEO, 08/2007)
[E12]	Generating and pursuing new project leads	Being able to acquire large new projects as key measure of success for the new executive board, particularly as exemplary salesmanship had been one of the most visible personal activities of the former founder-owner-CEO "To be honest, we haven't yet really figured out how to tackle this issue. We know it is on our agenda, but we don't know precisely how we will generate the fifth and sixth large customer in future. Up to a point, we simply lack experience." (CEO, 08/2007)
[E16]	Dealing with challenges in large government project	Overcoming a challenging and difficult phase in the development of the largest application project ever developed by the company, a large secure database for the Swiss Government, reinforced the company's key success indicator of "always delivering in time and running from day one" "I think the successful implementation of [the government database] was extremely important for our self-confidence as a company. Quite a large pressure had been built up, more and more it had become kind of a liability. Hence, it was like an act of liberation, because it went smoothly, that was really a success." (Executive board member, 12/2008)
[E21]	Holding strategy workshops	Push for more proactive strategizing "I think, we are on the right track, we've had discussions between the board of directors and the executive board, had some workshops, and I think the discussions were fine. They also resulted in programmes, activities were launched which now, how shall I put it, are in a phase of pregnancy, but at least, something is happening, we have set ourselves some goals for the future. I think, this way, success should ensue." (Member of the board of directors, 11/2008)

Management Knowledge: A Process View

Table 11.2b Patterns of justification: dimensions—innovation

Engagement		Implication and quote
[E15]	Pursuing new opportunity in the healthcare industry (e-Health), eventually unsuccessfully	e-Health initiative as trying a new approach of innovation, breaking with the company's established modes of pursuing opportunities: first, it was started without even having a potential customer at hand, which had for a long time been seen as precondition to develop new solutions in an effective way; second, it was announced as a strategic move up-front, whereas traditionally, strategic rationalizations had been produced ex post, trying to minimize uncertainty about company focus in the meantime "... these are interesting market dynamics, like in the case of e-health, which is related to e-government, personal health card and so on, certainly something with a catch-up potential, things like electronic patient records have been talked about for quite a while. We simply see all this as applications that should be built right now." (Executive board member, 08/2007)
[E18]	Pursuing opportunity and acquiring large new project in the logistics industry	For the first time, under the leadership of the new executive board the company secured a new big project with a new large customer in a new industry (logistics) and a new technology. In contrast to the e-Health initiative, this opportunity reinforced the traditional approach to innovation: committing to a new technology and a new industry only if there is a customer at hand "Usually, we first say, we need to know more [about a new topic]. Hence, we grow our expertise. Second, we try to place these issues more actively with customers, in order to instil need." (Executive board member, 01/2009)
[E20]	Driving technological and business innovation initiatives	Seeking ways of pushing technological innovation by striking a balance between customer-driven and proprietary development of new solutions, and in a break with past practice, selective investment of retained earnings "I'm still convinced that we are not good at developing solutions on our own. We need a customer as a kind of correcting force. We don't have an equally strong hand within the company at the moment, and I doubt we will within the next, say, three years." (Executive board member, 11/2008)

Table 11.2c Patterns of justification: dimensions—organization

Engagement		Implication and quote
[E1]	Establishing an interim executive board	Members of the newly formed executive board covering all important software engineering and project management functions, but with only limited experience in corporate management "To pick the four of us [as members of the interim executive board] was a decision by [the former founder-owner-CEO] based on history. For some years, there have been meetings of the four of us with him, in order to discuss certain issues of the company." (Executive board member, 09/2007)
[E2]	Allocating responsibilities	Pragmatic approach of allocating responsibilities among members of the executive board reflected a "problem solving" attitude

(*continued*)

Constructing Identity in and around Organizations

Table 11.2c Continued

Engagement		Implication and quote
	among interim executive board members	typical of Informatik AG, implicitly interpreting company leadership as yet another project *"We made a list of tasks that [the former founder-owner-CEO] regularly attended to, or what we assumed he would attend to, implicitly and explicitly, and then we distributed these tasks among ourselves quite haphazardly." (CEO, 08/2007)*
[E11]	Devising new organization chart	Challenging organizational identity by introducing a formal organization chart: Since its foundation, the company never had a formal organization chart with clearly defined roles and responsibilities, which the former founder-owner-CEO frequently proudly referred to as testament of its informal culture without many layers of hierarchy *"For the first time in the history of the company, there is actually a proper organization chart. That is, there used to be one before, just one large box containing numerous small boxes ..." (CEO, 08/2007)*
[E13]	Discussing and abandoning idea of employee stock ownership program	Intensive discussions on the (eventually abandoned) idea of employee stock ownership highlighting various implications: financial transparency among employees would nudge internal debates from a technological to a business focus and would emphasize financial performance indicators over engineering quality, while dividend participation would skew incentives and threaten further growth by dampening risk appetite *"Before [the former founder-owner-CEO] left, in his farewell presentation, he announced big time that there would be an employee participation scheme. It was a bit unfortunate to kind of burden the new owner with such a moral obligation. And for many employees, it has become a bit of a fixed idea." (CEO, 08/2007)*
[E17]	Establishing partnerships with major software companies	Entering in a number of partnerships with large software product companies challenging the company's traditional inclination toward independence from other software companies by developing proprietary open-source applications *"I have to cultivate these partnerships, and I'm realising how time-consuming this is. People are always visiting, and they always want to hear about new project or product opportunities." (Executive board member, 12/2008)*
[E19]	Involving seniors (nonboard members) in company leadership	Securing commitment of seniors who are not executive board members, hence fortifying a more collective approach to managing the company *"With these senior positions, with these new roles, we hope to create a few new evangelists, establishing more delegation and facilitating growth." (Executive board member, 12/2008)*
[E23]	Renaming "sharing experience" initiative as new business area "IT-Consulting"	New way of using labels: standard labels instead of proprietary labels and naming *"We have done consulting for several years already, but always a little obliquely, we called it 'sharing experience', because one didn't want to use the term 'consulting'. Now, either we do it, and then we call it consulting, or we don't do it. But something in-between, I didn't want to do that." (CEO, 12/2008)*
[E24]	Establishing permanent teams for IT-Consulting and 2nd level support	In contrast to traditional view of flexible, customer project-specific teams: permanent teams officialized. *"Now there is also kind of a balancing act between project team and specialist team, that is, like between standing organisation versus dynamic organisation." (Executive board member, 12/2008)*

- *Referencing "innovation"*: The interpretation of "innovation" and, in conjunction, of technology, quality, and engineering is also shifting; the firm-specific conceptualization of innovation has a technological ("at the edge of new technologies") and a symbolic dimension ("unconventional, science-related, radical approach to software engineering"). In 2007, we observed a shift toward a purely technological interpretation of innovation—the dimension of "innovation" that had been driven by senior management already for a few years prior to 2006 (the symbolic dimension was enacted predominantly by the former founder-owner-CEO). We also observe frequent and changing referencing of "quality." It is particularly difficult to objectify quality in a software company, because of the fact that software quality is only visible for expert software developers. On a symbolic level, it has thus been essential for AdNovum AG to insist on precision, simplicity, and elegance of its software, as resulting from good coding standards, the systematic use of bug fixing and software performance evaluation technologies, the use of robust software (in particular open source) if available, and a careful software architecture.
- *Referencing "organization"*: We observed frequent referencing to concepts of the "firm" or an "organization," the specificities of AdNovum AG and its boundaries, and the way the company interacts with partners. With the leave of the former founder-owner-CEO, who had often been seen as an impersonation of the company, and with the ensuing formation of a new governance structure, arguments revolving around organization became prominent. Before 2007, the company had been proud to eschew traditional approaches to formalized structures, and corporate bodies had been given proprietary labels (such as "eggheads meeting" for a meeting of senior employees). Beginning with the establishment of the interim executive board, we observe an officialization of structures throughout the company, with generic terms (such as "executive board") replacing proprietary labels: *" ... for the first time in the history of the company, there is actually a proper organisation chart ... "* (CEO, 08/2007). At the same time, we observe continuity in the ways in which the software company is seen as being built around the software engineering and development process as the structural core.

11.4.1.2 ROUTINIZATION

In parallel, management knowledge is enacted in multiple everyday activities. We distinguished three action patterns, which are routinized, de-routinized, and re-routinized over time: *governance*, which structures the interaction between owner, board of directors, executive board, and senior management; *decision-making*, which structures how decisions are taken, who is involved, and how managerial attention is allocated; and *resource allocation*, which structures how financial and nonfinancial resources are attracted, generated, and allocated to particular activities, projects, and themes. Tables 11.3a–11.3c offer more detailed descriptions on how managerial engagements relate to and highlight the three dimensions of patterns of routinization.

- *Routinizing "governance"*: The fundamental overhaul of the company's governance setup led to a multifaceted process of de-routinization and re-routinization of interaction structures between different management levels. The personalized web of interactions revolving around the former founder-owner-CEO essentially broke down, while the newly formed executive board and the enlarged board of directors constituted a mutually compatible interpretation of their responsibilities. Governance patterns established before the transition were reenacted and adapted (e.g., the close interaction between the former "inner circles" of seniors who became interim executive board members). New patterns were also deliberately established within weeks, such as meeting rhythms and formal information flows: " ... *[The interim executive board] established itself very quickly, because we met once a week* ... " (Executive board member, 10/2007). Furthermore, we observed a more hesitant routinization of emergent patterns, over a period of twelve to eighteen months, relating to strategic issues: in a first phase, the executive board and the board of directors showed a tendency of initiating uncoordinated strategic moves, followed by a hybrid pattern of partly formalized interactions in workshops and partly informal dialogue.
- *Routinizing "decision-making"*: We also observed a routinization of decision-making. We identified a shift from a markedly situated, managing-the-exception approach under the former founder-owner-CEO toward a more collective way of handling important decision-making processes, primarily triggered by the formation of an (interim) executive board. Within a few weeks of assuming their new responsibilities, a new pattern of mutually aligned communication, discussion, and enactment of relevant decisions emerged among the members of the interim executive board. To mitigate the risk of contradictory signals in on-the-spot decisions, they strictly separated spheres of responsibilities by implicitly adapting decision-making

Management Knowledge: A Process View

Table 11.3a Patterns of routinization: dimensions—governance

Engagement		Implication and quote
[E3]	Interim executive board stabilizing on-going activities	Immediately routinizing the work of the new executive board: meeting once a week, formal agenda and minutes, quickly routinizing collaboration among members, mobilizing a problem-solving mindset as well as disperse concepts and personal experiences from project management, software engineering, and other business contexts "[The interim executive board] established itself very quickly, because we met once a week and of course because of constant interactions in daily business, where often some issues emerged that needed to be discussed." (Executive board member, 10/2007)
[E10]	New board of directors assuming responsibilities	Establishing the independent board of directors as a new body through a routine of frequent meetings and formalized communication channels and formats with the executive board, with the new CEO taking part at every meeting and the former founder-owner-CEO sometimes as well "Many employees don't really understand why there is also a board of directors. It seems the average ETH software engineer knows very little about corporate law. I was really asked, like: who is [the new owner and chairman], and what is your role, who is the boss?" (CEO, 08/2007)
[E14]	Clarifying role of former founder-owner-CEO	For a good part of 2007, the former founder-owner-CEO and his (potential) ideas remaining a frequent topic and reference point in discussions among long-time employees "... [The former founder-owner-CEO] left the board of directors, which he had dominated. However, he has still taken part in a number of board meetings as a guest, simply to facilitate opinion formation." (CEO, 08/2007)
[E21]	Holding strategy workshops	Holding an intense series of off-site strategy workshops of board of directors and executive board, trying to establish a new way of more systematic proactive strategizing "I think, we are on the right track, we've had discussions between the board of directors and the executive board, had some workshops, and I think the discussions were fine. They also resulted in programmes, activities were launched which now, how shall I put it, are in a phase of pregnancy, but at least, something is happening, we have set ourselves some goals for the future. I think, this way, success should ensue." (Member of the board of directors, 11/2008)
[E25]	Establishing new sponsorship and branding initiative: sailing (instead of motor racing)	New brand campaign: sailing instead of motor racing, capitalizing on a more collective sport, yet retaining the image of racing and high ambition "[Sponsoring] Sailing is a good idea because it is relatively close to cars, to the racing idea. It is innovative, but more ecological than motor racing, and it also sets us apart from [the former founder-owner-CEO], showing our own idea of sponsoring." (Executive board member, 12/2008)

Constructing Identity in and around Organizations

Table 11.3b Patterns of routinization: dimensions—decision-making

Engagement		Implication and quote
[E1]	Establishing an interim executive board	Members of the new executive board covering all important software engineering and project management functions, but less explicit handling of corporate functions "[The interim executive board was] very much focused on operations from the beginning. We didn't think on how to develop the company in the longer term. It was declared as an 'ad interim' board. And so we pragmatically decided to hold a meeting once a week in order to synchronize." (Executive board member, 08/2007)
[E2]	Allocating responsibilities among interim executive board members	Pragmatic approach reflecting a "problem solving" attitude typical of Informatik AG, implicitly interpreting company leadership as yet another project "That went relatively well. There were quite a lot of side-activities which initially hadn't been covered, but the main activities and responsibilities, regarding major business domains, projects, people, that actually wasn't a big problem." (Executive board member, 10/2007)
[E3]	Interim executive board stabilizing on-going activities	Reroutinizing taking nonstandard decisions (financial and personnel) and dealing with uncertainty about medium-term perspectives of the company (both had been main focus of former founder-owner-CEO) "It wasn't about setting up some teams or establishing reporting structures between employees and members of the interim board, but it was always a question of who does employee A address if she has a specific question, or a problem in the area X. It was crucial that we could address these issues." (Executive board member, 10/2007)
[E4]	Interim executive board establishing leadership, setting priorities	Establishing a mutually congruent way of dealing with and communicating about fundamental issues among board members "That's something that many people haven't actually realised, but [the former founder-owner-CEO] was quite a dictator. He had very good relationships [with employees], but at the end of the day, he knew exactly where he wanted to go and he did take decisions, which was important. In that respect, there will be some kind of shift." (Executive board member, 10/2007)
[E19]	Involving seniors (nonboard members) in company leadership	Designating senior engineers and project leaders as heads of specific functions and initiatives (such as consulting, support, innovation), while executive board members retained direct responsibilities for core software development processes "With these senior positions, with these new roles, we hope to create a few new evangelists, establishing more delegation and facilitating growth." (Executive board member, 12/2008)

Management Knowledge: A Process View

Table 11.3c Patterns of routinization: dimensions—resource allocation

Engagement		Implication and quote
[E5]	Introducing new project controlling	Introducing a more systematic reporting structure with centrally consolidated data facilitated a collective mode of project oversight both within the board and with project leaders
"We now have a project portfolio report which gives an overview of all projects to the executive board. Hitherto, [the former founder-owner-CEO] somehow knew in his head: that project is in the red, but these three are performing well, so it will add up in the end. Now, no one has this overview in his head anymore, hence we systematized things and project leaders now report their data centrally every month." (CEO, 08/2007)
[E15]	Pursuing new opportunity in the healthcare industry (e-Health), eventually unsuccessfully	Reflecting the new executive board's push to establish a more proactive mode of strategizing, the way the e-Health initiative was set up, however, meant breaking with the company's established modes of pursuing opportunities: first, it was started without even having a potential customer at hand, which had for a long time been seen as precondition to develop new solutions in an effective way; second, it was announced as a strategic move up-front, whereas traditionally, strategic rationalizations had been produced ex post, trying to minimize uncertainty about company focus in the meantime.
"... these are interesting market dynamics, like in the case of e-health, which is related to e-government, personal health card and so on, certainly something with a catch-up potential, things like electronic patient records have been talked about for quite a while. We simply see all this as applications that should be built right now." (Executive board member, 08/2007)
[E17]	Establishing partnerships with major software companies	Partnerships, initially serving as door-openers for particular projects, implied lock-in effects as well: buying software licences, and building specific expertise, which could only be amortized by acquiring more projects with the same partner
"On the other hand, we shouldn't exclusively rely on partners. Our company has always set itself apart by an Open-Source focus." (Executive board member, 11/2008)
[E18]	Pursuing opportunity and acquiring large new project in the logistics industry	In contrast to the e-Health initiative, confirming the traditional business development approach: committing to a new technology and a new industry only if there is a customer at hand
"Usually, we first say, we need to know more [about a new topic]. Hence, we grow our expertise. Second, we try to place these issues more actively with customers, in order to instil need." (Executive board member, 01/2009)
[E22]	Defining and communicating four business areas	Defining four business areas (application development, security engineering, application management, IT-Consulting), also reflecting the new owner's view of strategy—that is, breaking the portfolio logic of a holding company down to Informatik AG
"The main discussion was: what do we want to offer? What precisely are our services, and what is our market, which industries? It was a rather prolonged process, but I think it was worthwhile to really arrive at a consolidated picture. And from there, trivially, the result were four business areas ..." (CEO, 12/2008)

practices from project management and software engineering, where formalized, collective decisions had been in place before 2006. As a consequence, operations were quickly stabilized. The shift toward a more diversified project portfolio and related discussions around creating a new focused innovation strategy during 2007 and 2008 also reflected changes in decision-making, particularly prioritising decisions on issues falling within executive board members' individual range of competencies.

- *Routinizing "resource allocation"*: Finally, we observed a routinization of action patterns that shape the ways financial and nonfinancial resources are attracted, generated, and allocated to important activities, initiatives and projects. In need of a consolidated project overview, the new executive board introduced a standardized project reporting and controlling framework. All projects are measured against the same set of criteria, with internal and external budget figures featuring prominently: *"...we now have a project portfolio report which gives an overview of all projects to the executive board. Hitherto, [the former founder-owner-CEO] somehow knew in his head: that project is in the red, but these three are performing well, so it will add up in the end. Now, project leaders now report their data centrally every month..." (CEO, 08/2007).* This approach helps to ensure smooth project work and streamline a previously hectic process of reallocating engineers between projects. However, the shift also marks a loss of flexibility to drive new opportunities. During much of 2007 and 2008, the executive board experimented with several approaches to push new initiatives in a proactive way, resulting in a more heterogeneous portfolio of projects and activities.

In sum, two observations are central for our understanding of management knowledge. First, management does not figure as a central reference in dealing with these issues; in our data, we hardly ever found a direct reflection on management. Rather, assumptions, interpretations, and concepts about the management of the company are debated implicitly, by relating to the references described above and enacting the functionally specific patterns of communication and interaction we set out. Second, it is in the on-going interplay between the enactment of different references and different routinized practices that management knowledge is mobilized. Management knowledge is thus mainly characterized by the complexity and heterogeneity of references and routines that are enacted, actualized, confirmed, and adapted. We further explore this last point in the next section.

11.4.2 Enactment of engagement regimes over time

Patterns of justification and routinization are constantly actualized in situated engagements; at the same time, they are questioned, confirmed, and adapted in those engagements. As our study of AdNovum AG reveals, these micro-changes on the level of individual references and practices reinforce each other and effect tendencies that shift the engagement regimes as a whole. In turn, changing engagement regimes feed back on the way specific situations and events are dealt with. In particular, we observed four major changes in the engagement regimes emerging from their on-going enactment during the period of our study at AdNovum AG from end-2006 to mid-2009. More background on emerging patterns of change of engagement regimes can be found in Table 11.4.

- *Formalization*: We observed a tendency toward formalization: *"... certain domains have now become more organized, for instance marketing, sales, where new responsibilities on a lower level (below the executive board) have been defined..." (Executive board member, 12/2008)*. The new executive board holds regular weekly meetings, on the basis of defined agendas and documented written minutes, while the board of directors reduced its activities to a defined number of meetings per year. The interactions are formalized, in the form of strategy workshops that deal with fundamental issues outside the everyday current of themes. Related to these formalized activities, we observe a dedicated naming of those bodies in the organization as "executive board," "board of directors," "strategy workshop," and "CEO," which is justified as " ... we call these bodies as they are normally called," and: *"Right now, we stick to our goals, because it is no use discussing a strategy and defining metrics, and then changing minds as soon as there is a little headwind" (CEO, 12/2008)*. Finally, we observed an explicit separation between project management and company management, implying that members of the executive board are involved in strategically important software development projects as experienced supervisors.
- *Collectivization*: These changes explicitly address a major managerial challenge of the past, namely the high reliance on one person, the founder-owner-CEO, which became a bottle-neck for the organization. Today, major managerial activities are distributed among a series of people at the levels of the board of directors and the management team: *"What I expect from [the CEO] is that he*

Constructing Identity in and around Organizations

Table 11.4 Engagement regimes: emerging patterns of change

Emerging pattern of change	Quote
Formalization	"There is a need among employees who are looking for some structure, I mean, they want to be allocated, they want to know who is nominally responsible for certain issues, you can call that organization or hierarchy or whatever."
	(Member of the executive board, 10/2007)
	"During the past two, three years, we have made quite an effort to furnish some technologies, also in the sense of a kind of catalogue, so that, for instance, projects may take from the catalogue whatever technology they need initially. We call that toolbox, engineering toolbox."
	(Member of the executive board, 11/2007)
	"It used to be one person alone who decided, yes or no, and today it tends to be a [corporate] body. I think having some more specific rules also conforms to employees' expectations. And it is not always easy, you know."
	(Member of the executive board, 10/2007)
Collectivization	"Having definitions of roles [within projects] and having written them down, we very much address these organizational issues in the sense that they cover a miniature project organization—or rather organizational aspects—that we say, there is a project leader, there is a technical project leader, an integrator, a business analyst et cetera. This also has to do with uniting the size of the company, the bulk of people under a common understanding again."
	(Member of the executive board, 10/2007)
	"My experiences are very positive, it works well. I mean, people are hungry, you have to feed them. That is, we've got, in a sense, also an informal or rather a formal middle management, we've got very good people who push a lot, which illustrates that delegation actually works well."
	(Member of the executive board, 11/2007)
Normalization	"... It is even much worse, not only do we have an executive board, we've even got—to be really precise—we've even got a middle management now. We have struggled quite a bit whether we should call this now 'organization'."
	(Member of the executive board, 10/2007)
	"I do believe that, over time, there will be certain aspects of becoming a quote 'more normal' unquote company. Because to a certain degree a broader reach implies more concerted action."
	(Member of the executive board, 10/2007)
Separation	"... these [issues] to a large degree imply questions of strategic positioning, which is defined by the board of directors to a much larger degree than it used to be the case in the past."
	(Member of the board of directors, 11/2007)
	"You first have to understand how the others work, what makes them tick, where they see their home turf, what they want to decide, what the sensitivities are, and, and, and. I think that were the issues, like, do we have to present this decision to the board of directors, yes or no."
	(Member of the executive board, 12/2008)

does not deal with complexities by introducing new fixed structures, but rather takes the existing structures and their ability to solve problems, and distributes these capabilities among several people" (Member of the board of directors, 12/2008). In addition, important strategic initiatives and new themes are allocated to experienced senior managers outside the executive board. As a consequence, we observed an explicit identification of managerial tasks, a substantial redistribution of activities among the management layers, and stabilized interaction patterns: *"We have lost our star salesman who catches the very big projects. Hence, we distribute sales among various people and fetch a deal here and there. Of course the result will no longer be a highly focused strategy ... " (CEO, 12/2008).*

- *Normalization*: Structuration, formalization, and collectivization imply also a process of normalization: in the past, the emphasis was on "being different," "being crazy," and "being exceptional," while today the argument goes more in the direction of "we are a normal company," "we do it in a similar way as other companies," and "we do what we are supposed to do": *"Sometimes I hear a reproach, or a comment—I don't know whether it is meant as a reproach—we have become a quite normal company. However, it always was a normal company, with a particular organization designed around one person, and now it has become somewhat different" (Member of the board of directors, 11/2007).* This occurs for several reasons: justification in terms of self-defined references, as it has been practiced by the former founder-owner-CEO, has been replaced by external referencing; the translation of former project managers' experiences as project managers into the definition of executive management has introduced formal tools and procedures; and the expectations of the new owner, who through his management holding company is engaged in other companies and ventures as well, have clearly emphasized "doing what has to be done."

- *Separation*: *"In my view, the way we operate is that we [the executive board] make proposals and the board of directors decides. I think there is enough industry experience on the board... " (Executive board member, 08/2007).* Issues and themes that had been identified as fundamental by the former founder-owner-CEO, are no longer at the core of discussion, including those associated with the particular "entrepreneurial" approach to management and strategy as it had been postulated in the past—that is, studying the deep structures and the underlying dynamics of the industry (including the increasing globalization of the software development value constellation). These "entrepreneurial" themes were delegated to the new owner. In a first phase, the board of directors tried to fill this gap, however, with speculative and philosophical debates and suggestions rather than tangible concepts and robust interpretations of what is going on in the software industry. In a second phase, these themes were eliminated from the agenda, leading to a situation in which not only the ways in which the company is managed but also the ways in which the future of the company is discussed are "normal."

These changes in the engagement regimes have interesting implications with respect to new, upcoming challenges and issues. As patterns of justification and routinization gradually shift, the on-going enactment of situated engagements gives rise to new controversies with respect to fundamental assumptions about managing the company. We identified four issues as particularly insightful and directly related to the ways in which the engagement regimes have changed over the three-year time period studied. More background on emerging patterns of change of engagement regimes can be found in Table 11.5.

- *"Remaining unique"*: It is increasingly difficult for the new management to identify in which respects AdNovum AG is unique. Being a "normal" company, which does what every company does, allows the new management to robustly justify what they do. Company-specific references in justification have been replaced by more general references, which can be found in many other companies: *"We have done consulting for several years already, but always a little obliquely, we called it 'sharing experience,' because one didn't want to use the term 'consulting.' Now, either we do it, and then we call it consulting, or we don't do it. But something in-between, I didn't want to do that"* (CEO, 12/2008). As a consequence, issues that had been enacted in the past in view of "being different" (e.g., comparatively low salaries, management has not been co-owning the company) are now discussed in terms of acceptance.
- *"Being different"*: Comparisons with major competitors become more important. The issue of "being different" is challenging in the context of the software industry, as the outcomes of software development projects are typically invisible, implying that competitive differentiation is relying on symbolic references. Being "normal" is in this respect both an advantage and a disadvantage. Through a comparison with other companies, the justification of certain initiatives is much more self-evident while challenging company-specific solutions is "special for its

Management Knowledge: A Process View

Table 11.5 Emerging controversial issues

Emerging controversial issue	Quote
Remaining unique	"I think the basic groove is still there and that's something that I find extremely important. [. . .] I was extremely concerned that the more pronounced structures could seriously harm that groove." (Member of the board of directors, 11/2007) "I never felt we were a unique firm. I know that was a sentiment. [. . .] I think there are a lot of things we do worse than other companies, but the image of being unique is also part of the hype, of marketing." (Member of the executive board, 10/2007)
Being different	"We don't want to become a 08/15 [i.e. average] firm in future, and I don't see a danger of us becoming one." (CEO, 08/2007) "It is indeed so [important], because there are certain things we are capable of doing which an other firm with another culture wouldn't be capable of doing." (Member of the executive board, 11/2007) "All the same, we have tried not to follow all conventions and remain a bit different in the way that, for instance, a [corporate] body may be defined along with certain responsibilities and domains, but besides, there are no further hierarchies or teams." (Member of the executive board, 10/2007)
Staying innovative	"Today, there are some rules and regulations which help keep channelling everything in ordered ways which, on some people, has already had the effect of behaving in a 'work-to-rule' ['Dienst nach Vorschrift'] manner." (Member of the executive board, 12/2008) "Does the company still believe in our being hip and leading-edge? Do university graduates still believe this is a hip and leading-edge company? That's the important thing." (Member of the executive board, 12/2007)
Acting entrepreneurially	"On the other hand, it is vitally important to bear in mind that we are precisely looking for and want to retain highly qualified employees who want to be taken seriously, who, I think, don't want to work in a fully hierarchical organization with an authoritarian boss. So there should not be an executive suite, and if you look around, there is none, which is very important." (Member of the executive board, 10/2007) "Of course, [the former founder-owner-CEO] very often and in a very forward-looking way, just said with this project I buy a new customer, or with that project I gain access to a new technology." (Member of the board of directors, 12/2007) "In the meantime, we have tried forays into completely new domains, which were not successful. So I think, we should market ourselves and not some fancy idea, and that's why the reduction or the focus on these four [business areas]." (Member of the executive board, 12/2008)

own sake." A case in point is a new propensity to enter formal partnership agreements with large software providers: *"On the other hand, we shouldn't exclusively rely on partners. Our company has always set itself apart by an open source focus ..." (Executive board member, 11/2008).*

- *"Staying innovative"*: It is important for any technology company to be "innovative." However, we observed multiple definitions of what it means to be innovative, both among companies within the industry, but also within one company over time (through comparative empirical research conducted by the two authors on other companies in the industry). Therefore, being "innovative" is often difficult to specify in tangible terms (all companies work with new technologies, solve new problems, address new issues, and develop new solutions), making the symbolic level very important. "Being unconventional" was productive in this respect, and it was open to many different interpretations over time, depending on particular situations, events, and opportunities; becoming "more normal" creates challenges and changes the culture and self-perception of the people in the company.

- *"Acting entrepreneurially"*: Acting entrepreneurially was highly identified with the former founder-owner-CEO and his emphasis on being unconventional. This makes it difficult for the new management to be perceived as entrepreneurial instead of just being "normal" managers. While this does not have implications on the operational level, it creates challenges for the self-understanding of the management team and the owner, as well as for the approach toward new opportunities. While a strong company-specific, entrepreneurial reference system allows being highly selective, a normal reference system is less specified. As a consequence, AdNovum AG is now active in a broader variety of fields. Furthermore, the focus is shifting from a close attention to the development of the company as a whole toward the realization of individual projects: *"I see it more like it is usually handled at consulting firms with their partner model: each partner is responsible for his part of the business" (CEO, 08/2007).*

In sum, we highlight two insights: First, it is not within a particular situation, or through the enactment of a specific task, or due to engaging in a specific controversy that engagement regimes are changing; rather, changes emerge over time—to some extent through the enactment of a series of situations, but more often as the result of multiple, contingent, situated interactions. Second, these changes lead to the disappearance of certain issues concerning ambiguous responsibilities, incoherent communication, or contradicting suggestions; in parallel, they lead to new issues with respect to taken-for-granted assumptions about management. Hence, shifts in engagement regimes, and thus in management knowledge as it is enacted over time, are a way to cope with action under uncertainty, at the cost of increased exposure to new uncertainty (Figure 11.3).

11.4.3 Shifting concepts of management

Changes in engagement regimes not only reflect and shape how multiple events and activities interact in the development of AdNovum AG over time but also imply shifts in the interplay of management knowledge and knowing, including shifts of concepts of management itself, that is, organization-specific theories (Tsoukas and Vladimirou, 2001) of what managing AdNovum AG implies. In this section, we explore how managerial engagements and firm-specific engagement regimes enact shifting concepts of management. It is important to note that these understandings are, most of the time, not explicitly reflected and discussed by those involved in management. Rather, they are indirectly and implicitly actualized, mentioned, and argued in the context of controversies concerning specific tasks, particular events, local situations, and precise episodes, as well as through the justification and routinization of engagement regimes. This makes it difficult to directly identify concepts of management; however, it is possible to indirectly find certain patterns relating to concepts of management.

- *Management as a profession*: The new management team interprets the management of a company as a profession addressing a defined series of tasks that are different from the tasks of project managers. Obviously, this shift is directly related to the careers of members of the new management team, who formerly acted as project managers. Further, it is a productive way of justifying their competence as managers, because by emphasizing not only the relation but also the difference between project management and company management, they are able to identify continuities and discontinuities between what they did before and what they do now. In this perspective, management knowledge is seen as largely independent of the firm.
- *Management as a normalized activity*: Management is conceived as a "normal" activity, which can be learned by referencing what is typically understood as managerial by the literature, by supervisory board members, by employees, or by colleagues in other organizations. While

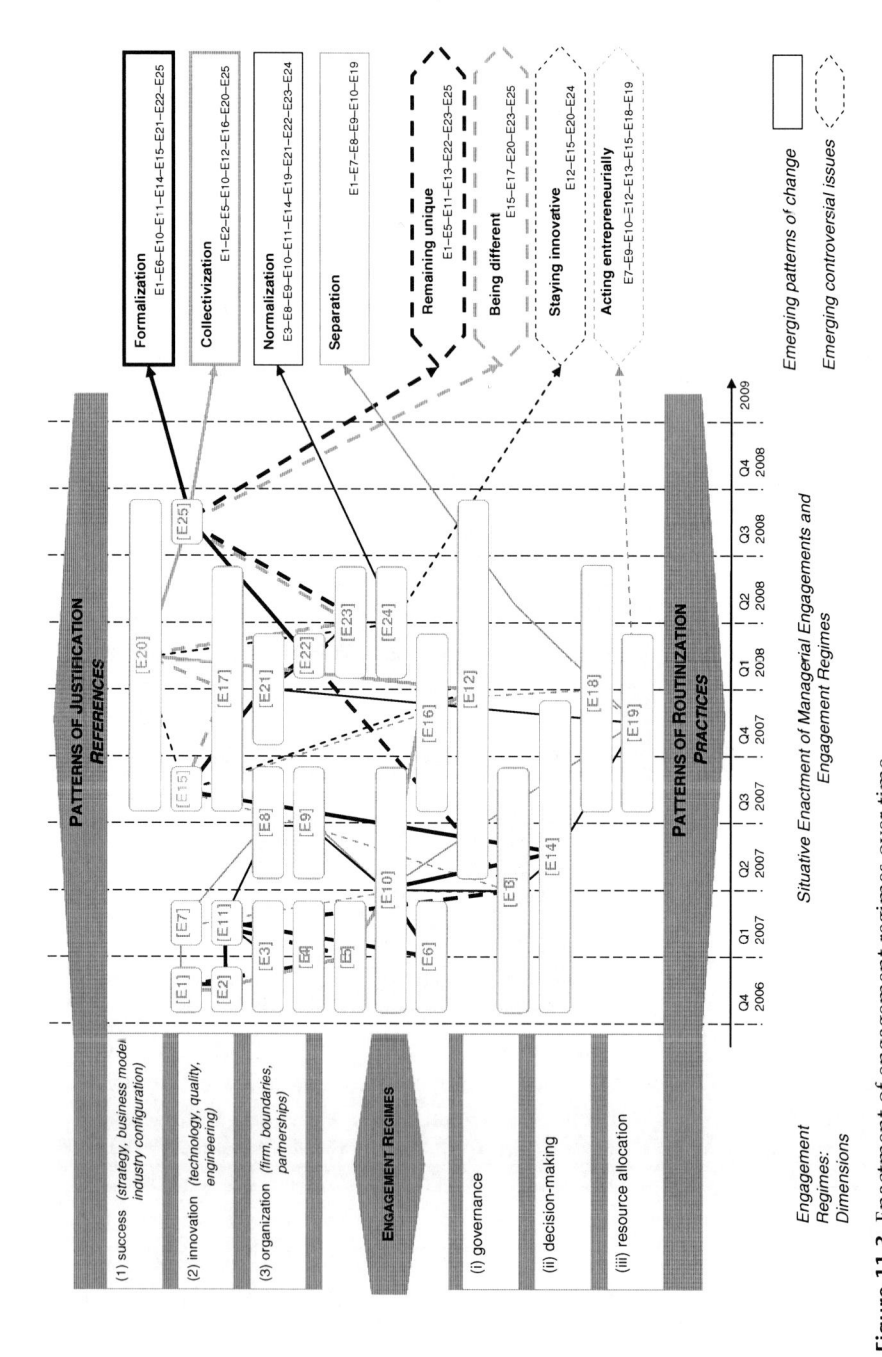

Figure 11.3 Enactment of engagement regimes over time
(For descriptions of the different managerial engagements, see Table 11.1)

the former founder-owner-CEO was emphasizing that entrepreneurial management must be invented in a firm-specific, unique way over time, the new management team tends to refer more to the management literature, institutionalized education, interactions with their colleagues and customers as their main references for characterizing management, as well as for identifying relevant tasks and priorities. Management knowledge thus implies an objectified and general body of knowledge, including given practices and formats.

- *Management as a collective effort*: For the new managers, management is a team effort, which implies that it is focused on how tasks can be distributed, differentiated, and allocated, as well as related, coordinated, and integrated. Management is interpreted less as a future-oriented activity, focusing on the creation, development, and transformation of new businesses and unconventional perspectives on technology; rather, it is seen as focusing on the coordination of distributed activities in a particular moment, as well as on the short- and mid-term acquisition of new customers and the generation of new projects, to ensure the survival of the company as it is. Management knowledge is thus seen as implying a jointly represented, collectively shared, broadly accepted concept and understanding of management.
- *Management as an organized process*: As a consequence, management requires a lot of organizing effort, including the structuration, tooling, representation, documentation, etc. of activities in the executive board and of their interactions with the board of directors and the senior management level in the company. This expectation leads to a situation in which new procedures, communication formats, and organizational arrangements are declared first and implemented later, whereas the former approach involved trying out procedures, formats, and arrangements, and only turning them into regular company-specific ways of doing things if they worked and were confirmed in practice. Management knowledge, as currently conceived at AdNovum AG, does not rely primarily on the personal competences and experiences of a CEO, but on tools and processes that ensure the systemic integration and coordination of company-related activities.
- *Management as distinct from entrepreneurship*: Because of the strong contrast established by the former founder-owner-CEO between management and entrepreneurship, the entrepreneurial qualities inherent in management are clearly separated and excluded from most discussions at AdNovum AG, except in the case of one or two people who continue to interpret themselves as having the responsibility to cover

these more entrepreneurial themes. This has two implications: on the one hand, certain themes are withdrawn as not relevant or as not appropriately allocated if discussed at the level of the management team; on the other hand, the former founder-owner-CEO remains a reference for these issues and questions which are outside the self-understanding of the new management. As a consequence, management knowledge is seen as a distinct body of knowledge that is different from knowledge associated with entrepreneurial management, and also from project management.

In a process view, management knowledge cannot be understood as a defined entity, and thus not "identified" empirically; seen as engagement regimes, it can only be studied in its situated managerial engagements. It is possible, however, to identify patterns of justification and routinization of these engagement regimes with respect to *explicit* references (i.e., in our case study, success, innovation, and organization) as well as practices (i.e., in our case study, governance, decision-making, and resource allocation). These engagements regimes allow for coherent, robust, and convincing managerial engagements in the face of uncertainty. The specific qualities of these engagement regimes can be studied insofar as they are shifting in the face of unexpected and unprecedented events, implying controversial issues that must be addressed in the light of management knowledge. In parallel, management knowledge consists not only of a series of engagement regimes but also of implicit concepts of management, which are essential for the self-understanding of management in its situated engagements under uncertainty, and thus as *implicit* references for routinization and justification (Figure 11.4).

11.5 Discussion

In this study, we explore one research question: *How is management knowledge justified and routinized in managerial practices and processes in the face of uncertainty?* More specifically, we explore how management knowledge is justified and routinized in the face of an unprecedented event and further managerial challenges over time. Our theoretical conceptualization, based on conventional theory and our empirical study, focusing on management succession from a process perspective, highlights that management knowledge can be understood as engagement regimes, that is, firm-specific ways

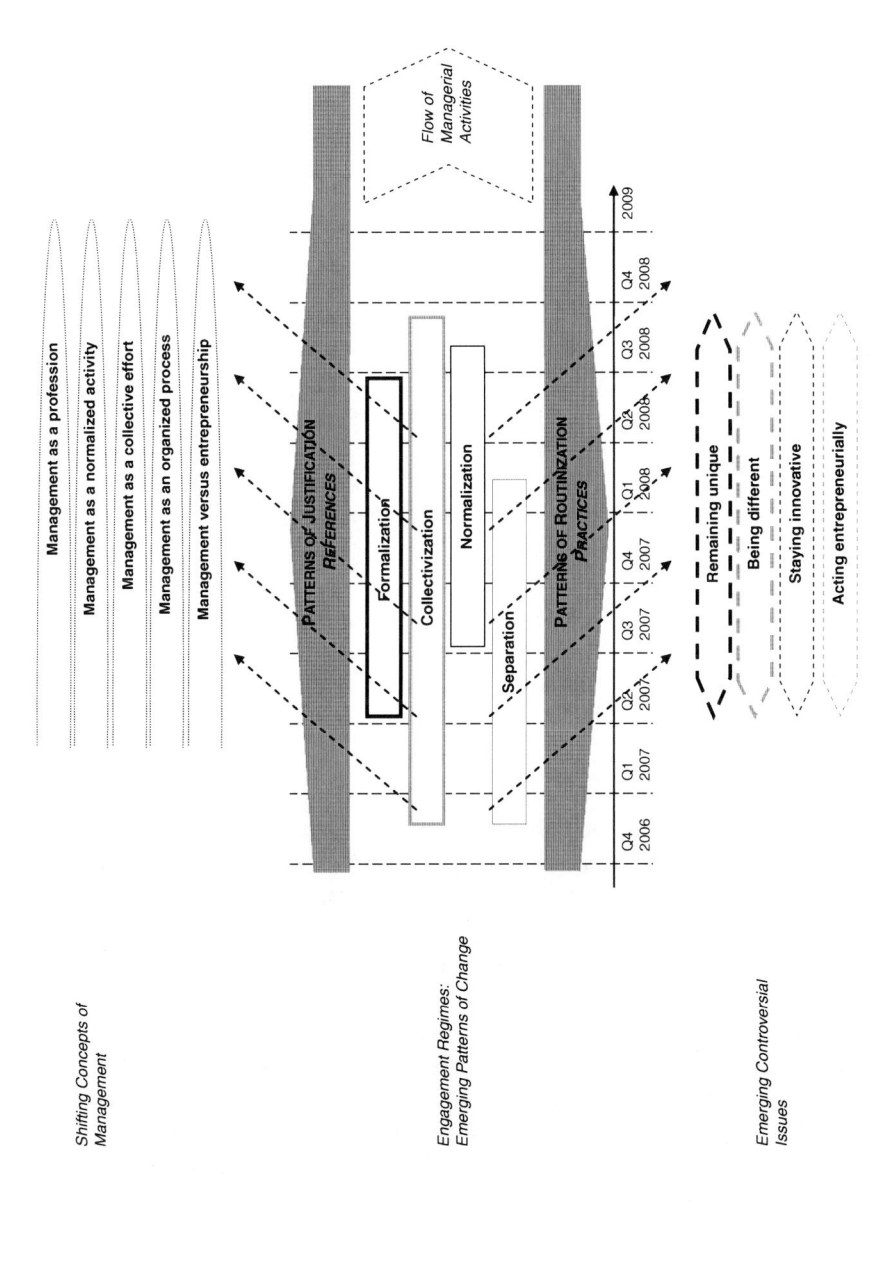

Figure 11.4 Flow of managerial activities, engagement regimes, emerging controversial issues, and shifting concepts of management

of enacting uncertainty through on-going, situated managerial engagements that mutually contextualize and shape each other. Engagement regimes encapsulate a particular, emerging and shifting interplay of managerial knowledge and knowing, at the same time actualizing—thereby challenging and justifying—central references of organizational purpose and legitimation, and drawing on—thereby de-routinizing and re-routinizing—key managerial practices. Over time, and in reaction to upcoming challenges, management knowledge enables the organization to effectively confront uncertainties of a certain kind, while provoking the surfacing of other controversial issues, an unfolding dynamic that in turn shapes the processes of its justification and routinization, as well as induces shifts in underlying, fundamental concepts of management.

Our study makes a series of contributions. First, we provide an empirical study of management knowledge as a particular type of knowledge that has so far not been explicitly addressed in management research. In so doing, we build on the recent differentiation between knowledge and knowing (Orlikowski, 2002); reinterpret both with respect to management knowledge and knowing; and describe the interplay of these phenomena in a single theoretical framework drawn from convention theory. We empirically show that management knowledge cannot be understood as stable and given, especially not in the face of uncertainty. Management knowledge must rather be understood as being justified and routinized in situated managerial activities.

Second, we introduce the concept of engagement regimes from convention theory (Thévenot, 2006) as a promising perspective for conceptualizing management knowledge. We identify managerial engagements as a fruitful unit of analysis for empirical process research, identifying twenty-five central engagements specific to our case. Focusing on managerial engagements allows for understanding management practices as they enact specific issues and controversies, while transcending the situational through referencing concepts of management. We observed justification taking place with respect to different major references (success, innovation, and organization); in parallel, we observed the routinization of governance, decision-making, and resource allocation, central practices in any management process (Bower, 1970; Burgelman, 2001).

Third, we describe management knowledge from the perspective of process research. We show how management knowledge is questioned in the face of an unprecedented event, and reestablished over time. The distribution of managerial engagements over time is, therefore, enacting and shaping changes in management knowledge; and this is leading to new controversial issues that have to be seen as specific to the case. We also identify formalization, collectivization, normalization, and separation as four essential change patterns, which characterize the new management knowledge emerging in the particular context of management succession.

Fourth, we provide a detailed in-depth process study of management succession, a very important managerial challenge in many companies today. We complement existing research by emphasizing the importance of management knowledge in this process. With new managers entering a company, or succeeding their predecessors, new engagement regimes of management are emerging. As a result, the ways in which managerial activities are distributed among different organizational levels, and how they are justified and routinized in the enactment of particular issues and challenges, is changing as well. A processual, systemic view of management succession is especially useful for revealing the complexities of such a process.

Our study also provides a series of interesting insights for related research areas. In particular, we see the following major contributions: First, our study contributes to research on organizational knowledge and knowing. It carefully describes how situated knowing and shifts in knowledge are related, thereby complementing and advancing recent research on the dynamic interplay between knowledge and knowing (Cook and Brown, 1999; Tsoukas and Vladimirou, 2001). In parallel, the study contributes to the theoretical conceptualization of this dynamic interplay, by introducing engagement regimes, a promising theoretical perspective from convention theory (Thévenot, 2006), and by arguing that knowledge cannot be empirically studied independent of processes of knowing.

Second, our study allows us to explicitly relate two important streams of organizational knowledge research—knowledge as "justified true beliefs" on the one hand (Nonaka, 1994), as well as "competence to act" on the other hand (Tsoukas, 2005). In the face of fundamental uncertainty, organizational knowledge is potentially or actually questioned and challenged, making processes of justification and routinization important in order to maintain to some extent the taken-for-granted, unquestioned, self-evident nature of knowledge (Gomez and Jones, 2000)—an essential precondition for managerial agency in the face of uncertainty (Spender, 1989, 1996).

Third, our study adds to attempts to understand management as routinized processes, following different "routinization modes" (Burgelman, 1983, 2001; Menuhin and McGee, 2002). While it is sometimes argued that the difference between managerial and operational activities lies in their degree of routinization (Zollo and Winter, 2002), we find that management is itself routinized, enacting firm-specific engagement regimes, which allow managers to do their "managerial work," while reinterpreting what is seen as managerial and identified as management (Ortmann, 2009). This confirms insights about the generative nature of organizational routines (Feldman, 2000; Feldman and Pentland, 2003).

Fourth, our study contributes to process research, by empirically describing important themes emphasized in process theory (Langley, 1999; Tsoukas and Chia, 2002; Hernes, 2008). Our study provides empirical and methodological insights into how process research could be reconciled with the practice turn in organization studies (Tsoukas, 2005) as well as in strategy research (Johnson et al., 2003; Johnson et al., 2007). We show how firm-specific engagement regimes are enacted and shaped in specific, local, situated incidences, events, and issues, while at the same time stabilizing and changing firm-specific, collective action patterns, concepts, and knowledge.

Overall, it is interesting to observe that managers seldom describe how they understand management per se (Pettigrew, 1985), but rather justify why they do what they do (Gomez and Jones, 2000) and explicate what they think they do (Mintzberg, 2009). Taken seriously, this insight has two fundamental methodological and epistemological implications: just reconstructing the ways in which managers explain what they do suffers from a "justification bias" (Tsoukas, 1994; Czarniawska, 1999; Ortmann, 2009); while describing what managers do (Mintzberg, 1971, 2009) suffers from a "routinization bias," as the situated enactment of events and episodes is always embedded in processes of referencing and justifying, explicit or implicit.

11.6 Conclusion

Our study contributes to the development of a theory of management, and of management knowledge from a process perspective. The limitations are manifold, but by explicitly studying "management in action," we can identify some promising opportunities for further research: on an empirical level, it will be important to increase the number of detailed, longitudinal case studies of managerial processes; on a conceptual level, it will be important to further specify the conceptualization of basic notions as management knowledge, engagement regimes, concepts of management, as well as their justification and routinization; on a methodological level, it will be important to add methods and representation modes, to better map the complexities of insights generated in a radical process view, in particular when engagement regimes are studied as they are enacted in mundane, situated, local interactions.

We identify four major arguments that underline the need for a closer empirical examination and theoretical conceptualization of management knowledge, and of management more generally, in a process perspective. First, a deep ambivalence with respect to the robustness and relevance of current management knowledge in dealing with contemporary uncertainties can be observed today (Mintzberg, 2009). Second, initiatives around management innovation argue for a need to create new management knowledge (Birkinshaw et al., 2008) that is appropriate for major managerial challenges today. Third, innovation and change processes inherently imply dispersed expectations with respect to management, controversies concerning legitimacy (Pettigrew, 1985), and changing concepts of management (Mintzberg, 2004). Fourth, management knowledge makes a difference (Birkinshaw et al., 2008): management is a strategic resource with competitive implications, with respect to the ways in which businesses are developed, opportunities are realized, resources are allocated, and companies are organized and governed internally and externally.

Management research is explicitly or implicitly participating in these debates, independent of whether it researches these issues or not. In our perspective, and in line with the epistemological considerations in recent knowledge research (Tsoukas, 2005), management research on management knowledge can only be conducted in a reflexive mode, exploring the implicit and explicit premises of investigation because these premises shape why and how scientific knowledge on management knowledge is created (Czarniawska, 1999). Therefore, instead of criticizing the lack of in-depth empirical studies of management in action (Mintzberg, 2009), it is important to epistemologically reflect the inherent difficulties of studying management and management knowledge. A direct study of management knowledge and firm-specific managerial practices is difficult, because these phenomena can only be studied in their situated enactment in management-related events and episodes. Furthermore, their explication must always be studied as part of ongoing justification and routinization processes. Without a direct, in-depth access to "management in action," it is impossible to uncover the subtle activity patterns, which describe the justification and routinization of engagement regimes. A reflexive, processual research approach, which involves researchers and managers in a joint coproduction process of knowledge, provides important insights and a promising research strategy.

Constructing Identity in and around Organizations

Note

1. We thank four anonymous reviewers, the volume's editors, and in particular Steve Maguire for their excellent comments and suggestions on earlier versions of this chapter, which were very helpful for us to better understand our study, as well as to clarify our argument. We are also grateful to Robert Chia, Martha Feldman, Robin Holt, Johannes Rüegg-Stürm, and our colleagues at RISE Management Research, in particular Daniel Bartl, for comments and suggestions on earlier papers and presentations on the empirical study. We thank RISE Management Research and the Stiftung zur Förderung der systemorientierten Managementlehre, St. Gallen for their support of our research. Our special thanks go to the owner-founder-CEO of AdNovum Informatik AG, as well as current management and employees who have always been enthusiastic about sharing their insights and discussing our findings.

References

Birkinshaw, J., Hamel, G., and Mol, M. J. (2008). "Management Innovation." *Academy of Management Review*, 33/4: 825–45.
Boltanski, L. (2009). *De la critique: Précis de sociologie de l'émancipation*. Paris: Gallimard.
—— Thévenot, L. (1991). *De la justification*. Paris: Gallimard.
Bower, J. B. (1970). *Managing the Resource Allocation Process: A Study of Corporate Planning and Investment*. Boston, MA: Harvard Business School Press.
—— Gilbert, C. G. (2005). "A Revised Model of the Resource Allocation Process," in J. B. Bower and C. G. Gilbert (eds), *From Resource Allocation to Strategy*. Oxford: Oxford University Press, pp. 439–56.
Burgelman, R. A. (1983). "A Model of the Interaction of Strategic Behavior, Corporate Context, and the Concept of Strategy." *Academy of Management Review*, 8/1: 61–70.
—— (2001). *Strategy is Destiny: How Strategy-Making Shapes a Company's Future*. New York: Free Press.
—— (2002). "Strategy as Vector and the Inertia of Coevolutionary Lock-In." *Administrative Science Quarterly*, 47/2: 325–57.
Callon, M. (1986). "Some Elements of a Sociology of Translation: Domestication of the Scallops and the Fishermen of St Brieux Bay," in J. Law (ed.), *Power, Action and Belief. A New Sociology of Knowledge?* London: Routledge & Kegan Paul, pp. 196–229.
Cook, S. D. N. and Brown, J. S. (1999). "Bridging Epistemologies: The Generative Dance between Organizational Knowledge and Organizational Knowing." *Organization Science*, 10/4: 381–400.
Czarniawska, B. (1999). *Writing Management*. New York: Oxford University Press.

Denis, J. L., Langley, A., and Pineault, M. (2000). "Becoming a Leader in a Complex Organization." *Journal of Management Studies*, 37/8: 1063–99.

—— —— Rouleau, L. (2007). "Strategizing in Pluralistic Contexts: Rethinking Theoretical Frames." *Human Relations*, 60/1: 179–215.

Eisenhardt, K. M. (1989). "Building Theories from Case-Study Research." *Academy of Management Review*, 14/4: 532–50.

Elkana, Y. (1986). *Anthropologie der Erkenntnis. Die Entwicklung des Wissens als episches Theater einer listigen Wissenschaft*. Frankfurt a.M.: Suhrkamp.

Feldman, M. S. (2000). "Organizational Routines as a Source of Continuous Change." *Organization Science*, 11/6: 611–29.

—— Pentland, B. T. (2003). "Reconceptualizing Organizational Routines as a Source of Flexibility and Change." *Administrative Science Quarterly*, 48/1: 94–118.

Gomez, P.-Y. (1994). *Qualité et théorie des conventions*. Paris: Economia.

—— (1996). *Le gouvernement de l'entreprise*. Paris: InterEditions.

—— (2003). "Recherche en action: Propositions épistémologiques pour l'analyse conventionaliste," in M. Amblard (ed.), *Conventions & Management*. Bruxelles: Éditions De Boeck Université.

—— Jones, B. C. (2000). "Conventions: An Interpretation of Deep Structure in Organizations." *Organization Science*, 11/6: 696–708.

Grand, S. (2003). "Praxisrelevanz versus Praxisbezug der Forschung in der Managementforschung." *Die Betriebswirtschaft*, 63/5: 599–604.

—— Rüegg-Stürm, J. and von Arx, W. (2010). "Constructivist Epistemologies in Strategy as Practice Research," in D. Golsorkhi, L. Rouleau, D. Seidl, and E. Vaara (eds), *Cambridge Handbook of Strategy as Practice*. Cambridge: Cambridge University Press.

Grant, R. M. (1996). "Toward a Knowledge-based Theory of the Firm." *Strategic Management Journal*, 17: 109–22.

Hamel, G. and Prahalad, C. K. (1989). "Strategic Intent." *Harvard Business Review*, 67/3: 63–76.

Hernes, T. (2008). *Understanding Organization as Process*. London: Routledge.

Joas, H. (1991). *Die Kreativität des Handelns*. Frankfurt: Suhrkamp.

Johnson, G., Melin, L., and Whittington, R. (2003). "Guest Editors' Introduction: Micro Strategy and Strategizing: Towards an Activity-Based View." *Journal of Management Studies*, 40/1: 3–22.

—— Langley, A., Melin, L., and Whittington, R. (2007). *Strategy as Practice: Research Directions and Resources*. Cambridge: Cambridge University Press.

Langley, A. (1999). "Strategies for Theorizing from Process Data." *Academy of Management Review*, 24/4: 691–710.

Langley, A. (2007). "Process Thinking in Strategic Organization." *Strategic Organization*, 5/3: 271–82.

Latour, B. (1999). *Pandora's Hope: Essays on the Reality of Science Studies*. Cambridge, MA: Harvard University Press.

—— (2005). *Reassembling the Social*. Oxford: Oxford University Press.

Law, J. (2004). *After Method—Mess in Social Science Research*. Oxon: Routledge.
Leonard-Barton, D. (1992). "Core Capabilities and Core Rigidities—A Paradox in Managing New Product Development." *Strategic Management Journal*, 13: 111–25.
—— (1995). *Wellsprings of Knowledge: Building and Sustaining the Sources of Innovation*. Boston: Harvard Business School Press.
Menuhin, J. and McGee, J. (2002). "Strategizing Routines in HSBC (UK)." Paper presented at the Nelson and Winter DRUID Conferences, Aalborg.
Meyer, G. D. and Heppard, K. A. (2000). *Entrepreneurship as Strategy*. Thousand Oaks, CA: Sage Publications.
Miles, M. B. and Huberman, A. M. (1994). *Qualitative Data Analysis: An Expanded Sourcebook* (2nd edn). Thousand Oaks, CA: Sage.
Mintzberg, H. (1971). "Managerial Work: Analysis from Observation." *Management Science*, 18/2: B97–B110.
—— (1979). "Emerging Strategy of Direct Research." *Administrative Science Quarterly*, 24/4: 582–9.
—— (2004). *Managers, not MBAs: A Hard Look at the Soft Practice of Managing and Management Development*. San Francisco, CA: Berret-Koehler.
—— (2009). *Managing*. San Francisco, CA: Berrett-Koehler.
Nelson, R. R. and Winter, S. G. (1982). *An Evolutionary Theory of Economic Change*. Cambridge, MA: The Belknap Press of Harvard University Press.
Nonaka, I. (1994). "A Dynamic Theory of Organizational Knowledge Creation." *Organization Science*, 5/1: 14–37.
Orlikowski, W. J. (2002). "Knowing in Practice: Enacting a Collective Capability in Distributed Organizing." *Organization Science*, 13/3: 249–73.
Ortmann, G. (2003). *Regel und Ausnahme. Paradoxien sozialer Ordnung*. Frankfurt a. M.: Suhrkamp.
—— (2004). *Als Ob*. Wiesbaden: VS Verlag für Sozialwissenschaften.
—— (2009). *Management in der Hypermoderne: Kontingenz und Notwendigkeit*. Wiesbaden: VS Verlag für Sozialwissenschaften.
Pettigrew, A. (1985). *The Awakening Giant: Continuity and Change in ICI*. Oxford: Blackwell.
Rüegg-Stürm, J. and Grand, S. (2007). "Handlung und Reflexion in Managementpraxis und Managementforschung: Konturen einer kreativen Beziehung," in T. Eberle, S. Hoidn, and K. Sikavica (eds), *Fokus Organisation. Sozialwissenschaftliche Perspektiven und Analysen*. Konstanz: UVK Verlagsgesellschaft mbH.
Schatzki, T., Knorr-Cetina, K., and von Savigny, E. (eds) (2001). *The Practice Turn in Contemporary Theory*. London, New York: Routledge.
Schendel, D. and Hitt, M. A. (2007). "Introduction to Volume 1." *Strategic Entrepreneurship Journal*, 1/1–2: 1–6.
Spender, J. C. (1989). *The Industry Recipes: The Nature and Sources of Managerial Judgment*. Oxford: Blackwell.
—— (1996). "Organizational Knowledge, Learning and Memory: Three Concepts in Search of a Theory." *Journal of Organizational Change Management*, 9/1: 63–78.

—— (1998). "Pluralist Epistemology and the Knowledge-based Theory of the Firm." *Organization*, 5/2: 233–56.

Strauss, A. L. and Corbin, J. M. (1998). *Basics of Qualitative Research: Techniques and Procedures for Developing Grounded Theory*. Thousand Oaks, CA: Sage.

Szulanski, G. (2003). *Sticky Knowledge: Barriers to Knowing in the Firm*. London, Thousand Oaks, New Delhi: Sage.

Teece, D. J., Pisano, G., and Shuen, A. (1997). "Dynamic Capabilities and Strategic Management." *Strategic Management Journal*, 18/7: 509–33.

Thévenot, L. (2001). "Pragmatic Regimes Governing the Engagement with the World," in T. Schatzki, K. Knorr-Cetina, and E. von Savigny (eds), *The Practice Turn in Contemporary Theory*. London: Routledge, pp. 56–73.

—— (2006). *L'action au pluriel: Sociologie des régimes d'engagement*. Paris: Editions La Découverte.

Tsoukas, H. (1994). "What is Management? An Outline of a Metatheory." *British Journal of Management*, 5/4: 289–301.

—— (1996). "The Firm as a Distributed Knowledge System: A Constructionist Approach." *Strategic Management Journal*, 17: 11–25.

—— (2005). *Complex Knowledge*. Oxford: Oxford University Press.

—— Chia, R. (2002). "On Organizational Becoming: Rethinking Organizational Change." *Organization Science*, 13/5: 567–82.

—— Knudsen, C. (2002). "The Conduct of Strategy Research," in A. Pettigrew, H. Thomas, and R. Whittington (eds), *Handbook of Strategy & Management*. London: Sage, pp. 411–35.

—— Vladimirou, E. (2001). "What is Organizational Knowledge?" *Journal of Management Studies*, 38/7: 973–93.

Watson, T. J. (1986). *Management, Organisation, and Employment Strategy*. London: Routledge.

—— (1994). *In Search of Management: Culture, Chaos and Control in Managerial Work*. London: Routledge.

—— (2001). "Beyond Managism: Negotiated Narratives and Critical Management Education in Practice." *British Journal of Management*, 12/4: 385–96.

Weick, K. E. (1979). *The Social Psychology of Organizing*. Reading, MA: Addison-Wesley.

Yin, R. K. (1994). *Case Study Research: Design and Methods*. Thousand Oaks, CA: Sage.

Zollo, M. and Winter, S. G. (2002). "Deliberate Learning and the Evolution of Dynamic Capabilities." *Organization Science*, 13/3: 339–51.

12

Aligning Process Questions, Perspectives, and Explanations

Andrew H. Van de Ven and Harry Sminia

> **Abstract:** This chapter describes different kinds of research questions, process perspectives, and types of explanations to argue pragmatically that the quality and coherence of process research will be enhanced when these ingredients of process research are aligned. A distinction is made between questions about process past (what has happened?), process present (what is going on?), process future (where are we going?), and process action (what should we do?); which are then associated respectively with the historical reconstruction, becoming/emergent, unfolding, and developing/control process perspectives. Each of these research questions requires a specific and distinct type of explanation, in terms of a unique sequence of events, a key event, a generalizable pattern of events, or a social mechanism. A hierarchy of logical relationships between questions and explanations is discussed, leading to implications for management research as well as management practice.

Process studies are undertaken to examine a wide variety of research questions dealing with how and why things in individuals, groups, organizations, and other things change, come into being, disappear, and also continue to be. These questions often focus on different temporal periods of what happened in the past (How did we get here?), what is happening in the present (What is occurring?), and what will happen in the future (Where are we going?). Some of these questions are descriptive (What's going on?) and others are prescriptive (What should we do when?).

A variety of process perspectives and conceptual explanations can be used to answer these questions. By using the term process perspectives,

Aligning Process Questions, Perspectives, and Explanations

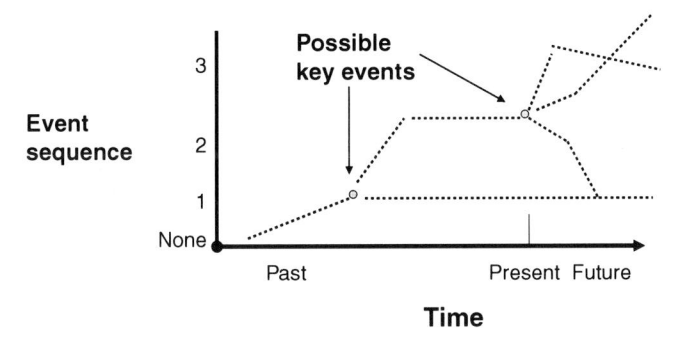

Figure 12.1 Illustration of events observed over time

we mean the epistemological approaches or methods that are taken to study processes; by using the term conceptual explanations, we mean the theories and inferences that are used as reasons in answers to process questions. In particular, we examine four perspectives on process (historical reconstruction, unfolding, becoming, and development) that Hari Tsoukas presented at the 2009 Academy of Management process research methods workshop. We consider also four different kinds of conceptual explanations: a unique event sequence, a key event in a sequence, a generalizable pattern in an event sequence, and a social mechanism that governs the pattern. Figure 12.1 illustrates three simple sequences of events (the dotted lines) occurring in the past, present, and for some organizational unit in the future, with Table 12.1 summarizing associated questions, perspectives, and types of explanation.

Table 12.1 Alignment of process questions, perspectives, and explanations

Temporal questions	Process perspectives	Conceptual explanation
Past: What has happened? How did we get here?	Historical reconstruction (of past events/experiences)	Unique sequence
Present: What is going on?	Becoming/emergent (describing the concurrence of circumstances)	Key event (in a unique sequence or generalizable pattern)
Future: Where are we going?	Unfolding (constructing/extrapolating a future from the past and present)	Generalizable pattern (with possible key events)
Action: What should we do when?	Development/control (intervening in the present to achieve a desired future outcome)	Social mechanism (motor governing a generalizable pattern and situations when it operates, plus key events that allow for interventions)

307

From the present time perspective, historical questions about the unit's past could be explained in terms of the initial simple linear sequence of events that was punctuated by a key past event that diverged the unit into following a parallel progression of two event sequences to get to the present. A historical reconstruction of the past consists of a unique sequence of events that the unit experienced. Contemporary questions about what is happening might focus on the unit trying to make sense of a key event that is unfolding at the present time. Finally, while addressing questions about what the unit might become in the future the unit members might envision the three possible directions shown in the figure and choose one of these based on the unit's past path-dependency, an environmental shock (as the key event might represent), and its future path creation opportunities. In addition to these three descriptive questions about the past, present, and future, the unit might ask a fourth prescriptive question about what it should do and when it should intervene to achieve a desired path and avoid an undesired path in the future. Answering this prescriptive question requires knowing the social mechanisms and conditions that govern these alternative process paths.

This essay examines relationships between these process questions, process perspectives, and conceptual explanations. We argue that we can increase the quality and coherence of our process studies by aligning our research questions, perspective, and explanations as outlined in Table 12.1. We take a pragmatic view in proposing that the perspectives and conceptual explanations that we use should be judged in terms of how well they address the intended question in its particular context (Dewey, 1938). We begin with a discussion of the four alignments of process research questions, perspectives, and explanations outlined in Table 12.1. After that, we discuss relationships between these alignments and their implications for advancing process studies.

12.1 Perspectives and explanations for different process questions

12.1.1 Questions about the past: How did we get here?

Historical reconstructions (of chronological events leading to a particular outcome) are needed to answer questions about the past such as, "How did we get here?" Longitudinal data obtained from archival records, real-time observations, and/or retrospective accounts are typically used to

Aligning Process Questions, Perspectives, and Explanations

historically reconstruct and narrate past events and experiences that led to a present situation. Chandler's seminal (1977) "invisible hand" would be an obvious example here. Historical reconstruction can also be found in Van de Ven et al. (1989) of the historical case studies of various innovations studied in the Minnesota Innovation Research Program, in Pettigrew (1985) in telling the story of what changed and stayed the same within ICI, and in Allison and Zelikow (1999) to describe decision-making during the Cuba missile crisis.

Howell and Prevenier (2001) describe an extensive methodology that historians have developed for constructing and narrating the occurrence of events and circumstances that led to a particular outcome. They point out that historians do not discover a past as much as they create it; they choose the events and people that they think constitute the past and decide what about them is important to know. Historians have paid careful attention to the sources and artifacts they use to interpret the past. They have developed sophisticated techniques for judging a source's authenticity, its representativeness, and its relevance. They have constructed typologies of sources, dividing them into genres that lend themselves to systematic comparative analysis, and they have invented ingenious strategies for decoding and interpreting sources. This technical work has long been considered the backbone of history writing in the West, and historians have traditionally judged the quality of their own or their colleagues' work in terms of its mastery of these skills. Seen from this point of view, the historian's basic task is to choose reliable sources, to read them reliably, and to put them together in ways that provide reliable narratives about the past (Howell and Prevenier, 2001: 1–2).

A conceptual explanation for historical questions typically consists of narrating a unique sequence of events that leads to the outcome under investigation. The explanation includes how one event leads to another and, by constructing a cause and effect chain of events, which events lead up to the particular outcome that needs to be explained. An example of a method which creates such a unique event sequence explanation is event history analysis (Heise, 1989; Griffin, 1993), which has found an application in research that tried to explain a policy change in a public body (Stevenson and Greenberg, 1998).

12.1.2 Questions about the present: What is occurring?

Questions about the present tend to view process as an emergent unfolding of a current situation. This moment could be viewed as a peak experience in kairos time or as a specific date in calendar time. In either case, the moment is a key event or immediate situation that demands interpretation and explanation connecting the past and the future. Howell and Prevenier (2001) note that historians think they need to know about a past key event because it seems to have had a direct role in making the present; sometimes historians choose their object of study simply because it seems central to a past that is important today. Historians always create a past by writing it.

When trying to make sense of a current situation, process is often viewed as an immediate becoming (Tsoukas and Chia, 2002). Relying on Bergson and Whitehead, organizational scholars such as Tsoukas and Chia (2002) and Hernes and Weik (2007) examine processes as tracing "the inner becoming of things": accounting for the process of becoming an event. Experiences are taken as the building blocks of reality. Whitehead has labeled this as "prehension," with past experiences building up and contributing to the what is happening in the present moment like the final chord of a piece of music being appreciated in a particular way because of the music that was played leading up toward it (Cobb, 2007; Langley and Tsoukas, 2010). This is a perspective that comes close to what has been referred to as "process metaphysics" (Rescher, 1996), the idea that the universe essentially is processual. Becoming methods examine manifestations of hopes, experiences, and inner workings to answer questions about the present such as "What is occurring?" To answer this kind of question, Czarniawska (2006) suggests that process scholars study structures of events rather than those of people or objects. Through sensemaking and sensegiving among organizational members, events may be interpreted as meaningful actions or random occurrences, but it is the connections among them that are central to organizing (Weick, 1995). "Events vanish if not connected to one another by the individuals to whom they happen—and they are connected with the help of expectations. Thus the structuring (connecting events) never stops and forever changes the shape of the event" (Czarniawska, 2006: 1664–5).

A conceptual explanation of the here and now typically consists of putting together a situation as a concurrence of circumstances and how this creates the key event. The sensemaking approach as put forward by Gioia and Chittipeddi (1991) and Weick (1995) is capable of creating such an explanation of the here and now (although often retrospectively). Ethnography or a painstakingly reconstructed account of what is present and happening at a certain moment in time is a favored method here, as can be gauged from Weick's account (1990) of the Tenerife air disaster or the tragic occurrences at Mann Gulch (Weick, 1993).

12.1.3 Questions about the future: Where are we going?

Answering questions about the future requires a robust understanding of how a process typically unfolds over time for a unit, the current condition, and the potential to create new paths in the future. Explanations of the future tend to be constructed by articulating and extrapolating a pattern of events from the past and the present and translating it into the likely future outcome. The plausibility of such explanations depends on whether the envisioned future reflects a generalizable pattern of past and present events and possibilities.

Scholars debate whether the future reflects a path-dependent or path creation process (Garud et al., 2010; Vergne and Durand, 2010). David (2001) defines a path-dependent process as a progression of events that is influenced by its own history. From a path-dependent perspective, Garud et al. (2010: 760) point out that actors become "locked in" by self-reinforcing mechanisms into paths whose evolution is determined by chance events and contingencies. Once locked in, actors cannot break out of self-generating feedback loops unless exogenous shocks occur. Path dependence has been used to explain both stability and change: existing institutions both persist over time and are created through novel recombinations of experiences (Arthur, 2009). Because path dependency emphasizes how history repeats itself and how contingencies and exogenous shocks influence temporal progressions, the explanations tend to reflect an outsider's, or exogenous, views of process (Hernes and Weik, 2007).

Another perspective that views change as coming from the "inside," or endogenous to the actors involved, celebrates human agency and teleology, such as found in studies of the "entrepreneurial mindset" (McGrath and MacMillan, 2000) where actors are driven by a "logic of control" to effectuate change (Sarasvathy, 2001). Such studies tend to portray leaders or entrepreneurs as heroes or victims of escalating commitments to courses of action that ended in successful or failed outcomes. Such explanations tend to be quite instrumental in assessing a progression of events in terms of some outcome determination.

In contrast, Garud et al. (2010) propose path creation as an alternative perspective. They examine process at a collective or organizational level that views agency as being distributed and emergent through the interactions of people involved in the process. Through interactions with others, people gain self-efficacy to enact, improvise, and bricolage "emergent ideas into action" and "emergent actions into ideas" (Garud et al., 2010: 762). "Emergent situations are not contingencies, but instead afford embedded actors the possibilities to pursue certain courses of action while making others more difficult to pursue. Self-reinforcing mechanisms do not just exist, but instead are cultivated" (Garud et al., 2010: 769).

12.1.4 Questions about intervention and control: What should we do when?

Questions about "What should we do when?" represent a more ambitious prescriptive undertaking than the more descriptive questions examined so far. It moves the purpose of the research from descriptive and explanatory to prescriptions of what is required to create a desired outcome. To be able to do that, there is not only a need to examine regularities in process patterns that make future courses predictable but also an ability to identify key events that allow for an intervention that sets the process toward a particular course and an ability to keep a process on course.

Managing processes assumes knowledge of developmental patterns and more particularly of controlling development. The possibility of intervention and control requires a social mechanism explanation. This type of explanation can be provided on top of both the unique sequence explanation and the two fixed sequence explanations above by concentrating on the process motor that makes these sequences occur in the first place and also by focusing on the socially constructed reality that generates the ongoing process that is created by this ongoing process. A social mechanism provides an underlying account of how cause and effect relationships come to exist between events. This mechanism provides a somewhat generalized explanation for the occurrence of the process under investigation (Mayntz, 2004) and also could provide opportunities to intervene in and control this process.

Van de Ven and Poole (1995) provide four social mechanism explanations for an organizational change process. They call the four social mechanisms process motors (teleology, life cycle, dialectics, and evolution), and each explains how a process takes shape and how a process is propelled forward through time. Each of these four process motors is based on a particular generator that is responsible for the movement in the process.

Teleology, or planned change, views development as a repetitive sequence of goal formulation, implementation, evaluation, and modification of goals based on what was learned or intended by the people involved. In this

Aligning Process Questions, Perspectives, and Explanations

model, planning or goal setting is triggered in response to a problem or opportunity that people perceive as being sufficiently important to put the process in motion. People are assumed to be purposeful and adaptive; they construct an envisioned end state, take action to reach it, and monitor their progress.

A *life cycle* model depicts the process of change in an entity as progressing through a prescribed sequence of stages or phases. Change in a life cycle tends to be morphogenic, involving qualitative shifts from one stage to the next as the unit develops. While there may be continuous development within stages in a life cycle theory, transitions from one stage to the next involve discontinuous changes in the unit and sometimes in the nature of the developmental process itself. Life cycle models comprise repeating milestones that take the unit from inception to completion or fulfillment. Once the end of a cycle has been attained, the process is set to commence anew, either with the same or a different entity.

Dialectical theories explain stability and change in terms of the relative balance of power between opposing entities (Van de Ven and Poole, 1995). Stability is produced through struggles and accommodations that maintain the status quo between oppositions. Change and innovation occur when challengers gain sufficient power to confront and engage incumbents. In dialectical processes, the current thesis or arrangement (A) is challenged by an opposing group espousing an antithesis (Not-A), that sets the stage for producing a synthesis (Not Not-A). This synthesis becomes the new thesis as the dialectical process recycles and continues. By its very nature, the synthesis is something new, discontinuous with thesis and antithesis.

Campbell (1969) introduced a model of variation, selection, and retention to explain *evolutionary* processes of change. Variations, the creation of novel forms, are often viewed as emerging by blind or random chance; they just happen. Selection occurs principally through the competition among forms, and the environment selects those forms that optimize or are best suited for the resource base of an environmental niche. Retention involves the forces and routines that perpetuate and maintain certain organizational forms (Aldrich and Reuf, 2006). Evolutionary change unfolds as a recurrent, cumulative, and probabilistic progression of variation, selection, and retention of organizational entities.

Whether and how each of these process motors operates and affects the course of a process is dependent on contingent circumstances (Tsoukas, 1989). Contingent circumstances identify when one or more of the social mechanisms are actually operating, and in more concrete terms what particular internal logic, end state, variation, or contradiction is driving the process. It is by way of manipulating the operation of these process motors that the process can be managed. Because we are dealing with social processes, the contingent circumstances that allow for such manipulation are essentially emergent social constructions and interactions; they appear as the process unfolds over time. It is also during the social construction of these contingent conditions that possibilities for managing the course of the process may be found. To be able to actually manage and affect the course of the process, the process pattern must feature key events that offer a possibility for intervention and changing the course or a possibility for control and keeping the course on track.

Many studies of various processes of continuity and change either implicitly or explicitly develop an understanding of the course of the process in terms of one or more of Van de Ven and Poole's process motors (1995). For instance, De Rond (2003) found that the process of strategic alliancing has been described in various ways, but each description fits with a particular process motor. There are not many studies that ask the extra question of how to harness the powers inherent in a process motor. One such a study has been done by Burgelman and Grove (2007). They describe the effect of variation as a consequence of strategic initiatives and the subsequent evolutionary process that dismisses or retains them as a powerful mechanism for corporate longevity, especially when it is synchronized with what is going on in the environment. It is this synchronization that they believe will enable top management to have the firm surviving through alternating periods of continuity and change.

12.2 Discussion

There are many different ways to conduct process studies. There is no single, best, or preferred way to conduct process studies. However, not every way is equally appropriate. We discussed four ways to align process research questions, methods, and explanations. We argue that researchers can increase the rigor and quality of their process studies by aligning their research questions, perspectives, and explanations. As different research questions beget different perspectives and explanations, it is important to align our conceptual explanations with the research questions that we ask and the methods we use to do a process study. A pragmatic approach to conducting process studies is to use the research methods that are appropriate for the questions being studied.

Aligning Process Questions, Perspectives, and Explanations

Some scholars may express preferences for certain process perspectives and explanations, and believe that others may be too objectivistic or out of date. The domain of process studies includes a "big tent." Given the great variety of questions, perspectives, and explanations being examined in this big tent, there is no need to state preferences and take sides on which perspectives and explanations to use. Instead, we argue that different perspectives and explanations are appropriate for different types of process questions.

There is a certain hierarchy in the type of questions and explanations that we have put forward, but there is not a strict one-on-one relationship between question and explanation. Take, for instance, the "How did we get there?" question. The unique sequence has been put forward as the most suited explanation for this type of question. There are many elements in the course of events that would have led up to the situation that needs to be explained. The elements can be expected to be unique to this course and give this process its individuality. However, this same process course can display communalities with process courses found elsewhere to the extent that it also conforms to a more general pattern. In that sense, the general pattern can be part of the explanation as well. A similar argument can be made for the key event explanation. The answer to "How did we get here?" could be that an earlier key event was pivotal in bringing about the present.

These (and other) alternative explanations reflect an ongoing tension between history and sociology in historical context (Griffin, 1993; Calhoun, 1998; Goldstone, 1998; Büthe, 2002). Should sociological theory (reflected in presumed general process patterns) inform historical reconstruction (Kiser and Hechter, 1998), or should historical reconstruction be a pure narrative without preconceived process theories about a course of events (Somers, 1998)? A related question is whether historical reconstruction can be used as a grounded theory-building methodology (Glaser and Strauss, 1967) to construct more generic process patterns or if it can be used to map alternative preformulated process theories in order to explain an observed event sequence (Van de Ven and Poole, 1995).

This tension was discussed in Whipp and Clark (1986) when they explained about how they reconstructed the innovation process that produced the Rover SD1 car. They described the various traditions and approaches that exist among historians, and decided to stay on the middle ground between narrative and analytical schema. With regard to the examples of historical reconstruction research mentioned earlier, the ambition of Pettigrew (1985) and Van de Ven et al. (1989) was to develop an understanding of the process of innovation and the process of strategy formation, respectively, which would be relevant beyond the cases that were investigated. In other words, historical reconstruction was a means of grounded theory building to develop and propose more general process patterns. Allison and Zelikow (1999) provide an example of three existing process models, labeled as rational actor, organizational behavior, and governmental politics that they utilize to understand one and the same process.

A hierarchy of logical relationships becomes apparent as we explore these process research questions and types of explanation. The process pattern or process theory that is needed to be able to articulate and extrapolate the future and answer the "Where are we going?" question could be generated and validated by earlier historical reconstructions from which these general patterns have been induced. The "How did we get here?" answer has to precede the "Where are we going?" question simply because without such a precedent, there is nothing to base any expectation on. Similarly, the argument can be made that to be able to answer the "What is occurring?" question in terms of concurring circumstances, there needs to be some kind of preconceived idea or process theory that informs the researcher which circumstances need to be taken into account and what each circumstance's contribution is. This process theory needs to allow some way for the identification of the key event that makes up the here and now. The "How did we get here?" question needs to be answered first in terms of some kind of process theory before we are able to do this. This is even truer for the "What should we do when?" question; this question relies on assessing with sufficient confidence that the here and now offers a key event with the possibility of changing the course of the process. With sufficient certainty, this assessment has to combine with its expected future trajectory so that the desired end can be expected to be realized.

It would be too much to expect that there always will be answers to the four questions. It was already noted that the "What should we do when?" question is particularly ambitious as it requires a level of predetermination and control that would not be realistic to expect all the time. If this was the case, the earlier process trajectory of path creation (Garud et al., 2010) would not be possible and the whole notion of creativity would be meaningless. There are and will always be instances and occasions when a process going forward simply is a journey into the unknown with no opportunity for management control. To a lesser extent, it could be possible to know in advance the various destinations where a process might end up, but the situation lacks the control to make it go off into a particular desirable direction. It could also be the case that to have a process remain on track, a continuous management effort would be required. Similar reservations can be made with regard to the other questions.

From a managerial point of view, the "What should we do when?" question is the most interesting one, because management can be seen as being about actively engaging with the course of a process, either by controlling it and keeping it on track or by intervening with the process and changing its course (Sminia, 2009). As it was stated earlier, to do that with some confidence about its effectiveness, an understanding of process in terms of regular patterns and key events is required. This demands a research effort to find out about process patterns and about the possibilities for control and intervention that might exist. An answer to the "How did we get here?" question in terms of a unique sequence by itself makes little contribution to finding a more general process pattern unless the explanation forms the basis for an inductive effort in theory construction. The same can be said about the "What is occurring?" question and the key event explanation. If there are generic qualities about the key event and if it offers opportunities for control or intervention, it can play a role in management theory. This means that from a managerial perspective, the purpose of process research should be finding out about regularity in process patterns and validating them into process theory while specifying whether the process allows for the creation of key events that offer a possibility for control or intervention.

References

Aldrich, H. and Ruef, M. (2006). *Organizations Evolving*. London: Sage.

Allison, G. T. and Zelikow, P. (1999). *Essence of Decision: Explaining the Cuban Missile Crisis*. New York: Longman.

Arthur, W. B. (2009). *The Nature of Technology: What it is and How it Evolves*. New York: Free Press.

Burgelman, R. A. and Grove, A. S. (2007). "Let Chaos Reign, then Rein in Chaos—Repeatedly: Managing Strategic Dynamics for Corporate Longevity." *Strategic Management Journal*, 28: 965–79.

Büthe, T. (2002). "Taking Temporality Seriously: Modelling History and the Use of Narratives as Evidence." *American Political Science Review*, 96/3: 481–93.

Calhoun, C. (1998). "Explanation in Historical Sociology: Narrative, General Theory, and Historically Specific Theory." *American Journal of Sociology*, 104/3: 846–71.

Campbell, D. P. (1969). "Variation and Selective Retention in Socio-cultural Evolution." *General Systems*, 16: 69–85.

Chandler, Jr., A. D. (1977). *The Visible Hand: The Managerial Revolution in American Business*. Cambridge, MA: Belknap Press.

Cobb, J. B. (2007). "Person-in-Community: Whiteheadian Insights into Community and Institution." *Organization Studies*, 28/4: 567–88.

Czarniawska, B. (2006). "A Golden Braid: Allport, Goffman, Weick." *Organization Studies*, 27/11: 1661–74.

David, P. A. (2001). "Path Dependence, its Critics and the Quest for 'Historical Economics,'" in P. Garrouste and S. Ioannides (eds), *Evolution and Path Dependence in Economic Ideas: Pas and Present*. Cheltenham: Edward Elgar, pp. 15–40.

De Rond, M. (2003). *Strategic Alliances as Social Facts*. Cambridge: Cambridge University Press.

Dewey, J. (1938). *Logic: The Theory of Inquiry*. New York, NY: Holt.

Garud, R., Kumaraswamy, A., and Karnoe, P. (2010). "Path Dependence or Path Creation." *Journal of Management Studies*, 47/4: 760–74.

Gioia, D. A. and Chittipeddi, K. (1991). "Sensemaking and Sensegiving in Strategic Change Initiation." *Strategic Management Journal*, 12: 433–48.

Glaser, B. G. and Strauss, A. L. (1967). *The Discovery of Grounded Theory: Strategies for Qualitative Research*. Chicago, IL: Aldine.

Goldstone, J. A. (1998). "Initial Conditions, General Laws, Path Dependence, and Explanation in Historical Sociology." *American Journal of Sociology*, 104/3: 829–45.

Griffin, L. J. (1993). "Narrative, Event-Structure Analysis, and Causal Interpretation in Historical Sociology." *American Journal of Sociology*, 98/5: 1094–133.

Heise, D. R. (1989). "Modelling Event Structures." *Journal of Mathematical Sociology*, 14: 139–69.

Hernes, T. and Weik, E. (2007). "Organization as Process: Drawing a Line between Endogenous and Exogenous View." *Scandinavian Journal of Management*, 23: 251–64.

Howell, M. and Prevenier, W. (2001). *From Reliable Sources: An Introduction to Historical Methods*. Ithaca, NY: Cornell University Press.

Kiser, E. and Hechter, M. (1998). The Debate on Historical Sociology: Rational Choice Theory and its Critics." *American Journal of Sociology*, 104/3: 785–816.

Langley, A. and Tsoukas, H. (2010). "Introducing 'Perspectives on Process Organization Studies'," in T. Hernes and S. Maitliss (eds), *Process, Sensemaking, and Organizing*. Oxford: Oxford University Press, pp. 1–25.

Mayntz, R. (2004). "Mechanisms in the Analysis of Social Macro-phenomena." *Philosophy of the Social Sciences*, 34/2: 237–59.

McGrath, R. G. and MacMillan, I. (2000). *The Entrepreneurial Mindset*. Boston, MA: Harvard Business School Press.

Pettigrew, A. M. (1985). *The Awakening Giant: Continuity and Change in ICI*. Oxford: Basil Blackwell.

Rescher, N. (1996). *Process Metaphysics*. Albany, NY: State University of New York Press.

Sarasvathy, S. (2001). "Causation and Effectuation: Toward a Theoretical Shift from Economic Inevitability to Entrepreneurial Contingency." *Academy of Management Review*, 26: 243–63.

Sminia, H. (2009). "Process Research in Strategy Formation: Theory, Methodology, and Relevance." *International Journal of Management Reviews*, 11/1: 97–125.

Somers, M. R. (1998). "'We're no Angels': Realism, Rational Choice, and Relationality in Social Science." *American Journal of Sociology*, 104/3: 722–84.

Stevenson, W. B. and Greenberg, D. N. (1998). "The Formal Analysis of Narratives of Organizational Change." *Journal of Management*, 24/6: 741–62.

Tsoukas, H. (1989). "The Validity of Idiographic Research Explanations." *Academy of Management Review*, 14/4: 551–61.

—— Chia, R. (2002). "On Organizational Becoming: Rethinking Organizational Change." *Organization Science*, 13/5: 567–82.

Van de Ven, A. H. and Poole, M. S. (1995). "Explaining Development and Change in Organizations." *Academy of Management Review*, 20: 510–40.

—— Angle, H. L., and Poole, M. S. (eds) (1989). *Research on the Management of Innovation: The Minnesota Studies*. New York: Harper & Row.

Vergne, J. and Durand, R. (2010). "The Missing Link between the Theory and Empirics of Path Dependence: Conceptual Clarification, Testability Issue, and Methodological Implications." *Journal of Management Studies*, 47: 736–59.

Weick, K. E. (1990). "The Vulnerable System: An Analysis of the Tenerife Air Disaster." *Journal of Management*, 16/3: 571–93.

—— (1993). "The Collapse of Sensemaking in Organizations: The Mann Gulch Disaster." *Administrative Science Quarterly*, 38/4: 628–52.

—— (1995). *Sensemaking in Organizations*. Thousand Oaks, CA: Sage.

Whipp, R. and Clark, P. (1986). *Innovation and the Auto Industry*. London: Frances Pinter.

Index

Figures and tables indexed in bold.

abduction 202–3, 205–6
actions 26, 73, 197, 208, 253
  theory 265
actors 37, 73, 75, 155–6, 205, 215, 311
  and changing environments 246–7
adaptive instability 96, 97
After Virtue (MacIntyre) 128
agency 15, 144, 248
  and uncertainty 265
  distributed 311
  triadic 202
  see also human agency
agentic momentum 238, 246, 250**t**, 256
agentic power, *see* human agency
Albert, S. 24, 67
Amburgey, T. L. 241, 244, 246
American Dream 73, 74
Anderson, B. 130
architextual frames 209, 223, 229
artisan 110, 111, 117
asymmetry 182, 183–4, 191–2, 194
Atkinson, J. M. 170
audiences 115
  preferences and social judgment 108, 110, 111, 116
  authoritative insider identity 108, 109, 112, 115

Bakhtin, M. M. 133, 213, 214, 216, 252
  theory of chronotopes 201–30
bankers 13, 147–8, 149–50, 157, 158, 159, 166, 169, 173
  moral character 163
  seen as villains 7, 13, 74, 147–74
Banking Crisis meeting (2009) 159
Barings Bank 157–8
Barley, S. R. 213
Barry, D. 206
Bartlett, F. 138, 139, 140, 142
Bartunek, J. 80

Beck, N. 241
becoming 1, 4, 10, 16, 36–7, 211
  and identity 53, 182, 184
  multiplicity of 14, 181–2
  of things 310
being 51
  and *becoming* 3–4, 10
belief structures 244, 251
Bergson, H. 210, 211, 213, 310
Bhattacharya, C. 72
Billig, M. 136
Bogen, D. 156
Boje, D. M. 167, 206, 209
both-and framing 53
boundaries 75, 76
BP plc 63–4
Bouchikhi, H. 254
Break Even Time (BET) 224
breweries 109–10, 111, 116
Britain, *see* United Kingdom
Bronze Soldier (statue, Tallinn) 131–4, 134**f**, 135, 136–7, 143
Brown, A. D. 155, 156, 157, 158, 167, 168
Brown, G. 170
Browning, R. D. 203
Brüderl, J. 241
Bruner, J. 128, 129, 206
building blocks 69, 83, 90, 115, 118, 148, 310
building safety 204, 219, 224–7
  time schedule 224**f**
  traditional chronotopes 225, 225**f**, 226**t**, 228–9
Bull organization 219, 221, 223
bureaucractic state 77
bureaucracy 254
Butler, R. 215, 216

Campbell, D. P. 313
Canada 104
  pipeline accident 154

321

Index

Cartesian body-mind dualism 211
categories 75, 150
causality 184, 186
   symmetrical concept of 184
Cerulo, K. A. 68
chain of events 309
Chandler, A. D. 309
change 8–9, 53, 58, 120, 237, 301
   emerging patterns 274, 288**t**
   evolutionary 313
character assassination 160
character definition 204
character-defining commitments 35
Cheney, G. 40, 41
Chia, R. 53, 57, 66, 213
Chittipeddi, K. 310
Chomsky, N. 58
chordal triad 248
Chronos 212–3
chronotopes 14, 201–30
   building industry 225, 225**f**
      traditional 226**t**, 225–6
   Deleuze on 216
   of manufacturing 222**t**
   new 222**f**, 223**t**
cinema 186–7, 189
claim-making 66
Clayman, S. E. 161, 170
Cloudswitch 34–6
cognition 138, 140, 141, 143, 149, 151, 172
collective actions 72, 137, 205, 300
collective identities 27, 119, 120, 129–30, 145, 155–6, 168
collective memories 141, 142–4
   "we-ness" 142
collectives 144–5
collectivization 287, 289, 299
complexity 2, 36, 40, 79–80, 83
   of time 188, 192
competition 290–1, 313
computer industry 203, 219–20
   chronotopes 221, 221**f**
   manufacturing 220–2, 222**t**, 223
conflict management 41
confluence 149
contingency perspective 81, 83, 251, 257, 311
continuity 8, 15, 24, 27, 93, 144, 182, 281, 314
contradictory identity 151, 153
controversial issues 264, 276, 296, 299
   emerging 291**t**, 275, 297**f**
convention theory 264, 270–1, 296, 298
   and engagement regimes 264–6

Conversational Analysis (CA) 168, 171, 172
Crabtree, C. 136
Critical Discourse Analysis (CDA) 171
cultural capital 76–7
cultural frames 72–3, 80, 81
cultural psychology 128
cultural repertoires 73, 79
cultural resources 11, 63, 81, 82
culture 76, 92–3
   as toolkit 99, 139
   definition 68–9
   forms 69, 79–80, 81
   mechanisms 63–70**t**–1**t**, 71–79, 79**f**, 80–88
   models 10–11
   theory 69, 75
Cunliffe, A. L. 209
customer service 223
Czarniawska, B. 310

Davis, G. 71
De Rond, M. 314
deadlines 242, 251
Dean, J. 153, 154
decision-making 115, 241, 243, 261, 282, 309
   and routinization 284**t**, 282–3
Deleuze, G. 180–97, 216–18
democracy 77
description, as identity discourse 148, 153–6, 167
description of events 160
destiny 186
dialectical theories 312, 313
dialogical interactions 202
diegesis 209
Difference and Repetition (Deleuze) 182, 184
discursive devices (DDs) 147, 148, 158, 166–7, 173, 174
discursive psychology (DP) 13, 148–9, 163, 165–6, 167–70
   and discourse analysis 171
   and language 172–3
   identity perspective 152**t**, 173–4
disidentification 113, 114
division of labour 202, 205, 206, 215
doing 26
dualism 2, 210
   Cartesian body-mind 211
duality 10, 90
Dukerich, J. M. 27, 72
Duncan, R. B. 245, 246, 250, 251
Dunn, R. E. 136
Dunnett, A. 153

Index

Dutton, J. E. 27, 72, 245, 246, 250, 251

Edwards, D. 155
elite positioning 76–7
Elliott, R. 215
Elmes, M. 206
Elsbach, N. 72
emergent momentum 243–5, 246, 248
  present focused 252
Emirbayer, M. 238, 241, 246, 247, 248, 249, 251, 252, 255
empathy 163, 166–7
emplotment 204, 212
enacted identity,
  see identity enactment
engagement regimes 16, 266, 271, 274, 275–6, 290, 296, 298, 299, 301
  and emerging patterns of change 288**t**, 290
  and management knowledge 264–6, 274–5, 296, 298
  and management 275–6, 277**f**, 298
  firm-specific 275–6, 293, 299–300
  managerial activities 297**t**
  multiple 272–3**t**
  situated 290, 296
  over time 287
entrepreneurs 268, 269, 289, 290, 292, 295–6, 311
environmental adaptation 93, 96–7, 110, 111, 116, 119, 314
  and role of peers 113
epistemology 52, 207, 211, 229, 300, 301, 307
Estonia, and Russia 130–3, 137
eternal return (Nietzsche) 186
ethics 155–6
ethnocentric narcissism 141
ethnographic studies 16
ethnomethodology 168, 172, 173, 229
exploratory momentum 15, 235, 238, 243, 245, 246, 254–6

Fairclough, N. 170, 171
fascism 132, 133, 138, 139
Feldman, M. S. 253
financial crisis 147, 148
  and bankers 159
  described as tsunami 154–5
  policy responses 166, 174
  public hearings into 148, 153–4
  sensemaking 157
Fine, G. 73, 75

flow of time 182, 182
  emergent momentum 249
  inherent momentum 253–4
  momentum 248**f**
folk tales 138–9
footing 160, 162, 166–7, 170
formalization 254, 287, 299
Forray, J. M. 215, 216
Foucault, M. 211, 212
frame-breaking change 237
Friesen, P. H. 239, 241, 242
Frye, N. 129
Fuld, R. 154
future 246, 247, 251, 254–5, 306, 311, 312, 316
  dimensions of 195, 196–7, 237–9

Garud, R. 311, 312
Geertz, C. 68
generalized other 36–7, 38
Genette, G. 208
Gephart, R. P. 154, 173
Gergen, K. J. 149, 150, 151, 169
Gersick, C. J. F. 242, 243, 255, 256
Gilbert, N. 169
Gioia, D. A. 310
Glynn, M. A. 80
Goffman, E. 172, 173
Goodman, M. B. 236
Goodwin, F. 161, 162, 163
governance 268
  and routinization 283**t**, 282, 298
government inaction 253
Greenwood, R. 252
Gregory, D. 214
Grove, A. S. 314
grounding strategies 58

Halifax 159
HBOS 159, 160, 163
Heisenberg Principle 52
Heraclitus 183
Hernes, G. 71
Hewlett-Packard (HP) 223, 224
historical perspectives 315, 316
Honda 36
Hornby, A. 159, 160, 161, 163
Howell, M. 309, 310
human agency 25, 93, 96, 108, 119–20, 238, 311
human beings 211
Hume, D. 189
Humphries, M. 167, 168

Index

Hutchby, I. 151

identification 25, 26, 28, 41, 42
identity 2, 5–6, 17, 27–8, 170
  and *becoming* 53, 182, 184
  concepts of 7, 8, 24, 31, 51–2, 54
  definition 56
  dialogical approach 168
  discursive psychology 148–51, 53
  as process and flow 50–60
  processes 2–4, 5, 9, 10, 12, 21–2, 23, 25, 27, 30, 31, 33**f**, 39, 39**f**, 40–1, 43, 51, 55, 181
  uses made of 150
identity and time, Deleuze on 13–14, 180–97
identity claims 10, 11, 26, 35, 37, 63–4, 76, 77, 78, 98, 100, 104, 105**t**, 106, 109, 110, 112, 114, 115, 117, 119, 149, 151
  collective 168
identity construction 28, 29, 54, 78, 81, 171–2
identity dynamics 4, 5, 26, 31, 42, 43, 55–6, 60, 96
identity enactment 98, 99, 106**f**, 108, 116, 117, 120, 121
  audience judgment 112
  disidentification 113, 114, 116
  image-vision alignment 109–10
identity formation 11, 26, 27, 90–1, 92, 99, 110, 111, 119, 121
  dynamics 117–18
  processes 107**t**
identity imprinting 99, 100, 106**f**, 108, 110, 115, 116, 119–20, 121
  causal chain 106
  critical decision-making 108–9
  strategic emulation 113
  value proposition 111
identity reservoirs 98–9, 108, 109, 111, 112, 115, 116–17, 121
identity sources 115–16, 121
ideology 72
image 109, 120, 144
image-vision alignment 109–10, 112
imaged communities 130
inconsistencies 153
incremental change 237, 241, 242, 244, 245
individual identity 168
individualism 93
  modern 129
induction 202–3
inertia,
  see momentum, and inertia
informal organization 93–4

inherent momentum 241, 242, 246, 254, 257
  and flow of time 253
  see also momentum
innovation 237, 279**t**, 286, 292, 301
  process 315–6
  and technology 281
inquiries 202–3
  critical 229
  pragmatist sense 205, 208
institutionalization 67–8
institutions 77
  mechanisms 78
intellectual property 129
interactions 120, 205, 221, 245, 274, 282, 286, 311–12
intervention, and control 312–14, 317
interviews 101–2, 102**t**, 103–4, 109, 121–2**ap**
intuition 211
Iran-Contra hearings 154
isomorphic alignment 78, 79, 80
isomorphic process 6, 68, 69
isomorphism 210
iterative cycles 100

James, W. 142, 143, 144
Jansen, K. J. 236
Justification 15, 16, 262–3, 265, 266, 274, 275–6, 290–1, 296, 299, 300–1
  bias 300
  innovation 279**t**, 276
  management 276
  organization 279–80**t**, 276
  success 278**t**, 276
  uncertainty 296
justified true beliefs 299

Kairos 212–13, 309–10
Karnoe, P. 311, 312
Kelly, D. 246
key performance indicators 276
Kihlstrom, J. F. 142
Kimberly, J. R. 246
knowing 262, 265, 298
Kornberger, M. 155, 156
Kraatz, M. 36
Kumaraswamy, A. 311, 312

labels 80, 166
Langley, A. 58, 59, 149
language 4, 21, 23, 28, 29, 34, 129–30, 132, 170, 172, 173, 211, 252
Lawson, N. 155
learning cycles 211

324

Index

Lefebvre, H. 212
legacy 80, 194–5
legitimacy 141, 167, 173, 174 , 191, 301
legitimation 11, 77, 78, 79, 82, 117
lifecycle 34, 81, 119–20, 22, 241–2, 312
linguistics 50, 52, 80, 148, 158, 168, 171–2, 173
liquidity 255
Lloyds TSB 161
logic of control 311
logical relationships 316
logistics 223
Luhman, J. T. 209
Lynch, M. 156

MacIntyre, A. 128, 129
management 264, 271, 286, 289, 301
  concepts 274, 296, 297**f**, 300–1
  multiple engagements 271, 272–3**t**
  research 268
  succession 299
  team 287, 289
  uncertainty 268, 298, 299
management-in-action 264, 301
management knowledge 261–302
  uncertainty 293, 298–9, 309**f**
management research 268, 301–2
management practices 14, 15–16, 298
managerial activities 297**f**
managerial agency 246
managerial knowing 16
managerial knowledge 15, 16
  process view 275**f**
  uncertainty 267
managers 251, 253
  actions 243–4
managing 261–2
Mann, J. (MP) 159, 160, 161, 162, 170
manufacturing,
  see computer industry, manufacturing
markets 77, 80
Markus, H. 25, 32
Marquis, C. 7
McAdams, D. 128, 129
McKinlay, A. 153
Mead, G. H. 31, 32, 33, 36, 37, 38, 246, 247, 250
meaning-making inquiries 205, 229
  diegetic levels 205
mediation 204
membership categorization 161
memory 143
  individual 141–2, 144

"me-ness" 142, 143, 144
Merleau-Ponty, M. 211
metalepsis 217–19, 220
metaphors 52, 142, 148, 236, 241, 244, 246, 252, 284
metaphysics, Deleuze on 182, 183
microbrewers 5, 11
microbreweries (Netherlands) 91, 98, 100–2, 115, 119, 121
  promotion of local region 109
middle-aged women 151-2
Miller, D. 239, 241, 242
mimesis 205–6, 209
Minor, A. S. 241, 242, 244
minor chords 249
Mische, A. 238, 241, 246, 247, 248, 249, 251, 252, 255
mnemonic communities 7, 12, 141, 142, 145
  Russia 139, 140, 141
  and Estonia 130, 132–3, 135–8, 143
modern bureaucracy 93
Mohr, L. B. 22, 56
momentum 15, 256
  and agency 245, 247–9
  and inertia 235–7, 241, 242, 243, 256
  and time 237
  agentic 238, 246, 250**t**, 256–7
  change-based 244
  definition 239
  future–oriented 242
  of organizational change 235–6, 240**t**, 241
  stasis-based momentum 236, 244
  typology 256, 257
  see also emergent momentum; exploratory momentum; flow of time; inherent momentum
moral character 156, 162–3
morality 155, 157
moral positioning 148
  contradictory 155
Mulkay, M. 169
myths 74, 115

narrative inquiries 229
narrative mimesis 205
narrative processes 204–5
narrative templates 138, 139, 141, 143
  and Russia 139–40, 141
narrative tools 130, 136, 137, 138, 144
narratives 6, 7, 8, 11, 12, 13, 14, 27, 43, 58, 65, 69, 74, 75, 79, 80, 82, 128–9, 137, 138, 157, 192, 194

Index

narratives (cont.)
  competing 167
  as cultural tools 144
  financial crisis 148
  studies 203
Nash, G. B. 136
nation-states 12, 130
national identity 130, 136, 138
national narratives 130, 136–7, 143
  and collective memory 142
natural laws 184
Navis, C. 80
Nayak, A. 211
Netherlands 11
  microbreweries 91, 98, 100–4, 115, 119, 121
New Zealand, and racism 151, 173–4
Newton, I. 202, 239, 242, 244, 247
Nietzsche, F. 186
nonfalsifiability 140, 143
normalization 289, 299
North, O. 154, 156, 157
not-for-profit organizations 156
nouns 28, 50, 51
NVIVO 8 104

O'Connor, E. S. 237
old institutionalism 90–1, 93, 100, 106, 115, 121
  and organizational identity 94–5**t**, 97, 102, 108, 119
ontology 2, 56, 57, 92, 118
  of action 207
organizational change 14–15, 52, 53, 56–7, 167, 237, 241–2, 252, 256
  radical 242
organizational culture 32, 52, 92, 251
organizational identities 10, 11, 55, 114, 120–1, 168
  construction 63–70**t**–1**t**, 71– 88
  culture 10, 11
  definition 99
  theory 79, 90, 93, 97
    model 99**t**
organizational image 26–7, 104
organizational knowledge,
  taken-for-granted 263–4
organizational self 33**f**, 38
organizations 186
  and normative core 93, 96
  in flux 96
  form dynamics 118
  not-for-profit 156

peer identities 108, 113
uncertainty 298, 299
organizing 1, 10, 14, 15, 17, 57, 67
  chronotopes applied to 201–30
  narrations 206
  praxeological view of 206, 229
  processes 203, 206, 207–8, 215, 229
organizing strategies 58
  toolkits 92–3
Orlikowski, W. J. 213

partnerships 292
past 193, 196–7, 257, 306, 308, 310
  and meaning 247–8
  and relationship 248
  in organizations 237–9, 246, 249–51, 254–5, 311
path creation 311
path-dependency 16, 308, 311
peer organizations 113, 115, 116, 118
Peirce, C. S. 202, 205, 206
Pentland, B. T. 253
Perlow, L. 212
Pettigrew, A. M. 315, 316
phenomenology 51
Plato 182, 183
plotting,
  see emplotment
policy changes 309
politicians 159, 166, 170
Poole, M. S. 312
Port Authority of New York and New Jersey 72
post-structuralism 171
Potter, J. 151, 156, 173
practice theory 265
Pratt, M. G. 9, 16, 36
prehension 310
present(s):
  multiplicity of 190–1, 193–4, 195, 196–7
  organizational change 237, 238, 239, 251
  studies 247, 249–50, 257, 306, 308, 309–11
Prevenier, W. 309, 310
Principles of Psychology, The (James) 142
problem solving 111
process metaphysics 310
process motors, *see* social mechanisms
process perspectives 1–2, 7–8, 9–10, 24, 301–2, 307, 307**t**, 315
  and identity 4, 5–6, 13, 43
  macro-level 10
process philosophy 1, 13
  identity and time 180–97

326

Index

process studies 306, 314
process theories 3, 7, 8, 22, 24, 27, 28, 43, 56, 58, 90, 120, 300, 316–17
 and DP 169
process thinking 4, 5
process worldview 1, 24, 25
processes:
 expecting and accepting 37
 expressing and reflecting 37
 identity dynamics 42–3
 integrative processes 37–8
 unique to identity 41–2
products 218–21, 223–4
project management 287
pronouns 162–3
 collective 166–7
Propp, V. 138, 139
proto-identity attributes 98, 100, 104, 106, 108, 109, 110, 111, 112, 113, 114, 117, 119, 121
public hearings 166, 167, 173
 into financial crisis (UK) 148, 153–4, 158–9
punctuated equilibrium 243
pure past 192–4, 195, 196
 see also past
Putin, V. 134–5

questioning 4, 9, 10, 16–17, 22, 23, 41, 43, 50, 54, 103, 129, 155, 156, 162, 203, 306, 307**t**, 310, 312, 314, 316–17
 alignment of process 308
Quinn, R. E. 53

Ravasi, D. 54
RBS Group plc 161, 163
reality 183
reflexology 211
relationships 254
religion/science 77
replicating strategies 58
Report of the Congressional Committee (USA) 156
resource allocation 285**t**, 282, 286
rhetoric 252
Ricoeur, P. 206, 207, 209
river (as image) 182
roadblocks 252–3
Roberts, K. H. 206
roles 25–6
 organizations 34, 66
 peers in 113
routinization 264–5, 266, 274, 275–6, 281–2, 290, 296, 299–301

 and decision-making 284**t**, 282
 and governance 283**t**, 282, 298
 resource allocation 285**t**, 286
 uncertainty 296
Rubin, E. 34, 35
Russia 130
 and Estonia 131–7, 143
 revision of history textbooks 136

Schacter, D. 138
schemas 25, 72, 73, 138–9
schematization 253
Schult, M. 54
screams 216, 217, 218, 226, 229, 230
self 4, 6, 9, 23, 26, 31–2, 37, 38, 73, 143, 168
 accounts of 155
 presentation of 172–3, 174
self-formation 36–7, 40, 42
self-making 155, 170
self-process 32
 identity 38, 39**f**, 40
Selznick, P. 67, 68
sensegiving 40, 42, 92, 115, 119, 120, 310
sensemaking 5–6, 26, 40, 41, 42, 52, 65–6, 92, 115, 117, 119, 154, 166, 310
 and organizing 202
 collective 92, 97, 98
 disaster 173
 financial crisis 157
separation 289–90, 299
Shotter, J. 168, 252
Silicon Valley 237
Smith, R. 140
social actions 151, 169
social actors 57, 115, 118–20
 organizations 65, 66, 69, 76, 82, 99
social constructions 28, 57, 68, 96, 115, 118–20, 149, 172, 245, 314
social identity 150
Social Identity Theory (SIT) 172
social interactions 149, 150, 159, 168, 211
social mechanisms 312, 314
social worlds 52–3, 54
Socrates 183
Software AG 267–8, 281, 295–6
 data collection 269–70
 ownership 269
 research setting 268–9
software companies 268, 281
software development 287
Solzhenitsyn, A. 140
Soviet Union 130
speakers 150, 155, 156, 160, 161

327

Index

speaking 129, 140, 153, 154
  and identity position 155
specific narratives 138, 139, 140, 141, 203
  see also narrative templates 139
specificity 138
Spicer, A. 215
stakeholders 26, 60, 65, 75, 115, 244, 254
stasis-based momentum 236, 244
Staudenmayer, N. 212
story-telling 12, 58, 65–6, 74, 75, 128–9, 133, 140, 141, 166, 167, 173, 180–1, 203, 204, 206, 212, 218, 229, 271
  as epistemological tool 208
strategic emulation 113, 116
strategic issue diagnosis (SID) 243–4
strategic issues 245, 250–2, 282
strategic resources 73
strategy 255–6, 289
  alliancing 314
  formation 315–16
structuration 289
Suddaby, R. 252
supply chain 223
Swart, W. 72
Switzerland 268
symbolic boundaries 75–6, 80
symbols 82, 90

talk 148, 149–50, 168, 173
talk-in-interaction 150–1, 157
Tallinn (Estonia) 131–4, 135, 136–8
Taylor, S. 157
Taylorism 210
technology 281
teleology 242, 312–3
temporality 2, 5, 6, 9, 10, 11, 205, 237, 238
Thatcher, M. N., Baroness 155
Theaetetus (Plato) 182, 183
Thévenot, L. 264
thinking/thinkers 2, 4, 129, 140, 183
thought 217
time 5, 14, 186
  accounts of 192–3
  dimensions of 184, 186, 188**f**, 189, 237–8, 246, 248–9
  events observed over 307**f**
  multiplicity of 184–5, 196
  Newton on 247
  periods 33–4, 36, 38–40
  philosopy of 187, 193, 195
  processes in 2
  syntheses of 195–6
  first 184–5, 185**f**, 189, 192

  second 193–4
  see also flow of time
time and space 14–15, 229–30
  Cartesian view 209
  chronotopes 203–4
  Deleuze on 14
  equivalence between 210
  framework 211–13
  identity in 4, 5
time-space frame, *see* chronotopes
time to market (TIM) 223–4
Toulmin, S. 2
Toyoki, S. 215
Treasury Committee Hearings 157–8
Treasury Select Committee 148, 159**t**
Tsoukas, H. 53, 57, 66, 149, 251, 264, 307
tsunami, *see* financial crisis
Tulving, E. 142
typology 65, 238, 256, 257, 309
Tyre, M. 212

UK Treasury Committee 158
United Kingdom 147
  financial crisis, public hearings into 148, 153–4, 158–9
  public opinion 161, 162
USA 136
  identity with flag 72–3
USSR 137, 138
utterances 169, 208

value infusion 90
value propositions 111
Van de Ven, A. H. 309, 312, 314, 315, 316
Van den Berg, H. 153
variance theories 22, 23, 56
velocity 244
venture capital 242, 255
verbs 9, 28, 29, 30, 31, 38, 51
Vladinirou, E. 264

Walsh, I. 80
Watergate inquiry 154
Watkiss, L. 80
"we" 162–3
Weick, K. E. 53, 202, 203
Wetherell, M. 151, 156, 171, 173
wealth creation 11
Weick, K. 53, 202
Whetten, D. 24, 67
Wiebe, E. 254
Woodilla, J. 215, 216
Wooffitt, R. 151

Index

work-identity 26
world-making 155, 170
worldview 1
Woywode, M. 241

Wurf, E. 25, 32

Zerubavel, E. 130
Zhang, R. P. 173